Second Edition

THE MAN
WHO TRANSFORMED
AFRICA

The Rebirth of a Continent

A NOVEL BY
PETER D. CIMINI

Halo
PUBLISHING
INTERNATIONAL

ISBN: 978-1-63765-116-2
LCCN 2020: 2020904010

Halo Publishing International, LLC
www.halopublishing.com

Printed and bound in the United States of America

This novel is dedicated to a dear friend and mentor, Charles Margolis. He is a teacher, a creative artist, an author, a poet, a project consultant, and a performance coach who helps adults reach their life goals. But these skills and attributes are not what defines "Charlie." His most significant characteristic is his concern for the welfare of all human beings who enter his life.

I am deeply grateful for the excellence editorial assistance of Ms. Cara Adair. Her keen understanding of proper grammatical structure, book formatting, sentence structure, and plot sequence has been a valuable asset and helped improve the flow of this novel. This learned English language specialist resides in Wales in the U.K. and Massachusetts in the U.S.A.

Reader Reference

In this novel there are some topics that might be confusing and/or difficult to follow if using only the written word. To aid comprehension and enhance clarity, the author has included six pictures, maps and illustrations, designed, and footnoted on the page numbers below.

1. A picture of a Solar Thermal Electric Power Plant
   Footnoted on page 205

2. Africa's Intra-Continental Highway
   Footnoted on page 224

3. Africa's underground water Aquifers
   Footnoted on page 270

4. Location of MASH-type tent hospitals
   funded by B.A.T
   Footnoted on page 282

5. Location of MASH-type tent hospitals
   funded by The World Bank
   Footnoted on page 293

6. Africa's vast Tropical Savannas
   Footnoted on page 301

PREFACE

For many years, going as far back as my Social Studies classes in junior high school, teachers described Africa as a continent with a great wealth of natural resources, beautiful landscape and resilient population. It is also identified as being in constant turmoil, upheaval, and poverty; there seemed to be no end to the horrors African citizens face daily.

Then in 1991, with my AARP card in hand, I tuned into a new television fictional drama "The West Wing," about an American presidency. Then in 1998 during the television program's final Episode, which was about the frantic pace of one administration preparing to leave the White House as the newly elected president prepared to move in. In this last episode recruiters were vying to entice top outgoing administration employees with attractive new employment opportunities.

In one scene, a plutocrat named Frank Hollis was interested in using a portion of his vast wealth to help humanity. He asks the outgoing president's chief of staff, C. J. Craig, played by Allison Janney, for suggestions on how to use his money to help the neediest people of the world. She hesitates, obviously unprepared for this surprise question, then said. "I would probably go to Africa and build roads."

That simple brief answer from Allison Janney caused a light bulb to click on, in my mind. I began thinking of what other projects a plutocrat might want to accomplish on the African continent. With pencil and paper in hand, strategies began to fall neatly into place; safety, protection for African families, providing dependable electricity for the first time in Africa's history building an intra-continental highway. My final thought was, if Africa has sixty-four percent of the world's arable farmland, why is the continent not an agricultural giant.

I decided to use a fictional narrative explaining my story about building a strong middle-class African society, and here is that story.

Part I the Vatican

CHAPTER 1

Giancarlo Barzinni was born in 1938, the only child of Leopoldo and Anna Barzinni. The Barzinni family lived in Piedmont, south of the mighty Alps in the northwestern region of Italy. Giancarlo's parents were domestic workers for a wealthy family who owned a villa overlooking Lake Maggiore. His father tended the villa's grounds and his mother worked as a house cleaner.

When Giancarlo learned to walk, he accompanied his mother to morning Mass. By five years of age, Giancarlo became deeply influenced by his mother's devotion to her Catholic religion. When Giancarlo began his schooling, he also started playing European football and soon became the dominant player among his peers. People from the Piedmont region of Italy heard of a young talented footballer from Lake Maggiore, and many traveled to watch the ten-year-old soccer phenom. At fifteen years of age, Giancarlo became the youngest player invited to Italy's national team tryouts. Coaches from the national team had been impressed with his exceptional football skills. During the final week of tryouts, Giancarlo seriously injured his hip in a collision with another player. The injured young player returned home without qualifying for a spot on the national team, with the assurance that he would receive an invitation to the national team's 1965 trials.

Giancarlo, now twenty years of age, received his invitation to the Italian national football teams 1965 try-outs. The coaches once again were impressed with Giancarlo's skills and noticed an improved maturity in his approach to game of football. During the third week of trials, Giancarlo was participating in a kick on goal drill against a defensive player, he cut sharply to his right to avoid a defensive team member, and suddenly fell to the ground in severe pain. The team medical trainer accompanied Giancarlo to the medical facility for an ankle x-ray. The x-ray showed a broken ankle-bone. That evening during a coaches' meeting, it was decided to exclude Giancarlo from further competition with Italy's national team. The coaches were unwilling to hold a spot on the team roster, for an injury prone player, no matter how skillful he was. Giancarlo was sent home and informed that he would not be considered in the future for Italy's national team.

During his final two years of high school, Giancarlo would often pray in an attempt to make sense of why God would have given him such remarkable athletic skills, and then suddenly take away his opportunity to become famous. At the same time, his mother Anna, was increasingly infuriated with changes made during the Vatican II council in the mid-nineties, when the Catholic Church liberalized its procedures and practices. The new liberal practices would diminish sacramental requirements, and encourage Catholics to interpret religious regulations, rather than following the strict decrees handed down to the people by the Catholic hierarchy. Her major fear was that Catholicism would no longer maintain its status as the one, true religion.

Giancarlo followed his mother's advice and frequently prayed to the Blessed Mother, imploring her to help him decide what to do with his life as an adult. A year after graduating from high school, Giancarlo entered a seminary in the Italian province of Cuno, an hour southwest of the Tanaro River, in Italy's main wine country, to study for the priesthood. He believed the Blessed Mother had answered his prayers. God wanted him to become a cleric and work to remove the new liberal church practices, returning Catholicism to its conservative roots, and its status as the one true religion.

CHAPTER 2

The news was predictably calm on this second Monday of October 2001. At 11:22 A.M., a press release from Vatican City streamed across the wires of all major news outlets. Pope Gregory XVII would be resigning his position as leader of the Roman Catholic Church. The press release further indicated that Pope Gregory was suffering from a rare disease, polymyalgia rheumatica. A corticosteroid drug would be useful in reducing the intensity of painful and weak muscle symptoms, but there was no cure for this inflammatory disease. The news release stated that due to the onset of this illness, Pope Gregory XVII would be unable to continue with the demands of the office of the pope. In addition, a conclave to select a new pope would take place as soon as possible, so that a new pontiff would have sufficient time in office prior to the Christmas season.

There is no law or religious regulation that states a pope must remain as leader of the Catholic Church until death. However, the centuries old tradition of the pope remaining in office until death had evolved into a quasi-expectation.

Therefore, Pope Gregory was not at all surprised that his resignation would be the cause of confused feelings among Catholics and some Catholic clergy. However, he was surprised at the numerous reactions of resentment to his resignation announcement, and even some feelings of betrayal. There were some clerics stationed at the Vatican who felt his voluntary decision to retire was treasonous. Pope Gregory was a loving and forgiving man. His dominant personality trait was to be non-confrontational, which far too often allowed Vatican prelates the freedom to manage their duties without proper oversight.

Two days after the announcement of his resignation, Pope Gregory called a meeting with three powerful Vatican cardinals he had selected to manage the closed-door conclave of cardinals, the formal process for selecting a new pope. Over the years, Pope Gregory had a cordial but unsatisfying relationship with the three cardinals, soon to arrive in his office to obtain their assignments. Cardinal Alejo Alejandra from Spain was director of the Vatican Bank, Cardinal Fabien Diudonn from France was Secretary of State for the Vatican City State, and Cardinal Giancarlo Barzinni from Italy was director of the Holy See. The Holy See is the diplomatic and governmental office within the Vatican state.

Pope Gregory XVII welcomed the three influential cardinals as they entered his office. "I have a good deal of material to go over with the three of you, but first let us move to the alcove section of my office for our meeting." Pope Gregory opened the meeting by thanking the three cardinals for their availability and immediately began. "I want to ensure that the rules of the conclave to select my successor are followed exactly as prescribed by church tradition. I am therefore delegating each of you with the following responsibilities. Alejo and Fabien, you will be responsible for each eligible cardinal's travel arrangements to and from Rome, including housing and meals. This task will include transportation from the Rome airport directly to their living quarters at the Vatican. During this procedure, I expect you both to remind each cardinal that any conversation relative to the voting process before, during and after the conclave is not permissible. I will expect all cardinals to be in their individual rooms by the twenty-fourth of October. When they are brought to their rooms, I expect you to remind them that they are to remain secluded and not speak to anyone, other than their fellow cardinals, until a new pope is selected."

Pope Gregory turned to Cardinal Alejandra. "Alejo, prior to the opening ceremony of the conclave, I want you to gather all the cardinals in one location for the purpose of reminding them of the rule that there is to be no discussion regarding who their choice of pope will be. Also, at this gathering, I expect you three to remind all cardinals they are not permitted to use their influence to promote specific candidates for the office of pope."

Pope Gregory poured himself a cup of espresso, took a sip, and proceeded to give further instructions. "Alejo also emphasize that once a conclave has begun, cardinals are required to remain silent during the selection process, and continue their silence, even as they leave the chapel, breaking their silence only after arriving at their rooms or the eating area. Remind them that conclave regulations specifically require that the selection process have the nature of a sacred retreat. There must be no event causing the cardinals to be distracted from their sacred duty."

Pope Gregory then turned to Cardinal Barzinni. "You will, along with other duties, be responsible for preparing the Sistine Chapel for the voting procedures, chairs, tables, the necessary voting paraphernalia, and other miscellaneous material that should be placed on each cardinal's table."

Pope Gregory handed a box to the Italian cardinal. "In this box, you will find informational material needed by the cardinals, explaining the proper procedure for completing their ballot. One of every item in this box should be placed on each cardinal's table."

The pope then turned to Cardinal Diudonn. "Fabien, when all cardinals are seated at their tables, you will first lock the entrance door and then proceed to lock all the other doors. Then at the conclusion of each session, you will be responsible for opening the main chapel door, allowing the cardinals to march silently, and in single file, back to their rooms and eating area. Once the last cardinal has left the Sistine Chapel, you will again lock the main doors. This procedure will be followed for each session until selection duties have been completed, by the selection of the next pope."

Pope Gregory once again looked in the direction of Cardinal Barzinni. "Giancarlo, you will be responsible for explaining the correct procedures for the conclave. All cardinals will be properly dressed in their formal robes as they walk each day in single file to the Sistine Chapel. Once in the chapel and seated on the morning of the first day, you will explain the format of the voting process, during the first morning session. The Pope then handed Giancarlo a prepared list of instructions explaining the voting procedures of each conclave session. Giancarlo, when explaining the procedural steps of the voting, emphasize they are expected to follow each step as outlined in the documents that you gave to them."

Pope Gregory clarified a point for Giancarlo. "The voting cardinals of the conclave will vote twice daily, except for the first afternoon session, which will consist of one vote. During the remainder of the first afternoon session, I will celebrate the conclave Mass."

Pope Gregory handed Giancarlo a second document that included the voting ballots, and commented, "God help us if this number of ballots turns out to be insufficient. I am praying that we will not have to deal with a long, drawn-out conclave."

It was clear that Pope Gregory was determined that this conclave would run in the prescribed manner.

He was concerned that his resignation placed him in the unusual position of being alive during the conclave to choose his successor. For that reason, he was determined that this conclave would not experience mishaps or errors.

Pope Gregory then poured himself a second cup of espresso and continued directions to Giancarlo. "Notice at the very top of each ballot there is a Latin phrase, *Eligio, Summum Pontificem*, (elect a Supreme Pontiff). Ask if any cardinal needs this Latin phrase interpreted. One of you three should be able to clarify these Latin words in whatever language is needed." Pope Gregory was disheartened that a significant number of cardinals needed this clarification. He commented. "It's a sad day when something so important written in Latin would have to be clarified for cardinals of our church, but I'm afraid bringing this to their attention is necessary these days."

Pope Gregory sat up straight, remembering one point he almost forgot. "It's also necessary to point out that the blank line underneath the statement is where they place the name of the person, they are voting to be their next pope. They are then required to fold their ballot and, one at a time, walk down the center isle of the chapel, holding their ballot high above their head for all to see, and place their ballot in the urn in the center of the altar. Remind them that as they are returning to their seat, they are also required to declare loudly, and Giancarlo, please stress the word *loudly*, 'I call as my witness Christ the Lord, who will be my judge that my vote is given to the one who, before God, I think should be selected as the one true pope.'"

Pope Gregory hesitated for a moment to allow for questions, and then continued. "Once the last cardinal has voted and completed these rituals, the four cardinals chosen by lot to process the ballots will then proceed to the altar. Oh, Giancarlo, one other thing, remember that if the voting process goes beyond three days, you will be required to randomly select four new cardinals to perform the final voting procedure until a new pope is selected."

Pope Gregory felt he needed to mentioned another important point. "When the ballots have been collected, they must match the number of voting cardinals seated in the chapel. If not, the ballots will remain unopened and burned, producing black smoke, and proceed with second ballot. Assuming the tally shows that all cardinals did properly voted; the cardinals chosen by lot will open each ballot and read aloud the name of the person written on the ballot. Make sure the two other cardinals also chosen by lot are keeping a written tally of the names called out. Giancarlo will be responsible for announcing the number of votes for each cardinal. If no cardinal has received the required two-thirds majority plus one vote, Giancarlo will add the chemical to the stove, producing black smoke indicating no cardinal has received the required number of votes. Balloting will continue in this manner until one cardinal has received the required two-thirds plus one vote. When that has occurred, Giancarlo will add the chemical that produces white smoke to alert the crowd waiting in Saint Peter's Square that a new pope has been selected."

The three cardinals assured Pope Gregory that the process was clear and they would follow the procedures as described. Pope Gregory requested that the cardinals remain seated. "I wish to speak informally before we end this meeting. You no doubt have noticed how quickly the 'fortune tellers' have been reporting on the likely candidate to replace me, and that the three of you are high on their list. I must agree that I too suspect that one of you may be my successor. Whichever one of you is selected please feel free to call on me if you desire counsel on any matter."

Pope Gregory quickly changed the subject. "Remember the words of John Paul II after he was selected to lead our church. 'God will forgive you all for what you have done here today.'"

CHAPTER 3

Six weeks had passed since Pope Gregory XVII announced his retirement. Conclave preparations were completed. Cardinal Alejandra, Diudonn, and Barzinni were in Giancarlo's attractively decorated apartment for a final review, for the opening of the conclave. Giancarlo was at his liquor cabinet, pouring three scotch whiskeys in tumblers. The three tired men were pleased that their tasks had been completed. After taking his first sip of scotch, Cardinal Diudonn stroked a thick clump of bright reddish hair off his forehead and spoke. "During my various car trips bringing cardinals from the airport to the Vatican, the conversation always seems to eventually center on selecting a younger man as pope, one with an appreciation for diversity, and the energy to promote Catholic social justice; which would help improve the churches public relations, eventually removing the negative press of the clergy sex scandals."

Cardinal Barzinni was intrigued by Cardinal Diudonn's comments regarding the conversations between the cardinals. Giancarlo had an organized, deliberate, quick thinking mind, able to envision a plan, and the sequential steps needed to reach its desired outcomes, as well as the ability to explain the reasons that would allow his plan to reach a successful conclusion.

An idea began to form in Giancarlo's mind, as Cardinal Alejo Alejandra discussed the completion of arrangements for housing for the hundred plus cardinals. When Cardinal Alejandra had finished his remarks, he nodded to Cardinal

Barzinni, to inquire if the voting paraphernalia was collated and ready for placement at each cardinal's seating area.

Giancarlo, with a sinister smile on his face, and his usual piercing eyes, as though they were searching in the darkness, ignored Alejo's question. He slowly placed his glass of scotch on its coaster, and asked Cardinal Diudonn, "Are you sure that the visiting cardinals were unanimous in their preference for a younger cardinal, interested in diversity, and Catholic social justice?"

Fabien replied, "Well, I'm not able to drive and count heads in the rear seat, but it sounded to me as though the vast majority of cardinals seemed to be agreeing each time this comment was mentioned."

Giancarlo, still ignoring Alejo's question remarked, "It would appear that Pope Gregory's opinion that one of us will be selected pope, may not be correct. We certainly are not young cardinals, nor do I believe that other cardinals see us as young and interested in diversity and Catholic social justice. Our cardinal brethren sounded as though they are not interested in abolishing the theological harm done by Vatican II over these past fifty or so years. I'm convinced it's time for us to take matters into our own hands, reminding Catholics around the world that Christ died on the cross, so that we could proclaim his father to be the one true God.

Cardinal Alejo Alejandra, no longer concerned about voting paraphernalia, asked Giancarlo. "I don't understand. How are we to take matters into our own hands?"

Giancarlo picked up his scotch from the coaster, and said, "Gentlemen, let me encourage you both to join me in a toast." Cardinal Diudonn, and Cardinal Alejandra looked confused. Both men were thinking, *would we be toasting the statement to take matters into our own hands?* Slowly the two cardinals picked up their drinks, and as the three glasses touched, Cardinal Barzinni said, "My friends let us join in a toast to Cardinal Sunjaya Prantata of Indonesia."

Cardinal Diudonn and Alejandra, upon hearing the subject of the toast, reared their heads back in wide-eyed confusion not knowing what their friend Cardinal Giancarlo Barzinni, was referring to, when he suggested a toast to the Indonesian Cardinal.

Giancarlo immediately continued, "If the conclave of cardinals were determined to select a young, diverse, energetic pope, willing to follow a social justice course, then their man could very well be: Cardinal Sunjaya Prantata of Indonesia.

Fabien Diudonn inquired, "I still don't understand how this Cardinal Prantata, as pope would enable us to take matters into our own hands?"

Cardinal Barzinni was ready with an explanation, "The Indonesian is a convert to Catholicism. As a convert, he lacks the basic theological foundations, we learned in seminary, allowing us to understand our faith as the one true religion. Without these theological principals, a convert does not appreciate the importance of adherence to the sacraments, and the religious interpretations Jesus Christ bestowed on us through his apostles. These infallible interpretations were handed down to us directly through Jesus Christ's words." Giancarlo went on to explain how the selection of the Indonesian cardinal would allow the three European conservative cardinals to restore the Catholic Church to the theological principles practiced before Vatican II.

Giancarlo was convinced that a seminary trained student would be better able to lead the Catholic Church than the convert, Cardinal Sunjaya Prantata, but this in fact is the basis of my plan. If Cardinal Sunjaya Prantata were to be selected pope, he would have to turn to the three powerful Western European cardinals at the Vatican for consultation. They would be responsible to recommend practices, dogma, and proclamations based on the words of Jesus Christ. The uninformed Indonesian, would need to confer with the three of us for clarification and advice on religious matters. We in turn, can inform him how important it is to abolish the regulations and decisions established after Vatican II, by Pope John XXIII. We can bring Catholicism back to its rightful place, as the single, only true religion, and the only true God. The Indonesian convert, under our supervision, can accomplish this, without him even realizing that he will be responsible for beginning this long journey back from chaos, to a new stable conservative rule."

Giancarlo's plan would not be difficult, since the majority of cardinals were already inclined to approve a younger, liberal leader, ready to take the church in the direction of social justice for all. Conclave regulations ban the cardinals from forcing their opinions relative to the selection of a pope. However, the conclave welcomes discussions among cardinals on church direction and qualities of a leader.

At this point in the conversation, Giancarlo discussed implementation strategies. "First, in general discussion with other cardinals before and during the conclave; we could mention if we were to select one of the many qualified cardinals of color this could very well dispel the prevailing notion that the College of Cardinals are a group of stuffy, old, white men living in the past. A popular criticism we all despise. Among the cardinals of color, there is only one young, energetic cardinal, the Indonesian, and I am confident this will become obvious as others consider all the various cardinals.

On the first ballot, we three can vote for the Indonesian, this will bring the Prantata name to their attention."

Cardinal Diudonn and Cardinal Alejandra were no longer as hesitant about Giancarlo's plan, as they were before his explanation. Giancarlo was highly skilled in his use of phrases and ideas, and his enthusiasm seemed to encourage Alejo and Fabien to accept his creative plan of action.

***

The conclave began the following day. The three cardinals spent a good deal of their time interacting with their fellow cardinals discussing their opinion on the type of man they would like to see lead the church. They were pleased that no clear leader had emerged after this first vote, and the Indonesian cardinal, surprisingly managed four votes, which was a positive start.

Cardinal Prantata was shocked at the fact that he had received four votes to be pope. He was sure many cardinals hadn't even known his name.

Black smoke rose from the smoke stack twice the next day. The following day was the same.

On the third day, the three Vatican cardinals were pleased to see a steadily rising vote for the Indonesian, even though some cardinals questioned his relatively young age.

The morning session on the fifth day began with the ninth conclave vote for a pope. The crowd gathered anxiously in Saint Peter's Square around eleven in the morning when the first vote of the day was expected. The hushed crowds stared at the smoke stack, anxious to see the color of the emerging smoke. At 11:22, A.M. white smoke burst from the chimney. The jubilant crowd began to scream, applaud, cheer, and soon the chant of "Il Papa, Il Papa" began. Automobiles moving on the streets surrounding the Vatican could hear the chanting, and drivers began leaning on their car horns, joining the celebration. All were unaware of the complete surprise they were soon to receive.

Sometime later, as the glass doors of the pope's residence opened to a balcony facing the people in the square. The excitement of the crowd heightened to its peak. The identity of the new pope was anyone's guess. A short, dark-skinned, smiling man, dressed in stately, imposing garments and elaborate headwear, stepped onto the balcony, and began waving to the jubilant crowd.

The chanting began to diminish as the powerful loud speakers in the square came alive with sound. A booming voice blared out the announcement. "People, allow me to introduce Pope Francis Xavier 1."

The crowd erupted once again, as the newly selected pope stood at the microphone. Once again, passing automobiles joined in the celebration. The unassuming new pope had a look of passive confusion as he continued waving to the cheering throng in Saint Peter's Square.

A member of the clergy standing next to the pontiff leaned his head in the direction of Pope Francis Xavier's ear, and said, "The crowd will begin to be silent if you say, Thank you, a number of times. That usually quiets them, knowing you are about to speak."

That brief comment seemed to shock Pope Francis Xavier out of his immobility. He used the powerful microphones, repeating the words "Thank you." The crowd soon settled and became quiet, and the powerful speakers blared the first comments of the new pope, with his appealing Indonesian accent. "I'm from the island of Indonesia, and I stand before you with an anxious heart, determined to serve the

Lord in my new capacity as pope. I expect to speak with you often, and I pray that my service to people, and God, will in some small way help to heal the many wounds we all face while living under far too many indifferent, selfish, uncaring leaders."

With that brief announcement, Pope Francis Xavier blessed the people in the square.

Meanwhile in Hamburg, Germany, a very different regretful atmosphere was prevailing in the office of former Pope Gregory, XVII. He continued to ponder his decision to retire. It was at this moment that he decided it was his responsibility to be of assistance to the new Indonesian pope.

CHAPTER 4

Saint Francis Xavier was the first Jesuit missionary to reach the shores of Indonesia, spending a good deal of time as a missionary priest in Makassar, on the island of Celebes in 1545, today known as Indonesia. Indonesian Christians revere Saint Francis Xavier as the man who brought Jesus into their lives.

The day before Pope Francis Xavier was to begin his duties as pope, he received a call from former Pope Gregory, XVII, who suggested they meet at the convenience of the newly selected pope to discuss the numerous duties and requirements expected of him. In addition, if the new pope was open to the idea, Pope Gregory Emeritus would be willing to act as a mentor to Pope Francis Xavier. The new pope immediately accepted both offers. The scheduled meeting was to take place the following Monday morning at Pope Francis Xavier's office in the Vatican.

The following day, Thursday, was to be Pope Francis Xavier's first day as leader of the Roman Catholic Church. Excited, and very nervous, he arrived at the door to the hallway leading to his office, expecting to introduce himself to his staff and commence his reign. Much to his surprise, the hallway leading to his outer office was an unlit, pitch-black pathway. He moved his hand along the inner wall of the hallway, found a switch, and turned on the hallway lights. The hallway area was an attractive, off-color yellow, with elaborately framed paintings hanging on the walls, adding to the attractiveness of the area leading to his office. On either side of the door of the pope's outer office, stood two black bronze ionic pedestal columns, one holding a white marble bust sculpture of Aristotle and on the other was a white marble bust sculpture of Dante Alighieri, the famous Italian poet and writer.

The new pope was able to see into the outer office, through an elongated window in the door. The room was dark, with tall-silhouetted structures outlined by the hallway lights. He reached for the door- knob, and found the room unlocked. Opening the door and moving his right hand on the inside wall his fingers found a light switch. Much to his astonishment, the high-silhouetted structures turned out to be stacks of cardboard boxes covering the entire outer office floor and desk with a narrow walkway leading to a second solid wooden door. He stopped to examine the contents of two boxes, finding papers and folders. He quickly discontinued his search and continued on the small narrow winding path between precariously stacked boxes leading to a solid wooden door. He turned the doorknob, and found it also unlocked. He slowly started to open the door, which quickly hit an obstacle; he could see a second dark room, more tall-silhouetted structures and he heard a phone somewhere in the room ringing. Moving his hand along the wall, he found the light switch, and turned on the light. As he angled his body to squeeze through the partially opened door, the pope was surprised to see a second room full of stacked boxes. The only wood floor he could see was on a narrow pathway leading to a desk, with cluttered stacks of stapled papers, small boxes, various empty containers, and a constantly ringing phone.

He moved a box from the desk chair and sat. Confused, he glanced around the room. Suddenly realizing the phone was still ringing, he had to move clutter to reach it. As he was about to pick up the receiver the phone went to a message, someone was offering congratulations to the new pope. Oddly enough, this voice mail message convinced the confused pope, that this was definitely his office! He had no idea what to do next.

He told himself, *I had better wait for someone to come and tell me what I should do. How am I ever to make sense of this chaos? How could I have been selected pope, leader of the Roman Catholic Church, and on my first day in office, here I sit, alone, engulfed by cardboard boxes and a continuous ringing phone?*

He felt frustrated and depressed at the hopelessness of what was before him. Seating motionless for what seemed like an eternity, he thought. *Why should I sit here alone, like a child waiting for someone to come and tell me what I'm supposed to do? This is insane. I was selected as pope. Something is terribly wrong. Why would I be selected as pope and then find that people here at the Vatican ignore my existence? The answer must be that this this room is not my office. I'm going to leave, and hopefully find someone who can direct me to the office of the pope.*

Sunjaya spent the better part of the next hour roaming through the building, turning on lights, calling out to see if others were on the floor. By 10:30 A.M., exhausted, frustrated and angry, he finally gave up.

He returned to his room, wondering who he could contact to explain his dilemma. Slumped in a soft

chair in his room, he thought of his friend Budi. *If only he were here, he would correct whatever this is.*

Desperate for a logical reason to his situation, he also wondered, *I must have misunderstood the directions to the location of my office that must be the answer.*

The experience was depressing and humbling. He spent the remainder of the morning and now late afternoon alone in his room, with nothing to read, no breakfast or lunch, and no appetite, but that was fortunate, because if he were hungry, he would not have known where to obtain a meal.

It was now 4:00 p.m.; the pope, slumped in his chair, his confusion now turned into a dark feeling of what drowning must feel like. Slowly, stark terror surrounded him. *I cannot leave. What am I to do?* The hours passed slowly; thankfully, his exhausted body fell off to sleep. After a restless night, the sun finally rose on a new day. He was now quite hungry and determined to find someone who could clarify his situation, but first, he desired some coffee and breakfast. He dressed in his Indonesian priest cassock and walked west along a Vatican sidewalk. Almost immediately, Sunjaya saw a man who was dressed in working cloths he stopped the older man and inquired where he could get some breakfast. The kind man, who did not recognize the new pope, referring to him as Father, directed the pope to the Vatican cafeteria. Once in the cafeteria, Pope Francis Xavier was immediately recognized and welcomed respectively. He was encouraged at his reception, after one of the longest days of his life.

As he joined the rear of the line of people waiting to fill their plates with food from long shallow stainless-steel pans, the persons in line in front of him, bowed before the pope and encouraged him to pass. The next twelve people in line did the same. Soon the pope was moving hot food onto his plate, which rested on a tray he could slide forward until he reached the end of the food line, where coffee and espresso was available. He looked out to the many tables where clerics and workers were enjoying their breakfast. He moved toward an empty chair in the large room with many windows inviting the early morning sun to warm his confused mind. He was dumbfounded as the people at each table he passed stopped eating and stood to say, "Good morning, Your Holiness." When he finally arrived at the table with the empty chair, the three people at the table stood, bowed respectfully, and remained standing until the pope sat in the empty chair. They expressed their gratitude to him for choosing their table to join them in a meal. It was at this moment that Pope Francis Xavier began to feel some relief. As the pope was eating, yesterday's disturbing thoughts gradually faded.

When Pope Francis Xavier finished his large breakfast, he excused himself from the cafeteria table. As he was leaving the cafeteria, a long line of people had gathered to thank him for his presence in the cafeteria this morning. As he left, he thought, *this is not a dream, apparently, I am pope.* Sunjaya was anxious for the Monday morning meeting with Pope Gregory Emeritus to arrive that would finally confirm his selection as pope.

He passed the time over the weekend enjoying long walks around the Vatican grounds, admiring the beautiful Vatican architecture, and was pleased to recognize those individuals who bowed or tipped their hat, saying, "Good morning" and "Good day, Your Holiness," the many salutations seemed to validate this extraordinary, unimaginable event in his life.

On Monday morning, former Pope Gregory XVII arrived to find Pope Francis Xavier waiting for him in the hallway at his office. Pope Gregory introduced himself to the pope. His first comment was to inquire where the pope's secretary was. Pope Francis Xavier had no answer; obtaining a secretary was one of the first items on his list of questions for the former pope.

Gregory was surprised that a secretary had not been in place as of day one of the new pope's reign. After the pope turned on the office light, the two men now staring at a full room of cardboard boxes. Francis Xavier apologized for not having chairs available, and he asked Gregory if he knew of an area close by where they could sit and chat.

Gregory looked puzzled, "Have you been informed why your outer reception room is completely full of cardboard boxes?"

Pope Francis Xavier was mortified by the Gregory's question, but not wishing to show his ignorance at the situation, he said, "I apologize for the room's appearance, but I had no idea what was expected of me, regarding the boxed material, when I arrived last Thursday."

Gregory had a strange look on his face as he asked, "Your Holiness, can I see your inner office?"

Pope Francis Xavier reluctantly agreed, feeling shameful and at the same time distressed at what Pope Gregory Emeritus was about to see. Pope Francis Xavier slowly opened the door, which was blocked except for about foot. Pope Francis stretched to turn on the lights, and then Pope Gregory Emeritus squeeze his body into pope's inner office. Gregory looked in horror, and without saying a word, quickly turned off the lights, and with a hopeless look on his face said, "Holy Father, there has been a horrible mistake! I can't believe what I have seen."

Pope Gregory Emeritus immediately took complete charge of the situation. "Your Holiness, not having an experienced secretary ready to greet you on your first day, and now the mess that someone has placed in your office, is inexcusable. Do you mind if I act on your behalf and find out who is responsible for this terrible reception?"

Pope Francis Xavier was pleased to accept the assistance of the former pope. Gregory immediately pulled a mobile phone out of his inner vestment pocket and made several calls; attempting to seek answers. He then made one other call and spoke in a more polite tone of voice to the person at the other end of the line. He explained what he had encountered upon entering the pope's office. He thanked the person on the phone for their help in arranging a crew to clear the office.

Gregory then called the Vatican Library and, after a warm and gracious short conversation, asked if they had a room available for him to conduct a meeting with the new pope. The person at the other end of the phone line assured him that space was available. "We'll be over in five minutes, and, yes, we would appreciate a pot of your special coffee."

Gregory had a confused smile on his face as he turned once again to face the bewildered pope. "Please accept my deepest apology for what looks to me like a series of errors made a few days ago. I'm embarrassed that you had to experience these unexplained errors, but rest assured, all will be taken care of by the end of today. Once in your office you can decide who you would like as a permanent secretary."

Both men were now more relaxed and spoke casually as they made their way to the Vatican Library.

The Vatican Library entrance was a small plain area with a door on one side, which opened to a reception area. Gregory was welcomed warmly, as he introduced Francis Xavier to the cleric at a small desk. The priest immediately moved from behind his desk, and knelt before Pope Francis Xavier. The kneeling priest then grasped the pope's hand, and was surprised that there was no ring on Sunjaya's finger. When he rose, he escorted both men through a beautiful large room, accented by elaborately carved old wooden shelves containing very large leather-bound books. The receptionist opened a glass door leading to a foyer lined with chairs. At the end of the foyer, the receptionist unlocked a door and invited the two men into a conference room with a large table, chairs, and a brass easel that held a large blank, unlined, white paper pad. Gregory invited Francis Xavier to a seat at the head of the table.

The receptionist said, "Please excuse me, I will return to my desk and have some refreshments brought to you shortly."

After a lively discussion on the responsibilities awaiting the new pope, former Pope Gregory placed two beautiful wooden boxes on the table. "This box contains keys you keep in your possession. They are all marked, and I am sure these keys will come in handy someday when you wish to enter a building or need a certain confidential document." Gregory handed a card file to Pope Francis Xavier containing all the number codes for various doors and cabinets. He then handed the pope a small box full of alphabetized index cards containing computer passwords and usernames for access to selected Vatican documents.

Gregory took a ring of keys out of a second box. "These are extra, labeled keys to the various departments at the Vatican. Department heads have keys along with the passwords and codes that are included on the labels attached to each key."

At the end of their long conversation, a grateful Pope Francis Xavier thanked former Pope Gregory for his kindness and willingness to be so helpful. Gregory responded, "The pleasure was all mine."

Gregory then asked Pope Francis Xavier if he would mind sharing some details about his background, and what made him choose the priesthood as a vocation. Pope Francis Xavier stared at the ground for a moment, somewhat embarrassed, that his choice of a priestly vocation had more to do with Indonesia poverty than religious fervor. He was quick to explain that he, and his childhood friend, Father Susanto accepted all their priestly vows, and hoped their life as Indonesian priests, would be able to help other Indonesians living in poverty. Pope Francis Xavier added, "If Father Susanto and I had remained a part of Jakarta's poor citizenry, we would have been unable to have an effect on future unjust acts by Indonesian leaders. However, as Catholic priests, we would be able to lead efforts against future Indonesians political leaders, who may not understand our poverty, or who might decide to promote unjust legislation or actions."

At this point Pope Francis Xavier felt it necessary to elaborate on the interrelated elements of South Asia's cultural history "Having lived in Germany, prior to becoming a priest and then pope. It's helpful to understand that South Asia is home to the better part of a billion people, all belonging to hundreds of different ethnic groups, speaking different languages, practicing dozens of religions, and living in countries with radically different forms of government, and political leaders ruling with a narrow view of South Asia, resulting in countries distrusting each other."

Former pope Gregory spent the following three hours explaining the basic duties of a pope, and many of the formal responsibilities' Francis Xavier would be expected to perform as pope

Before leaving the library, Gregory said, "Although I am in semi-retirement, ministering to the retired clergy of Europe, my home base is in a parish in Hamburg, Germany. My secretary always knows how to reach me. If I am visiting somewhere on the continent, all you need to do is call this number to reach my office, she will know how to contact me, and I will return your call as soon as possible. I am sure you are going to have many questions, feel free to call me any time. I would be most happy to help in any way that I can."

***

A Jesuit missionary priest, stationed in Indonesia for the past thirteen years, and a trusted dear friend of the new pope, picked up his ringing phone on the fourth ring and spoke. "Father O'Bannon speaking."

The pope anxiously spoke. "Jerome, have you heard?" Jerome joyfully shouted in response, "I heard it on CNN yesterday. Sunjaya, oh, I mean Your Holiness, I didn't believe what I was hearing. I'm still in a state of shock." "You're in state of shock, what about me? I'm still shaking my head and pinching myself, wondering if this may be a dream, instead of reality." Jerome immediately responded, "I don't know what to say. Do I congratulate you or give you, my condolences? Has it sunk in yet? I mean, do you realize what lies ahead for you? Oh, for God's sake, what a stupid question, you're probably still traumatized yourself.

Have you figured out where your bed is?"

The pope responded, "You don't know the half of it. Someday I'll explain." The pope quickly changed the subject. "Jerome, you've met my soon-to-be-secretary, Budi Susanto, haven't you?"

"Yes, I've met him a number of times," responded Jerome.

"Good. I expect him in Rome in three days. He's packing away some of our belongings, in Indonesia for storage and then will join me at the Vatican as my personal secretary. I need people like Budi here in Rome that I can trust. And that brings up the other reason I've called you. At some point, I may ask you to transfer to the Vatican to assist me, but that's in the future. For now, my thoughts are only on setting priorities for myself as pope. However, should I need the assistance from an efficient problem solver like you, I may ask you to consider temporally leaving your ministry in Indonesian, and join me and Budi at the Vatican?

A still shocked Jerome said, "Your Holiness, under my vow of obedience, I don't have the option of considering."

Pope Francis Xavier smiled, "My friend, you know no matter what the situation might be. I would never force you to come to Rome if you preferred to remain with your missionary in Indonesia. If I were to call, I would respect your right to make a decision about where you are most needed."

The Jesuit missionary priest agreed to think about the possibility of an invitation to work at the Vatican. Before Jerome ended the conversation, he thanked his former cardinal for taking the name of the Jesuit, Saint Francis Xavier, and added that Jesuits around the world were very grateful that you had chosen the name of the founder of their order.

CHAPTER 5

On Tuesday morning, Pope Francis Xavier placed a phone call to Pope Gregory Emeritus, thanking him once again for coming to his rescue. He then apologized for not inquiring about Gregory's health during their visit.

"Please, it's not necessary for you to apologize. It must have been very disturbing to face what you encountered on your first day in office."

Pope Francis Xavier, in a pleasant, non-accusatory response to Pope Gregory's statement, assured him that his intervention resulted in the entire situation being resolved to his satisfaction.

Pope Francis Xavier then said, "Enough about me, tell me how you are feeling."

The former Pope Gregory answered by explaining, "My polymyalgia rheumatic symptoms are being helped by medication; my joints are painful, but tolerable, but the worst part is the weakness I feel in all my joints. However, that has not as yet interfered with my ministry here in Europe." He wished Pope Francis Xavier well, and reminded him not to hesitate to call if he could be of any use to him.

On 4 September, 2009, Pope Francis Xavier had been in his new position for fourteen days. Budi Susanto, the pope's close friend and secretary arrived the previous afternoon and was at his desk sharply at nine a.m. the following morning, along with his accompanying jet lag.

Pope Francis Xavier immediately came out to his secretary's desk. "Budi, it's not necessary for you to be at work this morning. I expect you to take some time to get over your jet lag."

A weary but anxious Father Susanto said, "Your Holiness, I feel pretty good and would prefer to get started. By the way, when we are alone, like now, is it okay for me to call you by your first name, or do you wish for me to refer to you as Your Holiness?"

"I would prefer that our past history remain as it has been all these years, so when we are alone, I would like you to call me Sunjaya. And although it may seem awkward at first, when others are present, please refer to me as Your Holiness." The pope smiled, "Okay, if you're ready for work, I have some hand-written letters I need typed immediately, and when you've finished with the letters, call Cardinals Alejandra, Diudonn, and Barzinni and schedule an immediate appointment for them in my office."

Father Susanto responded, "You got it, boss."

Budi Susanto and Sunjaya Prantata had known each other since they were five years of age. Their families lived in the same rat-infested, fragile tenement building in Jakarta, Indonesia. Budi Susanto lived one floor below his friend Sunjaya. They entered first grade together, and over the next twenty-four years they remained inseparable friends, going through lower grade school, and both earning a scholarship to attend a nearby Catholic private high school. They decided to become Catholic priests, not out of a deep religious vocational desire, but rather the practical realization that the priesthood was their only way to escape the severe poverty of the streets of Jakarta. This decision was not as selfish as it might initially sound. Sunjaya and his close friend talked extensively about this step, and they decided to join the priesthood together and fully commit to all the rules, regulations, and vows of a Catholic priest, including celibacy, as their part of a bargain.

Early the following morning, the pope's landline phone rang. It was Budi. "I've finished the letters you wanted me to type, and I have set a meeting between you and Cardinals Alejandra, Diudonn, and Barzinni for tomorrow in your office at 2:30 P.M., oh, and by the way, they sounded as though they were expecting your call. Are they aware of the nature of the contents of these letters?"

"No, you and I are the only people who know the content of these letters,"

"Well then, tomorrow's meeting should be interesting, and I hope you've made the right decision."

That evening, the three European cardinals met in Giancarlo's room to discuss their meeting the following day with Pope Francis Xavier. When Alejo and Fabien arrived, a smiling Giancarlo greeted them warmly.

"Welcome, my friends, let's move to my work table. I have some wonderful brandy that I guarantee will take the chill out of your bones on this September evening."

The room was not large, but attractive furniture made the surroundings very inviting. A large square oak pedestal table sat in one corner. A bottle of expensive brandy sat in the center of the table along with three brandy glasses in front of comfortable cushioned wood chairs with armrests. Giancarlo poured brandy for the two cardinals and himself. After placing the shapely glass decanter back on its silver tray, Giancarlo reminded Alejo and Fabien that he had predicted the new pope would call on them for assistance. The only miscalculation on the of Giancarlo was that he never expected the pontiff to be crawling to them so soon after his selection. Giancarlo raised his glass for a welcoming toast.

"To the return of the Catholic Church to its rightful status as the one true religion. In addition, I also want you to know that we are toasting the return of Mother Church to its greatness with Riedel Vinum brandy snifters, perfect for swirling, sniffing, and enjoying only the finest brandy." The three smiling cardinals touched their brandy snifters in a toast. They swirled, sniffed, and finally tasted their fine brandy, which did indeed warm their bodies as Giancarlo had suggested.

After the cardinals were comfortable in their chairs, they discussed how they planned to set the tone of their meeting with the pope. When the pope enquires about the responsibilities of their departments, they planned to add duties that would put them in control of key procedural decisions that would move the church closer to their desired conservative policies.

The following afternoon, the three cardinals entered Pope Francis Xavier's office. They were surprised to see the diminutive man sitting rigid and looking stern behind his very large desk. They were expecting a more pleasant looking man and for the meeting to be more informal in the alcove section of the office, with its upholstered furniture, rather than at his desk. The three cardinals simply assumed this was an Indonesian custom and gave it no further thought. After the three cardinals were seated facing the pontiff behind his desk, the pope opened the conversation briskly.

"I intend to get right to the point of this meeting. I do not wish for you three cardinals to be part of the Vatican staff because I don't trust your intentions."

The three men were so surprised at his opening statement that they became confused and were not sure they had correctly heard the Indonesian man behind his desk. They were ready to ask for clarification, but the pope did not hesitate for a microsecond.

Continuing to speak, he reached to the right side of his desk and picked up a set of papers, and said.

"I have for each of you a composed letter, as though written by you to me, requesting a voluntary transfer from your positions here at the Vatican. You will note the letters state that each of you would like to transfer to a new assignment as soon as possible."

The shock of the pope's terse explanation, still did not immediately register with the three European cardinals, and they stared mutely at the Indonesian man. There was a very long pause before each cardinal reached for the letters placed before them. Each read their letter, written as though it had originated from them to the pope. They looked up, wearing frowns and wrinkled brows, glanced quizzically at each other, and then turned their attention back to Francis Xavier.

During this long awkward silence, Francis Xavier picked up another set of papers from the left side of his desk; these letters included his signature, and the following day's date. Pope Francis Xavier handed one to each of the three confused cardinals.

"This second letter is signed by me and contains my acceptance of your desire for a transfer to a different ministry, away from the Vatican."

The three cardinals read the second letters handed to them. Francis Xavier waited until the three men had a chance to digest the content of this second letter and then continued. "If the three of you sign your letters requesting a reassignment now, here in my office, this afternoon, you may keep my signed letter stating that I accept your reassignment request, which is dated tomorrow." Francis Xavier hesitated a few more moments, allowing his last statement to register, and then continued. "The three of you do have a second option. If you decide not to voluntarily request a transfer, I will begin a number of inquiries regarding your previous activities. First, Cardinal Alejandra, if you choose not to sign your voluntary request for reassignment immediately, I will proceed to bring in outside auditors to reopen the 2002 Vatican Bank civil court-ordered agreement to pay two hundred and forty-two million Euros to three credit banks as compensation for the money laundering affair of Roberto Calvi's Banco Ambarosiano."

Pope Francis Xavier then turned his gaze to the French cardinal. "Cardinal Diudonn, if you choose not to sign your letter of voluntary re-assignment right now, here in this office, I will be asking for a public auditing of the 2009 Peter's pence collection of $82.5 million. The audit will provide information on how much of the $82.5 million did in fact find its way to the poor."

Cardinal Diudonn did not look up from the letters he had received. Francis Xavier then looked directly at Cardinal Barzinni. "Cardinal Barzinni, if you decide not to sign your letter of voluntary reassignment, I will be publicly asking you as director of the Holy See, to explain your 2009 operating budget, which shows a surplus of $3.2 million despite a loss of $9.5 million relative to the value of the euro against the dollar. Moreover, if any of you three choose not to sign your letter of voluntary reassignment immediately, I will release a public statement to the general media in Italy, stating that my first act as pope will be to accuse you three of taking part in a planned effort to convince other cardinals during the past conclave to vote for me. I have statements from other cardinals that you intentionally violated conclave regulations regarding deliberate 'politicking' during a conclave to select a new pope."

Pope Francis Xavier hesitated a minute, staring hard at each of the three cardinals. "Gentleman, I expect your signatures on the letters you have in your hands, in which case, keep my signed letters agreeing to your reassignments. On the other hand, if you choose to leave without signing, you will find included a copy of the statements I have prepared, which I will release tomorrow to the Italian media, relative to my accusations toward the three of you."

Pope Francis Xavier placed his pen on his desk pad in front of him, leaned back in his chair, and continued to look at the three stunned cardinals.

Cardinal Barzinni stood, as he spoke, "Your Holiness, may I borrow the pen on your desk?"

Pope Francis Xavier continued to focus his ire on the cardinals and, without looking down at the pen, reached out with his right hand and slowly slid the pen across his desk toward Cardinal Barzinni. As Cardinal Barzinni signed his letter, Cardinal Diudonn rose from his chair and moved a step behind Giancarlo. He crossed his arms over his chest, his head turned, and eyes staring at a far wall in the office, as though the space in the pope's office was not large enough to hold the anger churning in his gut. Cardinal Alejandra remained seated with a guilt-ridden stare toward the same wall.

Cardinal Barzinni handed the pen to his fellow cardinal and addressed the pontiff. "We certainly misjudged your character, never expecting to have a knife thrust into our backs."

"Fortunately, I believe I judged the intentions of you three quite accurately." The pope responded softly but firmly.

Cardinal Alejandra took the pen from Fabien and signed his letter, then, placing the pen on the pope's desk asked, "Holy Father may we be excused?"

"Yes, you may," the pope replied.

CHAPTER 6

Due to their long tenure in such valuable Vatican positions, most Vatican prelates and workers were surprised to hear the three European cardinals had requested voluntary reassignment. The buzz around the Vatican involved numerous plausible reasons, unsubstantial speculation, and a good amount of wild conspiracy theories. Rumors continued through the Vatican for the following several weeks.

Eight days had passed since the three long-established Vatican cardinals had submitted their requests for transfer from their current positions. Pope Francis Xavier called his secretary and asked if he was free to come into his office.

Father Susanto knocked on the door to the pope's office, waited a long moment, and then entered. The pope's office had two oversized windows facing east, so that the morning sun always welcomed the pope's arrival. Centered in front of floor to ceiling shelving covering the back wall of the office sat a large mahogany desk. The center section of the shelving was a stylish maple cabinet with two doors, highlighted by shiny brass lion heads for cabinet door handles. The very old polished antique maple wood of the carved shelves and cabinet lent a charm and warmth of great antiquity to the office. Next to the entrance door on the right side was an alcove area that included two deeply cushioned seats and an equally cushioned small sofa. Between the cushioned chairs and sofa sat a beautiful low 18th century, table with intricately hand-carved legs. On the wall of the alcove, over the chairs hung a 14th century original oil painting depicting Jesus with a baby lamb straddling his shoulders. On the wall over the sofa was an original painting by Raphael, *The Angel Delivering Saint Peter from Prison.*

The pope invited his friend to the upholstered section of his office. "Put your notebook aside for a minute," he said softly, then approaching his old friend, the pope embraced him and gestured to one of the deeply cushioned seats that faced the Raphael painting. Once Budi sat down, Francis Xavier began speaking. "I am aware we have not had the opportunity to chat as old friends. Lord knows I've missed you! Tell me how things are going for you here at the Vatican."

Budi said, "I'm a little surprised, and pleased to say, that I have found the people quite pleasant and friendly. I must admit, I was not sure how people here at the Vatican would react to an Indonesian. I was expecting some racial tension, but that does not seem to be the case. Regarding the work, I'm still adjusting to the faster pace of almost everything. I'll have to swim harder against the tide, but I think I'm going to be able to keep my head above water."

Budi hesitated before continuing. "There is one concern I have, which may initially sound comical, but I'm really serious about this. We have remained thin because we usually didn't have enough food to eat. However, here in Rome, people get upset if you don't finish the mounds of food they put on your plate, and what makes this problem even worse is that the food is so delicious! It's very tempting to easily overeat. I'm afraid that I'll soon become, like American people! Remember when we used to call them the 'balloon people,' because Americans are so overweight. Well, if I keep eating like this, and here is where I may sound like I'm trying to be the comic, but I'm dead serious, you'll soon be calling me your 'balloon secretary.'"

Even though Budi was genuinely serious, when he finished, both men couldn't help but laugh at what could in fact become a problem for both of them. "Okay, enough with the kidding."

"Whose kidding. Now what is it that you need from me?" asked Budi.

The pope became serious. "I can't tell you how much it means to me that you are with me.

We go back so many years through some hard times. It's so comforting to know I have you at my side. You're the one person I can completely trust, someone that I can confide in and know you won't hesitate to tell me what you're thinking. Even when we were youngsters, you always were the one with sound judgment and understanding. I thank God every day that you are with me. Even though I know I was selected pope through devious methods, I still can't help but wonder what God has up his sleeve for me, during my reign as pope. I will strive to be as completely transparent as possible in the matter of pedophile clergy. The legal settlements, over and above the insurance policy reimbursements, have overwhelm me. I still can't believe the number of innocent people who have been abused by our priests. First America, and then Ireland. I have to admit, I'm nervous when I wake up each morning, wondering in what country the next shoe is going to drop. A clear message is necessary regarding sexual abuse by our clergy. Please give this some thought over the next week, and perhaps between us we can develop a clear, effective response that meets legal standards."

The pope then expanded on the question of sexual abuse by Catholic clergy. "One thing is for certain, I will not permit known pedophile priests, to ever again interact with parishioners."

The Pope and his secretary talked informally regarding the vast number of people that were sexually abused by Catholic priests. The decision arrived at by the pope and his secretary, was that a policy statement on pedophilia, applying to all Catholic clerics. This document would be the first official document from the new pope.

The cover letter for the policy statement included an opening statement that asked for forgiveness from the abused and then a stern condemnation of the cover-up that followed. The first paragraph of the policy statement made it clear that, starting immediately, priests, pastors, bishops and, where appropriate, cardinals, who know or suspect that a pedophile member of the clergy is functioning under their jurisdiction, they will be required to contact civil law authorities regarding their concerns and allow the civil legal process to move forward uninterrupted.

The second paragraph of the opening statement would be very controversial. It stated that the long-standing, accepted practice of confessional confidentiality, no longer applies to a confession of sexual abuse. "I'm inclined to follow the process established in secular institutions. Suspending the accused cleric until a full investigation has taken place by the civil authorities. If the civil police file charges against the accused cleric, at the conclusion of their investigation, and if the cleric requests a civil trial the church will provide funds for legal assistance. If found guilty, the church will abide by the sentence given by the civil judge; if found innocent, the cleric will be returned as a priest in good standing."

The policy statement concluded with a summary statement. *Any sexual act on the part of a priest without voluntary consent will be considered as a civil crime, and will be adjudicated as such. All individuals associated with a Catholic institution will no longer be under the supervision of a cleric's decision if the complaint is of sexual abuse. From this day forward all sexual abuse cases will be forwarded to civil law enforcement.*

Both men understood that the reference to criminal acts was a drastic change in policy for the church. However, they felt it was necessary so the public would understand that this issue was no longer going to remain an internal matter within the church. The message from the pope to pedophile clergy was direct and clear.

Pope Francis Xavier made the message public in October 2009, his second month in office. However, the message from the pope on pedophile priests left numerous unanswered questions. What would happen to a cleric after conviction and incarceration? Is there a cure for pedophilic disorders? If a priest is serving civilian prison time, should their ecclesiastical status be revoked? After a priest serves their prison sentence, does the church have a responsibility to provide food and shelter, if the cleric is unable to support himself?

Pope Francis Xavier held a news conference a day prior to the dissemination of his policy statement on pedophile clergy.

That evening, Pope Francis Xavier remained slumped in the easy chair, disturbed and perplexed by the staggering number of victims over so many years. This issue had caused such confusion that he was unable to rid his mind of the image of innocent children injured in such a vicious manner by an institution dedicated to love and compassion. Would the church ever be able to heal the scars caused by church leaders, who allowed these heinous, immoral acts to continue in the privacy of a confessional.

The financial implications were not a part of his public apology. The pope chose not to infringe in any way on financial settlements to the injured parties, but he understood that the Vatican would have to help some bishops and dioceses with the financial restitution to the injured. Pope Francis Xavier refused to deny any injured person the financial settlement handed down by the civil court.

***

Two days after the new policy on sexual abuse by clergy, Pope Francis Xavier and Father Susanto had an informal meeting to discuss the topic of sexual abuse by Catholic priests. Budi opened the conversation. "Our new policy brought up a feeling I've had since coming to the Vatican. It has to do with some members of the Curia and the issue of priestly celibacy. Remember our many conversations in Indonesia regarding our vow of celibacy, and the difficulty we had remaining true to this vow. Now that I'm in my fifties, I have to admit it's a lot easier, but it was tough on me in the beginning, and I know from our conversations over the years, it was difficult for you as well. Although I will admit, I do still enjoy looking at these lovely Italian, long-legged women, dressed to kill. Perhaps if I had been born in Italy, I'm not sure I would have had the will power to join you in our vocational choice."

The pope responded to his close friend and confidante, "Yes, I often recall those difficult years and, like you, I was very glad I had you to talk with, but right now I think you're starting to ramble. Get to the point about the Curia that seems to be bothering you?"

Budi agreed, "Okay, you're right, my point. I wish you would consider doing something about that brazen group of homosexual priests that seem to hold the power within the Curia. I don't know if you are aware, but they even have a nickname. Others refer to them as the lobby. Now we've both come across good devoted homosexual priests who have accepted the church's stand on homosexuality and made a choice not to act on their desires. I admire those guys, but these cardinals who are part of 'The Lobby,' they strut around openly hinting how they act on their sexual instincts, as though they have some special dispensation permitting them to disregard church teaching."

Pope Francis Xavier now noticed anger in the eyes of his friend, which was quite unusual. Budi continued, "And to make matters worse, this small group of Curia members act as though they have complete control over Curia policies and practices. They seem to ignore the equal status of the other members of the Curia. Perhaps I take it too personally, but you and I struggled with our sexual desires, and I know many other priests struggle with their desires as well, but this group seems to disregard their vows. In fact, they seem proud that they can ignore the church's stand on Celibacy for clergy members, simply because their cardinals."

Pope Francis Xavier responded to his annoyed friend, "I'm glad you brought this to my attention. I have not paid attention to these individuals, or maybe when I am around them, they are more cautious and remain on their best behavior. I must be more attentive; and if your feelings are accurate, I will certainly stop this behavior."

The pope hesitated, pouring himself a cup of coffee. He was disturbed by Budi's explanation of the atmosphere within the curia. Budi noticed his friend's troubled expression and went on, "In your role as bishop and cardinal in our homeland you tend to look more at the larger picture. Having been stationed in smaller communities, I am more aware of individual behaviors."

The pope responded, "You're probably correct, you have much more experience with smaller groups of clergy and communities of like-minded priests. I've been away from that type of ministry for the last eight years. I must pay more attention to how matters evolve in relations between priests."

CHAPTER 7

Pope Francis Xavier awoke from a deep sleep. Sitting erect in his bed, he touched his night garments and found them drenched with perspiration. Now fully awake, he sensed a feeling of dread throughout his entire being.

He thought, *I must have had a bad dream, but I can't recall what it was about, and I have a terrible feeling, I feel so frightened. I had better change these pajamas and dry my body. While in his bathroom, he continued to speculate about his dream, and if this dream was so terrifying that it woke me up, why can't I remember it?*

After drying his body; he drank two glasses of water and put on dry pajamas. He sat in a chair in his bedroom, still a bit shaky and upset, not quite ready to return to sleep. He remained seated, attempting to remember his nightmare. He still had a feeling of total apprehension and confusion. He took some deep breaths and tried to relax his body, which a few minutes ago had been trembling. His sense of disturbing fear was beginning to subside, but the frightful experience still occupied his mind.

During the next twenty minutes, his mind and body, and probably his blood pressure, returned to normal. Suddenly he thought of the deceitful way he had received votes from the other cardinals. He remembered his bewilderment during that second and third vote at the conclave. He was afraid to make eye contact with other cardinals, or was it embarrassment that caused him to continue staring straight ahead, focusing on the back of the head of the cardinal sitting in front of him, and wondering how could I, an unknown

Indonesian cardinal, be receiving so many votes to be pope. Entering his mind was a favorite phrase when he heard the vote total announced at the conclusion of the Conclave's third vote: *Wonder is to marvel at a mystery, and to be in awe before the unexplained.* He recalled his feelings at that time, not believing how or why his vote count was rising. Yes, I am in awe of the unexplained. Snippets, small morsels of awareness of the nightmare that awakened him, by entering his consciousness. *This frightening feeling that disturbed my sleep earlier is it solely due to my being Pope of the Catholic Church?*

As Pope Francis Xavier began to recall his nightmarish mystery, he decided that his subconscious mind was reliving those constant thoughts of not being prepared to be pope. These feelings of inadequacy had been a part of his mental process since that unbelievable moment now almost three months ago, when he had to rise from his seat at the Vatican Conclave and accept his fellow cardinals' vote for him to be leader of the Roman Catholic Church. Then as now, he was unsure of his ability to administer the duties of his position. It was a nomination he could not refuse, but in his mind, his selection was the most unlikely event to happen to an Indonesian.

Sitting in his bedroom easy chair, alone at 3:45 A.M., he spoke aloud, "Is this Indonesian capable of running the office of the pope. I'm Sunjaya Prantata, a cardinal from Indonesia. Being pope is preposterous!"

He continued talking aloud to himself, as though he was struggling to learn a newly formed concept. "I'm not the type of person who believes God comes down from heaven, juggling things around to make events happen the way He wants, yet how can this ridiculous event have ever happened? I'm not sure that I even believe in papal infallibility, God knows this, why Lord why?"

Pope Francis Xavier 1 started once again to perspire. He rose from his chair, walked to his bathroom removed a hand towel, and returned to his chair, while patted dry the perspiration from his forehead and underarms arms. He remained in his bedroom chair until dawn, asking himself. *Is there no way to correct such a terrible error? Will the remainder of my life be a series of foolish mistakes? What am I to do?*

When he arrived in his office after eating a light breakfast, he immediately called his secretary.

"Budi, finish what you are currently doing, then clear an hour, no, you better make that at least an hour and a half. I need to talk with you in private, and it's important. And put all calls to voice mail, I'll wait for you here in my office."

Father Susanto did not like the tone of the pope's request. He could tell something was bothering his friend. Budi then said, "I'll be in your office in about ten minutes."

Right on time there was a knock on the pope's office door, and after a brief moment, the door opened.

"Come in, Budi. Let us sit in the office alcove chairs."

They both settled in their chairs, Sunjaya explained his disturbed, restless night, continuing for approximately thirty minutes, recalling his anxiety, doubts, and fears. The conversation was serious. Budi understood what his friend was experiencing, and in some instances, sympathized with him. Budi decided to respond in practical, positive terms. "What alternative was there? You had been selected pope by other cardinals. You have no alternative but to remain as leader of the Catholic faith and if necessary, learning as you go along. Resigning your position after six months, is not an option."

The conversation progressed from the reality that Cardinal Sunjaya Prantata was now Pope Francis Xavier I, and whether real or perceived, he would have to deal with his dilemma of competency. Budi felt his role was to resolve, support, and reassure the pope by providing sensible suggestions and solutions. Budi expressed a suggestion, "If you feel unsure of your ability at this time, I urge you to take on projects that are realistic, workable, and, above all success-oriented. In this way, you will be building confidence in your leadership position."

Sunjaya continued to disagree with Budi's suggestion. He felt his secretary's suggestion would result in menial tasks, lacking in substance. Each idea seemed to Sunjaya to diminish his position as pope. The pope's reasoning was that his actions needed to be progressive in nature; this would be the only way to show members of the Catholic faith that he was capable of leading, willing to put into practice his belief system, proving to all the faithful and non-Catholics alike that the Indonesian pope was competent. Above all, he did not want to go down in history as the first brown skinned, South Asian pope, to be a mediocre failure.

Sunjaya was now in a different place than his secretary, which was unusual. Sunjaya seemed to have evolved over the past twenty-four hours, from being seen as a bureaucratic fool, to a young leader willing to show the world what Indonesian leadership can accomplish. The two men remained deep in conversation, nothing seemed to disturb their problem-solving strategies until they suddenly realized it was past the noon hour. An hour and a half had extended to three hours. Both men agreed it was time for a lunch break.

The pope ordered two light lunches delivered to his office, and both men continued their lengthy discussion as they enjoyed their lunch. The conversation began to center on the priorities the pope wished to establish as he moved forward in his position as pope. Sunjaya seemed to favor unpredictable ideas, completely opposite of what his secretary had been suggesting.

Budi realized his attempts to suggest productive ideas that would not rock the boat, seemed too to be going nowhere. Budi finally brought up the topic of dealing with lack of vocations. "Well, since your position seems to be more in line with disturbing the bureaucratic Vatican system and the Catholic laity around the world, how about you confront the inevitable problem of lack of priests? I know I'm in the minority on this issue, but the lack of priests may not be as traumatic as everyone seems to believe. With the median age of priests in the Catholic Church in the high seventies, and the fact that the number of men entering seminaries to replace this generation of priests, is so minimal, in probably ten to fifteen years, you will become the pope known for closing churches due to lack of priests. However, this fact alone may not necessarily be the end of our religion. It's possible that a lack of priests will turn out to be a blessing in disguise. Lack of priests may simply change the way Catholics worship."

Father Susanto then projected what the future might hold for his friend. "I believe that in your lifetime you may be forced to come up with a new definition of what constitutes a congregation. It could mean women priests or permitting existing priests to marry. If you choose to ignore both of those actions, then the question that you may face is simply a change in the way Catholics congregate to worship the Lord. It could very well turn out to become a new, more personal way of worship. Who knows what the Lord has in store for his people?"

Budi's reasoning came as a surprise to the pope. "If there are no priests, who will accept the leadership for gathering

Catholics for worship services, and there will be no one to concentrate the communion wafers?"

Budi responded, "If you consider the priesthood as it exists today, and the catholic teaching behind the consecrating of communion hosts, then your question is a valid one. However, look back on the period when Jesus walked the earth. There were leaders in the temples, but Jesus never became one of them. For that matter, if you were to read the gospels closely, you will find that Jesus never once referred to himself as a priest. Nor did he ever make reference to his disciples as priests."

The pope asked for clarification of Budi's statement, "What are you suggesting?"

Budi continued, "My feelings about priests may be unusual, but I often wonder where the need for priests came from, and how they became so important in our religion. Think about all the things Jesus spoke of when he was on earth. The disciples and other followers never called themselves priests. After the crucifixion of Jesus, when the disciples preached to the people, they never referred to themselves as priests. Luther may have had a point when he abandoned Catholicism. He wrote that *priests are not lords, but servants, and that the Eucharist does not belong to priests, but to all the people.* While I am on the topic, I don't believe that Saint Peter ever declared himself a pope or the bishop of Rome. During Saint Peter's time, bishops didn't exist, same for cardinals and popes; these categories came into being when some Catholics decided they wanted to establish a hierarchy. My point is that if there were no priests when Jesus walked the earth, perhaps Catholics can still worship, and maybe this worship may become stronger. If this were to occur, you or the pope that follows you may have to redefine the connection of priests and the administration of sacraments."

At the end of their planning, Sunjaya informed Father Susanto that he would take all the notes and ideas that they had discussed to Castle Gandolfo over the coming weekend, where he could think without interruption.

CHAPTER 8

The residence at Castel Gandolfo that Friday afternoon was quiet. The pope and the uniformed Swiss Guards traveling with him were the only residents. Castel Gandolfo is a small compact area, with a small piazza and an equally small church. Horse-drawn carts sell souvenirs, while other carts and vehicles sell their sandwiches and trinkets to visitors that arrive daily in huge tour buses. They come to Castel Gandolfo whether the pope is in his summer residence or in Rome.

The actual residence is a three-story villa overlooking the immediate gardens and cultivated landscape surrounding the building. The views from the various rooms in the villa are quite beautiful. The town of Castel Gandolfo is located fifteen miles southeast of Rome in the Lazio region of Italy. The pope's summer villa is high on the Albian hills overlooking Lake Albano. There are discreet rooms for visiting dignitaries which are plain except for the interesting artwork that adorns the walls. A small cafeteria functions when the pope is on holiday, during his summer stay or at special occasions, most often entertaining dignitaries during the summer months.

There are some very valuable benefits to being pope and one of these benefits is extended weekend vacations. Pope Francis Xavier called his secretary on Sunday afternoon and explained. "I've decided to remain at Castel Gandolfo an extra day. I plan on completing paperwork in the morning, then taking an afternoon break. The weather in this area of

Italy is wonderful, a beautiful sun, and a lovely light breeze that makes the gardens and trees inspiring. Budi, I'd appreciate if you would keep an eye on things at the Vatican on Monday. I plan to leave Castel Gandolfo after dinner, and I will be in the office first thing Tuesday morning."

Sunjaya Prantata was an uncomplicated person, but he also had an accessible personality. The severe poverty of his early years on Makmur Street was a factor in forming his attitude and behavior. He was almost three years of age before he realized there were other streets, families, and boys his age living in dilapidated apartments on streets other than his. During this time, his life revolved around his mother and two older sisters. He loved and respected his stern father, who died at the early age of fifty-three.

Sunjaya was very fortunate to gain the friendship of a boy on his first day in school, Budi Susanto, who, as it turned out, lived in the same apartment building on Makmur Street one floor below. Their friendship would become permanent, even though the two boys were quite different in personality, temperament, and sense of humor. Budi was not academically gifted or a motivated student, but even at the age of six, he was clever beyond his age when it came to managing, influencing, and controlling his peers. Budi helped Sunjaya understand and accept the early death of his father by sharing the harsh rules of poverty on Makmur Street. Soon, the two boys became more like brothers. They graduated high school together, learning quickly that a high school diploma was not a guarantee to enter middle-class Indonesian status. They both chose to enter a Catholic seminary and study to become priests. Their choice of priesthood was primarily a practical decision. Becoming a priest was the only way they knew of escaping the severe poverty of Jakarta. They learned at an early age that empty stomachs easily led to unsavory behavior, which became a part of life for the poor of Jakarta and, more often than not, would end in a jail sentence.

***

On Tuesday morning, at 8:00 a.m. sharp, there was a knock on the door of the door of the pope's office. Father Susanto, with writing pad in hand, entered and joined the pope, who was sitting in an upholstered chair in his office alcove. The two men exchanged morning greetings as Budi took a seat facing Sunjaya. The pope moved uneasily in his chair, Budi noticed a familiar determined look on his face, which was not always a good sign.

The pope said, "You won't need your pad. This will be a confidential discussion meeting for the immediate future. No one at this time must know of my plans."

Budi was surprised at the pope's opening comment; he had assumed they would be talking about papal priorities, not secret plans.

Budi said, "Know of your plans? What plans?"

The pope looked at his secretary with a curt half-smile and a look of toleration. "Budi, I have moved so far from my concerns and doubts of being pope of the Catholic Church. I now understand these fears were only roadblocks. I've decided to be aggressive and bold. I'm concerned if I become a pope who only takes part in ceremonial, events and parades, it will be said the brown-skinned South Asians have no initiative. If I strive to accomplish large projects or make changes, criticisms from others will no doubt follow. Therefore, either way, I'm going to be branded as a failure. So, if failure is a guarantee, why not be progressive in my actions, helping to improve the life of others."

Budi interrupted his friend. "I understand your thinking. However, a word of caution, don't make race your motivation for whatever task you have in mind; your decisions or this plan you speak of, should be motivated by correcting injustices, not promoting Indonesians."

Sunjaya smile was deep, almost sinister. "My friend, I couldn't agree with you more. What I came to understand at Castel Gandolfo was that my anxiety was not rooted in a fear of failure, but rather, in the fact that this overwhelming power and authority fell into my lap, through the illegal actions of three cardinals. Now that I understand where my fear is coming from, it has freed me to dream thoughts of empowering the less fortunate."

"Umm... I have one question, said Budi. Would it be in my best interest to request an immediate transfer back to Jakarta?"

The pope wagged his finger in his friend's face. "No such luck, you scoundrel, you're going to ride this out right alongside me. I now believe it would be a mortal sin if I failed to use the authority and power given to me. What I plan will be difficult, and it will not happen overnight, but I feel reinvigorated. It is as though I am twenty years younger and ready to embark on a great journey that will make a real difference in the lives of many people."

Pope Francis Xavier was ready to share his decision, that he arrived at over the past three days. He first reminded his friend of the numerous discussions they had in Indonesia, believing that God does not directly intervene in people's lives, causing them to act in certain ways or involve themselves in purposes because they believe this is a direct request from the Almighty. He assured Budi this was not the case, regarding what he was about to explain.

"I needed those three days away to understand the meaning of that terrible dream I recently had. My anxiety that evening had nothing to do with my qualifications to be head of the church. What frightened me during my dream was the intimidating power and authority of a pope."

Sunjaya then opened a brown folder holding a yellow lined pad of paper. He glanced down at the top page and then looked up at Budi. "I am determined to move forward with this radical idea, because I believe it is the right thing to do." Sunjaya certainly hoped God agreed, but right or wrong, the decision was his and his alone. He told Budi that while at Castel Gandolfo, he remembered the reason they both become Catholic priests. They would devote their lives to helping other poor Indonesians.

Budi interrupted his friend's explanation. "When I entered the office this morning, I immediately noticed that look in your eyes, and I said to myself, 'Here comes trouble.' So please, get to the point, which I am not sure I want to hear.'"

The pope grinned and continued. "So much has rumbled through my thoughts since the night I experienced that creepy nightmare. Perhaps the most important thing I learned was the fact that it would be cowardly of me to run away from my newfound power and authority. The courageous thing to do was to grab it, use it, and do what we vowed to do when we became priests, help the poor and the suffering"

Budi looked at his friend and said, "Hold on, I think I'm going to need a cup of coffee." Pope Francis Xavier followed his friend's example and filled his cup with hot coffee. While filling their cups, Budi could see that Sunjaya seemed to be very reflective in mood and appearance. This was Budi's clue not to interrupt; his friend had something very important to explain.

The pope continued, "In those three days at Castel Gandolfo, I was able to reflect on our youth in Indonesia and my priorities as a priest. As early as seven years of age, perhaps even earlier, as you and I lived in that death trap of an apartment house, we understood we were children of poverty, and that there was no way we could ever change the immorality of our state in life. I thought a great deal about my father and his only possession, his rickshaw taxi, propelled by his own legs to run wealthy people from place to place in Jakarta for miserly pennies so his family could have some food that evening. I believe his body simply wore out from all those years of pedaling his rickshaw causing him to die at an early age. I know he also felt the hopelessness of our existence, the same hopelessness that encouraged us to become priests. We convinced ourselves to choose this profession so we could help others in poverty, but equally important, we also understood the priesthood was the only way we could ever escape that rat-infested neighborhood."

Budi felt compelled to ask a question. "What was it that brought you back to our childhood?"

"As I was thinking of various priorities, I would like to accomplish over the next ten to twelve years, I kept coming back to the fact that poor people have no options. We chose the priesthood and vowed to remain true to our sacred promise. Then, suddenly, those three cardinals thought they could use us, and in turn, take over the Vatican."

Pope Francis Xavier put his cup of coffee back on the table and looked directly into Father Susanto's eyes. "You may have noticed I have been using the word we, rather than I. I know we talked about always remaining as a team, but what I have in mind will cause us to be hated and branded as traitors."

Budi was now anxious for the pope to continue. "Okay, let's have it. Explain what's in that head of yours. Enough with the preliminaries, I know you well enough to know that this must be something unusual, so please, explain what you have in mind."

The pope sat up strait, his eyes and facial expressions were beaming with excitement as he continued to speak. "This may not be the best reason for a decision such as this, but it was fueled by the fact that I want to show the world that an Indonesian has the ability and endurance to see a big project through to its completion."

Budi slumped in his chair. "Sunjaya, will you please stop with the theatrics!"

"I've decided to do something for the poor on a grand scale. I believe you and I have the opportunity to take almost a billion people out of poverty. Think about how we felt as youngsters on Makmur Street. Remember how it was when we were seven or eight knowing we had no options because of our position in life? Through the power and authority of the office of the pope I believe I can remove that same stigma we felt, from a billion people in Africa."

The pope treated himself to another taste of coffee, primarily to lubricate a dry throat that resulted from the intensity of this discussion.

Budi's face contorted in a doubtful expression as the pope continued. "Before you react, I know full well, the implications of removing poverty from the continent of Africa no, let me take that back. My idea is to save a continent that is disintegrating as we speak."

Budi was speechless for a moment and then responded. "Do you really think funding soup kitchens throughout Africa is going to remove the stigma of African poverty? You know as well as I that feeding the poor through handout food only reminds them how desperate their life really is! Food alone is misdirected aid. It alone creates an unsettled and disturbed way of life, forcing the poor to sink further into their inability to make the adjustments toward a more productive lifestyle. If you really want to stop the bleeding of Africa, it would take billions, no, multiple trillions of dollars, to even come close to lifting Africans out of poverty. And if you think, for one minute, your annual Peter's pence world-wide collection is enough to do what you are suggesting, you're wrong."

"Before continuing, I have to use the toilet, I'll be back shortly exactly, hold that thought." Budi used this excuse to give him time to think for a moment. He moved away from the door to the pope's office and with his back against the hallway wall. For a moment he thought through what the pope had just said about the continent of Africa. *My friend is about to explain the outline of his next step, implementing food kitchens for an entire continent, which is crazy, I need to bring him down to earth to protect him. His idea would only make him look like an overreaching fool. How do I explain that soup kitchens in Africa would only move him in a direction that would be self-destructive? His decision could very easily become a serious miscalculation. This idea is strangely out of character for Sunjaya; everything he does is deliberate and planned, but this is frivolously vain, and self-indulgent. I wonder if his idea of being inadequate as pope is ripping at his gut. I can only imagine how desperate and lonely he must be feeling to consider such a preposterous notion. He is not thinking clearly, not processing events with his usual clarity. That's okay. I have to find the right words to clear his head. It's time for me to get back to our discussion, God give me the correct words to help my friend.* Budi returned to the pope's Office, and sat down in his chair. The first comment by the pope to his friend was, "Budi, I want to assure you, I am not planning to establish soup kitchens on the African continent. My plan is much more complex and expensive than that."

Suddenly, Budi's mind stopped. *A terrifying thought popped into his head, a topic the two men had talked about often, but understood would never happen. Now he was really concerned.*

Budi interrupted Sunjaya, his eyes open wide, an expression of fear on his face. He said, "Hold on a minute. Please tell me you're not thinking what I think you're thinking. Please say you're not. You'll be crucified." The pope only responded with sly grin and then said. "You got it, my friend. I am thinking what you think I'm thinking!"

Budi tried his best to discourage Sunjaya by saying, "Our discussions were always hypothetical, and we understood the barriers. On paper, it looks good, but not only would the Catholic Church be outraged, the Western world would also gang up on you. Can't you just see a group like ISIL selling their oil to get their hands on a Michelangelo statue only to smash it to pieces with sledgehammers and post the video on YouTube? It will be the same as al Qaeda did in Afghanistan when it blew up the largest Buddha statue in the world."

Sunjaya would not allow his friend's caution to deter him. "They selected me to be their pope, and that gives me a certain amount of authority. It also gives me something called *ex-cathedra*, or papal infallibility as it's referred to, which will allow me the justification for selling the treasures of the Vatican and using the money to build a strong middle-class African society, and save the continent of Africa before it's too late."

Budi now understood Sunjaya was quite serious. "I can't argue with your idea as a matter of principal. But if I, were you, I would first find out if they can impeach a pope."

"Impeach me? On what grounds? I'm infallible, incapable of error in matters of faith and morals, and what is more immoral than our experience growing up in Indonesia? What I'm more concerned about is that someone might feel justified in assassinating me, before I sold their precious treasures. Accomplishing this won't be easy, but I have been given the power of accomplishing something meaningful for a great number of poor people. Suppose I decide not to go forward with this idea, and when I meet Jesus, how am I to answer if he says, 'You little squirt, those three cardinals misjudged you, by putting you in a seat of power. You had a great opportunity to accomplish something worthwhile, instead you get cold feet and blow it.

The pope's secretary, still in a bit of a haze at his friend's rationale, but knowing that leaving him was not an option, said, "Okay, boss, tell me what you want me to do first."

The pope looked directly into the eyes of his friend Budi. "Are you sure you want to be a part of this? You were right a few minutes ago when you said this might not work. Budi, don't agree to be part of this if you have doubts."

It was true that Budi was concerned about the success of this task, but he also wondered about the pope's ability to accept the aftershock of this announcement. *Budi knew, no one would be successful talking Sunjaya out of his idea.*

"Sunjaya, "My personal opinion is that your idea is far too radical, maybe even crazy. I'll be damned if I'm going to let them hang you alone. We've been together too long for me to bail on you now. I'm in with both feet, ready to support you to the fullest, even though I'm concerned for your safety."

Budi was about to make one of his classical wisecracks, but he stopped himself at the last moment, and then said. "All I have to say is I'm very proud of my bizarre friend. Tell me what it is you want me to do first."

The pope touched the hand of his dear friend. "Budi, I don't know what I would have done if you had chosen not to be with me on this. Can you believe we're going to try to do something that will help almost a billion people?" The pope's eyes watered slightly, as he said to his friend. "First, go to the Vatican library and request from Father John, the librarian, the entire packet for Vatican I. I'm interested in reading the minutes relative to the proclamation on the decision made at Vatican Council I, in 1869, regarding papal infallibility."

Budi responded cautiously "Making a statement based on your infallibility in matters of faith and morals? That's going to be tricky."

"Perhaps," answered the pope. "A good deal depends on what I read in the minutes. I'm interested in why this American scholar from Wisconsin claims the vote on papal infallibility was invalid. I think his name is Williams or Wilkins."

Budi said, "Wills, Garry Wills is the name of the man I think you are referring to. How can you forget his name? You have read all his books on Catholicism."

"Good man, Budi. You're right."

As Budi was leaving the office, the pope called out to him. "Budi, wait. Ask Father John for both Vatican Councils I, & II. I don't want him to assume there is something in Vatican I that interests me. Make it a casual request; pretend I wish to familiarize myself with the matters of both councils. In this way, he will be less likely to question my motives."

Budi took a step toward the door; he suddenly stopped, turned, and said, "By the way, I've noticed you've been acting very cynical lately. You seem to imply that everything directed at you negatively is due to you being Indonesian. You do know, when introducing your idea, everything is going to come down on you personally, and I'm worried about your long-term health. Think seriously about this. I'm not trying to talk you out of your plans, just letting you know, I'm worried about your health."

"Thanks, Budi. I think I'll be okay as long as you hang in with me, then I'll be fine."

Father Susanto looked doubtful. "You may need more than me. Let's hope Jesus is as confident as you seem to be. I'm just concerned for you personally. If you truly believe in what you are proposing, then only focus on the impact this could have for the African people and let the criticism of the Indonesian pope roll off your shoulders."

"Didn't I ask you to go to the library? So, get moving."

"You got it, boss," said Budi, knowing Sunjaya fully understood his concern.

CHAPTER 9

When Budi returned, he handed two the thick packets to the pope, labeled Vatican Council I and Vatican Council II. Pope Francis Xavier stopped what he was doing and cleared his desk, including the Vatican Council II folder. He turned to Father Susanto. "How does your afternoon look? Can you give me a half hour or so? I'd like to read the minutes of Vatican I and then discuss my thoughts regarding papal infallibility."

"For you, boss, I'll make time. How about three?"

"That'll be good. See you then."

Once Budi left, the pope opened the thick, musty-smelling packet labeled Vatican Council I. He shuffled papers, making sure not to disturb the order of the various documents, until he found the information having to do with the proclamation on *ex-cathedra*, or papal infallibility, and he began to scrutinize the official minutes.

Pope Pius IX called Vatican Council I into session in 1869. The purpose of the council meeting was to deal with contemporary problems such as the rising influence of rationalism, liberalism, and materialism. The council also dealt with two amendments. The first dealt with the topic of dogmatic formation on Catholic faith, which passed unanimously on the second vote. The pope carefully read the second amendment, *ex-cathedra*, primacy and papal infallibility, numerous times.

The pope hoped each word would be able to give him an understanding of the outcome, as well as the atmosphere in the room in 1869. There were 529 authorized cardinals eligible to vote on both amendments. The vote on the second amendment was unable to meet the two-thirds majority needed for approval. One of the cardinals who had voted in the affirmative asked to be recognized. He proposed that a committee of ten voting cardinals, five who voted yes on the amendment and five who voted no. The task of this ad-hock committee was to clarify the intent of the amendment, so that it might be more agreeable to the body of cardinals. They would meet during the remainder of the afternoon, and after dinner. This suggestion received a unanimously affirmative vote, and the afternoon session ended.

Pope Francis Xavier was startled when he read the continuing minutes from the morning's meeting. The minutes read, *five complaining cardinals were to leave Rome early the following morning, prior to the scheduled opening of the morning meeting to vote on the disputed second amendment.* The second vote later that morning, on the second amendment, ex cathedra primacy and papal infallibility, was able to meet the two-thirds required votes for approval.

The pope read the minutes for a second and third time. Pope Francis Xavier had to conclude that papal infallibility, a legally adopted principle, agreed to by the cardinals in 1896, had been flawed.

That settled a question that had been nagging him since his ordination to the priesthood. The vote on papal infallibility was inaccurate since five cardinals who had voted no, were not present for the second vote. The question lay heavy on the pope's mind. Papal infallibility was to be the cornerstone of his African plan, but now he knew it to be false.

Pope Francis Xavier stared at the two folders behind his desk for approximately ten minutes recounting in his mind the conclusive evidence relating to *ex-cathedra*. The scholar from the University of Wisconsin, Garry Wills, was correct in believing the second amendment voted on at Vatican Council I, ex-cathedra primacy and papal infallibility was illegal. This thought continued to interrupt his afternoon work.

The following afternoon, the two men from Indonesia huddled in the pope's office. Pope Francis Xavier explained. "I will need more time to determine if I should use *ex-cathedra* as part of my plan for Africa. I was very disturbed by the minutes of Vatican Council I.

Father Susanto responded to Sunjaya's predicament. "I know once you have made up your mind, I will be unable to change it. I'm not concerned if papal infallibility is right or wrong. After a hundred plus years, there's nothing you can do to change what has been accepted for many years. My concern is the resistance from the church hierarchy to the plan in general."

Pope Francis Xavier looked up from his desk and said, "I need a few days to decide if I want to use information, I now know to be false, I need some time to let the information sink in before deciding. Meanwhile, I would appreciate if you would return the Vatican, I and II folders to the library and continue as though our discussion on Africa is on hold."

Budi agreed there was no rush to come to a decision on Africa. On the third day after their discussion on Africa, the pope called Budi into his office. As Budi entered, Pope Francis Xavier was at his desk, a signal to Father Susanto that the pope was ready to work.

He said, "I've made my decision to use papal infallibility, as it is known to the general public, as the rationale for my Africa plan. However, I have decided to stay away from the public's term papal infallibility and use the term established during Vatican Council I, *ex-cathedra* when explaining the topic to the public. Vatican Council I defined *ex cathedra* as a teaching tool for popes and that is how I will use it. In addition, I have come to terms with the ethical principle of the means justifying the ends, and it is my intention to move forward in spite of that. I want to be clear, so you can decide if you can morally work alongside of me in what I expect to be a challenging endeavor."

The pope used the next few minutes to explain his position. "I do realize that using the term *ex-cathedra* implies I will be teaching the faithful to accept poverty as an immoral act against all humans. I have accepted the fact that using a doctrine falsely established by Pius IX would assist me in accomplishing what I have in mind for the poverty-stricken people on the African continent. I have made my decision, and I need to know if you can accept my reasoning. I have not heard your opinion, and I would like to know where you stand before I go further."

Budi responded to his friend, "Don't you think it's odd that no one else other than this Wills fella, has exposed the actions of Pious IX on such an important amendment?"

"No, I don't think it odd at all Budi. After my experience with those three European cardinals, I would not be surprised at anything human beings say or do either in God's name or in their own need to hold onto power. Pope Pius XII used papal infallibility for the first time in 1950, declaring the Immaculate Conception was true. He was not challenged in 1950, and I don't believe I will be challenged in 2009. The hierarchy fears negative publicity more that it fears me saying poverty is immoral."

Father Susanto was still concerned. He sat slumped in his comfortable chair, looking confused, and remained silent for a moment.

Then he abruptly sat up straight and said, "Appreciate for a moment how it will feel knowing we actually, could make a difference in the lives of the poor in Africa. Well, my friend, you sound determined to make one hell of a big difference. Therefore, I want you to know I'll be coming along for the ride, as you are being accused of treachery and whatever other evil acts others will claim. Let's get started."

CHAPTER 10

Pope Francis Xavier called his secretary to his office. He handed him a paper that had written on it seven names.

"Would you please find the phone numbers for these individuals then call their offices and give them my direct line? I'm concerned that if they are called directly and I say this is Pope Francis Xavier, their secretary may think it's a prank call. If the secretary is given a direct line phone number, it is more likely the person will get back to me."

Budi smiled and started walking out of the office, looking at the names on the paper. Before closing the door, his prankster mind kicked into high gear.

"Wow, you're traveling with the big shot elites of the world. Soon I'll have to make an appointment two weeks in advance just to speak with you. I'm impressed. I wish you luck!"

After his whimsical remark, Budi quick-stepped it out of the pope's office leaving pope with only the air to rebuke.

"Get back in here, you mischievous rascal. I'm not finished."

In a moment, the pope saw the familiar thin, handsome face with a devilish smile and full thick head of shiny black hair peering around the wood door molding.

"You called, master?"

A laughing pope said, "You're impossible, but I guess I'm stuck with you. There is one other thing. When you're inquiring about a place outside of Rome for these people to meet, ask the Vatican workers if they know of a nice peaceful place. Explain that you need to get away for a weekend, somewhere rural and secluded with good scenery for strolling, and a place that is about an hour from Rome. Don't ask the clergy. They still see us, or at least they still see me, as an intruder, especially since the three European cardinals were re-assigned, and frankly, I don't have much trust in many of them, and I'm afraid the feeling is mutual. If I can convince some of the names on the list, I gave you, to come to Italy and work on a plan for helping the poverty-stricken Africans, I want them to work outside of the city of Rome. As you can see from the names of the people on the list, they would, without question, attract media attention, and that will be distracting to their work."

The pope then thought of another detail. "Oh, one other thing. If I can convince them to come to Rome, you will also need to contact Italian customs officials at the airport and see if you can arrange for the people on my list to be able to pass-through Italian customs in an out-of-the-way area where our cars can park and hustle them off privately to their destination."

"Good point. No wonder your pope and I'm secretary," replied Budi.

The pope looked up from his desk.

"And if any of their secretaries believe this to be a prank call, I expect you to work your pleasant, seductive charm and convince them that it really is the pope's office calling."

Budi, with names and phone numbers in hand, started his calls. The first call was to retired Bishop Imamu Okote-Eboh from South Africa, then onto Amarie Maalout, South African anti-apartheid leader and a former president of South Africa. Next was Graham Quinlan, former prime minister of the United Kingdom, during the George W. Bush presidency, then Greta Ivar, former Swedish prime minister. He also called the most recent former president of the United States, Roscoe Ayala, Deidra Conrad, president of Germany; and Noah Lukas, former Belgium ambassador to Algeria.

The following day, the pope called his secretary into his office and asked him to bring along his notepad.

The pope began, "Budi, I would like you to contact the president of Sotheby's Auction House in New York City. Explain that I wish to speak with the president only, and on a secure line. I'm assuming whoever answers may also believe the call to be a hoax. In that case, work your amusing charms and get it done. Then I would like you to call a Ms. Sharon Wasserman. She is a preeminent world expert on rare books and antiquarian documents, she also resides in New York City. Leave the same message with her."

Later that afternoon, the pope received a call on his private line, from the president of Sotheby's Auction House, Mister Matthew Walkin. The pope responded warmly, thanked Mister Walkin for promptly returning his call, and took a moment to assure him that, in fact, he was Pope Francis Xavier. He began immediately informing Mister Walkin that he had a proposal for Sotheby's, and immediately qualified the auction proposal with conditions.

"Mr. Walkin, before I explain my proposal, I want you to know that confidentiality regarding this matter is the most critical aspect of our arrangement. If we can both agree on Sotheby's handling this sale for the Vatican, the contract must include a statement indicating that if the confidentiality of my proposal is broken before our agreed upon date, I would have the right to terminate our agreement, and furthermore exclude Sotheby's from participation in all future Vatican sales. I don't mean to be rude in this matter, but it is essential this transaction remain confidential. At this time, confidentiality is my highest priority."

Mister Walkin understood. "No need to apologize for wanting this stipulation in a contract. Over half of the contracts Sotheby's enters into, contain a similar clause relative to confidentiality; this will not be a problem for us."

Mister Walkin further elaborated, "Privacy is clearly high on your list of priorities so let me guarantee once again that a confidentiality agreement will be included, if and when we arrive at a contract."

The pope replied, "Perhaps I have gotten ahead of myself, but I need confidentiality from you personally that our conversation is also to be confidential. This must be absolutely clear, before I go any further in this conversation."

Mister Walkin began to suspect that perhaps this was not a general phone call for simply gathering information. *Could the pope be inquiring about selling one of the Vatican's prized possessions?*

"Your Holiness if you are thinking of selling an item of value, understand that Sotheby's integrity and reputation is also at stake, and, furthermore, if this matter were to become public, it would also mean the end of my employment, my reputation, and most likely my career. "Your Holiness, all I have to offer is my word, and my reputation as president of Sotheby's. I am honor bound not to repeat anything that we may discuss, even if you decide not to utilize our services."

The pope was still nervous about prematurely divulging what he had in mind but also realized at some point that he would have to trust someone. "I am seriously considering disposing of the Vatican treasures. All items located in the Vatican Museum, the Borghese Gallery and a few other rooms, and most of the artwork located in Saint Peter's

Cathedral, as well as the antiquity books and other rare documents now located in the Vatican Library. Word of this must not become public until after I make a declaration to the Catholic community around the world, a statement in a form that our constitution refers to as *ex cathedra*, which signals to Catholics that the statement is a part of my holy teaching."

Mister Walkin was relieved the pope followed his disclosure with a few sentences, which allowed him to catch his breath. Mister Walkin could only imagine, what it would mean for Sotheby's to supervise an auction of this magnitude. *This would be the most prized auction of art and antiquities ever to take place, not to mention the largest financial reward Sotheby's has ever earned.*

Mister Walkin, still silent took a long moment to get his bearings, realizing what the pope had just proposed, but he quickly regained his composure.

"Your Holiness, although I am not a practicing Catholic, I believe I understand the implications of an *ex-cathedra* statement. Doesn't that imply papal infallibility?"

"Yes, it does, Mister Walkin. And I must say I am impressed by your understanding of this Latin phrase."

Hesitating a moment longer, the pope continued, "Now that I have explained what I want auctioned, I hope you can appreciate my concern for confidentiality. I may be repeating myself, but this only emphasizes how strongly I feel about the issue of strict adherence to secrecy regarding this auction proposal."

Mister Walkin now up from his desk, walking around his office, holding his mobile phone close to his ear, finding it hard to concentrate on his conversation with the pope. His mind trying to grasp the enormity of such a sale. He finally said, "Now that you have explained the outline of your intentions, I can certainly appreciate your insistence on confidentiality."

The pope then explained a second requirement crucial to the sale of the Vatican property, "Mister Walkin, let me add, not only will this sale be controversial, but also the project, which will be financially supported by the proceeds earned from this sale, will be equally controversial. Therefore, I must make certain that the announcement of the auction at your facility in America and my announcement at a news conference in Italy begin at exactly the same time, which will be different in both countries. Not to mention that the questions asked of us both, will certainly be different. You dealing with the process of the auction, I expect to be dealing with resistance, which I fully expect to much more controversial."

Mister Walkin, continuing to pace up and down in his office, with the mobile phone glued to his ear, now had sufficient time to allow this financial opportunity sink into his reality. His thoughts began jumping into planning mode as he spoke. "I do understand the necessity of your cautious approach in this matter, and I guarantee that both Sotheby's and I will honor your unique needs going further in this matter."

With Mister Walkin's thoughts still swirling in his mind said, "Your Holiness, I am honored you have called on Sotheby's for such an event, and I will once again assure you my employees and I understand and respect the need for absolute confidentiality in this matter."

The pope immediately interrupted Mister Walkin in a raised tone. "You and your employees? You said nothing about informing employees."

Mister Walkin instantly realized he had made an error by interjecting the word employees before fully explaining the process necessary for such an event.

"Your Holiness, are you able to give me few minutes of your time to explain what needs to be done in preparation for arranging a sale of this magnitude?"

"Yes," replied the Pope.

"The art and statuary experts in our employ constantly deal with confidentiality in their work. They have experience with many clients who wish to remain anonymous. Some require their names not be associated with a sale before and after. In fact, our experts have an agreement in their employment contract precluding them from discussing names of sellers and/or buyers with the press and even their families, and that includes their spouses. However, it will be essential for these experts to travel to the Vatican to examine what you are planning to auction. A price range on each item will need to be established and included in an auction brochure. This, of course, is part of our service to our clients. The only other person who will be made aware of this event is our computer technician, who also has a confidentiality agreement in his contract."

"Another employee," said a disgruntled pope. "I'm afraid so," replied Mister Walkin. "For an auction of this size and quality, it will be to your advantage to be able to construct this auction as a global event. For this to be accomplished, my technology person will have to develop a new piece of software that would allow any interested party around the world to be able to become connected, via computer, to view and bid on each item. I believe global accessibility will be a critical factor if you are to realize the true value of your items. It would be essential for institutions, schools, museums, and the public in countries around the developed world to be able to view an item of interest. If you plan to dispose of every item in the Vatican's collection, I believe institutions and museums may have to collaborate on sharing the price of some of your more valuable pieces. A worldwide audience will be essential, and we can only accomplish this, using current technology."

Mister Walkin wanted the pope to hear some words of encouragement. "We have seen high prices for old-master paintings. For example, in 1987, the Van Gogh's *Sunflowers* painting sold in a London auction house for $40 million. In 2017, a Leonardo da Vinci painting sold through Christie's auction house, in New York City for 450 million plus dollars. I'm familiar with the Vatican collection and know you have a number of da Vinci's paintings."

The price of the da Vinci painting did not seem to be of any interest to Pope Francis Xavier at that moment, his mind occupied by another concern, the pope interrupted Mister Walkin. "One of my concerns is that a terrorist organization may purchase a valuable piece of art, with the sole intention of destroying a piece of Western Culture. Is there some way for you to ensure that only legitimate art dealers, art lovers, and organizations are allowed to bid on the various pieces of art for sale?"

"That's an excellent question, Your Holiness. The person designing the software for this sale will require certain information from individuals, organizations or museums wishing to participate in an auction of this magnitude. Also, let me add that we are familiar with over ninety-five percent of legitimate individuals or organizations we would expect to participate in this auction. Individuals or organizations Sotheby's are not familiar with, will receive a careful and detailed screening procedure, prior to entering the bidding process. Remember, Sotheby's and my personal reputations are on the line, especially in an auction of this size. So, let me assure you, our security department is quite thorough. If there is the slightest question about a bidder or their affiliation, they will be excluded from participating in your auction."

Mister Walkin continued, "Sotheby's would be proud to introduce to the art world to a never-before concept. A worldwide auction, which I feel is necessary in order for you to obtain the true value of the one-of-a-kind pieces in the Vatican collection."

Mister Walkin then added, "Your Holiness, let me say one last thing in the way of assurance of the confidentiality of an auction such as this. The reputation of our art and statuary experts would also be at stake. They cannot afford to break confidence in this matter, and the evaluation of the art and statuary you choose to sell, allows us to pull an item out of the auction if bidders do not meet the listed minimum price in our pre-auction brochure. Our experts and I fully understand that our personal reputations are on the line, along with Sotheby's reputation."

The manner and the understanding of Mister Walkin somewhat relieved the Pope. He told himself, *He sounds like a man who appreciates my need for silence in this matter.*

Mister Walkin continued, "I hope I have removed any concern regarding the private nature of our agreement. For an auction of this immensity and value, I want you to know we are honored you chose to speak with Sotheby's about your plans. We completely accept the stipulation that the disclosure announcement of this auction will remain as your prerogative, not ours. I would also wish to assure you; Sotheby's will not do anything foolish to damage our reputation or our relationship with you."

Mister Walkin closed the phone conversation by saying, "If you decide to use Sotheby's services for this auction, call me on this same secured phone line. If we are fortunate enough to be chosen, please allow me as much time as possible in advance so we can make certain all details are covered."

Mister Walkin gave the pope the number of his secure phone line.

The pope then asked Mister Walkin a question. "A Ms. Sharon Wasserman has been recommended to me as the preeminent expert on rare books and antiquity documents. Have you heard of her?"

"She would be an excellent choice, Your Holiness. I have met with her a number of times. She will be a valuable asset in reviewing your material. I can also vouch for her understanding of the need for confidentiality. Remember, any indiscretion on her part will only serve to destroy her reputation as well, and we both have been in this business far too many years for us to be indiscreet. I'm confident she would never do anything to destroy a reputation she has built over her many years of work, as a professional in her field."

Both men agreed the necessary information was covered, and the next step would be for Pope Francis Xavier to contact Mister Walkin with his decision.

After terminating the Sotheby's phone call, Pope Francis Xavier immediately called his secretary and informed him to let the library director and the Vatican Museum director know of the closure of both facilities for approximately a week, dates to be determined.

"Think up a plausible reason for this closing, but under no circumstance do I wish them to know the real reason for the expected closure. Also, inform them they will be told the dates of this closure as soon as possible so they can prepare properly."

CHAPTER 11

The pope's private line rang early on Tuesday afternoon. He answered and heard a firm but hesitant voice asks, "With whom am I speaking?"

Suspecting this may be Ms. Wasserman, the pope responded, "This is the pope of the Roman Catholic Church, Francis Xavier speaking."

Now a softer, more pleasant voice at the other end of the line said, "Good morning, Your Holiness. I must admit I had my doubts about this being a legitimate call. I could not imagine why Your Holiness would want to speak with me. So please forgive my initial tone of voice."

The pope, now much more relaxed about the question of confidentiality, explained the reason for his call. Ms. Wasserman was silent during the pope's description of what he needed from her.

When the pope was finished, Ms. Wasserman said, "Your Holiness, you have my word as a professional and one who understands the inherent value of rare documents, not a word spoken this morning will ever be discussed without your personal approval."

Ms. Wasserman assured Pope Francis Xavier his offer of travel expenses, along with room and board, was sufficient compensation for her work.

***

From 21, March to 28 March, 2010, the Vatican library and museum, the Borghese Gallery, Saint Peter's Cathedral, and a few small chapels located in Vatican City were closed to the public. Three evaluators, Ms. Wasserman, Mr. Raymond, and Mr. Ritter, were excited at the privilege of being able to evaluate many rare and beautiful works of art and historic written documents.

They wore plastic garments, headpieces covering their hair, and special latex gloves, which protected the works of art from the natural oil of their skin and other particles of sediment from infiltrating the open pores of the works of art they would be touching and moving. The artwork included pieces they had only read about in books or seen in film and video. They never imagined they would have the enormous privilege of examining the works of the masters, close-up and in person.

On March, 29, Ms. Wasserman was in the pope's office, delivering her written evaluation of the Vatican's library documents. She was a short, slight woman, with full grey hair neatly tied back in a precise bun. The sixty-six-year-old woman wore a simple solid light blue dress, flat leather shoes, and plain non-rimmed glasses. She was flushed with excitement as she handed her written report to the pope.

The pope thanked her for her work and asked her to summarize her findings. A half hour later, the frustrated pope was sorry he did not request a time limit on her verbal summary.

"Oh, my heavens, where to begin. I was surprised to see the library collection contained secular as well as religious documents. Initially, I assumed the Vatican collection would be only religious documents. How wrong I was. I came across a book of poems by John Keats the famous English Romantic poet. Now this would not necessarily stand out as unique, since Keats wrote extensively in the mid-1800's, and libraries, institutions, and private collectors own a number of original works of Keats. However, what makes your volume by Keats unique is that it includes a poem by his younger brother George, 'Value of Soul-Making,' which Keats must have included in this early volume of his work.

Ancient Greece produced more than a hundred plays, which is where Western civilization literature began. Only twenty-two original plays exist today, owned privately or in museums. The Vatican collection owns sixteen original Greek plays. Of significance in the Vatican's collection is an original single play and a trilogy by Aeschylus titled The Persians. Can you imagine the significance of this document becoming available to the public?"

Ms. Wasserman looked and sounded as though she was only now warming up and during a moment of hesitation by Ms. Wasserman, the pope said, "Ms. Wasserman, I know you are planning to leave this afternoon, and I am sure you have much to arrange before you leave the Vatican. So, let me suggest that I can read your exciting information in your comprehensive written report."

"Your Holiness, these past six days have been the most exciting days of my life. I must cover one last item; I promise to be brief. There are twenty-one documents of literature listed with an asterisk. Unfortunately, I don't have the technical equipment to authenticate whether these documents are monks' copies, or copies of original work. Experts believe that Christian monasticism began in the fourth century in the area of Egypt, as early as 251 to 365. Christian monasticism established as a solitary, eremitic ideal, probably originating from the word *Heremos*, which means desert. The word used for these early communities of men was *monachoi*, which means lone ones, who lived together in a *monestarion*, what we now refer to as monasteries."

The pope questioned Ms. Wasserman's last statement. "Does that mean your report is incomplete?"

Ms. Wasserman, a bit flustered, answered the pope's question. "I would like to discuss with you the possibility of engaging the services of another individual, whom I know would agree to enter into a contract that includes the same confidentiality clause I have. He also would not think of damaging his reputation, which we both have worked long and hard to earn. He has equipment not available to me, which can date the paper and ink used in these documents, identifying them as monks' copies or original works. I can assure you he would be happy to perform his examination, accepting travel expenses and room and board for his services. And finally, I want you to know you have made this old woman's life worth living, by allowing me to examine the Vatican's collection."

The pope reluctantly agreed.

The two men from Sotheby's were to meet with the pope for a luncheon meeting that same afternoon to share their report and explain some of their findings.

Mr. Ritter was a slight man, five feet six inches tall. He wore sloppy, soiled jeans and a solid-colored shirt that was soon due for the old rag department. He was the first to speak.

"You have historic, valuable, and beautiful paintings, sketches, and vestments in the Vatican collection. I have to mention that I got goose bumps handling a number of these vestments, especially a fourteenth century Byzantine dalmatic vestment of Charlemagne. I have included each item I evaluated in my report, detailing some of the important features of each piece. I want to thank you for access to the Vatican collection.

Mr. Raymond, the statuary expert, was an older man in his mid-fifties. Compared to his companion, he was well dressed. His ironed pants had colorful suspenders holding them in place. His full head of dark brown hair was neatly combed in contrast to his partner. He and Mr. Ritter kept their verbal presentation to a minimum.

"Your Holiness; I second Mr. Ritter's comment regarding his evaluation. I too was very excited evaluating the paintings and statuary located in the Vatican's collection. I was thrilled to examine the extensive statuary pieces in the Vatican's collection. I was so tempted to touch some of Michelangelo's pieces without my latex gloves, especially his *Pieta*."

With a broad smile, the pope asked Mr. Raymond to explain his fascination with Michelangelo's *Pieta*.

"It's very difficult to precisely describe the intricacy of Michelangelo's *Pieta*. Close examination enabled me to scrutinize every vein, sinew, muscle, and bone of Christ's dead body, and every pleat in Mother Mary's cloak. I have seen other Pieta statuary, but Michelangelo's *Pieta* proves he understood the human body as an organism in harmony with each of its various parts as he sculpted a dead body. Christ's limp form in death appears more vital and symmetrical than any living form depicted in art history. The piece of marble Michelangelo chiseled and crafted into the Blessed Mother and her dead son truly tells a profound story."

Mr. Raymond, flushed with excitement, continued. "I would like to mention a few other pieces of statuary that I had never expected to see in person. For example, a half-length angel by Giotto, a bronze bust of Sixtus IV by Pollaulo, the torso of Belvedere, first century Roman Sculptures, and I would be remiss, if I did not mention Michelangelo's Moses in this category; in addition, another personal favorite, a statue of Saint Augustine's detail of the reliquary with chair by Bernini. My written report details the necessary information needed for the auction. I remain ever grateful for these exciting two days of work."

Mr. Raymond made one last comment before the two men left.

"Mister Walkin told us you are considering removing some of your frescos to allow contemporary artists to show their work next to the old masters. I congratulate you for allowing this comparison to take place, I know of no other museum or gallery where this concept exists. However, I must warn you that removing a fresco is possible, but you must be sure the person who does this work is an experienced and talented restorer, or these valuable frescoes will be damaged."

"Thank you both for the reports and comments, I'm sure you want to get back to your rooms and prepare for your evening flight. In addition, you can be sure the reason for entering into this auction is of the greatest importance to me. I choose to say no more, except soon you both will understand the reason for this auction."

Mr. Ritter entered the conversation by saying, "I don't know if you use this expression in Indonesia but what do you want first, the good news or the bad news?"

A smiling pope was suddenly concerned, regarding what the bad news would be.

"Yes, I'm familiar with the saying, and no, that expression in not common in Indonesia. Please explain what you mean by bad news."

Mr. Raymond said, "Phil, stop foolin around, you got His Holiness worried now."

"Your Holiness, what Mr. Ritter is implying is that we wonder if there is enough expendable capital among the nations in the developed world for your church to receive the true financial value of some of the more important works of art. It is standard procedure to place a minimum value on original important pieces. I believe Mr. Ritter is correct in implying it may be impossible for anyone to estimate the minimum value on Michelangelo's pieces, such as his Moses statue, or Leonardo de Vinci's paintings."

Pope Francis Xavier now had a worried look on his face.

"I never considered that aspect. I will need to discuss this with Mister Walkin after I have reviewed your report."

Phil Raymond then said, "Mister Walkin did ask us to mention that after you've had the opportunity to review our report, he would like the opportunity to speak with you regarding the procedures we use for shipping such items as the *Pietà*. Sotheby's does carry insurance for all its deliveries, however, in this case, there are some pieces that, for humanity's sake, cannot be damaged, but you are correct, that is a topic you will have to discuss with Mister Walkin."

CHAPTER 12

The first-person Father Susanto called was retired Anglican Bishop Imamu Okote-Eboh of South Africa. "Good afternoon, I am Imamu Okote-Eboh."

Budi was a bit surprised that the retired bishop answered his phone, rather than a secretary.

"Bishop Okote-Eboh, this is the office of Pope Francis Xavier 1. He would appreciate the opportunity to speak with you. Could you tell me when that would be convenient for you?"

The bishop replied, "If he is free, now would be a good time for me."

Budi quickly responded, "He is in his office, and I know he is anxious to speak with you. Just hold for a moment, and I'll transfer you over to his direct line."

Budi called the pope and informed him that the bishop was available to speak with him. Pope Francis Xavier told his secretary to put the call through to his direct line. The pope picked up the receiver, introduced himself, and after Bishop Okote-Eboh congratulated him on his appointment as pope, followed by some brief pleasant exchanges, then the pope explained the reason for his call.

"I am hoping you will consider being part of a small group, a maximum of seven other distinguished individuals, for a special task I have in mind. My idea is to have you and six others meet in the near future for the purpose of developing a comprehensive plan to eliminate poverty from the continent of Africa."

Before the pope could continue, Bishop Okote-Eboh said, "Oh, I see. And how would you go about doing that?"

The pope was surprised and somewhat annoyed by the bishop's rude sounding interruption of his opening statement, but he decided to ignore the sarcastic tone.

"Well, that would be the point of bringing you and six other people together to design a plan that would accomplish this purpose. I have never been to Africa, and so it seemed reasonable to me, to get expert advice of others, who are familiar with the continent, before I begin such a project. My thought was to invite people like you, and others to meet and outline a plan of action for me to follow rather than me blindly intervening on a continent and into a culture that I know very little about. Bishop, I'm not a worldly man, living in Indonesia all my life and having experienced Indonesian poverty first-hand, I am more familiar with the effects of poverty on my island. Having said that, from my experience in Indonesia, I strongly believe that education is an essential ingredient in the initial steps to remove poverty, whether in Southern Asia or Africa, but beyond that, I need direction from people like you."

The pope continued, "I would like to give Africans the opportunity to earn a living wage, be part of a community, and be free to improve their status in life. I would hope that eventually my intervention on the African continent would produce a strong middle-class society, along with restoring security and peace for the African people."

The pope, now cautious and still defensive, said, "I simply would like to know how to stop the erosion of what should be, in my opinion, a powerful, vibrant continent that seems unable to provide security and prosperity for its people. I hope you are not offended by my statement, but I am simply doing my best to respond to your questions."

"No, Your Holiness, I am not offended in the least." Then the bishop remained silent, still seeming to be indifferent and unresponsive.

The silence lasted a few seconds, but it seemed like minutes to Pope Francis Xavier. "Excuse me, Your Holiness, before you go further, I have a question."

The pope, still frustrated with the conversation, thought, *Oh no, not another question. Am I to experience this reaction with the other people I plan to contact?*

"My question is central to your desire to introduce education in this plan you have in mind.

Do you expect the children to be taught religious practices in African schools?"

The pope, surprised at the comment, responded firmly. "O heavens no." *the pope suddenly realized he may have insulted a distinguished member of the clergy with his quick response, and had better apologize, and then explain himself.* Please excuse my last quick response, I meant no insult to your religion, when I used such a terse answer to your question on religion. It is just that I feel teaching the young children of Africa about religious systems or practices might be confusing to them. Based on my preliminary reading on Africa, religious education would not be appropriate for African pre-school children because of the many different languages, and many different Gods and different religious practices they grow up with. Burdening young African children with western or Asia religious practices would be counterproductive. I prefer that African children who enter school for the first time, be exposed to basic learning, and about the value of accepting other children as equals, and in a friendly manner.

My intention is to hire experienced African educators who are fluent in more than one African language; and concentrate their instruction on encouraging the proper use of their native language, along with learning the rudiments of the English language, hopefully encouraging their students to someday become bi-lingual."

The pope continued to explain another objective that he felt important for African children to learn at their early age.

"A second area that I feel would be very beneficial for young African children is the process of building trust in their classmates. Having faith and confidence in one another, I believe will serve them well as they grow into adulthood."

Bishop Okote-Eboh was surprised and genuinely pleased by the pope's response. He had initially assumed that the pope's interest in Africa was to make Africa a Catholic continent, and that perhaps this was the pope's reason for wanting to develop a plan for Africa.

The Episcopalian Bishop Okote-Eboh surprised the pope with the first expression of encouragement by responding to his last comment on pre-school education with a typical South African phrase, "Smashing, Your Holiness, perhaps we will be able to get along."

Get along, what did that mean, thought the Indonesian pope?

The bishop continued, "Your Holiness, your idea is a splendid one, but what you are suggesting will require an enormous financial commitment. Have you given much thought to that aspect of your intentions?"

The bishop's tone was now suddenly more sympathetic and had a calming effect on the pope.

"Yes, I am very aware of the financial implications, and although I have anticipated this issue, I'm not ready to announce how I intend to procure the necessary funds.

However, let me assure you, I will shortly be publicly announcing the source of the necessary funds for this project. In addition, let me say I expect those men and women who choose to be a part of this planning team will do so with no financial restrictions. I feel strongly that decisions made with the burden of fiscal limitations are doomed to failure. And for this reason, I will be encouraging the planners to suggest what would be required to make this plan successful, not how much it will cost."

Bishop Okote-Eboh said, "That is very generous of you, but let me respectfully suggest that you may not realize the significant costs that would be needed to, as you yourself suggested, develop a strong middle-class society."

At this point in the phone conversation, the pope was determined not to be apologetic; he would remain guarded but understanding. Perhaps the bishop was correct; that the pope did not comprehend the implications, but that would be for the planning team to decide. He was determined to remain hopeful that he could reach this wild dream, in spite of this surprisingly negative man. He was not about to abandon his idea based on a fifteen-minute conversation over the phone with a retired African bishop he had never met.

As the bishop continued with his statement, the pope's mind was on a belief he had formed while in the seminary that remained with him as a code to live by as a priest, bishop, cardinal, and now pope. *Hope is finding the light in the darkness and trusting in a positive ending.* The pope knew only one thing, he was willing to accept the burden of changing the lives of a great number of poverty-stricken people, and it was unfortunate the first person he spoke with seemed initially, to have a negative attitude toward his idea.

The pope suddenly remembered he had not mentioned reimbursement for this team of men and woman, so he quickly responded before the bishop could rebut once again.

"Bishop, I failed to mention that I intend to pay for your transportation, room and board, and provide a stipend to each of the planning members. I will leave the matter of the amount of the stipend to the members of the team I have in mind, but it does sound to me, you will not be interested in an invitation to participate in the planning process. However, I want you to know that I appreciate your ambivalence toward my offer, and I wish to thank you for your time."

Bishop Imamu Okote-Eboh replied, "Your Holiness, a stipend is unimportant to me at this point.

However, what is important to me is your understanding of the enormous number of resources needed to build a strong African middle-class society. If, in my opinion, the amount is sufficient to accomplish what you have expressed today, then I would be most happy to be a member of your planning team. In addition, I would be willing to volunteer my services as an informal secretary and note-taker. May I make a brief observation before we end our conversation?"

"Of course, I'm interested to hear any thoughts you may have on the subject."

Bishop Imamu Okote-Eboh said. "Earlier you mentioned making Africa a powerful and vibrant continent. I have a strong core conviction that governments must foster equal opportunities in order to build and sustain a strong middle-class. I do hope that will be one of the long-term objectives of your efforts in Africa.

Pope Francis Xavier agreed fully with the bishop's conviction on his important last question. Having time to reflect on Bishop Imamu Okote-Eboh last comment, the pope realized, once again, how ambitious his idea was, but he remained resolute in moving forward.

The following day, the pope heard from Amarie Maalout of South Africa and Graham Quinlan, former prime minister of the United Kingdom. He returned their calls, and when the pope finished explaining what he had in mind, they both agreed on the spot. Pope Francis Xavier was not sure how the other individuals would react to his proposal, but he was delighted with the positive introductory phone calls.

Over the next week, Greta Ivar, former prime minister of Sweden; Roscoe Ayala, former president of the United States, and Deidra Conrad, president of Germany agreed to be part of the planning team. The pope was very pleased that six out of seven people on his original list agreed to participate. The only person on the pope's original list was Noah Lukas, former Belgium ambassador who thanked the pope for considering his name for planning purposes but could not participate due to poor health.

CHAPTER 13

Due to a pope's extensive travel schedule, planning an advance work schedule for multiple days was always difficult. Especially now in early December, soon the Christmas season would be upon them, which meant no time for anything but the duties of the pope during this holy time of the year. He was determined to begin the preparation of the *ex-cathedra* statement and have it ready for release in January, prior to his initial Indonesian tour scheduled for the end of February.

Time, however, would not be the pope's biggest problem. Any pope would have difficulty writing an *ex-cathedra* statement, but for Pope Francis Xavier, the task would be especially difficult. All during the writing process, the knowledge of the minutes from the 1869 Vatican I Council haunted him mentally. Although the pope had made the decision that an *ex-cathedra* statement was an essential ingredient to his plan for Africa, which did not mean, he never experienced occasional twinges of guilt about his actions. It's no wonder in the past 147 years only one pope had invoked ex cathedra. Most people, especially Catholics, do not understand that the idea of infallibility does not mean that the pope as man is infallible. Rather, his teaching authority is unchallengeable. It's therefore not the pope himself, as a human being, or as the bishop of Rome, who is infallible, but the pope's teaching, cannot be challenged. The operative words here is *teaching*.

On their first day of work, Pope Francis Xavier and Father Susanto found it difficult to complete a first draft by six that evening. They decided to come back to the statement the following day. The pope asked Budi to cancel an appointment he had scheduled in two days; this was going to take longer than anticipated. The following day, both men were writing a new draft copy. By lunchtime, they still had not produced anything of merit, and they were both feeling discouraged. When they picked up their work after a short lunch break, gloom seemed to resonate throughout the pope's office. Pope Francis Xavier slouched in his chair, gazing out his window, and his hand lay limp at his side. His secretary mentally noted how uncharacteristic his posture and window gazing were, certainly not consistent with the task-oriented man Budi knew.

Budi could not recall a time when he had seen his friend so anxious, filled with misgivings. Father

Susanto was surprised by the pope's frame of mind during these days. He decided that he would have to be especially attentive to the needs and state of mind of his friend as planning progressed.

After approximately an hour of discussion a wastebasket, and floor were filled with crumpled balls of discarded paper, both men remained in disagreement on an introductory paragraph.

Suddenly, the pope stopped writing, looked up from his desk toward his secretary, and said, in a startled, disturbed tone, "Oh, I have forgotten. Budi, I just remembered I have failed to name a replacement for my position as cardinal in Indonesia. Our country has been without a cardinal for almost a year."

With this surprised distraction to the content at hand, Father Susanto realized the pope was far too distraught to accomplish anything meaningful.

Reaching across the chair and placing a gentle hand on his shoulder, Budi said, "My dear friend, let's stop for a moment. I promise to make some calls today after our meeting to some of our clergy friends back home and get their opinion on possible names for you to consider for Indonesia's next cardinal. A year has gone by without a cardinal in our home country, and the Catholic Church in Indonesia has not disintegrated, so stop worrying. It was good you thought of this, but I would like you to consider the context under which this question entered your mind. Here you are, facing perhaps the most critical decision of your papacy, maybe the most critical decision of your life, and suddenly you recall something that is no doubt important, but completely irrelevant to the task before us. Now, don't you think you need to try and approach this question in a more relaxed, unruffled manner?"

Father Susanto put down his pen, frustrated and knowing his friend was not thinking productively said. "In the past hour or so, I have not been planning with the stable, well-grounded, sure-of-himself friend I have known for almost fifty years. Now, take a deep breath and return to the Sunjaya I know."

"Thanks, Budi. The truth is I have been pondering this statement since the moment I decided to use this doctrinal principle. I must have mentally formulated this paragraph a thousand times, thinking of the precise words to use. I guess my major problem is I know this statement will be based on a fraudulent question of our faith, yet I have embraced this deceit, knowing the words we decide to use are permanent."

Budi seemed to have lost patience with his friend and responded sarcastically, "Perhaps I should get my confessional cloth and hear your confession. Knowing you as I do, it's probably a bit scary for you to know you've gone this far, agreeing to do something you know is deceitful. You would not be human if you were not intellectually and emotionally focused on this aspect of what we are trying to accomplish. Would it help if you could accept the fact that this principal has for many years been an approved rule of faith of the Catholic Church? Isn't it more important to focus on the results of your statement than whether or not you are being deceitful?"

The pope answered his secretary's question. "When put that way, it is helpful. We're working with a long-standing accepted doctrine of faith. What I have interpreted from old minutes from the Vatican Council should not be a hindrance. It should be freeing. The basic problem may be that I am a human being, not perfect or infallible but trying to write something that will be considered infallible."

Father Susanto started to chuckle. "This thought just jumped into my head as you were talking. Now picture this for a moment: Imagine our teacher back in high school in Indonesia, Father Hermanto, standing in a long line of people waiting their turn to speak with the Lord. Its Big Hermanto's turn, his arms resting on his big belly, and he says to God, *'Are you nuts, putting those two hoodlums from Makmur Street in charge of your church on earth. What made you do such a crazy thing?"*

Now the two men were laughing hysterically at the picture of their old teacher, who had been so instrumental in them becoming priests.

Pope Francis Xavier still laughing, said, "Thanks, Budi. That's just what I needed, a good hard laugh! I guess I'll have to keep you around after all."

Budi responded by saying, "Okay, it's time we got back to work."

The pope was still laughing as he tried unsuccessfully to review what he had last written. His laugh slowly started to leave his face. His facial expression just moments ago was full of cheer, but slowly his face began turning to a frown, Then the frown disappeared, and his eyes became bright, his jaw dropped, his mouth opened, and he dropped the pen to his desk.

"That's it, of course, how foolish of us. The problem we're having with writing this statement is that we are imperfect human beings, but here we are trying to be infallible.

Budi looked at his friend with a sarcastic grimace and spoke. "Ok, so tell me what I'm missing!"

"We won't use our words. We'll use His words. Jesus spoke often of our responsibility to the poor. He's the infallible one. Why not simply tell the people I am speaking through our Savior in proclaiming poverty, as we know it, to be immoral. We'll just go back to His words as the basis of our teaching statement, or what Catholics call papal infallibility."

Budi said, "Way to go, boss. You nailed it. We can't go wrong using our Lord's own words."

Using the Bible as their main reference, their statement began to take on a new dynamic form. They were now doing less writing and more biblical research.

On the afternoon of the third day, Budi entered the pope's office with the final typed draft of the statement in hand. The pope slowly read the statement twice, as Budi relaxed in an upholstered chair. The pope looked up from his desk blotter.

"We'll leave this as it is for tomorrow, then we'll read it one more time, and if we both agree we have our *ex-cathedra* statement, we'll then prepare our next steps."

The following morning, the first thing the two men did was to read and then reread the statement they had prepared. When finished, they both decided it was suitable for mailing to all cardinals and bishops, instructing them to share Pope Francis Xavier's doctrine of *ex-cathedra* with all Catholics around the world. Budi prepared the copies for mailing, including copies for the Italian media to use during the coming press conference. The press conference would focus mainly on the definition and an explanation of the term *ex-cathedra*. Moreover, for now, there was only a vague reference to the pope's decision to use resources at his disposal to begin to eradicate the immoral condition of poverty, on the continent of Africa. He expected to be questioned about what he meant by resources, but he would not at this time announce the selling of the Vatican treasures or the remodeling and reorganization of Saint Peter's cathedral; this would be for another time in the very near future. Both men decided to do nothing more that day. They would leave the document as is, have a good night's sleep, and read the statement one more time, first thing the following morning.

Pope Francis Xavier was pleased with the work accomplished. That evening, alone in his room, he prayed to Jesus for guidance and thought about Jesus' time on earth. It was late and with thoughts of Jesus still fresh in his mind his body was telling him, *enough with your thoughts, it's time to rest your weary mind and body.* Surprisingly, sleep came quickly that evening.

After breakfast, he arrived at his office early, ready to share his thoughts with Budi. On his desk blotter was a white envelope, with the name Sunjaya written across the front of the envelope in Budi's left-hand scribble penmanship.

It read, *Dear Sunjaya:*

Remember in our senior year at Saint Joseph's school when both of us were drawn to the Catholic faith because of what Jesus preached. We both felt we had a responsibility to the poor of Jakarta. We thought it a good idea to become priests and help other poor kids like us, rather than going back to our Jakarta slum and being stuck in a life of poverty leading to crime. Remember how we felt that we could actually make a difference. Well, my friend, you are going to make one hell of a big difference.

Your friend for life, Budi

The pope reread the handwritten note a number of times, thinking of that time and the vow they made. Now they were soon to embark on the task of eliminating poverty, not for the street children of Jakarta, but for a large continent. Somehow Budi's note made it all worthwhile. He rose from his desk and walked to the outer office where Father Susanto was working at his desk.

"Good morning, Father Susanto," said Pope Francis Xavier,

"And good morning to you, Your Holiness."

The broad smile and the peaceful look on the faces of both men were the results of a very satisfying and personal feeling of accomplishment.

Budi looked around the room to make sure no one was present other than himself and the pope, and remarked, "You did a nice job, boss."

"Budi, let's go into my office. I wish to share with you the many thoughts I had last evening before I was able to fall off to sleep."

Both men entered the inner office and sat in the alcove section on the upholstered chairs.

Pope Francis Xavier was first to speak. "After yesterday's focus on the period when Jesus walked this earth, I could not help but reflect how, over many centuries, man has misinterpreted the religious teachings of their founders. In the Quran, Muhammed praises the status of women, but today Islamic clerics use the Quran as justification for violently removing the genitals of young women. I am sure Buddha would not have approved of the apartheid practices against various Buddha minority sects. Judaism seems to be one of the few religions that has chosen not to magnify or misinterpret what the great profit Jesus taught. Moreover, as I thought about Christianity, we may be the guiltiest religious institution in our encouragement of strong personalities who are able to acquire power and money, though Jesus lived a humble life and did tell us to turn the other cheek. As far back as the Roman Empire, we know from the writings of Tibulus and Horace that homosexuality existed among individuals and there is no written indication that Jesus condemned this practice. Yet in modern times, our church leaders have determined that these actions are serious offenses against God. Catholicism seems to be more interested in doctrine and regulations than in loving your neighbor. Why have we become so strict regarding our rules and regulations and less concerned about our actions?"

"Wow! Someone was up late last night."

"You're right Budi, it's time for me to stop philosophizing, so let's get to the matter at hand, but before that let me say a special thank you to my friend, not only for your kind note, but for all you do for me."

1 May, 2010 — EX-CATHEDRA DECREE ON MORAL REC-IPROCITY

When Jesus walked this earth, he told us of many truths. He preached that the human body is a vessel, and therefore needs protection from harm and death. Poverty prevents many people from being able, as Jesus preached, to protect their body while on this earth. Yet millions are not able to protect their body through no fault of their own.

Two thousand five hundred children die each day from lack of clean water.

Seven hundred and thirty-eight million people in the world lack access to clean water.

Approximately three million children die each year due to poor nutrition.

Eight million people in the world do not have enough food to lead a healthy active life.

Five hundred eighty million people in Africa have no access to electricity.

I, Pope Francis Xavier 1, speaking from the chair, and teaching that living in poverty prevents many humans from following this truth spoken by Jesus. For this reason, I, Pope Francis Xavier 1 using the teaching power of ex cathedra, *which cannot be challenged, proclaim poverty is immoral.*

In response to God's teaching, I, Pope Francis Xavier 1, proclaim that all people have a responsibility to demonstrate to the world, and in so doing, teach the world, that God has proclaimed, through his son, the immorality of poverty on our earth.

I, Pope Francis Xavier 1, as a start, will direct financial resources to the continent of Africa to help remove the immoral stain of poverty that afflicts the people of this continent. Furthermore, we can read the words of Jesus, the son of God, who taught us that poverty is immoral. Believers can understand more clearly the immorality of poverty by referring to the actual words of Jesus our Savior in the following scripture writings:

> *Jesus teaching the Pharisees and other religious leaders - Matthew 19:21*
>
> *Jesus begins his public ministry (chapter 61): Luke 4:18*
> *From Jesus' discourse at a luncheon: Luke 14:12-15*
> *From Jesus teaching his disciples: Matthew 25:34-40*
> *Old Testament references: Psalms 72:12*
> *Old Testament references: Proverbs 14:31*
> *Old Testament references: Proverbs 31:8-9*
> *Old Testament references: Psalms 140:12*

The pope's *ex-cathedra* statement went to all church leaders throughout the developed world on 8 June 2010 with a cover letter instructing all priests to read this statement to their congregations and Catholic institutions. The cover letter also included an introduction and a brief explanation of the meaning of an *ex-cathedra* statement as the infallible teaching of Pope Francis Xavier 1.

A news conference was to take place in the conference room at the Vatican Library two days after the ex-cathedra statement was sent to cardinals and bishops in the developed world.

The pope made a brief statement relative to the meaning and definition of speaking *ex- cathedra*. He clearly explained the difference between papal infallibility and a statement from his chair, formally known as an *ex-cathedra* statement. The pope had no illusions that drawing the distinction between the two would result in correct headlines in the various papers. It was more important to media outlets to use the word infallibility, which was an interesting and intriguing headline. *Ex-cathedra* was a phrase few individuals would recognize, but he had tried his best and would have to accept the explanation in the media that he was infallible in proclaiming poverty as an immoral condition.

CHAPTER 14

On the morning of 27 July, 2010, a smiling Father Susanto walked into the pope's office to let him know the car was waiting to take them to the airport for their first visit to Indonesia since Cardinal Prantata became pope.

"Time to go," said an excited Father Susanto.

The pope's party arrived at Rome's Fiumicino Airport to board his flight to Sumatra in Indonesia. Pope Francis Xavier had scheduled a grueling twelve-day tour, with plans to visit the five major islands in Indonesia. The reception received by Pope Francis Xavier and Father Susanto as they disembarked from the plane in Indonesia, was beyond their wildest expectation.

Budi whispered to the pope, "This reception is reserved only for kings and queens, certainly not for two rascals from Makmur Street in Jakarta.

The pope's first stop would be Sumatra, a major metropolis and Indonesia's fourth-largest city. Here the pope would make his first public appearance at Masjid Raya Medan, an impressive grand mosque commissioned by Sultan Ma'mun Al Rashid Perkasa Alam in 1906. The Moroccan style building has a grand entrance, towering ceilings, ornate carvings, Italian marble, and stained glass from China.

Next on his itinerary was a stop in Semarang, a port city on the north coast of Java. The schedule for the pope began in Semarang's old quarter, featuring Dutch colonial architecture and the Sam Poo Kong fifteenth century temple.

From Semarang, his party boarded a boat to Kalimantan, for his second two-day visit, including a major stop in Borneo, the third-largest island in the world. Borneo is primarily mountainous with a dense rain forest. The agenda in Borneo called for a meeting with both the non-Muslim Dayaks and the Islamic Malays.

The following day the pope was scheduled to visit Irian-Jaya, and then on to New Guinea. In Papua New Guinea, the pope visited a number of the tribes that inhabit this island. From New Guinea, he would proceed to Sulawesi for a one-day visit. Then he would take a flight to Jakarta for a two-day visit to the city of his birth.

In Jakarta, Sunjaya celebrated Mass, his homily focused on his childhood in Jakarta. After the Mass, a parade took place to honor the pope. The pope stood in the Pope mobile with two sisters at his side. They waved to the people, as he gave continuous blessings to the welcoming crowds along the parade route. Father Susanto rode in a large black car directly behind the Pope mobile. The parade moved on to a boulevard with people crowded together behind police barricades on both sides. The modest former cardinal was close to crying at the site of the crowds that came out to wish him well. At one point, the thought entered his mind, *is it possible for miracles such as this to happen to a once-poor street child from Jakarta?* He suddenly understood, perhaps for the first time, the strange and unbelievable twist his life had taken. As his motorcade continued, his emotions built stronger and stronger, until he experienced teardrops flowing down his cheeks, teardrops not of sadness, but in awe of the impossible.

The Jakarta parade ended at the Jesuit missionary church to meet with Father Jerome O'Bannon. The pope entered Jerome's room wearing a broad smile, with both arms extended. He prepared for a warm embrace from a dear old friend. Instead, Father O'Bannon grasped the Pope's hand, preparing to kneel to kiss his ring on.

"Jerome, what are you doing? Stop with the formality. You're my dear friend, and when we are alone, I expect a big hug."

After a mutual sentimental embrace, a more relaxed Jerome said, "So, how is my old friend, Sun…" His voice trailed off, and he spoke. "Ops, I mean, Your Holiness?"

The pope looked at Jerome once again with a wry face. "Oh, please, I hate to be greeted in that way. I know it's the so-called proper thing to do, but not from you, Jerome. Please, when we are alone or on the phone, I wish to keep our greetings as they used to be."

Jerome was born in Queens, New York City. He was in his mid-forties, much taller than the pope, and beginning to lose his once-thick head of brown hair.

He responded, "My greeting did feel strange, but I wasn't sure how to act."

The two men sat across from each other, talking about Jakarta and Jerome's work and Sunjaya's path to the Vatican.

After approximately ten minutes, Jerome could wait no longer.

"Is this a catch-up on things visit? Or are you about to ask me for the favor you mentioned about a year ago?"

Jerome was curious about Sunjaya's long ago comment. "Jerome, I'm about to do something quite radical that I know will offend many people in Vatican City and, I suspect, many Catholics around the world, as well as art historians. Please don't share the following conversation with anyone, including your superiors."

The curious Jesuit missionary priest cautiously agreed.

Sunjaya continued, "My *ex-cathedra* statement, on the immorality of poverty, is going to be my rationale for selling the Vatican treasures at auction."

Jerome looked wide-eyed at his friend.

"When you say radical, you're not fooling around."

The pope continued. "I don't expect much reaction to my *ex-cathedra* statement, other than those who may not agree with the concept of infallibility. During my news conference introducing my *ex-cathedra* statement, reporters asked about my use of the word resources, but I refused to clarify or expand further on that word, as it was not the time for details. I want you to know I plan to use the money received from the auction sale of the Vatican treasures to make a major effort on the African continent to eliminate poverty, which will show the world I am willing to put into practice what I stated in my *ex-cathedra* statement. I feel I must be proactive and demonstrate I am not only declaring poverty a moral issue, but I also plan on taking steps to eliminate immoral conditions, and I have chosen the African continent for this purpose. If we are successful, my hope is others may follow our example. I am planning to announce the auction of the Vatican treasures sometime in October 2010."

The pope hesitated a moment, expecting some reaction from Jerome, but Jerome was so surprised he simply stared at his friend, not sure why this was to be so secretive.

The pope continued. "My news conference will not only include an announcement of the planned auction, but also the renovations to the empty Vatican Museum and library, as well as the remodeling of Saint Peter's Cathedral."

Jerome had a few moments to recover from the shock of the pope's comments, before saying, "You're willing to open yourself to the heavy criticism from within the church, and the Catholic laity? I can already hear the vile protests from Catholic clergy around the world! You will also be criticized severely by the Italian media, that's their culture you will be selling."

"Yes, Jerome, I am prepared for the negative response."

Sunjaya was now ready to explain Jerome's involvement in his grand plan. "Jerome, I would like you to accept an assignment at the Vatican for a two-year period. In this position, you will act as the manager overseeing a renovation project that will remodel the current Vatican library and the museum into a hotel. You will also oversee the remodeling of Saint Peter's Cathedral.

Jerome was quick to respond, "Oversee the Vatican Museum and library renovations? Why in God's name would you want me for that? I'm a missionary priest with absolutely no knowledge of construction and renovations. Surely there are more qualified clergy, who have a background in those areas, one who could serve you much more efficiently than I?"

Jerome's reaction was not unexpected, Sunjaya responded to Jerome's questions, "Let me explain something you may find difficult to hear. I have very little trust in many Vatican prelates, and I need someone I can trust, someone to be my eyes and ears, during this renovation and remodeling process."

Sunjaya could see that Jerome remained puzzled, and even uncomfortable. The pope decided that he needed to be perfectly candid with his friend. "Jerome, I understand you have no experience in renovating facilities. I don't expect you to be directly involved in the evaluation of the construction of these two projects. I envision your primary responsibility will be twofold, one, ensure that workers meet their building deadlines, and second you will act as the protector of the Vatican treasures, from being looted by individuals who believe they are protecting church property."

Jerome's facial expression was now even more contorted as he said. "You believe people at the Vatican would openly defy you by pilfering items from the Vatican?"

The pope answered, "Yes, I do. I expect intense opposition once my plans become public. I'm concerned some at the Vatican or from outside of the Vatican, may be so against my actions they may feel justified, in interrupting the implementation of my renovation plans, and the auction of valuable Vatican art. Jerome, I don't believe I'm being neurotic in my assessment of this situation. There are some among the Vatican hierarchy who are disloyal, self-promoting individuals, who see me as a treasonous enemy."

The pope hesitated at the look of surprise on Jerome's face, and then continued. "Jerome, let me be clear on another aspect of my proposal to you. If you choose not to interrupt your missionary duties in Indonesia for this assignment, or if you believe this assignment will result in a setback of your missionary work; or if this offer seems unreasonable, just say the word, and I will understand. You do not owe me any vow of obedience, regarding this request. All you have to say is thanks, but no thanks, and that will be enough for me. If you decline my offer, I will not question your friendship or your loyalty; and I will find another for this assignment."

Jerome responded with another question, "You mentioned a two-year assignment at the Vatican. Do you believe the renovations will take two years to be completed?"

"Once the auction has taken place, you would be responsible for overseeing the Sotheby's personnel during the shipping procedures of the statuary and art items. Once that has been completed, the renovation and construction will begin. The architectural firm of Gerasina and Lombardo are responsible for the design and construction of the renovations. During that time period, I would like you to remain alert for any sabotage attempts to the remodeling schedule."

Sunjaya then took a moment to explain his experience during his time at the Vatican. "The Vatican can be a deceptive place in terms of honor, loyalty, and unselfish service to man and God. Obtaining power seems to be the most important thing in the lives of some prelates at the Vatican. I know you don't want to hear that, but unfortunately, it's true. Moreover, because of my doubts about others at the Vatican, I need someone in this position with your integrity. Before you say a word, I want to emphasize once again that you're free to decline. However, if you do accept this offer, don't do it because of your loyalty to me. Do it because you believe in what I am trying to accomplish in Africa."

Jerome responded with unexpected enthusiasm. "Sunjaya, what a wonderful thing to do. Talk about a mission that can make a difference! I accept the challenge to be a part of your plans for Africa, now that you have clarified my duties, and I am sure my provincial will agree."

"Thank you, Jerome, I want you to know you have taken a great weight off my shoulders, and finally one other thing, my rascal of a secretary is also looking forward to enjoying a few nightcaps with you, and he wants to know if you prefer bourbon or scotch."

Both men now laughing. "I'll take care of Budi's request, said Jerome.

The smiling pope muttered, "I can't seem to do anything about that rascal. Perhaps you may be a good influence on him, although I have my doubts.

CHAPTER 15

On the nine-and a half hour flight, returning to Rome from Indonesia, the pope and his secretary were exhausted but grateful for the enthusiasm of so many Indonesians. The size of the crowds to view the pope on his first major tour suggested Catholics and non-Catholics alike celebrated the pope's visit. The percentage of Catholics in Indonesia was in the single digits, but public participation at the various events was unexpectedly larger, fifty million people had filled the various venues where Pope Francis Xavier celebrated Mass. The trip was truly the most fulfilling experience in the lives of the two boys from Makmur Street. The only disappointment was that the parents of both men, were not alive. to enjoy their children's

During the flight from Jakarta to Rome, Budi slept as the pope finished his mandatory news conference, which took place in the rear of the airplane with the reporters who were assigned to accompany the pope on his tour. The pope's frustration with news conferences stemmed not so much from the chore itself, but rather the foolish, inane questions he would often receive. He understood reporters were interested in asking personal and controversial questions, hoping for personal and controversial answers, which would result in increased sale of newspapers, and magazines.

When the news conference ended, he returned to his seat at the front section of the plane, hoping to get some well-earned sleep. Sitting comfortably in his first-class seat, the pope estimated he could get three welcome hours of sleep, unlike Father Susanto who had been in restful slumber for the past hour.

The pope was not so lucky. His mind was unable to relax and free itself from the changes facing him back at the Vatican. His expectations of the next few months would be a series of chaotic days, upheaval from cardinals, and most likely uproar from Catholics and the Vatican staff, once the changes became public.

As the plane continued on its way back to Rome, he tried to stop his mind from rambling from one crisis to another, without much success. Sleep during these supposedly restful hours was not going to happen. He noticed that the t-shirt he wore under his papal garments was wet from perspiration and clung uncomfortably to his body. He turned the knob over his seat to blow colder air directly onto his body, and soon the blowing air turned his wet shirt into a chilly, uncomfortable garment that now needed to be changed.

He stood, opened the storage space above his seat, and shuffled through his carry-on luggage until he found a clean white undershirt. He left the carry-on at his seat and proceeded to the men's room, dabbed his chest and arms dry with paper towels, and put on the dry shirt, buttoned up his white robe, returned to his seat and placed the cold wet shirt into his luggage, and stored the bag above his seat. Now feeling more comfortable, but still unable to calm his mind, he turned to some scripture reading, hoping that would help him relax. However, the negative thoughts kept interfering with his reading. What would happen if his idealistic plans unraveled and failed, or if his planning team changed their minds and he was back to square one? In addition, what if the African plan, for any number of plausible reasons somehow backfired, or simply failed? The headlines would be most unkind: *Young Indonesian Pope Sacrifices the Vatican Treasures in a Failed Attempt to Help African Countries!*

Sitting erect staring at the blank grey back of the seat in front of him, the pope saw only the crumbling of all the plans he had so cleverly designed since he first conceived of his idea. Sitting alone, he was no longer the young, confident Indonesian cleric, who had shocked the world by being selected pope of the Catholic Church eight months ago. He was now a man consumed by foreboding. Budi had teased him when he came up with the idea of his impeachment as pope. He began to wonder if his friend might be on to something. All he could see was Cardinals Alejandra, Barzinni, and Diudonn forcibly removing him from his position and having to return in disgrace to Indonesia. Prominent in his mind's eye was the old rat-infested apartment on Makmur Street in Jakarta, Indonesia.

His thoughts remained negative. *People will refer to me as the unqualified Indonesian who ruined the Vatican by selling their precious collection of priceless items.*

He was still in this negative, dark place as the plane made its final approach to Rome's international airport. *Would I be responsible for shattering the very foundation of the Catholic Church?*

The pope was no longer glaring at the back of the grey seat in front of him; his undershirt once again was wet with perspiration. As the airplane wheels bumped on the runway, he felt only pangs of defeat and and disgrace.

CHAPTER 16

The second week of August, 2010 was warm and sunny in Rome. The pope and his secretary were walking back to their office from lunch in the main cafeteria. The workers responded in the customary manner as they passed. The worker would stop what he or she was doing, then give a slight bow and the greeting, "Your Holiness," or "Holy Father" and the pope would respond in kind with a cheerful smile and a polite, "Good afternoon." The worker would then address Father Susanto in a similar fashion, but without the slight bow of the head and only, "Good morning, Father." Each worker who greeted the pope's secretary would have a bright smile on his or her face, a smile one might expect a person to have after a good-humored teasing. Budi had a pleasant and comic demeanor, always finding something to say to each person to make him or her laugh, the same way he could make his friend laugh with a brief story or a quick tease.

Pope Francis Xavier said, "I wish I could have the type of relationship that you seem to have with the Vatican staff."

Budi responded, "One big difference between us that makes the workers more cautious when they speak with you is your office. The popes in the past have been elite authority figures who seemed to want to retain their august reputation. Pope John XXIII had started to chip away at that attitude, and you are continuing this approach simply by eating your lunch in the workers' cafeteria. Habits are hard to break, but they'll come around, you'll see. Continue making an effort to be one of them, and they will respond.

Sunjaya was more cautious. "I'm not sure I will ever be as successful as you. Your personality seems to draw people to you, I unfortunately have a more reserved personality, and I'm not as good a comic as you, but I'm trying my best. Your skin is as black as mine, and they seem to love you, so that's one stigma I can't use as an excuse."

Budi continued, "I understand our personalities are different, but I see you are trying to be more engaging.

The Italian workers at the Vatican were all very loyal. Rarely did Vatican workers resign. There was a great deal of pride surrounding their employment in Vatican City. Employment at the Vatican meant friends and family generally held the Vatican employee in high regard. Vatican City employed numerous civilian personnel such as gardeners, gift shop and museum employees, caretakers, servants, clerical workers, drivers, and the world-known Swiss Guards, with their long and dedicated service over many centuries.

Father Budi Susanto had a pleasant manner; he was a sociable man who enjoyed talking with people and making them laugh, and he was never too busy to stop and introduce himself to any new face in Vatican City. He had the unusual trait of being interested in the lives of the staff and their family members. This made it easy for the common workers to feel connected to the friendly secretary of Pope Francis Xavier.

The pope and his secretary continued on their way toward the Baroque stone building that housed their office complexes. They were now passing the grassy knoll. Visible from the top of the knoll were helicopter blades. At the end of the knoll, a bright black helicopter was in full view on its concrete heliport. Adjacent to the heliport pad on the far side were railroad tracks, 862 meters (about a half mile) in length, which joined the Italian railroad track system to Rome's railroad terminal, used solely for the distribution of freight.

As the two men rounded the corner, the walkway changed from a concrete path to a wide, brick-lined path leading to the pope's office facility.

Before arriving at their office, the pope said. "It's time for you to start locating a nice, rural, comfortable place for the six planners to meet. Try to find a location that is about an hour outside of Rome, which would not have the distractions they would encounter in Rome. I'd appreciate if you can take care of this matter in the next few days, and please make sure you ask the workers, not the clerics. I'm still leery about involving them in anything, especially at this stage, when soon, I expect all hell will break loose."

"Oh, and one last thing, arrange for a private car service to pick up the planners from the Rome airport. If we were to use our drivers, it would be all over the Vatican that special dignitaries have arrived, and the rumors will start. Budi said, "Got it boss," and began moving towards the pope's outer door. Pope Francis Xavier called out to his secretary, "Budi, please come back. There is one other item I need to speak to you about."

Father Susanto returned to the chair in front of the pope's desk. Sunjaya opened the conversation with an anxious tone.

"Chaos is likely to soon erupt around here, and we haven't discussed the expected reaction to my foray into Africa since our return from Indonesia. Are you still in agreement with my plans? Have any doubts crept into your mind in the past month? If so, now is the time for me to hear from you. Once the auction starts, there's no turning back."

Budi did not hesitate for a moment. "Hey, what kind of a question is that? I have gone this far with you, and after all these years, I'm surprised you would even ask such a question. No matter how hot it gets, know that I have your back. I'm in until the end, I thought you understood that!"

The pope dropped his head, took a long breath, and exhaled. Then lifting his head, the pope stared directly into the eyes of his dear friend.

"It's going to get rough, but I guess you know that. I asked that question because I'm going to need your strength in the coming years, are you up for me leaning on you."

"Yes boss, I know we are entering the rough part of your plan, and I'm ready to blast forward, now can I please get back to my work."

Thank the Lord that you are at my side Budi. The pope continued. "After the six planning members see my *ex-cathedra* statement, and then the dual news conferences announcing the sale of the Vatican treasures in Rome and New York City, I expect they will know where the finances will be coming from. I'm hopeful this will signal to the six planners that I'm serious about the African plan. I expect to call each member of the planning team the day following the news conferences, and I will hopefully get a firm commitment from each of them."

"Good thinking, boss," said Father Susanto as he rose from his chair to return to his desk in the outer office. "Hold up Budi." the pope asked his secretary to sit back down. Budi sat.

"Budi, there is one other important thing I need for you to do! Contact Mr. Walkin at Sotheby's in New York City and remind him that the scheduled news conference announcing the worldwide auction of the Vatican treasures is to take place precisely at nine a.m. New York City time, and the Rome news conference will begin at three p.m. allowing both news conferences to occur simultaneously.

Budi's frustrated reaction to the pope's last-minute requests looked puzzled at his friend. "Sunjaya, stop for a minute, having me rise up and down from my chair is not like you. Tell me what's going on."

The pope lowered his shoulders and relaxed his body for a moment, then said, "You were fast asleep when I returned from my news conference on the plane. I was tired and had hoped to get a few hours of sleep before we arrived in Rome. I could not fall off to sleep. My mind was racing, thinking of all the little details I was going to have to accomplish when we got back here. The more I thought about what was needed to be done in this next month, the more doubtful I became. Soon I began perspiring, and I had to go to the men's room to change my undershirt. It was a most discouraging three hours of my life. I could only think of the fact that this entire effort could very easily blow up in my face. I believe I had for the first time accepted the gambling aspect of what we are planning and the likelihood of how easily this entire project could fail and what that would mean for the church. I'm frightened. So many things can go wrong. I'm thankful that I got this far before my thoughts zeroed in on the fragile nature of the project. If I had considered the comprehensive variety of tasks needed to build a middle-class society in Africa, I may have never decided to move forward with this idea. Lately, negativity seems to be consuming my thoughts about my plans for Africa. I am no longer focusing on the positive aspects of my plan, now only thinking of the many things that can go wrong.

Budi responded to the troubled Pope. "Are you thinking of not going through with the auction?"

The pope had a disturbed, slight grin on his face. "No, I'm going forward. I'm just not as confident as I was a month ago. Perhaps only now do I fully understand the magnitude of eliminating poverty in Africa. Those three hours on the plane were a wake-up call for me. Maybe it was the fact that you were enjoying your sleep, and I could've used someone to talk with."

As the pope continued, Budi noticed tiny beads of perspiration forming on his forehead and the desperate expression on his face. The pope's body language was unusually calm and subdued, but now the look on his face was one of apprehension, no longer the look of excitement and achievement. Budi noticed fear and doubt for the first time. "Perhaps if you had thought more carefully, you never would have considered such a wonderful Christian act. This might be one of those crossroads in your life when you internally understood you were the only one who had a chance of being successful. Perhaps you need to remember what you told me many months ago: you have the power and authority to do something spectacular and worthwhile for almost a billion people. Since no one else was going to try, why not you, and if you fail, so what? Didn't Jesus say, 'What you do for the least of my people, you do for me'? Remember those words and think how proud Jesus is of you."

Pope Francis Xavier leaned against the back support of his chair; he considered Budi's comment for about ten seconds, and then sighed.

"As usual, you always seem to say the right thing when I get myself into these critical places. Thanks, Budi. You're a valuable friend. However, I disagree with your comment that I'm going to do something spectacular. We are going to do something spectacular. There is only one thing that still bothers me. If this whole thing fails, people won't be saying it was the fault of the pope. They'll be saying it was the fault of the brown skin, *Indonesian pope.*"

CHAPTER 17

The press mingled around their chairs in the conference room of the Vatican library. As usual, a large pot of coffee rested on a table in the rear of the room, with a short line in front of the table. Promptly at 2:58 in the afternoon, Pope Francis Xavier entered the conference area, for his 3:00 P.M. news conference. At the same time, Mr. Walkin walked up to the microphone at Sotheby's Auction House at 8:00 A.M New York City time.

The pope placed his notes on the podium and began his news conference at the precise hour. He opened the news conference by referring to his *ex-cathedra* statement released in January, in which he proclaimed poverty to be an immoral state of the human condition. He would try once again to clarify the difference between "speaking from the chair" and papal infallibility, which was commonly misunderstood by Catholics and non-Catholics alike.

"First, I would like to discuss the general misconception surrounding the phrases *ex cathedra* and its oft-mistaken title papal infallibility. This misunderstanding is largely due to the title first described during the first Vatican Council in 1869."

He explained the difference between papal infallibility and an *ex-cathedra* statement. After a number of questions to clarify the topic of papal infallibility, the pope introduced the second item listed on the news conference agenda, *Vatican treasures*.

"As pope, I have decided if I were to proclaim that poverty is immoral, then it is my responsibility to become an example of my teaching statement. With that in mind, I intend to intervene where people have experienced various levels of poverty for many centuries through no fault of their own. It is my intention to provide a significant number of resources to stimulate the African economy, so that Africans have the opportunity, through hard work, to become members of a broad middle-class African society. A plan to accomplish this objective will become operational shortly. The expected time of implementation for this plan will be approximately fifteen years. The financial resources will come from the sale of the Vatican Treasures, which I believe is justified, to remove the immorality that now exist on the African continent."

At the end of the pope's statement, murmuring occurred, and shortly thereafter, raised hands, followed by loud cries from the Italian media, to gain the attention of the pope. The pope quickly called on a reporter in the first row knowing everyone wanted to hear the first question.

The reporter stood and asked a question on how and when the sale of the Vatican treasures would take place. The pope responded, "Through a worldwide auction by Sotheby's Auction House, located in New York City, on 3 October, 2010."

The long, boisterous news conference ended with a final question, relative to the reorganization and remodeling of Saint Peter's Cathedral, the Vatican Museum and Library. The pope explained the need for the hotel, and the new, unusual configuration of Saint Peters Cathedral, in using its specific design, to encourage all religions to use the cathedral.

***

The public reaction to the two news conferences, one in Italy and one in America, were received quite differently. The announcement by Mr. Walkin in New York City was enthusiastic. There was genuine excitement along with a great deal of speculation, especially within the art world. There was a great deal of discussion about the various pieces of art which might become available and speculation on the amounts of the various bids. The speculation and interest in the United States was lively. Activities at Sotheby's were brisk during the morning hours after the news conference. The following day telephone calls lasted into the evening hours.

However, when the Italian newspapers reported the same news, the mood in Rome and throughout Italy was one of gloom, with talk of deception and treason, especially vigorous in the Vatican City State.

During breakfast, the morning after the news conference, Father Susanto and the pope, who usually ate at different tables, found the usual polite and joyful formalities had changed to a breakfast in unusual silence. When someone did speak, it was in hushed tones. The pope and Father Susanto were at the receiving end of odd, distrustful looks. A dark cloud seemed to hover low over the cafeteria. People at the Vatican were expressing their indignation toward the Indonesian pope, who did not understand the significance or historical implications of selling their treasures. The news the following day implied that the pope had betrayed the Vatican, as well as Italy. The pope and his secretary knew some would not accept this news, but now they were surprised at the visceral negative feeling of the Italian people. Father Susanto's phone was busy with complaints for the remainder of the week.

***

The Vatican Bank is a relatively new creation within the Vatican. At the beginning of World War II, Pope Pius XII established the Vatican Bank for funding charitable services around the world, never intended to support Vatican activities. However, in the latter part of the twentieth century, the Vatican Bank, with significant resources, was found to be involved in banking activities that, at best, were labeled as dubious, and at worst, unethical. Pope Francis Xavier understood the Vatican Bank would become the depository of huge amounts of money to support a single charitable effort in Africa. The pope needed a compassionate and experienced banker who understood the role of banks in modern society. Pope Francis Xavier was unwilling to appoint a permanent bank director from current Vatican clerics.

The pope's secretary called Doctor Muhammad Hasson, PhD, the director of the Osteen Bank in Bangladesh, and received Doctor Hasson voice mail. Father Susanto left the following message:

"Doctor Hasson, this is the office of Pope Francis Xavier 1 at Vatican City in Rome, Italy. Pope Francis Xavier wishes to discuss an important matter with you and would like you call him on his direct secure line, which I will now share with you."

Budi made a point of assuring Doctor Hasson this was in fact a legitimate call from the Catholic leader. The recent news conference may have intrigued the Bangladeshi banker, since he called back within the hour. When the pope's desk phone rang, he picked up the receiver and said, "Hello, this is Pope Francis Xavier speaking."

"Your Holiness, this is Doctor Hasson. Am I speaking to the pope of the Catholic Church?"

"Yes, Doctor, I can assure you I am Pope Francis Xavier and I can understand your initial skepticism. You must be wondering why my secretary requested you to contact me, but I do have a specific question I need to ask you."

Doctor Hasson responded, "You must admit it is rather unusual for the leader of the Catholic Church to have a question for a Bangladeshi banker."

"Yes," answered the pope. "I'll agree, this is quite unusual. If you have no objection, may I take approximately ten minutes of your time to ask you a rather large favor?"

Doctor Hasson answered with genuine surprise, "A favor, yes continue.?"

The pope quickly responded in an understanding tone. "I suspect you are confused by my call, but I promise not to take-up much of your valuable time to explain?"

"Confused would no longer be the correct word. I am now curious and would like you to proceed with your explanation."

The pope referred to his recent *ex-cathedra* statement. He inquired if Doctor Hasson had heard of the announcement of the auction of the Vatican treasures.

Doctor Hasson responded with a slight tone of insult. "Uh, we do have some fine newspapers here in Bangladesh, and I am aware of your recent comments and your auction activities."

The pope quickly apologized if his question was misinterpreted.

"Please pardon my awkward question, I meant no offense."

Doctor Hasson, still curious, said, "Please proceed, Your Holiness."

"The Vatican expects a significant amount of money to be deposited in the Vatican Bank through the sale of Vatican treasures and I have a most challenging position to offer you as director of the Vatican Bank for a two-year period. I would like to continue with some details if you are willing to listen. May I continue?"

Doctor Hasson responded in a more pleasant manner.

"Well, your ten minutes aren't up, but I must warn you that I am not looking for a new job."

The pope quickly continued, "The reason for selecting you is we both have an identical philosophy about helping the poor raising themselves from poverty. Your philosophy in Bangladesh providing loans to entrepreneurs with the hope of building a stable middle-class society, is similar in outcome to what I wish to do in Africa. I have six people, two African leaders, Bishop Imamu Okote-Eboh and Amarie Maalout, and four other former leaders of countries; Mr. Graham Quinlan, former Prime Minister of the United Kingdom; Ms. Greta Ivar, former Prime Minister of Sweden; Ms. Deidra Conrad, German president; and Mr. Roscoe Ayala, former American president. They will be arriving in Rome in a few days with the specific objective of developing a plan, which is to include, steps leading to peace, order, and security on the African continent; along with efforts to build a middle-class African society. The plan I'm referring to, will include strategies and construction projects, all designed with a strong middle-class society in mind.

"I understand the difficulties I face in implementing the plan's goals and objectives. I realize the plan will be ongoing and take approximately fifteen years to complete. Implementing this plan will be a huge undertaking but I'm confident that with good leadership and a great deal of resources, we may have an opportunity to strengthen the African continent. I have no illusions as to the amount of time a project of this magnitude will take, and have decided to approach this project in two-year segments, understanding that the various skills of personnel hired to complete certain objectives will be very diverse and it would be unreasonable to expect skilled personnel like yourself to give more than a two-year commitment."

"As for your role as Vatican Bank director, I would expect you to manage the money coming from the auction, set up a bill payment system to fund our African projects, design a program that can transfer money into various African banks, enabling the banks to pay suppliers, contractors, importers, and workers in local currencies, such as African CFA francs, dinars, pounds, cedis, shillings, rupees, dollars, and a few other minor currencies. There would be an accounting firm, not associated with the Vatican, hired to complete audits at least once a year. And of course, you would be in charge of all personnel and the day-to-day bank operations, which I don't believe I need to go into, since you are an experienced banker."

The pope followed up his last statement immediately. "I understand I may be asking a great deal, but I'm hoping the concept of what I want to do would be of interest to you."

The doctor, dubious of what he had just heard, reiterated, "You're expecting me to leave Bangladesh and live in Italy for approximately two years to manage your bank?" The pope firmly asserted, "Yes, and I am willing to pay a desirable yearly salary, a salary equivalent to your current salary in Bangladesh. I will also provide you and your family free-living quarters here at the Vatican, or, if you prefer, in Rome proper. I will be responsible for the rental fee of any residence of your choice. Moreover, I'm not ashamed to say, I'm also appealing to your humanity. Think for a moment of the importance of your role in this effort to bring peace, security and work for an African population. I believe after two years we will be able to say we are on the way to accomplishing our goals and objectives, and you will have been instrumental in helping us to move to our next step, that of building a strong middle-class society in Africa."

A thought entered Doctor Hasson's mind. *Am I talking to a realistic person with a dream, or a very naïve, delusional religious leader?*

The pope continued, "I'm convinced if we do this correctly, in time, Africa could become a major economic power, and you can be a key part of starting that process. I know there will be bumps ahead, but I believe someone has to come forward and make this effort, and I would love to have you on my side."

Doctor Hasson cleared his dry throat with a quick drink from a glass of water, on his desk, before replying.

"Your Holiness, I will not say no at this point, but you should know a negative response is my inclination as of this moment. However, before giving a positive no to your kind offer, I would like to see the African plan. That would help me put this commitment in some perspective. To be clear, I will, for the present, only promise to think about your kind offer. That's as far as I am willing to go today."

Doctor Hasson added, "And please understand if I decide even to simply consider your proposal, I will have to share your offer with my board of directors, who will also have to agree to a two-year separation from my current duties in Bangladesh."

Doctor Hasson thought to himself. *Now, why did I agree to look at his plan? Taking my family to Rome for two years seems out of the question.*

"Your Holiness let me be frank. Yes, I believe you will be able to raise a considerable amount of money, but I also believe you may not understand the task that lies ahead, if you were to attempt such a project. I'm not convinced your efforts can be successful, no matter how much money you put into the continent. There are just too many variables and problems to overcome."

This comment brought back the despair and doubt the pope had experienced on his trip returning to Rome from Indonesia, but he decided now was not the time to question Dr. Hasson. Pope Francis Xavier had agreed to share the information the banker had requested, and after that, he would pray and hope.Francis Xavier hesitated before his final comment.

"I'm confident you are the person for the job I outlined. I know what I am asking will be a burden. All I can ask is that you take some time to consider my proposal. I will send you the final copy of the plan. My secretary has your contact information. I would appreciate if you would be so kind as to let me know your decision as soon as you have made up your mind. I am willing to wait for your answer until after you have an opportunity to review our plan."

CHAPTER 18

On 2 August, 2010, the pope's secretary sat at his desk opening and arranging mail into three piles: important, review later, and don't bother. He picked up a white business-size envelope addressed to Pope Francis Xavier I, Vatican City State, with the familiar special delivery overnight mail sticker attached to the front of the envelope. Father Susanto had seen many of these stickers on envelopes while at the Vatican, and although he did not know some of the Italian words, he understood the meaning of the notice: important mail. He then looked for a return address, which indicated the letter came from *Palazzo di Giustizia, sede della Corte Suprema di Cassazione, Rome, Italy (Italian Supreme Court of Appeals)*. Budi knew the word *corte* meant court in Italian, suggesting the letter was from the Rome judicial system. He slipped his letter opener under the back envelope flap, unfolded the four pages, and began to read. When he finished, he immediately went to the office of the pope, this time not bothering to knock,

As the pope's door opened quickly, Francis Xavier was a bit startled at the unusual entrance of his agitated friend.

"You better look at this immediately," Budi said, thrusting the special delivery letter on top of the papers on the pope's desk blotter. There were two copies of a court order from the *Corte Suprema di Cassazione*, one in Italian and one in English. The pope read the English version of the document.

Il Palazzo di Giustizia, sede della Corte Suprema di Cassazione, 9/8/210

REQUEST FOR AN INJUNCTION

The Plaintiffs in this matter are Cardinal Alejo Alejandra, Valladolid Province, Spain; Cardinal Fabien Diudonn, Paris, France; and Cardinal Giancarlo Barzinni, Puglia, Italy, who have requested this injunction to halt the auction of Vatican property scheduled for 3 October, 2010 in New York City, U.S.A. The Plaintiff's request for this injunction has been granted. Defendants in this matter will be Pope Francis Xavier I and the Vatican City State. A tribunal of three judges from the Corte Suprema di Cassazione will hear testimony from both the plaintiff's barristers and the defendant's barristers on the question of the legality of the sale of property owned by the Vatican City State.

This injunction hearing will take place at the Palazzo di Giustizia, sede della Corte Suprema di Cassazione, at 9:00 a.m. in courtroom 4 on 19, September 2010. The plaintiffs and defendants must submit a request for delay of this tribunal no later than 18, August 2010, for review by the magistratures'.

The decision to call this injunction is based on the plaintiffs' need for clarification of whether the definition of poverty is a question of morality or a personal matter of circumstances, which individuals have the ability to alter. The plaintiffs argue that Pope Francis Xavier I speaking ex cathedra is illegal if the statement does not meet the definition established by Canon Law.

The tribunal of three judges of the Roma Italy judiciary system will rule on this question, which may have an effect on the decision by Pope Francis Xavier I, as head of the Catholic Church, to auction Vatican property.

The adjudicated question of conflict between the plaintiffs and the Vatican City State, located in the Rome Judicial district, is via a normative act of a region through an incursion in their respective spheres of authority. This normative act must fall within a juridical infringement on the constitutional Canon rules previously estab-lished by the Vatican City State.

The infringement of the bounds placed on the plaintiffs in this matter relative to the exercise of the rights of power, whether secular or religious, constitutes a possible conflict regarding the plaintiffs claim and thus needs resolution by a panel of three judges of the Constitutional Court.

With respect, Angelo Marchello, Clerk of the Corte Suprema di Cassagione

After carefully reading the Request for an Injunction, the pope motioned for his secretary to take a seat. "Give me a few minutes, I wish to read this statement one more time. When the pope finished the second reading, he looked up to Budi and spoke.

"I can make out the Italian spelling that this injunction is from Italy's Supreme Court, and so it would seem our three friends have decided to retaliate against my authority to sell the Vatican treasures. I should have been prepared for some-thing like this from those three, even though I can't think of anything I could have done differently that would have pre-vented them from using this legal tactic. It looks like we have a new battle on our hands."

The Vatican employs the law firm of Vecchiolla, Rossi, and Rufino, the firm that had been handling civil matters for the Vatican for over fifteen years. The attorneys at the law firm very rarely, if ever, had occasion to deal directly with a chal-lenge to the action of a pope. The Vatican's law firm dealt almost exclusively with matters that involved the civilian staff or matters to do with the Vatican City State in which case the matter was the responsibility of the Curia, in con-sultation with the pontiff. However, in this case, the matter

144

in question dealt directly with a personal act of the pope in accordance with his authority to speak *ex-cathedra*.

Victor Vecchiolla, a partner in the firm, was to meet directly with the pope. Mister Vecchiolla is a respected barrister, with many years of experience in Rome's courtrooms. He is known as a man who dressed with impeccable taste, and was partial to expensive tailor-made outfits, but Francis Xavier was more interested in the fact that Mister Vecchiolla is considered a skilled and deliberate barrister, with a quick mind and imposing legal manner.

On 18, September 2010, Victor Vecchiolla entered the pope's outer office. Father Susanto moved from a seat behind his desk to greet Mister Vecchiolla. The pope's secretary escorted Mister Vecchiolla into the pope's office. The plan for this morning was to have Mister Vecchiolla explain the ramifications of the injunction and the strategy used to counter the plaintiff's injunction. When Mister Vecchiolla and Father Susanto entered the pope's office, they saw a tense, troubled, unsettled pontiff. After the appropriate and pleasant introductions, the three men gathered in the corner section of the pope's office on upholstered chairs as Father Susanto poured coffee and invited Mister Vecchiolla to help himself to the pastries on the coffee table in front of them.

Mister Vecchiolla began his presentation after a sip of coffee. "First let me say that I have never experienced such speed of the Roman judicial system to act on a legal matter. As you may be aware, many of Italy's current civil legal laws were established during the early Roman Empire, and due to the complicated regulations and laws of that period, our legal system could stand some changes. Modernization would be especially important. I mention this not to caution you both in any way, but simply to understand my surprise at the hast of this matter. Now let's deal with this specific injunction. After a plaintiff's request for an injunction is presented to the Italian Supreme Court, it always takes years for the actual case to be heard. I cannot explain the reason for their immediate attention to this particular case. However, I suspect it may be due to the fact that an auction of Vatican property is to take place in October of this year. The judicial system may be reluctant to ask a pope to stop the auction. Now the speed of this injunction could also be attributed to the fact that the judiciary in Rome, may be very uncomfortable on ruling on a religious matter and not a civil matter, if this is the case, it could be to our advantage. So, I prefer to accept the judiciary date and proceed as scheduled. I suspect I will be given plenty of latitude in my argument against the injunction. So, my money is on the discomfort factor. I say this because of one word used in the injunction notice, if you would refer to line twenty-three of the injunction, the words "may have an effect," rather than the usual "will have an effect." This wording makes me suspect there is some question in some judges' minds about the validity of a civil proceeding becoming entangled in a pope's decision regarding faith and morals."

The atmosphere in the room remained tense; the pope grew more concerned as Mister Vecchiolla continued with his explanation. "The question before the tribunal judges will be the narrow question posed by the three plaintiffs. Therefore, the three-judge panel hearing this case may realize they run the danger of becoming involved in a religious squabble, being heard in a civil court, and that helps our case. The plaintiffs' claim in the injunction is that poverty is an issue of circumstances, which is within the control of the individual person, and not a moral issue, since a poor people have the power to remove themselves from poverty by hard work and effort, and therefore you don't have the authority to sell Vatican property."

Mr. Vecchiolla stopped and reached for a sfogliatelle pastry. "Your Holiness, you don't play fair. Here I am watching my waistline, and since I have been sitting on this sofa, and talking, the beautiful sfogliatelle pastry has been interfering with my concentration, its thin-layered pastry dough looking at me and saying, quick, grab me before someone else does. I can no longer resist. I love these pastries, especially with this hot cup of black coffee!"

Mr. Vecchiolla then proceeded to take a bite, along with more sips of coffee, and then placed the unfinished pastry on his plate. "I'll save the remainder to have with my next coffee."

Mr. Vecchiolla was about to continue when Budi spoke for the first time. "Hey, Sunjaya," Budi hesitated, realizing his error by referring to the pope in such an informal manner. He looked at Mr. Vecchiolla and spoke. "It's okay; we have known each other since the fifth grade in Indonesia. I don't often make that mistake, but that was an error on my part, in your presence."

Looking back toward the pope, Father Susanto said, "I was about to say, Holy Father, I have a brilliant idea. The next *ex cathedra* statement you should write is to make it a mortal sin to eat sfogliatelle. And if you think the people in Italy are upset with you selling the treasures, this will really get you impeached!"

All were laughing, when Mister Vecchiolla said. "And don't call on me to defend you on that one, because I will be leading the charge for your impeachment!"

The three men were now laughing with good humor, for the first time at this meeting. The atmosphere in the room suddenly became more relaxed, as did the three men. Budi touched Mr. Vecchiolla's arm, and both men still with broad smiles on their faces. Budi said, "Now you know why he's the pope and I'm the secretarial comedian."

Budi had worked his comedy magic once again and poured coffee for all. He then got the meeting back on task by saying, "Okay, enough fooling around, let's get back to business."

Mister Vecchiolla moved to a verbal outline of his presentation. "The witnesses I plan on presenting are experts on the African continent. It seemed logical to our research staff to develop a response by using these experts. My opening statement will center on the manipulation, death, massacres, and the inadequate amount of food the African people deal with daily. I will also give some brief examples of how Western European countries, political dictators, and, in some cases, religious intolerance all played a role in forcing the African people to constantly remain in poverty, making it impossible for Africans to improve their standard of living."

Mister Vecchiolla hesitated as though he needed to recall a fact enabling him to continue his statement, but immediately he was back on his point.

"I plan on presenting two witnesses. The first is Jonathan Oliver, an American historian who specializes in African studies. He is a professor at the University of Michigan, and my questions will allow him to explain the history of two failed countries in Africa, The Central African Republic and an African country formally known as the Belgian Congo. His explanation will be able to bring out why poverty is not a matter of circumstances, but an actual condition that people have no power to alter."

Mister Vecchiolla asked to have his coffee cup replenished and continued "Based on my questioning of Mr. Oliver in our phone conversation, he feels strongly that the history of these two countries and their specific actions have forced their citizens to remain in poverty. I will then broaden the question from the two countries to include a similar historical summary of the following countries in Africa: Chad, Benin, Equatorial Guinea, Gambia, Togo, Djibouti, Rwanda, and Burundi. The tribunal judges, prior to the hearing, will receive this summary report, which in my opinion will help the court to visualize the horrors forcing African people in these countries, to remain in poverty, with no chance for escape from their brutalized existence."

Mister Vecchiolla continued. "The explorers in the seventeenth and eighteenth centuries, followed by the colonial powers later, established practices and regulations preventing the African people from rising out of their state of poverty. I will then introduce the existing period when African states gained their freedom, and how corrupt politicians, warlords, tribal militias, and ethnic massacres have all played a role in forcing the general population to remain in their current state of poverty with no opportunity to escape their brutal, destructive, immoral existence."

The pope interrupted Mr. Vecchiolla with a question. "If the tribunal judges agree with the cardinals' interpretation that poverty is not a moral issue, then my *ex-cathedra* statement would not fall under the category of what is known to the general public as papal infallibility. Is that an accurate interpretation on my part?"

Mr. Vecchiolla said. "Yes, that would be correct. However, if that were the case, I would immediately inform the three-judge tribunal that I intend to appeal, and I will have the appeal documents in my possession, ready to give the notification to the clerk of the court. My appeal would essentially say that, in our opinion, civil judges do not have the religious training to form a conclusion on whether poverty is or is not a moral issue. I would support the conclusion, that only trained religious leaders have this authority. As pope, you have the religious training, and by the constitution of Catholic and canon law, only a pope has the supremacy to speak with *ex cathedra* authority, which cannot be challenged. And that is the outcome the three judges fear the most, knowing I have this appeal argument ready for them. I'm confident if this issue goes to appeal, the three judges hearing the appeal would decide in our favor."

CHAPTER 19

At 9:07 A.M. on 18 September, 2010, the Italian court clerk loudly said, "All rise." The three judges hearing the case entered courtroom number four, in single file, and proceeded to a raised platform containing three black leather seats. The wall behind the judges consisted of four-foot-wide grimy oak wood panels. Above the wood panels on the bare wall was a pale outline shape of a cross that had hung in all Italian courtrooms, until removal of this religious symbol in the late twentieth century. Situated to the far left of the judge's platform, facing an empty jury section and an empty witness box. Two long tables facing the judges was reserved for the competing barristers. The two barristers stood behind their respective tables, Barrister Mario Salvati, representing the three plaintiff cardinals, and Barrister Victor Vecchiolla, representing the pope. The pope and three plaintiff cardinals had received prior permission not to be present during this injunction hearing, out of respect for their religious titles. Directly behind the barrister tables stood a decorative wood rail separating the spectators from the trial participants. The courtroom doors were closed to further spectators due to unavailable seating. After the three judges had taken their seats, the lead judge raised his voice saying, "Please be seated." The lead judge then gaveled the courtroom to order. "This tribunal hearing is now in session."

The lead judge informed the tribunal that under Rome's judicial regulations, tribunal hearings do not require a jury; the decision rendered by a tribunal hearing is the responsibility of a three-judge panel. The lead judge explained the parameters of this tribunal hearing, as an injunction motion offered by the plaintiffs to halt the auction of Vatican property, scheduled for 3 October, 2010 in New York City. The plaintiffs are contending that the definition of poverty is a secular issue, not caused by immoral acts. The plaintiffs' argument, therefore, is that Pope Francis Xavier does not have the authority to sell Vatican property to support his *ex-cathedra* statement or infallible proclamation. In accordance with Roman regulations of a tribunal hearing, each barrister may question any number of witnesses submitted to this three-judge tribunal panel for approval prior to the proceedings. In tribunal hearings, barristers may not cross-examine witnesses called to the stand but are allowed to make an opening statement.

The lead judge looked directly at the plaintiffs' table and said, "Mr. Salvati, do you wish to make an opening statement?"

Barrister Salvati stood and said, "Yes, Your Honors."

"You may proceed," said the lead judge.

"It's the plaintiffs' contention that poverty exists for numerous reasons, all of which are under the direct control of the individual and therefore cannot be the result of a third-party act, whether deliberate or inadvertent. Therefore, it is impossible for poverty to be a moral issue, because individuals can eliminate the existence of their poverty status through their own actions. I will be able to show that poverty is the direct result of numerous circumstances, none of which has anything to do with immorality or the acts of others. Finally, I will show that governments and/or states generously accept responsibility for the living conditions of handicapped individuals who may be living in poverty.

Therefore, no claim of immorality can be applied to their individual's condition."

Mister Salvati, a well-dressed, articulate young man of thirty years, moved from behind the table as he continued his statement. "The condition of poverty is the result of such factors as unemployment, underemployment, a freely agreed upon salary, size of a family, and, in some cases gender of the employee. In addition, it is true women are generally paid less than men are, but this is due to the fact the vast majority of women have a second income from a husband to provide for their family. If a woman has children and is not married, that too would be a situation involving circumstances, but certainly not morality. All of the above situations have the element of circumstances individuals have control over. Therefore, the plaintiffs' argument is that the state of poverty, as we know it today, cannot be a moral issue.

Barrister Salvati returned to his seat behind the plaintiff's table.

The lead judge looked at Mister Vecchiolla and asked, "Barrister Vecchiolla, do you wish to make an opening statement?"

Mister Vecchiolla stood behind his table and answered the lead judge. "Yes, Your Honors." Mister Vecchiolla turned and faced the spectator section of the court and began. "We intend to show the theological factors that motivated Pope Francis Xavier 1 to make an *ex-cathedra* statement declaring poverty to be an immoral condition. Therefore, he has the authority to sell Vatican property in order to remove poverty from the continent of Africa as a demonstration to show the world how governments and organizations need to provide conditions, and structural improvements in their countries, which will create the need for employment opportunities."

Mister Vecchiolla turned and faced the three judges and continued with his opening statement.

"It is poverty that causes forty million people in Africa to die of starvation each year, approximately half of which are children. Many people in rural Africa have no access to clean water, forcing individuals to drink polluted water, which is a direct cause of sickness and disease. Over half of the population of Africa has no direct access to health services. Poorly supplied African public hospitals lack certification as sterile facilities. As an example, Nigerian public hospitals, are one of many public African hospitals that do not meet minimum standards for sterility, due to the lack the proper supplies. Therefore, it is not surprising that Nigeria has the highest rate of malaria in the world."

Mr. Vecchiolla moved to a spot in front of his chair, and while standing, he placed both hands on the tabletop and continued.

"It is also important to note that in 2007, the Sudanese government sponsored genocidal attacks that resulted in the displacement of 300,000 Darfuris in their home country. The United Nations inspectors named Ali Kushayb, the leader of the Sudanese army units, as responsible for these attacks. The International Criminal Court for war crimes against humanity have an outstanding arrest warrant for Mr. Kushayb. These examples would seem to conflict with my learned colleague's assertion that, and I quote, 'It is impossible for poverty to be a moral issue, because individuals can eliminate the existence of their poverty status through their own action.'"

Mr. Vecchiolla now centered his gaze directly toward the panel of judges and said, "I have completed my opening statement, and I thank the court for its attention."

Barrister Vecchiolla returned to his seat.

The lead judge, looking toward Barrister Salvati, spoke. "The barrister for the plaintiffs may call his first witness."

The court clerk called out, "Will Ms. Maria Cagnina please take the witness stand?" A well-dressed attractive, middle-aged woman, with head held high, entered the courtroom from its double door entrance, and proceeded down the center aisle. She wore a dark-colored dress, her black hair swept back, away from her face, she carefully stepped into the witness box. The court clerk asked Ms. Cagnina to place her right hand on the Bible and pledge to tell the truth.

Barrister Salvati rose from his seat and moved toward Ms. Cagnina. He thanked her for her appearance before the court, and asked the witness a question.

"Miss Cagnina, what is your occupation and title?"

Miss Cagnina responded to Barrister Salvati's question. "Director of the Italian National Bureau of Social Assistance. I oversee twenty-one offices throughout Italy, which provides services to the poor and needy of Italy."

Barrister Salvati continued, "In your opinion, how likely is it for people to remove themselves from poverty?"

Ms. Cagnina responded. Official statistics show a significant number of people have escaped poverty in the latter part of the twentieth century. In 1950, world organizations that study the topic of poverty, estimated that one-half of the people living on earth were living in poverty, or in conditions of poverty, or near poverty levels. She then referred to a study completed in 2010, indicating that this number fell by half in developing countries, from 43% to 21% , a reduction of almost one billion people."

Ms. Cagnina was a poised and confident witness. Her testimony was formal, unemotional, and concise. Barrister Salvati had not expected the witness to respond to this opening question in such a detached manner. He could do nothing at this point, but to move forward with his questions. "Ms. Cagnina, please define for the court the term extreme poverty."

"This category of poverty is defined when a person's earnings are, in American currency, up to $1.90 per day.

Mr. Salvati then asked his witness. "Ms. Cagnina is it possible for individuals and or families to raise themselves out of extreme poverty?"

"It is definitely possible for individuals and/or families to raise themselves out of the extreme poverty category."

Barrister Vecchiolla objected to Ms. Cagnina's opinion on the basis of a personal conclusion and was overruled by the three-judge panel.

Barrister Salvati addressed his witness with a third question. "Is it accurate to say social agencies have statistical data showing how efforts on the part of poor people results in employment opportunities that culminate in the elimination of extreme poverty?"

Ms. Cagnina sat up erect in her chair, and with a raised indignant voice, gave an example of a successful program that is eliminating extreme poverty. She referred to the Lula launched Bolsa Familia, an Argentinian program that provides financial assistance to families in extreme poverty, provided they met a requirement that a percentage of the financial assistance be used for their children's school tuition.

Barrister Salvati moved toward the witness, placing his hand on the front panel of the witness box, asking in a warm, low manner, intending to relax the witness. He then proceeded to ask the following question: "What role does personal responsibility play in this question of poverty?"

156

Ms. Cagnina, not noticing Barrister Salvati's attempt to encourage her to respond with more feeling and sympathy continued her testimony. "Personal responsibility plays a major role for people who find themselves trapped in a lifetime of poverty; this situation is often attributed to a reluctance to work. Individuals who find themselves in poverty, I'm sorry to say, have only themselves to blame."

Mr. Vecchiolla quickly rose from his seat and said, "Objection Your Honors, calls for speculation on the part of the witness."

The lead judge responded, "Objection sustained."

Barrister Salvati moved away from the witness and toward the audience. He looked directly at the onlookers, as though he expected them to have the answer to his next question, and said, "Regarding this question of poverty, do you believe wealthier countries have a responsibility to assist nations that have a high percentage of their population in extreme poverty?"

Mister Vecchiolla called out as he stood. "Objection Your Honors, the question calls for speculation on the part of the witness."

The lead judge thought for a moment and then said, "Overruled. The witness has sufficient experience that enables her to respond authoritatively, to such a question."

Ms. Cagnina continued her testimony, stating that she believed it was a mistake to give financial aid or food products directly to the poor for two reasons. Direct aid to individuals can quite easily make them dependent on this aid, causing the cycle of extreme poverty to continue. Second, assistance to third-world countries all too frequently finds its way into the pockets of corrupt government officials.

Mister Salvati slowly approached the witness with a confused look on his face. It was clear from Mr. Salvati's body language, that Ms. Cagnina's response included a reference to corrupt government officials, a statement he had not been expecting.

Mister Salvati attempted to clarify a reference she made in her previous testimony with a follow up question. Mister Salvati asked Miss Cagnina, "Surely the minor incidence of corrupt behavior by some individuals is so isolated that it has no effect on the incidents of poverty in poor countries"

Mister Vecchiolla was on his feet before Mister Salvati's question was finished.

"Objection Your Honors, leading the witness!"

The lead judge, without conferring with the other two judges, said, "Sustained. Mister Salvati, your witness has answered the question. I suggest you move on."

Barrister Salvati, said, "Thank you for your scholarly comments, Ms. Cagnina." He quickly turned to the three-judge tribunal and said, "Your Honors that is all I have for this witness."

The lead judge excused Ms. Cagnina and said to Mister Salvati, "Call your next witness."

Barrister Salvati called his final witness, Dr. Anna Vitali. An elderly woman proceeded up the center isle of the courtroom and stood in the witness box. She was a short, very slender, with white curly hair and formally dressed in a delicate business suit.

Mister Salvati asked, "Could you tell the court your current position at Bologna University?" The elderly witness with a confident voice said. "I am the chairperson of the psychology department at the University of Bologna."

Mister Salvati than asked, "Please tell the court how long you have studied psychology, and other disciplines that you have specialized in over the years."

"I have been a psychologist for over thirty years and have specialized in the area of poverty for the past thirteen years."

Barrister Salvati then said, "Doctor Vitali, please tell the court in your own words, the causes of poverty among some people."

"People in poverty tend to enter into self-destructive behavior, dropping out of school, joining gangs, substance abuse, and bearing children, are but a few of the reasons."

Barrister Salvati then asked Dr. Vitali to share with the court important research studies completed on the subject of poverty.

"A few important research findings have shown that economic stress can be a factor in a person's cognitive capacity. A release of cortisol by the adrenal glands, occurs in response to fear or stress, as a part of the fight-or-flight body mechanism. If a person is anxious about bills, inability to buy food or other items, stress can cause the body to interfere with its ability to exert self-discipline. This can result in mental strain for many people. T. Sendhil Mullainathan of Harvard University and Elder Shafir of Princeton University discussed this thoroughly in their book, *Scarcity*."

Barrister Salvati thanked the witness for her participation this morning and informed the tribunal judges that Dr. Vitali was his last witness.

Barrister Vecchiolla stood and moved toward the panel of judges. He smoothed his silk tie and then buttoned his stylishly tailored suit jacket before addressing the court. Mister Vecchiolla was in his early fifties. His attractive hairstyle, his unwrinkled face, and his agile movements suggested he was much younger than his actual age. "Your Honors, I would like to call my first witness."

This statement was the cue for the clerk to call out, "Will Dr. Donato Assunto please take the stand?"

After Dr. Assunto's swearing in by the clerk of the court, Barrister Vecchiolla said, "Thank you for your time this morning, Doctor Assunto. Before I begin, please inform the court of your profession and give us an example of research work you have studied?"

"I am a psychologist with a practice in Rome, and have extensively published research in the area of personal behavior." Dr. Assunto was a bearded man with a high forehead from the loss of hair. He wore a light brown jacket with leather patches near his elbows, dark slacks, and casual loafers.

Barrister Vecchiolla asked the witness, "Would you be good enough to shed some light on the issue of poverty and how it relates to the personal behavior of individuals?"

Barrister Salvati jumped from his seat and called out, "Relevancy, Your Honors."

The lead judge, without conferring with the other judges, immediately said, "Sorry, Mister Salvati, but your previous witness introduced the topic of behavior, and therefore the objection is overruled. Dr. Assunto, you may answer Barrister Vecchiolla's question."

Dr. Assunto began his testimony with a strong voice, referring to his published research that overwhelmingly demonstrates that society fails the young before the young fails society. Governments are unwilling to provide the resources that could help people living in poverty. Political leaders have little interest in victims of poverty because their contribution to the tax base is minimal, and their voting record is spotty.

Barrister Vecchiolla thanked the witness and said he had no further questions for Dr. Assunto.

The lead judge said, "Call your next witness, Mister Vecchiolla." The court clerk, called out "Will Dr. Nuncio Manganiello please take the witness stand?"

A tall, well-dressed man entered the courtroom and proceeded to the witness box.

Dr. Manganiello, what is your occupation, and please add any special assignments you may have been given in your work."

"I am a professor of economics at Milan University. I am currently on a two-year leave of absence for the purpose of acting as chairman of the Economic Task Force on Technology and Labor."

Mister Vecchiolla said. "Would you please summarize for the esteemed tribunal of judges the work of the economic task force that you chair?"

Dr. Manganiello responded by discussing the impact of technology on labor as it applies to European markets. He chaired a task force that concluded increased global trade has had a disruptive influence on industry and workers. The task force findings suggested that countries with a cheap labor force provide tax incentives to businesses to relocate within their borders. This practice affects industries such as textiles, apparel, furniture, electronics, household appliances, automobile production, and the toy industry. Our task force found that computerized machines, and the use of robots have begun to have an impact on both the factory and non-factory labor market. He went on to explain that many sectors of factory production, using these new technologies, complete work faster and are more efficient than workers. He added that replacing secretaries with word processors, and along with access to voice mail, and e-mail has become more and more prevalent.

Hand held devices are a contributing factor in reducing the labor force in numerous ways.

He then added that machines now have the ability to measure with laser speed and efficiency, which, result in industry hiring fewer carpenters and plumbers. Electricians, who are not familiar with fiber optic use, are no longer employable. What is a tragedy for the unemployed textile workers in Venice, is very good news for designers in New York City?"

Mister Vecchiolla continued with a look of satisfaction on his face and posed the following question to his witness. "Does the manufacturing industry have a responsibility to prepare their workers for the implications of these new technological advances.

Dr. Manganiello replied, "It no longer is a question of preparing employees. Industries that quickly embrace technology and innovation, allows them to increase profits, while eliminating their labor force that was once indispensable. In summary, technological advances have allowed manufactures to maintain or increase profits, while eliminating skilled workers by the use of robots or on-line software."

Mister Vecchiolla asked his witness to elaborate on the European wage structure of today's unskilled labor force.

"Dr. Manganiello's work in this area allowed him to respond to the question with authority. "The average European wage has remained flat for the last two decades. Insecurity in the labor market is now common. More and more people find themselves with limited or no employment options.

At the completion of Dr. Manganiello's testimony, Barrister Vecchiolla turned to the judges and said, "You're Honors, I have no further questions for this witness."

The lead judge told Dr. Manganiello, "You may step down, doctor."

Before calling his next witness, Mr. Vecchiolla submitted an exhibit, which was a written historical description of two African nations. After the lead judge scanned the heading of the exhibit, he said, "Mr. Vecchiolla, you may call your next witness."

The clerk of the court called out, "Will Dr. Jonathan Oliver please take the witness stand."

A stately man with bushy grey hair and looked to be in his mid-fifties entered the courtroom and proceeded directly to the witness stand.

Mr. Vecchiolla thanked the witness for traveling so far in order to give his testimony in person. He then asked his first question, "Doctor Oliver, for the benefit of the court, would you please give a brief historical summary of the two African countries that you previously provided for the three-judge tribunal.

Dr. Oliver, sitting erect in his chair, began his testimony.

"The Central African Republic is a pathetically poor, land-locked nation of some two and a half million people. Only a tiny handful of the population of this country have ever had the slightest sense of physical or economic well-being, despite the country having vast natural resources, including diamonds, uranium, manganese, timber, and rich agricultural soil. The Central African Republic has no railroads, no telephone system; and only two hundred sixty-five miles of paved roads, causing the vast majority of its people to be trapped into subsistence farming. The Central African Republic, remains to this date, one of Africa's poorest countries."

Dr. Oliver then moved on to a brief oral history of Belgium's colonial rule of the Congo. He described in shocking, vivid detail how in 1914, the Belgian King's request for an increase of rubber tree leaves, which had the effect of destroying eighty kilometers of rubber plants, stripping the Congo of its valuable natural resource.

The lead judge interrupted the testimony. "Doctor Oliver, I believe you have made your point. We look forward to reading your more inclusive comments on these two countries in the exhibit you provided to the court."

Barrister Vecchiolla thanked the witness and said, "Your Honors I have one final witness to present, and permit me to suggest that we break for lunch before he takes the witness box. Without comment, the lead judge said, "Court will resume at 2, P.M.

The gavel came down on a wood pallet so all could hear the clerk of the court call the afternoon tribunal into session."

"The lead judge instructed Barrister Vecchiolla, to call his final witness." The clerk called out, "Will Mr. Thomas Kennelly please take the witness box?"

Mr. Kennelly entered the courtroom and proceeded up the center aisle and into the witness box.

Mr. Vecchiolla asked the witness to explain his background, which would verify his credentials for the judges and spectators. After Mr. Kennelly completed explaining his education and his work on the African continent, Mr. Vecchiolla asked the witness, "Are you the author of the book titled *Four Famines*, published in 2010?"

Mr. Kennelly answered, "Yes, I am."

"Mr. Kennelly, would you please explain the title of this book?" Mister Kennelly responded, "Four incidents of famine that occurred in different countries are the subjects of my book. I have studied the causes of these four famines because I believe them to be the worst famines in recorded history."

Mr. Vecchiolla asked, "Where did these famines take place and when?"

The witness replied, "The Irish Potato Famine began in Ireland in 1845. The Bengal Famine occurred in 1943, and into 1944 in India. the Great Chinese Famine took place in the mid-twentieth century. Finally, the Ethiopian Famine happened in the 1970s."

Mr. Vecchiolla said, "Based on your study of these horrible occurrences, can you explain what happens to the human body when it is deprived of food?"

The attorney for the plaintiffs stood and said, "Objection, relevance, Your Honors. This is not a biology class."

The lead judge looked to his two fellow judges. Placing their hands over their respective microphones, the three judges discussed the objection for a few moments. They separated, and the lead judge denied the objection, and instructed Mr. Kennelly to answer the question.

Mr. Kennelly began, "The physical symptoms of people when they are starving are consistent, and if allowed to continue cause death. A human body deprived of food will begin to consume itself. By that, I mean the body begins to consume its store of glucose, which is in the liver. After this, the body begins to use up the proteins in its muscles and cells. Soon after that, muscle protein breaks down, and the remaining fat bunches up in the stomach area which, as strange as it may seem, causes the enlargement of their stomach. The starved person will soon experience a personality change. They become disorderly and sloppy, followed by aggressiveness. The person will often separate from others. Judgment seems to disappear as anxiety rises. Eventually the person's mind becomes delusional. Finally, if by chance the starving person is given food, they may not recognize it as food, and may not accept it. And we know that after this stage, death comes quickly."

Mr. Vecchiolla asked the witness, "When we think of famine, we usually believe it is caused by an act of God such as a long drought or great floods. What was the cause of these famines?"

Mr. Kennelly responded. "These famines were all preventable. Those in charge during these famines, for various reasons, discouraged the production of food, and along with the failure to produce food, there was a failure to distribute food properly. This may sound confusing Your honors, may I briefly explain?"

"Yes, please do, Mr. Kennelly," said the lead judge.

"In each of the four famines studied, it was true the supply of food was limited by natural causes, but the limited food supply was not the reason people died of starvation. When the food chain became limited for various reasons, people actually took food from one group of people and gave it to another. An example is the Irish Potato Famine. In 1845, when the potato blight hit Ireland, the land was producing limited food, but there was enough food to prevent people from starving to death. However, the British Empire continued to ship cattle and corn from Ireland to England during the blight.

"In other cases, humans did not properly protect the food they had, and in fear of hunger, food was vandalized. In other situations, those in charge chose not to assist the starving people. They simply allowed individuals to starve to death. This was the case in the Bengal Famine in India, when the British protectorate chose not to respond to the starving Indian people during the famine."

Barrister Vecchiolla politely interrupted his witness, and asked, "Why would a country do such a thing?"

Mr. Kennelly replied, "Stubbornness, insensitivity, lack of understanding of the problem, poor judgments, any number of reasons. For example, during the Irish Potato Famine the British administrator of government relief is on record, saying. 'Famine had been sent by God to teach the Irish a lesson.' That type of attitude could very well explain why one would decide to either not intervene or disregard the consequence of shipping food from Ireland to the British Empire.'"

Mr. Vecchiolla asked the witness, "When food becomes scares in a country or region, can authorities prevent the starvation of their citizens?"

"We could if we were able to eliminate egocentricity, inflexibility, and a host of numerous, sometimes evil motives that can be part of a person's thought process or their motivation during a famine."

Mr. Vecchiolla asked the witness to explain further. "The best explanation I can give you occurred during the Great Chinese Famine, which was the direct result of the policies and procedures of one man, Mao Zedong. He had been warned that his program. *The Great Leap Forward* would cause starvation among many people in China. Unfortunately, Mao Zedong ignored the advice, believing his policies were right for China. Chairman Mao was known to punish those who disagreed with his policy and practices by death.

Mr. Vecchiolla said, "Thank you, Mr. Kennelly."

Mr. Vecchiolla then turned his attention to the three-judge tribunal and spoke. "The defense rests its case."

***

At 10:30 A.M., two days after the completion of the tribunal hearing, the two barristers sat at there tables in courtroom four, waiting for the arrival of the three judges.

After a ten-minute delay, the three judges entered the courtroom from a side door and took there

places on the elevated section of the room. The lead judge called the sentencing procedure into session with a single rap of his gavel and read a statement.

"In the case of the cardinal plaintiffs versus the Vatican pontiff regarding the authority of Pope Francis Xavier 1 to dispose of Vatican property, the tribunal finds in favor of Pope Francis Xavier 1 and supports his authority to dispose of Vatican property for the purpose of supporting his theological declaration that poverty is an immoral state of existence."

With a firm rap of the gavel, the lead judge said, "The Rome Judicial Court will not consider any further motions pertaining to this dispute."

The tribunal hearing and its decision received a reasonable amount of publicity around the world through various newspaper articles, the internet, and on radio and television news programs. Quite a few newspapers ran their article beneath the fold on the first page, headlines such as *Indonesian Pope's Declaration on Poverty Upheld in the Rome Court*. Pope Francis Xavier was thrilled with the verdict and surprised at the publicity the Italian court's decision.

CHAPTER 20

Father Susanto asked Mario, one of the cafeteria cooks at the Vatican, if he knew of a place for a weekend holiday. Mario told him of the town where he was born, a rural mountain town approximately an hour's drive from Rome called Opi, located in a valley surrounded by the Apennine Mountains in the Abruzzo region of Italy. Mario also mentioned to Father Susanto that if he chose to go to Opi, he should make a point of eating at the small local town bar. A woman named Maria Antonia Sgammotta, who prepares meals at the bar, has a local reputation as the best cook in Italy. Mario also informed the pope's secretary there was a small, ten-room hotel that was a clean and a pleasant place to stay on his weekend getaway.

Father Susanto was confident he had found a proper location for the six individuals to work on the African plan. The following day, Budi informed the pope of the Abruzzo location, and both agreed the town of Opi sounded ideal for the African planers. Budi arranged for a Roman car service to pick up the six planners as soon as dates and times of their flights were determined.

The planning session in Opi would begin on 16 November, 2010. Rooms were reserved for a five-day period with the stipulation that these reservations might be longer or shorter. Ms. Maria Antonia Sgammotta was contacted, and agreed to prepare meals in the hotel's kitchen for the six guests.

Mr. Amarie Maalout and Bishop Imamu Okote-Ebon had inquired if they could arrive a day early, as they wished to take a day to relax and familiarize themselves with Italy and the area where they would be staying. Budi, without consulting the pope, agreed to this change and contacted the vehicle service hired to bring the planners to Opi. The two were picked up at the airport in Rome on the morning of the 15th of November and taken to Opi. Along with the luggage of the two African planners, was a recording machine, paper, easel, large white pads, pens, pencils, erasers, staplers, transparent tape, masking tape, and a few other miscellaneous items.

The planes carrying the other four planners, landed in Rome's airport on the morning of the 16th. The team members passed through customs in a secure room and were escorted out a rear door, where a black limousine was waiting to take them to the mountain town.

After arriving in Opi that afternoon, the remaining men and women of the African planning team used a late lunch to become acquainted. The four planners who arrived on the 16th spent the remainder of the afternoon resting from the effects of their jet lag. The six men and two women enjoyed a delicious late evening meal, a refreshing sleep, and a light breakfast, before beginning their work in the small hotel.

There was enthusiasm in the room even though each participant harbored some doubts about this effort; but here they were, determined to follow through on their agreement with Pope Francis Xavier. Each participant had differing ideas as to how this venture could so easily end up being a useless undertaking, one full of hopes and dreams, and perhaps, eventually winding up collecting dust in some file cabinet because an unrealistic pope with a noble idea eventually realizing what he asked for, was impossible to accomplish. The planners decided they would complete their work as promised, each chose not include their pessimism as a part of their work.

The following day, Father Budi Susanto stood at the entrance to the pope's outer office late in the afternoon, talking to the director of maintenance regarding a roof repair to Saint Peter's Cathedral, when his desk landline phone rang. As Budi hurried toward his desk, he told the maintenance director to keep him informed. He picked up the phone and heard the distinctive voice of Bishop Okote-Eboh, who said. "Good afternoon Father Susanto, this is Bishop Okote-Eboh with a message for Pope Francis, our first work day was productive, and each team member was pleased with their room and, and the scenery in Opi was magnificent." Budi was pleased by the news and assured the bishop that he would pass the information on to the pope. When the phone call ended Budi made a mental note to thank Mario, the Vatican cook who recommended Opi.

That afternoon, as Budi entered the cafeteria for his lunch, he first moved toward the kitchen to thank Mario. After entering the kitchen, the first thing he heard was Mario shouting from a distance, "Ha, ha, so I caught the good priest in his little white lie! Oh, the poor the hard-working priest needed a weekend retreat, what a load of bull."

Father Susanto, looking sheepish and curious in the same moment, said, "You mean me, Mario? You should know by now I am the champion white lie teller."

"Never you mind, you bull thrower, and if you were not a priest, I would have used a different word, than thrower, I heard from my cousin, who lives in Opi, that big important people arrived in his town over the past two days. You can only fool Mario for a short time, but soon I know everything."

Budi smiled and said, "I'll have to remember to speak with someone else when I have another one of my white lies to tell."

With a broad smile the cook said, "Get out of my kitchen, you rascal! Get out."

As Budi left the kitchen, both men were laughing.

Three days later, Budi's landline phone rang and he answered. "Good morning, father, this is Bishop Okote-Eboh once again."

"How nice to hear your voice. I hope everything is well in Opi,"

The bishop assured the pope's secretary the planning was progressing well, but informed Father Susanto that two extra days will be needed to complete their work.

Budi questioned the bishop, "I hope that the setting for your work hasn't been the cause of your delay."

The bishop hesitated, as though he was considering how to respond, "Well, to some degree, yes, but the reason has been a most pleasant one. It's a bit difficult to explain over the phone, simply inform His Holiness that although we will need two extra days, we believe we will have a complete and workable blueprint allowing him to reach his goals. Please pass along our apology for the delay and be sure to tell him the delay has not been due to complications relative to our proposal, but rather, had to do with the warm welcome we received from the people of this beautiful little village."

"I'll be sure to pass along your message. I'm sure the delay will not be a problem in spite of the pope's anxiousness, but that was to be expected, as he tends to be a worry wart."

Pope Francis Xavier was not in his office during this phone conversation; he was visiting with the museum and library directors, explaining he had decided to bring in a Jesuit priest to coordinate the direction of both the library and museum. The pope, now not as paranoid about secrecy, now that his plan would soon be announced, was only concerned about the disappointing news he was bringing to the two clerics who would be relieved of their duties as temporary directors?

When Pope Francis Xavier returned to his office, Budi informed him of the message left by Bishop Okote-Eboh. Father Susanto made a point of mentioning to the pope that the bishop was confident they would be able to present him with a sound, workable plan upon their return, and that the delay was not due to problems with the plan.

"Well, that's very good news! The next hurdle will be for us to get a competent bank director in place as soon as possible. My first choice would be Doctor Hasson, but I expect him to decline. I have made some contacts with bankers in Rome, through recommendations from Cardinal Latina. These bankers have told me they will make contact with experienced bank officials in Rome, individuals who they believed might consider to be interviewed for the position of Vatican Bank director, but that decision will be made after we hear from Doctor Hasson. I promised to send him the African plan, which he wants to read before making a decision, but something tells me he will turn down my offer."

Pope Francis Xavier looked drawn and worried.

"I wish I had more time in this recruiting process but having to keep things so secret has really made this process much too compact. We really needed more lead time to get things in place."

***

That same afternoon, Pope Francis Xavier called the architectural firm of Gerisina and Lombardo, inquiring about the removal progress of the nine frescoes. Mister Gerisina explained that extreme caution had to be imposed when removing frescoes from their wall surface. The pope was disappointed that this task was still incomplete, but for now the African Plan was his main priority.

Mr. Gerisina then added that the empty spaces, once the home to three frescoes had been successfully removed, and properly prepared to receive contemporary art.

Pope Francis Xavier thanked Mr. Gerisina for the good news and asked him to pass along his gratitude to the men involved with their delicate work.

CHAPTER 21

The six planners arrived back at the Vatican as scheduled. They were taken to the Borgia building at the Vatican and received keys for their single rooms. Each planner found their luggage waiting for them in front of their room door. The remainder of that first day would be free for them to unpack, rest and visit the Vatican buildings at their leisure. Dinner would take place at 7:00 p.m. in a quaint small dining area on the first floor of the Borgia building.

The following day, a 9:00 a.m. meeting had been scheduled to take place in the Vatican Library conference room, with Pope Francis Xavier, Father Susanto and the planners. There were no other scheduled events for the remainder of this second day.

The following morning when the planners, along with the pope and his secretary, arrived in the library conference room, they found an easel holding a large white pad with the cover of the pad turned over exposing the first page, which had written upon it, in large black underlined letters, *GOALS*. Underneath the word goals was written: *PEACE, ORDER, SECURITY, and MIDDLE-CLASS SOCIETY.* On a large elaborately decorated table sat lined pads, pens, coffee cups and saucers, snacks, cloth napkins, three glass containers holding chilled water, and a large warm pot of coffee. Eight chairs circled the table, with one labeled Bishop Imumu Okote-Eboh.

The pope was the first to speak. "Please feel free to serve yourself at any time during our conversation. I do hope everyone was pleased with our breakfast, and if there are no preliminary questions, I'm anxious to turn this meeting over to Bishop Okote-Eboh."

The bishop began the conversation by explaining why the planning team needed two extra days to complete their task. Pope Francis Xavier was not at all concerned about the delay; only anxious to hear the plan's details.

"Speaking for our entire group, the weather was cold and snowy in our mountain retreat; the town was picturesque and invigorating. Opi had gorgeous mountain views. It was located in the center of a green valley with the Apennine Mountain range circling the entire valley and town. The air was pure and clear, and, if you can believe, it actually smelled sweet. We had one other experience so unique for each of us, I wish to take a few minutes to explain, and then I promise to get to our work."

Pope Francis Xavier, still quite anxious, and not pleased with the delay, but felt uncomfortable interrupting Bishop Okote-Eboh. Instead, he chose to respond with a slight bit of sarcasm, he knew only Budi would detect.

"Please bishop, feel free to share your entire experience. I have set aside the entire day for our discussion, and you seem very pleased with whatever delayed your work, so please continue. Father Susanto and I are interested in all that occurred in Opi."

The bishop continued, "The cause of the delay was a most pleasant experience. When Amarie and I arrived in Opi, we registered at a small hotel located in Opi. As we were resting, prior to lunch, we received a call, that the mayor of Opi was at the hotel desk and would like to introduce himself, before taking us to lunch. We felt it was only proper to accept his invitation. When we entered the lobby, a tall man in a full vintage World War II uniform greeted us, and proceeded to inform us that he was Nicoangelo Boccia, the mayor of Opi. He added that he had been a life-long resident of Opi, and as a young man, he worked as a Shepherd, tending a large sheep herd in the valley of the mountain town.

The pope used all his willpower to remain quiet and pretend to be interested in the bishop's comments.

"The mayor invited us to follow him along a cobblestone road, which led to the home of a Ms. Sgammotta. Entering her home, the room had a large dining table; sitting around the large table were Six men wearing suit jackets and ties. As we entered, the six men stood and moved behind their chairs. Mayor Boccia introduced the seven standing men as members of the town council of Opi. The mayor directed us to sit in empty chairs, also around the table. The six council members remained standing until we sat. The only person in Opi who spoke English was Mayor Boccia, who informed us he would act as interpreter during our lunch."

"We soon learned that the residence of this small town considered our presence in Opi to be a rare, special occurrence, and that a lottery had been arranged by the people in this mountain town, and the winners would serve dinner in their homes for the six of us each evening, along with a *passeggio*, which in Italian, means stroll."

Amarie Maalout picked up where the bishop had left off. "The people who accompanied us on this passeggio, were proud to show us the houses they lived in, their cemetery where their ancestors were buried in the valley area. After World War II the area, and the town of Opi became a major Italian national park, along with many indigenous animals. The people and the area were so delightful and charming that we could not turn down their hospitality, in spite of snow and cold weather. That, in summary, is why we needed two extra days to complete our work.'

This discussion ended abruptly when Bishop Okote-Eboh suggested it was time to discuss their work in Opi.

Pope Francis Xavier said. "Your reception was not planned by me or my office, so I must assume you were treated to traditional, old fashioned Italian hospitality."

The bishop began. "On the first day of our work session, the planners were bursting with enthusiastic energy, and numerous suggestions for moving forward. Amarie caught my eye and we both nodded. I interrupted the conversation and suggested that before going further, it might be useful for Amarie and me to share the cultural traits, habits, and especially the history of the African people. I could feel the frustration of the other planners, but they choose, no doubt reluctantly, to permit me to continue."

Pope Francis Xavier's also chose not to disrupt the bishop's introduction. The pope moved in his chair to pour himself a cup of coffee, hoping that might relax his impatient feelings.

Graham Quinlan interrupted Bishop Okote-Eboh. "Imamu, before you begin, I would like to share two points with His Holiness." Imamu nodded. "Your Holiness, I don't want you to think I am being disrespectful by referring to the bishop by his first name, so let me briefly explain. We quickly decided prior to our working task that we would dispense with formalities, which included using surnames and or titles."

Roscoe Ayala, former American president, smiled and added, "Our decision to be informal came about when Imamu angrily said, 'For God's sake, would you all stop calling me Bishop? We're going to be working closely for the next five days! We're not at a negotiating summit. We're in a small mountain town to do some good old-fashioned hard work.

Roscoe added a second observation. "I can only imagine how anxious you are to see the concrete objectives of our plan. I do understand, because I too was anxious and somewhat annoyed at the delay when Imamu and Amarie began their report on African culture and history. But fifteen minutes later, their comments and slide show were beginning to make sense. So, I would ask you to sit back, relax, and I believe you will find this information as valuable as we did."

There was a brief moment of silence. The pope interjected the following question. "Mr. Prime Minister, I mean Graham. I believe you have a saying in your country, you read me like an open book. Is that as your countrymen would say this phrase?"

Everyone smiled, as Graham said. "Yes, you are correct, Your Holiness." Well then, it is my wish that you stop referring to me as Your Holiness, and when we are together, please refer to me as Sunjaya. Father Susanto, do you agree?"

Father Susanto entered the conversation. "Now my first name is not difficult to pronounce. Say it just as its spelled Budi the pope's first name is a little more difficult to pronounce: Sun-ja-ya."

Sunjaya then said, "Before we get started, one last item. I forgot to mention, you may have noticed that Budi is planning on recording your comments. I do hope no one has any objection. We don't plan to share your words with others. Budi and I would like to be able to refer to your explanation if we find we have questions after we had the opportunity to digest your words."

Sunjaya stopped speaking, looked round the table, and said, "Well then, it would seem we are finally ready. Please, Imamu, proceed."

Imamu began, "These first three slides are of the Macumba cults that exist today throughout Brazil. The ceremonies, paraphernalia, practices, artifacts, voodoo, religion, art, and dance that you see in these slides are cultural traits of African's first humans. Moreover, these same actions and practices have been a cultural part of African people for centuries and are still practiced to this day on the African continent. Fossil bones, stone tools, and petrified footprints in mud have been found in East Africa and dated back three million years. The human species, *Homo sapiens*, evolved from African stock. You see, we are all Africans through lineage. The next slide shows the work of Svante Pääbo, a Swedish paleo geneticist, who found a way to extract the DNA of a Neanderthal fossil found in a German quarry. His research is attempting to uncover a genome relationship between Neanderthals and modern humans. If successful, he may be on the verge of finding the elusive 'missing link'."

Imamu moved to the next slide, which showed a drawing of an animal on the walls of a cave.

"Allow me to take a few more moments to introduce one other historical find. This discovery, by Dr. Christopher Henshilwood of the University of Bergen, in 1991, was of a wall drawing made of a female pig-deer in an African cave. The painting had been made by mixing pulverized ocher with animal bone marrow, charcoal, and water. This cave wall drawing was a two-dimensional outline of this animal, and the paint analyzed and dated to be 1.76 million years old. This find proved the origins of hominins on the African continent, and their ability to produce creative symbolic thought.

This cave drawing debunks the notion that creativity and symbolic thought began on the pre-European continent.

Amarie continued. "About a hundred thousand years ago, humans first left the African continent and eventually colonized the rest of the world. They moved across the Sinai Peninsula and settled in the eastern Mediterranean region, and around ninety thousand years ago, Africans reached Asia, and forty thousand years ago African's reached Australia. Thirty thousand years ago Africans arrived in what we now call Europe. They crossed the Bering Strait fifteen thousand years ago and reached the southern tip of South America. Africans finally reached the last remaining large habitable land mass, now known as New Zealand. And in 1969, African ancestors landed on the moon."

Team members were all smiling at Amarie's final comment.

The bishop took over the conversation and showed a slide of a fourteenth century sailing vessel.

"When the first white man stepped off his boat and set foot on the African continent sometime in the fourteenth century, he was greeted by the African people. The white man saw dark-skinned people for the first time. They were sparsely dressed, pleasant, easy-going, and had a docile personality. The African people were amazed by the unfamiliar white man and his boats that moved by the wind of the sea. These white men had unfamiliar weapons that made a loud noise when it exploded. The African people were confused by the white man's unusual customs, especially their cruelty to animals, killing them for pleasure, rather than food, African natives were also startled by the white man's violence toward their own companions."

The pope was a bit confused and somewhat frustrated at this point, but he did remember what Graham Quinlan had said, and was willing to be patient.

The bishop continued. "In the fourteenth century, when the white men arrived in Africa, they concluded they had come upon a high class of animal and referred to them as savages".

The similarity between the African animal-like savages and the white man was striking. These savages walked upright on two legs and spoke many languages, although the words were unknown. The savages gathered in groups that the white men called tribes. The white men of the fourteenth and fifteenth century saw these savages as sub-human creatures to be used for labor, a product, a new commodity."

"Now if you believe that I am being delusional when I say the white man saw the African savages as a high form of animal, let me tell you a brief, but a real story, which took place in 1904. I call to your attention that in telling this true story, I am jumping from the fourteenth century to the twentieth century. So again, in 1904, an African by the name Ota Benga, from the Congo, was taken to America and put on display at the Saint Louis World fair. When the world fair was over, the authorities had Mr. Ota Benga, a citizen of the African Congo, transported to a place in America, called the Bronx Zoo. The zoo placed Mr. Ota Benga behind a locked cage with orangutans, for the viewing by spectators."

Imamu continued to the next audio slide, which showed a black man shackled in chains on a platform before a white audience, being sold to the highest bidder. "During this period in history, it was common in Africa when various groups were low on food that their men would wander to find root vegetables and hunt animals to bring back to the tribe for food. However, a strange phenomenon began to occur since the white man's arrival. The African members of various "tribes" began to make a connection between the arrival of the white man and the fact that their hunters were not returning. They were correct in this observation, but they put the blame on evil spirits brought to their land by the white man."

Imamu continued, "Over time, the disappearing African men and women caused some groups to suffer from a lack of hunters, and they were forced to assimilate with other groups. The new larger groups eventually settled in one place, homes were constructed, and communities were established. These friendly, easy-going, trusting, docile people eventually came to understand that their men were actually being taken by the white man."

Prior to continuing, Imamu Okote-Eboh became emotional. Tears were visible in his eyes as he spoke of slavery on the level of a holocaust. The bishop was able to feel the despair, agony, and pain felt by the slaves. However, as he continued to speak, an urgent censorship of his emotions became apparent. It was as though he was attempting to drive away the trauma associated with these atrocious and immoral acts against his compatriots.

Imamu stopped for a moment, drank some coffee, and took some time to collect his thoughts before continuing. "This violence, this unjust carnage over time, this injustice took its toll on the African people."

Imamu seemed exhausted, and he was having difficulty continuing. Amarie picked up the topic, explaining they would soon be finished.

Amarie introduced a name, James Gordon Bennett, publisher of the *New York Herald*, who sent a reporter to Africa in 1871 to locate the British medic, missionary, and African explorer, Dr. David Livingston. The reporter, Mr. Stanley, did find Dr. Livingston, and quite soon became obsessed with the African continent. He began to write vivid articles on Africa for the *Daily Telegraph* of London. His dispatches to the London paper aroused a great deal of interest by Europeans about the African continent. European countries, aware of Africa's vast natural resources, began to colonize African territory, and increased their wealth by removing Africa's natural resources.

The next series of slides showed various aid agencies, men and women, many with good intentions, believing they were coming to the rescue of these African "savages." In the slides were old film footage of missionaries telling the African people they were wrong to believe that gods controlled African land, water, and animals, and that their environment was not to be worshiped as their higher spirit. The white missionaries told African natives they were to worship a supreme being, someone the white man referred to as God. Africans were encouraged, often against their best judgement, to follow a god who would make them suffer in an afterlife if they refused to follow the white man 's God.

Amarie Maalout ran the next set of slides. "As colonization spread, the African was introduced to corruption and bribery as a legitimate process in all business tractions. In the middle of the nineteenth century, Europeans, finally turned over their control of land areas in Africa, giving independence to the African people. Unfortunately, Africans were unprepared for the abruptness of independence, and they incorporated both the negative and positive aspects of European culture. Corruption and bribery used by the white man, remained a part of the African way of life, as they gradually gained full independence. Before long, the local African citizen was unable to tell the difference between an African politician, a war lord, or an African witch doctor."

The next series of slides showed life after colonial rule. Violence became common; gradually the strongest military leader eventually banished or killed off the competition and turned themselves into violent, ruthless dictators, and a new form of violence was now being committed by Africans against other Africans."

Budi took advantage of the brief pause to interject his concern. "I remember what Graham said about your talk, but I have to admit that I am finding it difficult to understand what all this has to do with eliminating poverty in Africa."

Imamu interjected, "If I'm not mistaken, this is about the same place in our history lesson where Deidra said very similar words, some ten days ago. Let me assure you, understanding the mind of today's African will be invaluable as we move forward with our objectives."

Although Budi did not understand Imamu's comment about accepting the mind of current African, he encouraged Imamu to continue. "This explanation is to prevent us from making the same mistakes that other white men have made, some with good intentions, and others using violence to control the African population. The purpose of this little history lesson was to convince the non-African planners that the objectives developed in their plan must move forward while always considering the historical biases embedded in the minds of the African people."

Imamu stopped for a moment and asked Budi to pass him the glass container of water. He filled his glass then looked directly at the pope. "If you move into Africa and tell the people you have a plan to remove them from their life of poverty, they will tell you how wonderful you are for being so generous. The next day, they will stall your efforts and cheat you in any way they can, because they believe you are also corrupt and have come to their land for the express purpose of cheating them. They believe the only reason the white man inhabits their continent is for the singular purpose of enriching himself, and when that has been accomplished the white man leaves the African land, leaving them bare and destitute."

He turned to Amarie Maalout. "It's your turn, Amarie."

Amarie moved forward in his seat and began. "Our plan was developed to accept Africans as they are. If we enter Africa and tell the people we are removing them from poverty, all we will accomplish is to reinforce what they believe about the white man. Words will not change the African mind, because most have nothing but contempt for white men. Don't be misled by the way Africans present themselves as respectful, polite, and agreeable. The truth is, Africans will not for a moment, hesitate to destroy all the white man's sincere efforts to improve their conditions"

Imamu noticed the pope and his secretary were not as jittery and inattentive as they had previously been, but were now listening patiently.

"The approach to our work in Africa must, therefore, be as unobtrusive as possible. We should go about our daily work, never promising to make their life better or telling them we are on their land to remove their poverty. Let our actions and our organization be our introduction to what we are planning, not words of explanation, but deeds of improvement. If we approach our objectives with honesty as a priority, it will truly be a new learning experience for the average African person."

Imamu looked at the pope and said, "We are finally finished, and I happily turn the conversation over to Roscoe and Amarie, who will begin the explanation of our plan."

CHAPTER 22

Amarie Maalout looked across the table toward Roscoe Ayala and with a big smile said, "Why don't you begin? I'll listen carefully and make sure you don't make any mistakes."

This remark was a welcomed interlude, after Imamu's enlightening but sad commentary. Members of the planning team laughed for the first time that morning.

Roscoe introduced the African plan. "Let me start by saying that we all agreed this plan will need to progress over a ten-to-fifteen-year period, if we expect to set this continent on the path to independence and prosperity. The first two years will be critical in setting the foundation of what is to proceed in the following years, and the first two-year period, is when a great deal of money will be spent."

From the expression on the faces of Sunjaya and Budi, the estimated length of time was unexpected. However, the two men swallowed hard, and did not object.

"This ten-to-fifteen-year plan, perhaps longer, will place Africa on the path to progress by providing a greatly improved continental infrastructure, improved health care, and most importantly, establishing an orderly, peaceful continent where middle-class employment opportunities are greatly enhanced and continental poverty will slowly be eradicated; a land where Africans no longer fear for their very existence, even in their own homes. If we are able to accomplish eighty percent of what we have planned, we believe the African continent will begin its move in the direction of realizing its great potential, which eventually will be a contributing agricultural global power."

Roscoe continued, "The African plan's goals and objectives were developed with a clear understanding of African history, culture, and attitudes toward the white man. We expect to approach and complete each objective efficiently, refusing to engage in graft, corruption, or bribery. Our refusal in this regard will speak much louder than any preaching we may do on the subject. Africans will be able to see that falling into the trap of graft, corruption, and bribery is not only wrong and illegal, but is also inefficient, wasteful, and hinders long-term stability and positive growth for the future."

Roscoe, pleased with his opening comment, continued with confidence. "The second advantage of building a strong middle-class African society is the fact that Africa has been blessed with the most fertile soil in the world and the gifts of an abundance of natural resources. Our plan objectives will, from the beginning, utilize, protect, and nurture Africa's soil, by introducing, preservation and sustainability as a main objective. Once again, it's our expectation that this message will be delivered more effectively by how we act rather than preaching."

Roscoe enthusiastically explained the third advantage. "And finally, we believe we have a powerful force on our side, to meet this objective; and that is the pluralistic nature of the African people. Except for radical terrorist groups, warlords, criminal militias, and corrupt dictators, the African people are still, and have always been, a pluralistic society. Africans may be citizens of a specific country, but they still maintain a strong connection to their continent and each other. They have consistently over the centuries, and even through colonial rule, accepted pluralism over the delusion of separation from their cultural roots. Let me try to be clear on this point, because it is a critical factor towards what we hope to accomplish in Africa."

Roscoe Ayala continued on this important concept of pluralism. "Most Africans can trace their lineage and culture back for many centuries, growing from bands of hunters and gatherers to tribal or clan formation, and progressing to chieftain/kingships, until finally organizing themselves into countries. Through this long cultural process of change, Africans remained connected to one standard of their continent. Our project must encourage their already strong pluralistic society of African people, held together by their land. We all agreed that this social formation will become a powerful aid in the success of the African plan, which Amarie will now explain."

The attention of the eight people now turned to Amarie. "We have structured our task objectives into two-year time segments, which we believe will allow the project to be operationally successful. During the first two-year time segment, we will focus our attention on removing those individuals and groups who control certain areas of the continent through violence, physical abuse, murder, rape and fear. African people must eventually see our military force as their protectors, and not as violent, vicious trespasses. "Secondly, during this first two-year period, we will begin the improvement of the existing African infrastructure: Roads, electricity, improving state-run hospitals, modernize existing train travel, and begin to build new infrastructures that will be permanent and lasting. These infrastructure projects will be visible proof that our only interest is improving their land and lives; while not destroying their natural resources, and nourishing their continental land.

Roscoe now moved to an explanation of the plans for infrastructure building. "As we begin to work on infrastructure projects, we will deliberately limit the employment of African workers and African suppliers. Now, this sounds contradictory to our goal of building a strong middle-class, but at this time in African history, using only African workers and suppliers of products and equipment may result in unreliable infrastructure, that the African people are most familiar with. Our priority in infrastructure construction in Africa, must be permanence. Once Africans experience this permanence, we expect African companies, and workers, will eventually follow our example, but until then, we feel it is most important to exclude most African vendors, and when this is not possible, vendors will have to accept our supervision at their location to ensure that all materials will meet our permanence requirement."

Amarie took over for Roscoe and moved to the purposes of their third segment. "We have planned this segment to begin during the first two years, but we expect it will take three to four years to complete. During this interval, our plan will continue its focus on the unfinished infrastructure, and removal of unusable infrastructure projects.

During the third to fifth years, we expect to hire more Africans, once we are certain that our infrastructure procedures and processes are free of graft and bribery. Our most important goal, farm towns on the land known as the tropical savannas, may begin in the first two years, and will hopefully be completed in year three or four. Development of this project will be the backbone of a strong middle-class African society, which has, as its core, making Africa a strong, competitive, agricultural giant, able to compete globally, with the completion of Africa's intra-continental highway."

Sunjaya and Budi were beginning to understand the context of the short history lesson on Africa.

Amarie continued, "We expect to be on the ground in Africa in early 2011 and continue our presence in Africa until the African people are able to see progress as beneficial to improving their personal lives on their beloved continent. After the third year, there should be less emphasis on financial spending and a slow increase in participation by African country leaders; as they begin to accept more and more responsibility for continuing the progress of our plan's goals and objectives. It's too early in this process to predict the exact number of years that African countries, and African leaders, will be willing to come together diplomatically to form districts that are willing to work together for the benefit of the citizens in these districts. In addition, it is our hope that soon after seeing district-wide benefits, governments may wish to consider a plan to form a union of African countries. This would be a great leap forward for the continent, but we must be careful to gather input from those directly affected. The benefits of this change can result in formal practices such as recognizing and protecting borders, establishing common standards and regulations, developing a single currency, and other positive actions developed by a new breed of African elected leaders.

"I would like to clarify one infrastructure project mentioned in our plan, railroad travel. In the eighteenth and nineteenth centuries, railroad transportation systems were built by those countries that colonialized Africa. The purpose of these railroads was to move the African natural resources to seaports, for export to their countries, or for sale to other countries. For this reason, you will not find any mention of new railroad construction, only modernizing and refurbishing rail systems that have been allowed to deteriorate, but we see this as taking place later in the plan, hopefully by individual countries."

With that brief clarification completed, Amarie distributed four copies of the Africa plan to Pope Francis Xavier. Roscoe told the pope and his secretary that the planners intended to remain at the Vatican until four in the afternoon on Thursday. This would provide the pope the opportunity to clarify any questions he or Budi may have, as well as provide personal input or changes to the plan. Roscoe then proposed his and Amarie's service as co-managers of the plan for the first two-year period. The meeting concluded, leaving time for all to return to their rooms to refresh and relax prior to lunch. The afternoon would allow the planners to continue their visit to the numerous buildings that make up the Vatican State. Pope Francis Xavier and Father Susanto would use the afternoon to review the written African plan and prepare questions for the planners on Thursday.

Budi had made reservations at one of Rome's popular restaurants for the evening of the second day.

This was to be a social evening; there would be no business discussed, just a hearty, delicious meal and some enchanting wine. That evening, three black Vatican sedans passed through Rome's back streets, headed for the Fortunato al Pantheon Restaurant on Via del Pantheon, a popular restaurant that frequently hosted Rome's politicians and notable persons in the arts and theatre. The pope's party of eight had reserved a secluded private room where the planning team, along with Sunjaya and Budi, would enjoy a special Italian dinner. The three sedans parked in spaces at the back of the restaurant. The maître d' was waiting for their arrival and held the rear door open for the special guests. As the planning team moved toward the open rear door, the pope touched the arm of Roscoe and Amarie, asking them to hesitate a moment.

He quietly said, "I've quickly read the plan and have many questions, which we can deal with tomorrow. However, for now, I would not only be happy, but eternally grateful, to appoint you and Amarie as co-managers of the African plan. I can't tell you how worried I've been thinking of the leadership positions since I decided to move forward with this venture, never thinking the both of you would be willing to attach your names and reputations to the plan. Now, no more talk of plans for this evening. Let us have an evening free of Africa and enjoy a wonderful Italian meal and each other's company."

The four men quickly joined the others as each was welcomed by the maître d.' During dinner, Sunjaya and Budi were feeling very comfortable with the six planners, whose cultural backgrounds could not have been more different, yet here they were toasting, laughing, eating, and sharing stories about each other. As time for dessert was rapidly approaching, the eight individuals seemed to have jettisoned their backgrounds and significant accomplishments and simply enjoyed a wonderful dinner in each other's company. Perhaps being on first-name basis helped to make them more relaxed. However, more likely it was the shared adventure they had experienced, a task that others viewed as improbable, while they alone truly believed history was about to be made.

At a momentary period of silence, Pope Francis Xavier spoke. "By the way, I have recently received some exciting news. The pastor of a church in Rome, where Michelangelo's *Moses* has been since the fifteenth century, informed me that the members of his church voted to donate their most valuable possession to our auction. I was in tears after reading the pastor's letter. The criticism I have been receiving for parting with the Vatican treasures no longer seemed to matter."

New precision tools, testing, and the use of modern technology allow knowledgeable experts the opportunity to remove valuable works of art from further damage due to weather conditions, reclamation projects, and now the charity of parishioners from and Italian church.

Michelangelo carved only three statues for the tomb of Pope Julius II, the magnificent *Moses* and *Rachel* and *Leah*. After completing these statues, Michelangelo was forced by Pope Julius II, to stop work on his tomb, and was given the assignment of painting the ceiling of the Sistine Chapel. He was not at all pleased by being reassigned, he saw himself as a sculptor not a painter. Three additional figures for Pope Julius's tomb were completed by Michelangelo's assistants, they were the statues of Raffaele da Montelup, Francesco Urbino, and Giovanni de` Marchesi. The tomb of Pope Julius II exists today, in the church of San Pietro in Vincoli, which reflects little of Michelangelo's original conception of the tomb, though the *Moses* alone has made this work prominent. One can only imagine if the frescoes painted on the ceiling of the Sistine Chapel, would have been different if Michelangelo had not been forced, against his will, to paint a ceiling."

Workers from Lombardo and Gerisina arrived two weeks after the pope mentioned the donation to his planning team. Removing the *Moses* and replacing the vacant space with Fra Angelico's altar and frescoes, was a delicate, tedious assignment. Both the removal of the *Moses* and Fra Angelico's altar and frescoes replacement were successfully completed, with no damage.

Many highly valued frescoes, such as the Giotto, located in the Scrovegni Chapel at Padua, or the Byzantine wall paintings in Greece were in grave danger of further deterioration due to excessive dampness. When a fresco is exposed to excessive moisture, which contains high amounts of sulfur dioxide, it causes the calcium carbonate in the air to become calcium sulfate, which causes the paint of frescoes to crumble and disintegrate due to the pressure of expansion.

The least invasive method of detaching a fresco painting from a wall is the "Lo Strappo technique."

The first step this technique is to heat bone glue into a pearled format using a double boiler, and mixed in a ratio of 350 liters to one liter of water. Cheesecloth is then placed over the fresco painting, and the heated bone glue is brushed evenly onto the cheesecloth. A restorer would use numerous layers of cheesecloth, anywhere from three to eight, depending on the size of the fresco, and each layer brushed with the heated bone glue. The restorer will usually lift a small corner of the layered cheesecloth, as a testing method to determine if the bone glue has sufficiently dried. Once dried, the painted surface of the fresco will attach itself to the numerous cheesecloth layers that the restorer removes.

CHAPTER 23

Jerome O'Bannon arrived at the Vatican on 15 September, 2010, and received a warm welcome from his two Indonesian friends. The pope and Jerome knew each other quite well, working together in Indonesia before the pope had been elevated to Bishop.

Budi had met Jerome five or six times, but he had never worked directly with him. Budi arranged for Jerome to be housed a few doors down from his room. They were both looking forward to spending some time getting to become familiar with each other since they would be working closely for the remainder of the next two years. Jerome and Budi enjoyed finishing their day with a nightcap of scotch and water, which usually encouraged a pleasant conversation encouraged by their soothing beverage.

One evening during Jerome's first week in the Vatican, Budi inquired if he liked watching American football games on television. Jerome, being from Queens, New York, told Budi that as a boy he and his father used to watch the New York Giants football games when they played in Yankee Stadium.

Budi said, "You're a New York Giant's football fan, what a coincidence. Wait until you hear this story. I became a lover of American football from watching ESPN on Indonesian television. When I came to Rome, I read that the Giants and Washington Redskins were scheduled to play their 2009 game in London. I had never attended an actual game, only watched it on television. I decided to use my position as secretary to the pope and try to obtain a ticket for the game. I contacted New York City Archbishop Benedict MacCarthy, who I had known was the chaplain of the Giants football team and asked if he could get me a ticket for the London game. I was very excited when he asked me to be his guest on the sidelines for the game!"

After taking a sip of Scotch, Budi continued with the best part of his football adventure. "That's not all, after the Giants game in London, Archbishop McCarthy asked me if I would consider taking my August vacation in New York City staying with him at his residence, and here is the best part. He took me to a Giants pre-season practice in a place called Albany, New York, introduced me to the players and we had lunch and supper with them. Isn't that a great story? I'm so glad I had the nerve to contact him in the first place for those London tickets. I felt like I hit the jackpot!"

Being a New Yorker, Jerome knew of Archbishop McCarthy, but their paths had never crossed.

One evening two weeks later, he and Budi were once again enjoying their Scotch and water and were becoming fast friends. Jerome questioned Budi about Francis Xavier's plans for the future. "Budi, may I ask you a question about the African plan that has me a little confused?"

"Fire away, Jerome. Sunjaya and I have gone over that thing so many times, I probably know it by heart."

"Sunjaya seems to place so much emphasis on building a strong middle class in Africa, yet I'm surprised to see African companies not being used to implement some of the tasks in the plan. Said Jerome. It would seem logical that if you want to build a strong middle class, you would hire African companies to do at least some of the construction projects, and using Africans as workers. That would keep some of the

198

money in Africa and provide work for the African people. Wouldn't that boost the African economy and help in the development of an African middle-class?"

Budi suggested, "Why don't you mention it to him? You know him almost as well as I do. He's always open to listen to others, especially you, Jerome. He respects you."

"Ah...well, I'm not sure questioning him on his plan is appropriate. He didn't bring me here to lecture him on his African plans. I would be very uncomfortable questioning him. After all, he's the pope, and we're not back in Indonesia dealing with one of our programs."

Budi suggested, "Okay, how about I say we were chatting over our Scotch, and you asked me the question about the African middle class, and I told you I would mention your thoughts to him?"

Jerome shook his head and hesitated. "Gee, that's going to make me sound like a wimp. I would not be comfortable with that approach, and it would sound like I'm not confident enough to speak to an old friend."

Budi smiled and said, "Well, I don't know what else to say. If you have questions and want answers, then it would seem you're going to have to speak with him. I think you're acting much too humble around Sunjaya. In Indonesia, when Sunjaya was bishop and then cardinal you were not reluctant to express your point of view. As I already mentioned, he has great respects you. You're being too, oh what's the English word? Oh, hell, I know it begins with something like, uh...def or defer...something like that."

Jerome said, "You may be looking for the English word deferential."

"There you go, that's the word. I love that word. I've got to remember; deferential, deferential."

A laughing Jerome said, "Budi, Sunjaya's right, you are impossible."

"Well, I may be impossible, but you gotta admit, I'm a handsome scoundrel."

After Jerome stopped laughing with his new friend, he asked Budi to help him. "Would you mind being present if I discuss the question with him?"

"Of course, but I don't think it's necessary."

"Thanks, Budi. I'd prefer to have you there. I guess it's difficult for me to shake the protocol about popes, we learned in the seminary, would you also set up a meeting for the three of us? I'd feel more comfortable with you present. I know this sounds unusual coming from a grown man and a friend no less, but I never imagined I would ever have the opportunity to kiss a pope's ring, never mind work for a pope."

"Consider it done," said Budi." I know he'll want to see you immediately."

Jerome then said, "Thanks for putting up with this old fool."

CHAPTER 24

The worldwide auction of the Vatican treasures took place as originally scheduled at Sotheby's auction house in New York City on 3 October, 2010. Sotheby's staff arrived on schedule the day of the Vatican treasures auction, fully expecting this to be a very long day and evening. One of the pleasant surprises for Sotheby's was the excitement that had been building not only in America but also around the world. In Mr. Walkin's attempt to schedule a beginning time for the auction, he had to account not only for the different time schedules on the various continents, but also allow for the six-hour difference between American and European time. The sale of the Vatican treasures had to coincide with Italian time, due to the great deal of interest by the people of Italy. Therefore, the Sotheby's auction would begin at 9 a.m. New York City time. Mr. Walkin had received word that a line of auction spectators had started at Sotheby's front door at approximately six a.m. that morning. He greeted this information with enthusiasm, thinking that perhaps public interest was going to be higher than anticipated.

There had been a buzz of interest, encouraged by newspapers, magazines, television, radio, and internet reporting of this once-in-a-lifetime auction. Even people who had no interest in art were excited about speculating on the price of some of the more famous pieces of art in the Vatican's possession.

All indications by Sotheby's public relations department showed there was very high interest in most foreign countries, especially in Western and Northern Europe and the Mediterranean countries of Spain, Greece, and Turkey. The report also mentioned there seemed to be a great deal of unexpected interest from quite a few Middle Eastern countries, but the biggest surprise was Russian interest.

The spectator doors opened earlier than usual to allow the spectators who were waiting to enter the enlarged spectator seating section. Among the spectators were the New York City art crowd, men dressed in tuxedoes, and women in evening gowns. The formally dressed art historians and art scholars came from as far away as San Francisco.

The Sotheby's software came alive at their auction house at 8:45 p.m., New York City time. The software developed for this unique world event was working quite well. There were three calls to Sotheby's indicating they could not get the televised feed from New York City, and they would have to participate using the thick catalogue sent to all requesting parties along with Sotheby's many open phone lines.

The Sotheby's auction house in New York City has a large auditorium type of room, with four folding, movable wall partitions that changed the large area into four separate auction rooms. For this auction, Sotheby's did not use any folded walls. The auditorium-like room began filling early.

Upon entering Sotheby's, each spectator was required to give his or her name and have a facial picture taken. With a picture, the new software was able to identify the spectator through their facial features, allowing for a thorough background check. If the software turned up nothing suspicious, the individual proceeded into the auction area. Those intending to participate by phone were required to divulge their name and phone number, which allowed a software program to examine their background. This procedure

202

eliminated any suspicious individual or group, by blocking their phone number from reaching Sotheby's during the auction period. Those authorized to participate in the worldwide auction and not present in the audience, used their Skype account to view each item and submit bids. Mr. Walkin was true to his word regarding security; the software worked to perfection.

Various people with diverse interests gathered in the spectator section. New Yorkers dressed casually, with their overcoats hanging from the back of their chairs. Art lovers were dressed in business suits and attractive evening gowns. Art scholars were anxious to know the monetary value of many one-of-a-kind, precious art pieces. Many art dealers representing all areas of the United States were also in attendance. Also in the spectator section were art enthusiasts who simply wanted to say they had attended the auction of the century.

The podium stood in the back area of the room. Normally, a revolving stage displayed the item for auction. In the Vatican auction, this stage area contained a sixty-inch, high-definition television, giving spectators a clear view of the Vatican art to be auctioned. A Skype screen became a valuable tool for serious bidders. To the left of the podium sat several phone tables consisting of fifty landline phones with a receptionist staffing each phone.

Sotheby's had a crew of six men at the Vatican site who would be responsible for arranging the various works of art corresponding to the order in the auction catalogue.

The auctioneer's gavel slammed down on the wood pallet at exactly 9 A.M. The first item, a Byzantine vestment from the fourth century went to the highest bidder for $100,000 dollars, much higher than expected. Many of the early items offered for auction went for their expected prices. The works of Fra Angelico and Botticelli were prominent, early in the auction. Many of Raphael's pieces sold for much more than anticipated.

Leonardo da Vinci's works, as expected, earned their share of very high prices, as museums in Denmark, Sweden, and Norway formed a consortium and successfully bid on two important da Vinci works of art. Other institutions collaborated on important pieces of work, causing delays in the bidding process, extra time was allowed for consortium bidders to communicate with each other via phone. There was considerable excitement over the sale of a number of Leonardo da Vinci's numerous original illustrations.

Next came an item the art world was waiting for anxiously, item number twenty-six Michelangelo's *Pietà*. The famous sculpture began its slow rotation on the television. The bidding war was intense and lasted an unusually long time. Finally, the gavel went down, as the auctioneer yelled into his microphone, "Sold to a consortium of Western European museums for $956 million dollars! The price became the highest bid of any piece of statuary ever sold at auction. Spectators were enthusiastic in their applause of the sale of this valuable piece of sculpture.

Two hours later, the auctioneer announced item number seventy-three. The *Moses* began to rotate on the television screen, slowly exposing Michelangelo's important work to spectators in New York City and many thousands of others around the world via their Skype television even though they did not participate in the actual bidding. There were gasps of wonder among the spectators in Sotheby's large exhibition room. The bidding quickly narrowed to four bidders; an anonymous individual bidder, another bidder rumored

to be a Middle Eastern Museum, the third was an anonymous consortium of Asian institutions, and a fourth bidder
was the Metropolitan Museum of Modern Art, which, for
this bid, was in collaboration with other unnamed important
New York City museums. All of these bidders were clearly
in this to stay. As the bidding time rose to almost an hour.
The individual anonymous bidder dropped out as the price
continued to rise. In the next half hour, the rumored Middle
Eastern Museum wore the bidding clock down to thirty-eight
seconds before it declined to meet the latest bid of $548 mil-
lion dollars. That left two remaining bidders: a collaborating
group calling themselves the Asian Institutions and the Metropolitan Museum of Modern Art and their partners. The
bidding continued for another forty minutes. At this point,
it seemed as though the entire world was focusing on the
final bidding for the *Moses statue*. After being on the clock
for twelve of the allotted twenty-minute bid time, the Sotheby's
auctioneer alerted the audience that a bid would shortly
come across the large television screen. In yellow letters
against the sky-blue background of the television screen the
message read, *The Asian Institutions accepted the auctioneers bid
for the Moses statue at $700* million dollars. The excitement
was now in the hold-your-breath mode. The auctioneer at
Sotheby's in New York City announced this dollar figure
at 11:03, New York City time, in the morning of the second
day. the message went out to each country less than a minute
later. The world waited to hear from the other bidder. During
this waiting period, a rumor started that a new bidder was
about to enter the bidding, but this never materialized.

The next twenty minutes was an exciting wait. Would the
Museum of Modern Art's consortium top the Asian Institutions unusually high bid? If so, would the Asian then bid

even higher, there was speculation that a statue might reach the one billion price tag. The large HD television screen finally lit up, and across the screen came a message: *The Metropolitan Museum of Modern Art accepts the auctioneers' bid* of *the* Moses of *$850* million dollars. The spectators at Sotheby's stood with a burst of applause. After the spectators returned to their seats, the Sotheby's clock was already at four minutes for the allotted twenty-minute bid time.

The spectators were unusually quiet, some gaping, others peering, and others not interested in the blank, black television screen, waiting until the screen took on its light blue background. At fourteen minutes on the Sotheby's bid clock, the large television screen suddenly changed from black to its light blue background. Now all were staring at the screen and in a few moments, the words appeared, *the Asian Institutions decline to meet the auctioneer's bid of* $850 million dollars for the *Moses*. The spectators stood, and once again, a long, loud standing ovation as all celebrated.

The auctioneer shouted into his microphone, "Sotheby's accepts the bid for Michelangelo's *Moses* from the Metropolitan Museum of Modern Art and its partners." Sotheby's also won a huge prize, a percentage of each item it sold!

The auction continued, and many of the spectators at the Sotheby's auction facility in New York began to leave after the sale of the two most desired pieces, Michelangelo's *Pieta* and his *Moses*. The auction continued with the successful sales of important art and statuary. Then, after the sale of all items that had been located in the Vatican Museum and Saint Peter's Cathedral. The twenty-minute bid time was waived, and a new bid time of fifteen minutes was enforced. A new auctioneer took over for the auction of documents and books located in the Vatican Library and the art and statuary located in the Borghese Gallery.

The action quickly picked up once again. The spectators remaining, were the few art dealers and the formally dressed art historians and scholars. They were soon to be thrilled at the high auction prices accepted for both original and monk-copies of rare documents from the Vatican Library. The library documents and manuscripts were sandwiched between the one-hundred plus art and statuary pieces from such artists as Veronese, Bernini, Rubens, Raphael, Caravaggio, Fontana, and Valadier, all located in the Borghese Gallery at the Vatican. The numerous pieces of framed artwork sold for generous prices.

The final pieces of art, the frescos removed by Lombardo and Gerisina, ended the twenty-nine-hour auction at 8:22 a.m.

***

Only after the auction was completed did Pope Francis Xavier realize the extent of what he had set in motion for historians and the art world in general. He also began to understand the workload he had placed on his key personnel at the Vatican. Father Susanto was frantically working long hours sorting out a new wave of fanatical hate E-mails, postal mail, text messages, and telephone messages that poured into the Vatican for many weeks after the Sotheby's auction. Letters were stacked in Father Susanto's office in four large post office bags. Ill-tempered postal correspondence was only part of the negative mail that arrived to the Vatican. Father Susanto's voice mail was full of violent, offensive, and dangerous sounding messages that Budi had to endure. The pope's secretary was thankful for the machine's quick acting delete button.

Jerome worked with the experienced Sotheby's shipping employees. Heavy wood containers were designed to hold and protect the valuable works of art. The delicate humming of the electric tool, used to securely hold together each container, with the use of special screws. These sounds became a constant reminder to Jerome, of his difficult undertaking. Although noise was not a factor in the shipping of the cardboard boxes, and metal tubes used to ship the library material, Jerome still felt a similar sense of loss when he numbered, catalogued, and registered each package, for insurance purposes. His final distressing feeling of loss, came during the construction of the empty Vatican Museum and library, into a Vatican hotel that would have no charge for their room, but would depend on each user paying what they could afford.

CHAPTER 25

Three weeks after the auction at Sotheby's, Pope Francis Xavier received a call from Doctor Hasson, who informed the pope that his board of directors were eager to granted him a two-year leave of absence to become Director of the Vatican Bank. Pope Francis Xavier was surprised but thrilled that Doctor Hasson accepted the position. The pope understood the important role that the Vatican bank was to play in the success of the African plan. The financial logistics of the plan would be difficult, especially since the source of financial arrangements would be located on the continent of Africa, not in Italy.

"Doctor Hasson, I want to express my deep gratitude for accepting my offer. I appreciate the fact that the financial details of our project are going to be quite important to the project's success. I must admit I had my doubts you would accept, but you said would make your final decision immediately after the auction, and as promised you did.; but I am curious, to know why you have decided to make such a sacrifice in the middle of your banking career in Bangladesh."

"Well, it was a combination of factors. My Board of Directors felt the temporary leave would be excellent publicity, so they were in favor of the temporary move. The other important reason was my family. My wife and especially my two daughters were very excited about spending two years in Rome. They had been encouraging me to accept since I mentioned your kind offer some four months ago. Encouraging is perhaps the wrong word, insisting might be more accurate.

The nagging by the three women in my household for these past months has made me realize the value of the Catholic clergy's vow of celibacy. In all seriousness though, I was also impressed with your plan. Although I'm still leery of its success, and thought it was a bit heavy on the military side, nevertheless, I found it was quite innovative. Finally, when I saw the news reports of the estimated trillions of dollars earned from your auction, I decided that if you were willing to gamble on me managing that amount of money for such a worthy cause, it would be selfish of me to say no. Apart from all the reasons I just mentioned, being a father of two teenage daughters, enthusiastic about shopping for clothes, using my money, may be the real reason for me accepting to live in Rome for two years men had a good laugh after Doctor Hassan's final comment."

The pope expressed his gratitude to Doctor Hasson, and immediately made plans to bring him to Rome the following week, too look for housing.

By mid-January, the Vatican Bank had liquid assets were estimated to be higher than any other bank in the world. However, the exact amount would have to wait until Doctor Hasson was on the job. After acquiring housing, Doctor Hasson spent his first two days meeting individually with each bank worker. He shared his expectations of them, made some different duty assignments, and allowed two employees to resign in good standing. The following day, he familiarized himself with the building, and when he entered the bank vault, he was shocked to find the long-rumored large stash of gold bullion. He knew that if he were to sell the entire amount of gold in one sale, the value of this precious commodity would easily lose some of its value. Instead, he systematically planned the slow sale of the gold bullion, which would force the world price of gold to remain at its current high value. Doctor Hasson's next task was to work out a system whereby all African banks would receive deposits to cover wages and expenses using various African currencies. He developed a PIN number system allowing workers to visit any African bank and collect their weekly salaries. Doctor Hasson then produced a system, in which vendors around the world could be compensated for delivery to Africa of supplies and goods.

Dr. Hasson had worked out a very rough estimated budget to meet the task objectives. His calculations included the pope's yearly worldwide Peter's pence collection, which had remained in the range of eight million dollars per year for the past ten years. He made a mental note to follow this amount closely over the next twenty-four months to determine what effect the selling of the Vatican treasures would have on this yearly collection. He then was able to calculate that $3.9 trillion dollar would eventually come into the bank via the auction sale, plus the eventual sale of all the gold bullion, which would raise the total Vatican Bank's liquid assets to slightly over five trillion dollars.

Placing that amount into perspective, a trillion dollars equals a thousand-billion dollars. Dr. Hasson, familiar with poverty from his Bangladeshi roots, had a keen understanding of the great financial resources it would take to reach down and lift a billion people out of poverty. He hoped that the trillions of dollars at the disposal of Pope Francis Xavier, would be enough for this mighty task.

After calculating the financial needs of the task objectives, Dr. Hasson's budget estimate for the first two-year period would easily cover the anticipated expenditures. Even though the first two-year period would be the most expensive period of the African Plan, he wondered if the Vatican Bank would have the financial resources for the subsequent two-year periods. Before leaving the Vatican at the end of his two-year period of employment, he planned to develop an estimated budget for the following two-year period, which would be based on the objectives and goals for that period of the African plan. Doctor Hasson was able to develop a rough estimate of expenditures, which would drastically slowdown in each two-year period. It was going to be a tight fit, but Dr. Hasson's calculations came very close to matching his expected outlay of funds. His calculations did not go beyond ten years.

In his short time in the Vatican, Doctor Hasson had come to admire Pope Francis Xavier, a gentle, good man who had risked a great deal in terms of his position as leader of the Catholic Church. The more he worked with the pope and observed his determination, the more committed he became to the African plan and the holy, pious, gentle Indonesian man.

He decided he would do everything in his power not to allow this courageous man to fail. His wife and children were enjoying their Rome experience. He silently, and privately considered expanding his anticipated two-year commitment, wondering how his board of directors would react to extending his leave of absence for a third year. That was not for him to decide now, his priority was the running the Vatican Bank operations.

His major responsibility at this time was to begin smart investment strategies, to allow the trillions of liquid assets to grow in safe investments over the next ten years, maximizing the growth of the existing assets. The only funds he would not be able to calculate at this time would come in the form of equipment donations and funds from plutocrats around the world. He encouraged Roscoe and Amarie, project co-managers, to hire a director of philanthropy as soon as possible. That position would encourage foundations and the wealthy to pick up some of the expenditures. He hated dealing with the unknown, but in this case, he had no choice but to accept his frustration.

The pope prayed daily, thankful for having these five men delivered to him: Father Budi Susanto, Jerome O'Bannon, Doctor Mohammad Hasson, Amarie Maalout and Roscoe Ayala. Had these men not joined the African project, the simple matter of logistics for such a complicated plan would have at the very least, interfered with the smooth beginnings of the plan. Pope Francis Xavier, having had no prior experience with such a venture, was unprepared for the beginning steps needed to set the African plan in motion. Only now did he understand that without these five men, the project might have never become a reality. It was now time to ponder the success or failure of his undertaking. Would the planned objectives move smoothly on the ground, or would unforeseen obstacles hinder the project? Only time would tell.

Part 2 - Africa

CHAPTER 26

Pope Francis Xavier picked up his phone to speak with his secretary. "Budi, what time are you leaving for the airport this afternoon?"

"I'm leaving at four forty-five for a six o'clock flight to New York City."

"Do you have about fifteen minutes to give me before you leave for America? I would like to discuss Archbishop McCarthy with you."

"I'll need ten minutes to finish what I'm doing, and then I'll be in."

Soon the pope heard the familiar knock, and a moment later, Father Susanto entered with his pen and notepad in hand.

"Have a seat, my friend. The pen and note pad will not be needed."

Budi sat across the desk from Sunjaya. "First, let me say how happy I am that you and Archbishop McCarthy have become such close friends. It's been a few months, since we both agreed to have you spend half of the year with me and the other half with Archbishop MacCarthy in New York. I think your work with the archbishop will been able to rekindle a new passion, a happy spirit for you, you deserve the joy these popular retreat programs, for married men and women will bring into your life. Perhaps it is time for you to consider, completely stepping away from your duties here at the Vatican. I may be holding you back from achieving your own personal achievement and happiness. I would be sad to lose you, but I encourage you to consider a full-time assignment with the archbishop in New York City. All that would be necessary for that to occur is for me to permanently assign you to his district, allowing you to continue your work with him."

The pope's words came as a surprise to Budi. "Sunjaya, we've been together all these years, and your offer is enticing, but I'm not sure I want to make a total break from you and the Vatican. The plan for Africa will begin shortly, and I would like to stay involved with the project until it is completed. I'm satisfied with my schedule for the near future. Sunjaya, you and I have such a long history together, which means a great deal to me. Please don't permanently separate us."

Sunjaya sat behind his desk, which was unusual, as the two men most often sat in the alcove section on the upholstered chairs. Francis Xavier stood and moved around his desk to sit in the chair next to his dear friend. "Budi, I'm very happy to maintain our half-year assignment, but I think you should give this idea continued thought. I love you more than anyone, and I don't want to interfere with your happiness."

Budi placed his hand on the pope's arm and leaned forward. "I really don't need to consider your offer; I am very content with my current arrangement."

***

In early February 2011 Roscoe and Amarie, co-managers for the plan, now referred to as Build Africa Together, had been on the job in Africa for only two weeks when Pope Francis Xavier, anxious to know what was happening, could no longer help himself. He called his co-managers and scheduled a Skype conference for later that afternoon at 2:00.

Pope Francis Xavier called members of his Vatican team and informed them to be in his office at 1:50.

The computer monitor screen turned to its soft blue background, and with a press of a key, the distorted faces of Amarie and Roscoe appeared. The pope's Vatican team, now at the Vatican, Jerome O'Bannon and Doctor Hasson, moved their excited and anxious looking faces into the small screen and sent their greetings. Jerome mentioned that Father Susanto had left for his half- year assignment in New York City.

The pope, uncertain of the news from Africa, was eager to hear what had been happening over the past two weeks. He asked, "How are your families. I hope they are all well." Roscoe Ayala responded, "My family is well and excited about their new surroundings." Amarie Maalout said, "My wife is doing fine. She will remain in South Africa until I can find a rental property that will be able to accommodate the both of us."

Roscoe and Amarie were interested in talking about the progress in Africa. "Amarie and I have been kept busy, but progress is not as fast as I had expected. Things seem to move a bit slower in Africa than I'm used to. Amarie keeps telling me to slow down, and I keep telling him how the others should pick up, but he assures me we will all meet in the middle someday soon. Having Amarie here has been a huge bonus to both the project and me. On a positive note, we have been speaking with some good people about taking on the role of project directors. We have discussed some interesting ideas with them so, all in all, I can say we have put the past two weeks to good use."

Roscoe then added, "I'm glad you called. Amarie and I were saying, just a few days ago. that it was time for a Skype conference with you. We have been discussing amongst ourselves our plans for the future, but once we have directors for many of our long-term projects, all facets of the project, will require regularly scheduled Skype meetings, so the Vatican team can be kept informed of our progress."

Without hesitation, the pope responded to Roscoe. "We agree, but for now fill us in on what has been happening these past few weeks."

"We have hired two retired American military special operation forces commanders who have convinced their former retired executive officers, to also sign on to our project. Their presence in Africa has taken a huge burden off our shoulders! Both men are anxious to get their units trained and operational before we start operations. We have outlined a few initial operations, to them, but before we start, they feel that a military presence would be wise for security purposes. They are with us today, and I would like to introduce them to you."

Sunjaya's personality was not that of a man who placed a priority on control and manipulation of every facet around him. Although he had been surprised at the decision to hold back on some of the projects until the military units were operational, he decided it was best to let the on-the-ground leaders make decisions, so he chose not to comment or show his surprise.

"Let me introduce to you retired American special operational forces Commander, Colonel Bruce McGruder." The colonel moved his chair closer to Amarie and bent his head into the picture on the computer monitor, and spoke. "Hello."

Colonel McGruder's face was more angular than round and serious looking. He had broad shoulders, which were evident even on the Skype screen.

Amarie then introduced retired commander Vice Admiral Jack Fisher. Vice Admiral Fisher moved his body to the left to get his face on the monitor screen and said, "Greetings, it's a pleasure to meet you."

The vice admiral had a slender, smiling face; he did not seem as serious as colonel McGruder.

Amarie explained. "Their executive officers are currently in America recruiting ex special operations forces for duty here in Africa, and I have plans, beginning tomorrow to tour African countries to recruit an African partner for each American special operations soldiers. After training, our commanders will assign partners, and each African soldier and American soldier will become a team working together. There will be two special operations forces units comprised of one hundred fifty Africans and Americans in each unit. Partner teams will be structured with one American and one African."

Sunjaya's reaction was a mixed bag; he understood the continent was going to need a military force capable of restoring peace and security. His concern was the large size of the continent and the almost one billion Africans who lived there. Could the military meet the goal of peace and security on such a large continent? At the same time, military forces were contrary to the pope's nature; he only associated military with violence. This part of the plan would always be the most troublesome for him. Even though he understood the need for military force, it nevertheless made him feel anxious.

His mind shifted to more optimistic thoughts. *After all this discussing and planning, I am finally getting to hear about others who will become part of the plan. This is somewhat reassuring, knowing we are now in this wild dream with both feet. Who would have thought, two years ago, Cardinal Sunjaya Prantata of Indonesia would ever be talking to a former American president and a distinguished, brave African leader, discussing military personnel?*

When the conference was finished and the line disconnected, Pope Francis Xavier thought. *What have I started? As this project continues, will I be strong enough to see it through to its conclusion?*

***

Two weeks later, the next scheduled Skype conference took place. Pope Francis Xavier, who was now more comfortable with Skype, welcomed the two co-managers. He had considered opening each meeting with a prayer, but at the last minute, he decided to abandon the idea. His reasoning was not a matter of practicality, but rather his unwillingness to impose on the private lives of others. *I will not ask others who may believe in a different God, or no God at all, to participate in a practice they may have no interest in, or who may feel prayer to be an unnecessary intrusion in their lives?*

Pope Francis Xavier turned the meeting over to Amarie Maalout, who introduced two retired American CIA employees who were to function as advanced intelligence operatives. The faces of Jon Edwards and Rick Kinsley appeared on the monitor screen, and they introduced themselves to the Vatican team. Amarie nodded to Roscoe, which was his cue to introduce the operations status of Building Africa Together. Roscoe began by commenting, "It feels good to be discussing actual steps relating to the progress we've made so far. Our initial steps were slightly delayed due to the logistics of getting around such a large continent."

He mentioned he was feeling a certain amount of frustration waiting for actual work to begin, even if only on an informational basis. He talked about the difficulty of re-inventing the continent so that in ten, or fifteen years, hopefully not twenty years, Africa could begin the process of competing agriculturally on a global stage.

Amarie then added quickly, "let us not forget, recorded history has shown the African people have suffered more abuse, mistreatment, and exploitation and have been deceived more frequently than any other race of people. These injustices have gone on far too long, and it's my hope that Build Africa Together, soon to be known by the acronym B.A.T., will be able to rectify this great injustice."

Roscoe, as co-manager with Amarie Maalout reminded those each person on the Skype conference line that the co-managers would move deliberately and quietly without promises, knowing that the timeline for some tasks might experience a delay and those tasks might require a new timeline due to situations on the ground. He was emphatic in the notion that due to the long history of deception against the African people, the beginning steps would meet with some resistance. "We are going into this plan knowing we have to earn the trust of the people before meaningful change can ever be expected."

Roscoe then moved to the operational phase of the plan.

"I understand we have all read the plan, and there may be questions, and hopefully not too many disagreements. So, as I discuss task objectives feel free to interrupt with your thoughts. Remember, opinions are always welcome."

This last comment set a relaxed, positive tone for what was about to follow.

Roscoe continued, "Their first task, once the recruiting process is completed, will be the training of Americans and their rookie African partners."

Amarie joined the conversation, "There will be two special operations forces to take on the difficult task of making my beautiful continent a secure safe place for every African."

Commander McGruder, sitting next to Roscoe, poked his head into the Skype screen. "Commander Fisher and I urged our co-managers to move slowly with their operations until both of our units have been trained to our satisfaction. During the training period, we will be assertive in ordering the necessary equipment and supplies our men will need to be effective. The special forces Commanders will also use the training time to decide which on-the-ground security operations need military attention."

Roscoe then spoke directly of B.A.T.'s first on-the-ground operation.

"Our first operation in Somalia will take place when military training has been completed. We hope the success of this objective will show African leaders we have a competent military force made up of both Africans and Americans who intend to restore an honest, governmental structure in Somalia, a government responsible for the safety and prosperity of all Somali citizens. With this in mind, we expect our initial operation will be to capture the leaders of militias who now control many areas of Somalia. And if we can locate evidence of crimes against the Somali people, we will make every effort to bring this evidence to the International Criminal Court in The Hague. It is important to note, our organization is an Italian Humanitarian organization, sponsored by the pope; and therefore, we must not be overpowering people or groups with a strong military operation, but strong enough to get the job done."

Muhammad Hasson interrupted, "I agree your military forces may very well be able to break the control of warlord activity in the various areas of Somalia, but I suspect you will have more difficulty when dealing with the tribal family clans of Somalia. The fierce loyalty of clan members and family leaders has existed for a millennium, and they have a long history of resisting all who are not one of their clan lineages.

I wish you and your men luck facing what I suspect will be very strong opposition."

Roscoe knew by this comment and the history lesson that here was a man who knew the history of Somalia.

Amarie joined the conversation after Doctor Hasson's comment on Somalia's history of clan family structure. "Doctor Hasson, the people of Somalia have been abandoned and have been living without a governmental structure to assist them with their basic needs. Gaining the trust of the Somali people will be most difficult and is our first important objective. If lives are to be enriched it is our intention to first build the people's trust, by accomplishing minor improvements in their day-to-day existence? Our military behavior will be as small as possible, and will not be violent and destructive. Soldiers will concentrate on breaking up the warlord organizations, which control local areas through violence and murder of the people in their controlled land area. The militia groups operate against helpless people, stealing, killing, kidnapping wherever a segment of the population looks vulnerable. They tend to be ruthless, violent, and attack those least able to defend themselves. In addition, we intend to deal with the Somali pirates, who perform their violent, illegal acts on the high seas. These three groups have a similar philosophy. They are illegal bandits that have moved into Somalia knowing they will not face resistance because there is no formal government."

Amarie was quick to remind the Vatican team that the family clans may disagree with our strategy, but as long as they do not feel threatened, they will not interfere.

Amarie then summarized his information to the Vatican team. "Stopping the bad guys from hurting the Somali people and demonstrating that we do not intend to leave them to be vandalized will be a new and refreshing experience for them. Our actions will demonstrate to other African countries that the humanitarian agency known as B.A.T. has not abandoned the African continent after one battle."

Roscoe Ayala took a moment to emphasize the deliberate tactic of keeping a low profile. "Using our military force only against those who threaten the Somali people will show the clan families, and the local people, that removing the 'bad guys' is B.A.T.'s lone objective in their country. It is our intention to have our deeds speak louder than our words, hoping to see more cooperation and less resistance from all Somalis, including the clan families."

Amarie continued by saying, "Now, I will be the first to agree that these high-sounding concepts will surely fall on many deaf African ears. When that situation arises, we will make an effort to meet with those leaders who are reluctant to change their behavior and make it clear they must change or face uncomfortable resistance. If they choose not to take us seriously and continue to govern in a manner that is not in the best interest of their people, it will then be time to demonstrate a more vigorous military capability, hopefully causing them to take notice."

Doctor Hasson then asked a second question, which gave those at both ends of the Skype line cause for reflection.

"What authority or jurisdiction gives you the right to detain and confine Somali warlords and militia leaders or, for that matter, the men or women you may determine to be criminal dictators and send them off to the International Criminal Court in The Hague for trial and sentencing?"

Roscoe indicated to Doctor Hasson that his thoughtful and important question was very appropriate. "Regarding our authority or jurisdiction, we feel if there are crimes committed by one individual or group, against innocent people. It is historically accurate, that in the past local prosecutors may be restricted in prosecuting these criminals due to the criminal acts occurring in numerous countries. In addition, these crimes are so brutal and violent; people are reluctant to testify, knowing their governments lack the resources or the will to protect them. The Hague is in place to prosecute these deliberate, unprovoked crimes against humanity, which fall outside of the jurisdiction of individual countries and, in many cases, happen when individual country leaders have no interest in protecting their people. One of the tasks central to our objective to provide a safe and secure environment, is to assist the prosecutors at the Hague in prosecuting criminals who commit crimes against humanity, ensuring they receive a fair trial and, if found guilty, pay for their crimes."

Amarie was quick to mention the difficulties facing the International Criminal Court at The Hague.

"Since its inception in 2002, the International Criminal Court at The Hague has been laden with a growing pile of cases, defiant government authorities, and a United Nations Security Council that has called for investigations and prosecutions of The Hague's personnel; but the U.N. Council has done little to assist in advancing the investigatory and trial process. The International Criminal Court has convicted a tiny fraction of those it has charged. Unfortunately, many more have eluded arrest altogether and the lead prosecutor at The Hague, Brigitte Beugnet, a Gambian citizen herself, has battled charges of her bias against African leaders, a charge the Hague lead prosecutor, has rebutted."

Amarie then added, "I am, as we speak, waiting for a return call from the lead prosecutor's office at The Hague. I hope, as an African nationalist who has fought for the rights of the South African people, she will grant me the opportunity to meet with her in the Netherlands and explain what we have in mind in Africa. It is my intention to determine the policy, procedural steps, and the evidence needed to legitimize the sending of criminals to the International Criminal Court at The Hague. We expect to obtain the authority from the ICC to arrest, deliver, and provide proper evidence, and African witnesses, against individuals who have committed crimes against humanity; after we have helped to make the area or district a safe environment, which will encourage witnesses to testify, knowing no harm will come to their families."

CHAPTER 27

The use of special operations forces evolved in every branch of the military during the Vietnam War in the 1970s. A rag-tag army of Viet Cong fighters, who survived on meager rations and moved like moles, undetected through an intricate set of underground tunnels, exposed, for the first time, the ineffectiveness of America's mighty standing army with its tanks, planes, bombs, napalm, and superior numbers of soldiers.

Then, in 1980, the disaster of Operation Eagle Claw occurred. This failed rescue attempt of hostages at the American embassy in Iran led some military brass to suggest a military force other than conventional forces, an alternative approach that would successfully engage a new type of enemy.

Over the next five to seven years, the Pentagon introduced strategies based on the acceptance that the American military would no longer be facing an enemy composed of massive units of soldiers, but rather, they would be confronting clandestine missions, counter-terrorism, unconventional warfare, psychological operations, and civil interactions.

The Pentagon required this new organizational structure of special operations forces to be comprised of volunteers who would find themselves in situations that fluctuated from minute to minute, and therefore, special operations force personnel needed to be independent, flexible small units having the capability to move rapidly when engaging the enemy. The initial version of special operations units does not resemble the Hollywood version of John Wayne's Green

Berets, and most certainly nothing resembling Sylvester Stallone's *Rambo*.

Full implementation of special operations forces met with early resistance by Pentagon brass. They were uncomfortable with the reality that special operations forces, would by the nature of their operational structure, independent, flexible, small units, and rapid enemy engagement, would in many instances, ignore chain of command and general military protocol, to be successful in some operations. This lack of enthusiasm by the Pentagon brass led to a weakening of the basic concept of special operations forces. A second military review found if the soldiers in these units were to become a serious part of Pentagon programs, this new military operation had to have a five-star commander sitting at the Pentagon table.

When this occurred, new requirements for these volunteer units were instituted: rigorous physical development, a minimum IQ of 120, a personality test, and special training in counter-insurgency techniques. The final important structural change came with the development of intelligence operations that allowed these special units to move in small groups as they engaged the enemy on their own turf.

The more recent methods of the Taliban, al-Qaeda, and the Afghanistan incursion, along with the occupation of Iraq, finally convinced the last holdouts at the Pentagon that America needed this new radical type of military force, known by its military acronym COIN, standing for Counterinsurgency Operations.

Afghanistan and Iraq taught American troops that abusing the local population is counterproductive to good, solid intelligence. Treat the locals well and they will tell you who doesn't belong in their village. One of the first lessons learned by the men of these units was that good soldiering begins with serving the local population and treating them respectively. Lawrence of Arabia, who was way ahead of his time, put it best when he said, "Better the Arabs do it tolerably, than for us to do it perfectly."

***

B.A.T.'s special operations force commanders and their executive officers were meeting with Roscoe in his home in Cameroon, Africa, on a late February evening in 2011.

The purpose of this meeting was to discuss the organizational procedures for establishing two special operations forces in Africa. Attending this meeting were the co-managers of Build Africa Together, Roscoe Ayala and Amarie Maalout. Joining them was retired Colonel Bruce McGruder, who had been hired to command B.A.T. 1 special operations force, with his executive officer, retired Lieutenant Colonel Rich O'Keefe; and Retired Vice Admiral Jack Fisher, hired to command B.A.T. 2 special operations force with his executive officer, retired Lieutenant Colonel George Andrucki.

Later that evening, when the beautiful Cameroon sunset had passed, the six men were discussing operational planning in Roscoe's living room, and each requested bourbon over ice. The six men toasted to the success of Build Africa Together. After placing their glasses on coasters on the coffee table, Roscoe began the conversation. "I'm thrilled that the four of you decided to come out of retirement to lead our military operations in Africa. I'm curious why you men chose to leave the good life in Arizona, California, Texas, and New York. Rich, I believe you were in Texas, weren't you?" Lieutenant Richard O'Keeffe said "That's correct, Mr. President, and George, you lived by your in-laws on Long Island, New

York. I hope I have this straight." Lieutenant Colonel George Andrucki responded, "That's affirmative, Mr. President." The four men nodded and smiled.

Commander Bruce McGruder said. "You seem a little surprised that we've made ourselves available for this tour of duty. No offense, Mr. President, but it's hard for a non-special operation forces personnel, even someone with your experience, to understand how much a trained soldier can miss combat, the camaraderie, the excitement of working out a plan, and then successfully closing the deal. Can be very personally satisfying"

Retired Vice Admiral Fisher added, "And don't forget, recounting the details of a successful operation with your buddies over a cold beer."

Commander McGruder added, "I guess the special operations forces world is like a small club with a sense of mission, and what you proposed to us, well, sounded like a very exciting mission. Once you experience a successful mission, you want that special taste back in your mouth."

Retired executive officer Rich O'Keefe, said, "Once these men and women experience combat together, they tend to develop a tribal mentality, the same tribal mentality that we're gonna be looking at in our first mission in Somalia. As the colonel said, it's hard to explain, but we become bound by our shared experiences in remote places, and replicating that mutual feeling is, for us, very rewarding."

Retired Colonel McGruder jumped back into the conversation. "A good example, sir, are the first two people I put you in contact with, the two ex-CIA operatives you hired, Jon and Rick. Once I explained the mission, they were on board and immediately had a new look on their faces. They were excited about having an opportunity to get back into operations. I'm sure the salary was also an incentive, but when they heard what the mission was, and who would be heading the project, they wanted in. They were both free, enjoying retirement and perhaps a bit bored. When we told them the mission, their response was, 'hell, kids are out of the house, and our wives would love the opportunity to spend a couple of years in Africa, count us in!"

Retired Lieutenant Colonel Andrucki expressed a similar reaction. "The response I've had so far during my recruitment of men from our military units has been very positive. I asked them how they would like a two-year special ops tour in Africa, room and board, and sixty grand a year, and the best part, no military regs. All you have to do is please Commander Bruce McGruder and me. When they heard that, they were hooked!"

Roscoe said, "Jon Edwards and Rick Kinsley, the two ex-CIA operatives, also surprised me with their enthusiasm for the job. What pleased me most was their experience was largely in the field, very little time spent at Langley."

Commander Vice Admiral Fisher added, "As you know, Mr. President, guys and gals in their field tend to remain unknown operatives, and they like to keep it that way."

Roscoe immediately jumped into the conversation. "You're right, I had never heard the names of Rick and Jon, mentioned in my eight years in the White House."

Amarie then said, "I've arranged with the president of Kenya for us to use a vacant military camp for your training site. When do you expect the training to begin for both units?"

Commander Bruce McGruder was quick to respond. "We expect to reach our quota of a hundred and fifty retired American soldiers in about two weeks. About thirty guys promised to get back to us by then. Give us a week to arrive in Kenya and settle in, and then, depending how fast the Africans can get up to speed with our guys, my guess is by early June we could be ready for operations."

Roscoe turned to Amarie. "What is your assessment of the recruiting of African partners who will be working with the American forces?"

Amarie Maalout responded with optimism. "As you know, my priority since I started in February has been the recruitment of Africans willing to partner up with American soldiers. I have a handful of Africans I need to contact, but after they get back to me, the African part of the force will be ready, and they all understand extensive training will be their first task. And now that our training facility is nailed down, I have every expectation that everything will be ready in days, not weeks."

Commander McGruder then asked, "Mr. Maalout, have you received the SERE training manuals for each recruit?"

"Yes, I have," Amarie replied, "and let me say that not only was each section, Survival, Evasion, Resistance, and Escape, explained very clearly, I was most impressed by the fact that you were able to get these booklets in English and in three of the most prominent African languages. Although one requirement of the African recruits is that they speak and read English, having them able to refer to some common African languages will help them to grasp some of the more technical terms. This manual will go a long way in helping the African recruits. How were you able to get manuals in the different languages?"

Commander McGruder responded in a nonchalant manner, "A guy at the Pentagon still owed me a favor from my active-duty days, so I called it in."

Roscoe Ayala said, "I'm aware that you both refer to me as Mr. President or Sir, and I know habits used throughout your military careers are hard to break. When we began our planning for this project, Bishop Imamu Okote-Eboh suggested we dispense with the formal titles and call each other by our first names. Since then, we have all fallen into this informal way of addressing ourselves. Would you mind using my first name as well as Amarie's?" Both commanders and both of their executive officers indicated they would not feel comfortable calling their former president by his first name and would prefer to continue to address him as Mr. President or Sir and Mr. Maalout or Sir. "Understood, and I'm happy to continue to address you four as Colonel, Vice Admiral and Lieutenant Colonel."

Roscoe changed the subject by referring to their first task. "Gentleman, I want you to know I understand we've stuck you with a bitch of an operation in your first mission. Somalia is going to be a very tough nut to crack, but that's the reason we chose this country to be our first venture into the continent."

Roscoe hesitated for a moment and clarified, "That didn't quite come out as I had intended. It's not that we chose Somalia so you would have a rough first task. We chose Somalia because they have resisted the establishment of a government for almost twenty years. Somalia is also strategically important for B.A.T. If we can revive the need for a formal governmental structure, we will have succeeded. It will also put other African leaders on notice that we are here to stay, continuing to work only for the African people. Equally important, we want to start demonstrating that Build Africa Together is one agency that will not accept bribes.

Someone has to break this African pattern of corruptness, and we believe our actions are the best way to start."

Roscoe cracked a smile as he said, "It's as much about establishing a reputation as it is about solving a tough problem. As I mentioned previously, after we begin formal intervention, our purpose will be to remain a mystery for as long as possible, just another humanitarian agency, with no military aspirations. No need to spook the clan families before we really get started. If we are successful with the Somali people, other Africans will be respectively curious. Although, at some point, our military is bound to become obvious."

Ex-Lieutenant Colonel George Andrucki asked for clarification. "This concept of being low-key still eludes me. Would you mind taking a few minutes to clarify your reasoning?"

Amarie was first to respond. "Considering both its advantages and disadvantages, B.A.T.'s planners in Italy felt playing down the efforts on the African continent was the best way to proceed. The reasons for this nuanced approach are African history and culture. In the past, aid to Africa has been, and I'll put it politely, overemphasized and lacking in effort. Africans have learned a loud presence usually means unscrupulous agencies collecting donations from abroad and then conveniently disappearing in the night once their coffers are full. Africans have learned to distrust aid agencies who promise big but deliver little. Build Africa Together will send a very different message, making no promises, and instead we will be establishing permanent facilities, practical and useful infrastructure, suggesting B.A.T. intends to be around for a while. Next, and most important, in place of promises, Africans will see and feel actions that make their lives safer, and enriching their lives, not by promises, but by our encouraging productivity."

Roscoe interjected, "Let me add one aspect of our intervention in Somalia. We hope to remain, for as long as possible, a phantom group, not interested in invading the country. Invaders are persona non grata among the clan families of Somalia, and they possess a fervent hatred of foreigners, especially Americans. The same goes for some African leaders."

Roscoe Ayala was uncomfortable by the fact that he was asking these men to accomplish something America and other countries did not have the persistence or political will to accomplish. He, as much as any man, understood that overcoming the tribal influence of Somalia, and making it a functioning country was a very difficult task. Since all else had failed, perhaps the use of a small, rogue group of ex-special operations forces stood a better chance of being successful.

Commander Fisher immediately interjected some optimism. "Mr. President don't get discouraged before we even begin. We understood what we would be up against when we first discussed the Somalia operation, and as to the fact that no country has been able to crack the dysfunctional nature of their political system, Commander McGruder and I kind of see this as a challenge. So, let's see if our outfit can do what other nations have failed to do."

A pessimistic sounding Roscoe said, "Well, I certainly can't argue with history. I'm thinking of our humanitarian efforts in the late 90s that wound up as the Black Hawk Down disaster."

Amarie and Roscoe shook hands with the four officers and topped off their drinks. Amarie was obviously anxious to begin as soon as possible and inquired. "Can you estimate when you will be ready to implement your tactical operation in Somalia?"

Commander McGruder responded. "No, we can't, Mr. Maalout. If it were just our guys being re-trained, we probably could give you an estimate, but given the fact we will be evaluating the training of our African partners, I'm afraid that's too much of an unknown for us at this time. The actual training progress is the only experience that will give us the answer to your question. I believe I can also speak for Commander Fisher when I say we will not put our guys into an operation without agreeing on their readiness and resolve."

Retired Lieutenant Colonel O'Keefe interjected a comment, "Please try to understand, a special ops soldier is not an automaton, as some people would like to think. Our training has taught us to be creative thinkers and quick problem solvers. When a soldier successfully completes training, he or she understands the extraordinary mental and physical accomplishment achieved. Perhaps that's why there is such an allegiance among our soldiers, only we can appreciate what has been accomplished. The commanders are on the money, refusing to speculate on readiness until they are satisfied with the results of the African partners in training."

When ex-Lieutenant Colonel O'Keefe had finished, Commander McGruder spoke up.

"Thank you, Lieutenant Colonel, that was well put, and I believe it will help the co-managers to appreciate the question mark we have about the African partners."

Commander McGruder then turned his attention to Roscoe and Amarie. "Once we begin the training, Commander Fisher and I will be able give you both an estimated ready date for our intervention in Somalia."

With that, the meeting ended, and the former American president and Amarie Maalout saw the commanders and their executive officers to Roscoe's front door, promising to stay in constant touch regarding the beginning of training in Kenya.

CHAPTER 28

On the twelfth day into training in Kenya, both commanders called an emergency Skype meeting with Roscoe and Amarie. They informed the co-managers that the June training has hit a snag.

Commander McGruder reported, "We have stopped training due to problems with some of the African recruits. The American recruits identified eighty-three African recruits as unable or unwilling to participate in training routines. Our American guys refused to continue training with them. This group of eighty-three men are washouts, and we thought it best to halt training until we could discuss the problem with you both. Some of the eighty-three African trainees had IQ difficulties, or perhaps it was a lack of sophistication regarding our methods. Others refused to engage in the physical fitness training, a few were unable to qualify on their personal weapons, and then there were a number of Africans who the American partners suspected were at training only for the purpose of reporting back to their country leaders."

Commanders informed Roscoe and Amarie that they had not as yet discussed any information relative to the first operation in Somalia.

Amarie was furious. He apologized to both commanders and assured them he would rectify the problem. He asked the commanders to name the countries where the washouts came from.

Amarie said to Roscoe, "My friend, let this be a wake-up call for us both. Let us proceed with caution and suspicion in all future dealings. Clearly, we cannot assume all African leaders are in agreement with our intentions. We will have to operate differently than we had originally anticipated."

The two managers of B.A.T. after must discussion decided on the following: Strict vetting of African leaders would become a priority, before new operations began in all countries.

All agreements, from this time forward, between B.A.T. and African country leaders would include written contracts. However, both managers understood that a signed contracts including penalties, was not a guaranteed solution, contracts would be just one tactic.

Rick and Jon would travel to a country before an operation or project was scheduled to begin. Their task would be to gather on-the-ground intelligence about a country leader.

Face to face meetings with African leaders would be a requirement before any operation in that country was approved, by B.A.T. This requirement includes regional projects, such as the electricity grid improvements, large construction projects such as the intra-continental highway. If the leader of a country refuses to meet with a B.A.T. manager than the project planned for that country, will be diverted to a neighboring country, whose leader is willing to confer with a B.A.T. manager.

Once Roscoe and Amarie agreed on these pre operational details. Amarie was off to find replacement partners for the special military soldiers. Amarie put a good deal of miles on his Land Rover, traveling to recommended police chiefs, commanders of army units, and a few leaders who he trusted. It took a full two weeks of constant traveling and personal interviewing, but eventually Amarie was able to identified eighty-three African men interested in becoming partners with the American soldier. Once the men were in place, Commanders McGruder and Fisher resumed training, and soon the operation known as "Welcome to Somalia" was scheduled to begin at a much later date than had been expected, February, 2011. Once operational, both military units would be able to supply the security for the start of two major construction projects: the intra-continental highway, and improvements to the existing African electricity grid.

CHAPTER 29

Now that B.A.T.'s training had restarted and a new approximate completion date had been determined, Roscoe Ayala used this time to arrange a meeting with the American Secretary of State, William Powell. Roscoe had previously contacted Bill Powell asking for a face to face to inform him of B.A.T.'s plans in Africa. Roscoe and Amarie both felt a trip to America to meet with the Secretary of State would be worth the travel expense. Roscoe could use his influence with the current administration, encouraging Bill Powell to view B.A.T. as a friendly tool, able to provide intelligence information on Africa and the region. If Roscoe was successful, the pope's plan for Africa could benefit greatly, in used military equipment.

Roscoe arrived in Washington D.C. on 12 April, 2011. On the day of his appointment with the Secretary of State, Roscoe arrived at the White House early in the morning to greet former employees he had not seen since he left office on 20 January, 2010. Many White House staff greeted former President Ayala with warm embraces, recalling memories of his eight years in office. At 9:50 that morning, Roscoe hustled over one section of the White House to meet with the Secretary of State Powell.

Secretary Powell welcomed Roscoe warmly, and they both moved over to a comfortable sofa in the secretary's office. After some casual catching up on government affairs, the two men began discussing Roscoe's new assignment in Africa.

Roscoe explained the reasons for this meeting. "Bill, I wanted to meet with you this morning to alert you to some of the plans we have on the African continent for Pope Francis Xavier's project."

Secretary Powell, aware of the African project from news reports, was interested in receiving first-hand, accurate information on the pope's plan.

"Yeah, we have been hearing all kinds of rumors about the pope's involvement on the African continent after that auction event involving the Vatican treasures. I would appreciate being kept in the loop on the activities of the project. I admire you for becoming involved in this project, and I know you understand that it will be a tough nut to crack, not to mention the danger involved."

Roscoe accepted Secretary Powell's kind words, and his admiration of Roscoe for attacking African poverty. "I think my father being born in Africa had a great deal to do with my decision to become involved."

"So, how can I be of any assistance?" asked Powell. "My visit today is to determine if the administration is open to cooperating with Build Africa Together. I have hopes you might see value in a confidential quasi-relationship between America and Build Africa Together. Perhaps we both can benefit. If you would consider this idea as a possibility, we are open to an informal relationship."

Secretary Powell responded, "Well, naturally, we are very concerned about some of the rumored activities occurring in that strategic area of the world. I would agree some type of relationship with your project could turn out to be beneficial to us both. I would be very open to maintaining confidential lines of communication between my office and your project. I can see the value of you keeping us up to date on activities in the region. I'm confident in your assessment of events there. President Barman and I both feel you and your people could be an asset to America. And for this assistance, I know I can speak for President Barman being open to some off the book resources getting into your hands."

"That sounds wonderful Bill. Would it be of any value if I took ten minutes of your time to review the purposes of our African project?"

Secretary Powell asked Roscoe to continue. Roscoe glanced at his wristwatch to note the time and proceeded with his explanation. When he had completed the concise project review, Roscoe stood, not wanting to take advantage of Secretary Powell's time.

The two men shook hands. "Let's both keep in touch Roscoe, and once you get established in the region I will look forward to your on-the-ground assessments. I prefer our contact to be on the phone. I would discourage e-mail communication. In addition, I would be especially interested in any activity of groups such as al Qaeda, Taliban, al Shabab, Seleka, Boko Haram, and Daesh ISIL. We can use your information to help us confirm our usual intelligence sources in Africa and the general region. Mr. President, I would ask you to stop at my secretary's desk. She has a special secure phone line for contacting my office. Use it freely to share information you believe significant."

Both men walked to Secretary Powell's office door, and as Bill Powell reached for the doorknob, Roscoe said, "Oh, I almost forgot. I need a favor."

"Fire away, Mr. President,"

"Can you give a heads-up to your CIA director, informing her we have two retired CIA field operatives working with our special operations forces? They have false CIA identifications, and if by chance anyone from Africa should call the CIA office asking for verification on these two operatives, ask her if she would be willing to give a non-committal answer such as, 'I can't confirm or deny their presence in Africa. Something simple like that is all we'd need. Needless to say, if she would like to speak with me or Amarie Maalout, ask her to use these two direct, secure phone line numbers or if she prefers to speak directly to the two ex-CIA guys, Jon Edwards and Rick Kinsley who I'm sure she knows, I'd be happy to also share with her their direct, secure phone numbers. Her cooperation would be most welcomed, but if she's not comfortable with this request, mention to her I understand. And, by chance, if she prefers to keep her distance, I know Rick and Jon will also understand."

After Roscoe received the number of a secure phone line number for reaching Secretary Powell's secretary, he gave her a warm hug.

CHAPTER 30

Somalia is a country with a long history of internal instability due in part, to clan family feuds that have lasted for centuries. This continuous fighting has led to a protracted divide between the major branches of the Somali lineage system. The six tribes include four pastoral nomad clan families: Dirk, Daarood, Isaaq and Hawiye tribes, plus two agricultural tribes, Digil and Rahanwayn. Somalians believe their present clan family structure comes from the Old Testament version of tribal segmentation by the children of Israel. The overwhelming majority of Somali people trace their genealogical origin to a mythical founding father, Samaale or Samaal.

The Somali people share kinship with other members of the Eastern Cushitic groups of the Horn of Africa through language, traditions, and way of life. This includes the Oromo, who constitute roughly fifty percent of the population of Ethiopia, along with Afar, which is between Ethiopia and Djibouti. Other Eastern Cushitic people belong to the Beja tribes of eastern Sudan and the Reendilli and Boni tribes of northeastern Kenya.

Some people who live in the coastal area of Somalia have no affiliation with clan families. Several thousand independent people live and work in the area from Mogadishu to Kismayu. There are other Somali citizens of Arab or Persian decent. Rounding out the Somali population in the coastal area are people not connected in any way to the cultural elements of Somalia. Many citizens in this group are the descendants of former tribal slaves given their freedom in the 1920s.

In the late 1970s and continuing into the 1980s, the Said Barre's regime, which had been propped up by Russia, ignored Soviet advice and invaded mineral rich Ethiopia, causing the Russian government to sever all ties with Somalia. The Russians sabotaged a great deal of the infrastructure it had constructed in Somalia before pulling out of the African country, an moving into neighboring Ethiopia. Tons of equipment and war material, along with Soviet advisors and several thousand Cuban troops, were part of the Russian pull out of Somalia. The newly restocked Ethiopian army soon had the Somali soldiers in full retreat. The last elements of the Somali army retreated to their home country in March 1978. Unfortunately, Said Barre foolishly and arrogantly decided to once again attempt expansion of Somalia into Ethiopia, which turned out to be a second military disaster.

Said Barre, still in control of the Somali government ignored the advice of his allies, as well as detractors, and unleashed a reign of terror against the majority of Somali citizenry abolishing all opposition to political parties. He then compounded his political problems by rewarding his Majertain sub clan family important government positions. They made up a large segment of the Somali secret police and began vicious and brutal campaigns against other clan family members. This caused the clan family members to militarily run the Majertain clan out of Somalia.

From that time forward the history of clan families resulted in unifying the families into an unrealistic state of paranoia. For the next twenty plus years, only family members were welcomed into each clan family. This situation helped to destroy all Somali political and governmental organizations. The clan families resisted all efforts to form a new government, fearful of who or what they may get as a leader. They preferred to remain in their local territories under the leadership of their clan family leaders, vowing to never again be under the control of a central government.

Somalia as a country soon collapsed into chaos, resulting in a Somali social order that existed largely along warring clan families. Soon, warlords and marauding militias moved into the vacuum, dividing control of the remaining land areas of Somalia.

With Somalia in chaos, foreign fishing vessels began illegally fishing in internationally recognized Somalian territorial waters. This illegal fishing activity caused depletion of the fish population off the Somalia coast. The Somali fishermen viewed foreign fishing ships as illegal and were forced to take matters into their own hands.

They attacked the illegal foreign fishing boats using armed fishermen and high-speed vessels, successfully driving out the illegal boats. With no Somali governmental structures in place, a criminal element moved into Somalia, and followed the pattern of Somali fishermen beginning the confiscating of large tankers and their crews, and demanding ransoms for the ship's return. What began as a protective maneuver of national territorial fishing waters, soon became a criminal piracy activity.

CHAPTER 31

In mid-July 2011, Jon Edwards and Rick Kinsley, the ex-CIA operatives, were the first B.A.T. personnel operating on the ground in Somalia, deliberately trying to look like American government employees, in the capitol city of Mogadishu. The two men with false CIA identification were dressed in dark business suits, white shirts, ties, and sunglasses and they traveled around Mogadishu in a black Yukon Chevrolet sport utility vehicle, which blatantly announced their status as American officials of some sort.

Their assignment was to evaluate area facilities for a permanent home for B.A.T. 1 Special Operations forces. Permanent sites were narrowed down to two old, Russian-built, abandoned airport facilities, one at Baledogle, near Mogadishu, and an airport facility further south next to the seaport of Kismayu. Soil samples at both facilities were analyzed to determine soil compactness for the landing of a large C-130 cargo plane, now part of the military fleet of Build Africa Together. The Kismayu facility had the advantage of being located next to an abandoned naval yard and being structurally sound. The disadvantage was the existing terminal building at this site was small, which meant quarters for the men would be tight. The terminal building at the Baledogle site was also structurally sound, but had been looted of anything that could be sold. The condition of airplane runways at each site, was in desperate need of repair, but temporally usable. Both facilities would be able to accept a fully loaded C-130 fixed-wing aircraft, after some repairs.

When Rick and Jon had completed their assessment of the two facilities, both special operations force commanders received the reports. The commanders decided to inspect the facilities before making a final decision. The Kismayu site was the first site seen, and both commanders were pleased with what it had to offer. After inspecting the Old Russian terminal building at the Baledogle airfield, which included a three-story U-shaped building with the shell of an air traffic control tower on the building's roof, both commanders agreed the Baledogle was their preference. The factor that made Baledogle more desirable was the size and shape of the building. The size would allow for three floors, with the top floor being a self-contained prison facility.

Once the commanders arrived at their decision, Jon and Rick's next task was to pass themselves off as CIA operatives delivering a bogus message from the United States to the Somali interim president of the provisional government. Mr. Bartari was the third interim president named by the United Nations since the official government of Somalia collapsed in 1991.

During their meeting with Mr. Bartari, Rick and Jon made up a hypothesized false chain of events involving the American government. "The Guantanamo Bay facility in Cuba had become a public relations headache for America. The United States would like to obtain official permission to remodel the Old Russian airfield facility at Baledogle into an airport and prison facility, which would house the terrorist prisoners currently being held at the Guantanamo Bay facility."

Mr. Bartari was pleased to agree to this request. They negotiated the final details and both parties signed the contract.

The Somali interim president had the responsibility of informing the Somali people that Baledogle facility would become a prison, for suspected Islamic terrorists. The interim president had false copies of credentials that showed Build Africa Together to be an Italian civilian humanitarian organization supported by the current Catholic pope.

The interim president was satisfied that this venture would benefit both countries, America would have a public relations fiasco removed ninety miles from its border, and Somalia would benefit economically from a venture that was not militarily threatening. Build Africa Together was especially careful to hide the real motives of the project, a facility to house a special military force which would soon become known as B.A.T. 1.

This rouge would not provoke the clan family structure or al-Qaeda. In fact, it was exciting news for al-Qaeda and al-Shabab leaders, having their brothers located on African land. Al-Qaeda could not have imagined such a promising reality. They were already planning their first operation, a mass protest of the incarceration of their brothers, and they eventually hoped to convince the humanitarian agency to release the prisoners into their custody.

Once the transfer of ownership of the Baledogle site was officially completed, Rick and Jon ordered a delivery of roadway patch compound for temporary repairs of the runway potholes as well as metal poles, wire fencing, and razor wire to be placed on the top of the fencing.

After the materials arrived, a detachment of special operations forces, six Americans dressed in civilian clothes, along with their six African partners, dressed in African attire, left the training site in Kenya bound for Somalia. They would spend the next three days completing the temporary runway repairs and installing the perimeter fencing around the entire Baledogle site.

Acquiring African laborers would be the next step in this cleverly designed two-pronged plan to renovate the Baledogle compound, and at the same time pacify the leadership of the clan families and the criminal gangs that controlled most of the Somali coastal area, from Mogadishu in the north, to Kismayu in the south. The key element in this operation was to permit the special operations forces of Build Africa Together to gain a presence on the ground in Somalia without a military invasion. Through this plan, Build Africa Together would be able to establish a military defensive presence in Somalia without a military frontal assault.

During the three days of temporary repairs at the Baledogle facility, Rick and Jon would have to arrange for African laborers to help B.A.T. 1 & 2 personnel in the renovation project. However, before laborers could be hired, Rick and Jon called for a meeting with Roscoe and Amarie. They met the co-managers at Roscoe's house the evening of the first day of runway repairs and fence installation.

Jon began the conversation. "We fully understand your insistence on never paying bribes for the tasks you complete in Africa. Getting the Baledogle site job done on schedule will require approximately one hundred laborers working with our American and African soldiers. Hiring these laborers will allow us to meet the schedule of our Special Operating forces.

Rick said, "And now the bad news. If you don't allow us to provide American dollars as bribe money to the criminal gang leaders, you can forget about getting the African laborers for renovations. Without laborers, the job's time-line is going to have to take a serious hit. I guarantee the warlord and militia leaders will never agree to supply laborers unless American dollars are involved. And expect the amount of the bribes to be in the thousands of dollars."

Amarie said, "There must be some alternative to get us the laborers without a bribe."

Rick answered abruptly, "Trust us when we say there are no alternatives. The real problems of meeting with these leaders without offering bribe money is one, no laborers, and two, if we refuse to hand over cash, they will immediately become suspicious that we actually are African government agents impersonating American, which could threaten the Baledogle ruse, and also our safety may be at risk."

Roscoe looked over to Amarie. "Well, Amarie, we knew it wasn't going to be easy, especially in the beginning. If you feel strongly about this, we'll simply tell our commanders they must come up with a different plan."

Amarie stared out the living room windows and was silent for a few moments.

Finally, he said, "Okay, it looks like we have no choice in this situation. Although I am against changing our philosophy of no bribes, I have to wonder if we were being naïve making that policy."

Roscoe and Amarie reluctantly approved the bribery money for the sake of the organization and the safety of Rick and Jon.

***

The two B.A.T. advanced intelligence operatives, in their dark blue business suits, white shirts, ties and sunglasses, drove their black Chevrolet Yukon into Mogadishu and parked in the parking lot of the popular, mostly outdoor Jangel nightclub. The nightclub had tables that were set under acacia trees trimmed to look like umbrellas. Patrons included every faction of Mogadishu nightlife. The advanced intelligence operatives, Jon Edwards and Rick Kinsley, strode into the nightclub looking very much like the American officials they wished to portray. They squeezed into two spots at the bar, forcing the two men on either side to adjust their position, although they didn't look happy about being inconvenienced, they also decided not to challenge the two formidable looking Americans.

The two Americans ordered Bedele Ethiopian beers and paid for their drinks with a generous tip. They deliberately huddled close together, sipping their chilled beer. Halfway through their drinks, they motioned to the burly bartender, who had a thick Australian accent, the bartender responded. "What's your pleasure, mates?"

Jon Edwards said, "We have been told that if we want to make a Somali contact, you're the man to speak with."

The bartender with a slight grin, quietly said. "Well, maybe." Rick Kinsley placed a folded American one-hundred-dollar bill under his beer coaster, trying not to be obvious, but making sure the bartender would notice his movement. Rick then pushed it halfway toward the bartender. The bartender glanced at Rick, and then glanced back to Jon.

Jon said, "We wish to contact a number of powerful men in Mogadishu. The boat leaders in Puntland and the warlord and militia leaders who control the coastal land from Mogadishu to Kismayu."

The big Australian bartender was surprised by Edwards's request. "Wow, mates. You're asking a lot from a lowly bartender. I'm sorry, mates, but I'm really not interested in getting involved with those sons of bitches."

Kinsley reached into his side pants pocket and pulled out a wad of American cash, making sure the bartender noticed. Holding the American currency in his left hand he peeled off a second hundred-dollar bill, folded it in half, and neatly placed it under the bar coaster. Both operatives looked up toward the bartender.

The bartender, without hesitating for a moment, said, "Mates, I'm really sorry, but you're best talking to someone else."

Edwards then spoke, "What's your name, big guy?"

"My name is bartender to you two gentlemen, not big guy."

Edwards apologized, "Sorry, I meant no offense. Just trying to be friendly. I can assure you we have a very lucrative financial deal to offer these men. Let me add, we're not interested in their activities here in Somalia. We would appreciate if you would mention that fact to them when you make contact to set up this meeting."

"Hey, fella, don't jump the gun on me. I may not know how to contact these men."

Jon apologized once again. "There I go again, sorry, me and my big mouth. Look, we're in a bind. We need to contact these men, and we'd really appreciate any help you could give us. You can also tell your contact we will come to the meeting unarmed, and we will not be insulted if they wish to travel with their own security. I promise you, they will thank you for the call, because our proposal will line their pockets with little or no work on their part. We're only interested in paying them for their influence, nothing else. As you can see, we intend to be very generous toward them, as we are being with you. All we want from you is a simple phone call. I can assure you, after tonight, you'll never see us again."

As Jon was pitching the idea to the bartender, Rick was slipping two more American hundred-dollar bills under the coaster.

The bartender hesitated, glanced around the bar once more, then looked carefully into Edward's eyes.

"How do I know you pricks are not fucking me over? If your meeting goes go south, I'm gonna take the heat along with both of you."

Kinsley moved his beer bottle from in front of him and leaned over the bar toward the bartender.

"This will not go bad. In fact, I know the people we want to talk to will be very grateful and maybe even be generous to you. What we will be discussing is an opportunity for them to earn some hard American cash, and you also could come out ahead."

Edwards slipped a fifth hundred-dollar bill under the coaster, then opened his jacket, pushing the left side of his jacket out in front of him, holding it forward so that no one but the bartender could see him removing his fake CIA identification from his inside suite jacket pocket, opened it so that it was visible only to the bartender.

Edwards said, "Don't let this make you nervous. We just want you to know that we have the resources to reward these men with more than pocket change. We'll say it again; we don't care about their business here in Somalia. We are concerned only with our business. And when our deal is completed, we are out of Mogadishu for good, never to bother you again."

Edwards closed his jacket and waited for the bartender to respond.

The bartender hesitated, noting the bills under the coaster. His head turned right and then left, his eyes quickly noting all patrons at the bar. He hesitated before speaking.

"Shit, you guys must be awfully desperate or awfully well heeled, maybe both."

The bartender then slid the coaster covering the five hundred American dollars off the bar and into his pocket. He then called out to his partner behind the bar.

"Hey, mate, I need to make a quick phone call. Cover me. I'll be back in two minutes."

The bartender then moved to his left, went behind a closed door, and, as he predicted, was quickly back behind the bar. He stood directly in front of the two B.A.T. operatives. "Come here tomorrow night. Get here a few minutes before seven. Come directly to the bar and order the same two beers you ordered tonight. There will be two guys in colorful keffiyeh scarves around their necks. They will look you over and decide if they wish to arrange the meeting. That's the best I can do, and you're going to have to financially take care of the both of them also. That will let them know you mean business."

The two B.A.T. intelligence operatives thanked the bartender without shaking hands, and moved quickly toward the entrance of the bar.

The next night they entered the Jangel nightclub, ordered their beer, and waited. Soon Kinsley felt a tap on his shoulder. He turned to see two tall, thin, very black-skinned Somali men with keffiyeh scarves around their necks. "We go outside to do," one man said quietly.

Rick and Jon followed the two men out the door. They walked about ten feet to an alley between the Jangel nightclub and an adjacent building. The Somalis held out their hands, and Rick Kinsley reached into his pocket and pulled out his wad of American bills, making sure the two men saw the cash in his hand. He handed two packets of three-hundred-dollar bills to each man. One of the men handed a piece of paper to Kinsley. It read, *tomorrow in nite take car Yemeni*

Street in Mogadishu pak car will pick up and met. When both intelligence operatives had finished reading, they looked up. The two Somali men had already started to walk out of the alley.

The following evening, Edwards and Kinsley were in their car on Yemeni Street. They had been waiting for approximately an hour, both men now nervous that the meeting would not take place. Then Edwards noticed a group of men coming down the street in the direction of their car. They both sat up straight, Rick wondered, *what will happen now? How the hell do we get out of here if they get violent?* Two of the men opened both front doors, two other men opened the rear doors and sat in the rear of the car.

The fifth man spoke to Jon and Rick, "Out car." Once out of the car the tall black man proceeded to pat the operatives down. He then ordered Rick and Jon to sit in the middle rear seat of the car. The man who patted them down quickly sat in the front seat. The car moved slowly down the street, three men in front of Rick and Jon and two men behind them, with pistols clearly visible. After moving about twenty yards down Yemeni Street, they stopped in front of a brown house.

Rick and Jon were ordered out of the vehicle and were escorted over a sidewalk and up four stairs to the front door of the brown house. The two operatives were pushed forward into the house. The tall black man ordered Rick and Jon, "walk". The operatives took a few steps until they entered a large, bare, open room. Two empty chairs sat positioned in front of ten seated men dressed in colorful African outfits. One of the seated men motioned for Jon and Rick to sit in the two empty chairs. The four men remained in the room with their guns at their sides, clearly visible from where Jon and Rick were seated. The fifth man was positioned in front of a door towards the rear of the large room. The two B.A.T. operatives remained silent.

A tall thin man with pitch-black skin spoke in understandable but awkward English. "Our ears open, so say. Edwards was first to speak. "Will you allow us to reach into our inside jacket pockets to show you, our identification?"

The big man once again responded, as the others remained silent and glaring, "Everything you do, do slow. Killing you, no problem."

As Edwards and Kinsley held up their identification, the big man swiped both identifications from their hands. Looking at them and then passing them to his left. Some of the Somalian men seemed interested in handling, touching, and rubbing the leather backing, and one man sniffed at the leather of the fake identification.

The tall black man who seemed to be the leader, or the one chosen to do the talking, returned the fake identifications to Edwards and Kinsley and spoke. "Tell us how you use us."

Rick Kinsley responded, "The United States Government wants to build a prison in the abandoned air base terminal site at Baledogle. The president of the transitional government in Somalia, Mr. Bartari, has approved the conversion of the old terminal building at Baledogle into a prison. This prison will hold Islamic terrorists, now located in Guantanamo Bay, in Cuba. The Cuban prison has become a big problem for America. America wants to close the Guantanamo prison and take these prisoners from Cuba to the terminal building at the former Russian air base at Baledogle. We need to hire men to help our American contractor make the old Baledogle airline terminal into a prison for these American prisoners."

The spokesperson interrupted, "And how does rich America pay us for men?"

Kinsley answered, "America will pay the workers you provide an agreed upon salary. If you agree to supply us with your men, the American government is also willing to pay you, two thousand dollars when your men begin construction and another five thousand dollars when the construction is declared finished by our construction manager."

The first offer was low, knowing that bargaining was about to begin; if bargaining were not part of the deal, the leaders might get suspicious.

"And we also want you to know that America appreciates your cooperation on this project, and for this reason, America promises not to interfere with your daily work in Somalia or anywhere else in Africa."

Kinsley added a few words of flattery, "America has been beaten twice by your people, and America has decided to never again interfere militarily in Somali activities."

The big man who had been doing all the talking for the other nine men was now puffed with pride as he responded, "American money, no. You pay twenty thousand dollars workers start, and fifty thousand work done."

Rick immediately counter-offered, "Five thousand when work starts, and fifteen thousand when work has been accepted by the American contractor."

The big man looked to the other leaders. "Let us stand away and talk of these monies."

The men rose and walked to the opposite wall, and the men who had been standing by the door, rushed immediately to the circle of chairs, now also pointing their pistols at Rick and Jon. There was a brief period of discussion, and the ten leaders returned to the line of chairs and sat down.

The big man said, "We take ten-thousand dollars, not one, each ten of us, then get men for work, and fifteen thousand, each us, when builder man happy. Each worker hundred dollars for six days he work, ten hours each day. Workmens will be at this building eight o'clock morning, back house six o'clock night. Money for workmens give to man with yellow keffiyeh and black hat. Give money him, no to workmens, we do each week."

Edwards and Kinsley moved their heads together and pretended to be whispering details to each other, understanding that bargaining was over. The operatives broke from their huddle, and Edwards said, "We agree to pay the amounts you said."

The spokesperson called out to the men standing at the side door; he ran and stood by the side the spokesperson. The leader then put his hand on the shoulder of the man standing next to him, and moved him so that he was facing Rick and Jon. "This people with yellow keffiyeh and black hat give money him, no workmens. Us Fifteen thousand dollars first, then say okay to you."

Rick and Jon looked at each other, nodding their heads in the affirmative. Jon said, "We agree with each of your final conditions."

The man who had been doing the bargaining then said, "I am Dayo Cisse. Now let me tell you one thing; men know where two each minute of day and night. If no receive American dollars on last day, both you die. Now tell Dayo how many of man you want for work."

Rick nodded in agreement and said, "We have a deal."

"No," said the tall, slender man. "I and my friends have deal. You are now doing as we want."

Rick and Jon again nodded in agreement, understanding that the spokesperson's last comment was to show his superiority to the other leaders.

Rick said, "We'll be here Monday morning at seven thirty with trucks and cars to pick up one hundred men for work and give the fifteen thousand dollars bonus for each ten of you to show our good faith."

Rick deliberately left out the time and date of the last payment, hoping the spokesperson would not notice. B.AT. had planned a different location, and time for the final payment.

The tall man said, "You get prison, we get American monies."

CHAPTER 32

In late July 2011, B.A.T. 1 and 2 military partners arrived at the Baledogle facility at 4:30 P.M. The men had an hour and a half before dinner to unpack the gear for their tent quarters, at the Baledogle site. The men of B.A.T. 1and 2 spent the morning of the second day, breaking down their gear and completing their unpacking, and arranging their temporary tent quarters for approximately three weeks. After lunch, the soldiers of B.A.T. 1 and 2 were scheduled for a meeting with both commanders, to organize work groups, after which the soldiers were free to rest, catch up on e-mail, and contacting family members until dinner, with free time after dinner.

At approximately ten fifteen A.M. of the third day B.A.T.'s C-130 airplane was scheduled to touch down on the temporarily repaired runway; the plane contained the first shipment of construction supplies for the renovation of the three-story terminal building. Three hundred American special operations soldiers and their three hundred African partners gathered a good distance from the runway, anxious about the safe landing of the C-130 on the worn, cracked, pothole repaired runway without ground radio contact.

The roar of the C-130 jet motors announced its descent at the scheduled time. Three minutes later, the big plane was low, roaring over the security fence, and heading nose first to the repaired runway. Both commanders and soldiers were very nervous about the hazardous, but necessary landing conditions. Soon there would be a newly constructed cement runway and an operating communications tower, but for today, everyone had their fingers crossed as the C-130 cargo plane with its important freight, touched the dangerous runway, and came to a bumpy, but safe stop in front of the U shaped, empty building. Spontaneous cheers of the men from B.A.T. 1 and 2 were long and loud as the pilot and co-pilot opened their cockpit windows and waved encouragingly to their buddies. The cargo plane would have a much smoother landing in mid-August. B.A.T. personnel unloaded the cargo plane, and after a two-hour stay, the empty C-130 was rumbling down the bumpy airstrip to collect its second load of equipment.

A Helicopter would be arriving the following day with a delivery of more supplies and equipment,

The following day at eight in the morning, the one hundred Somali laborers bordered the vehicles on Yemeni Street, five trucks, and a number of sport utility vehicles. The workers tended to be teenagers and young men in their twenties. Three older men, who appeared to be in their forties acted as quasi leaders, and interpreters. When the trucks and SUVs were loaded, the caravan of workers headed for Baledogle, Somalia.

After breakfast, B.A.T. 1 and 2 soldiers quickly formed their work groups, and began stacking and grouping construction materials. A rotation schedule had been posted for guard duty, at the entrance and exit openings during construction. Visitors were not welcome, and guards were kept busy dispersing inquisitive neighborhood visitors that frequently arrived to observed construction from outside the fence perimeter.

The entire facility, when renovated and secured, would comprise the headquarters of B.A.T. 1, with troop living quarters located on the ground floor. The second floor would house the computer operations center, conference rooms, storage facilities, plus several rooms used for group meetings. The third level was to be renovated into a prison facility, and on the roof, would be a functioning control tower, set up with the proper equipment for guiding incoming aircraft onto the soon to be completed concrete runway.

The Somali laborers seemed to be independent and did not need much encouragement from their African leaders. The special operations forces soldiers were dressed in civilian work clothes, not wanting to give away their military function. During the renovations, military vehicles remained covered with tarpaulin, concealing their presence; primarily due to fact that B.A.T. had entered Africa as an Italian humanitarian organization.

Renovation of the terminal building began with a forklift vehicle delivering construction material to all three floors, and the control tower. During the renovation of third floor, which was being prepared to house the jail cells. Workers under the supervision of the engineer teams of B.A.T. 1 and 2 built cement block walls partitioning each jail cell, and two days later, final construction of the jail cells began. Bolting floor-to-ceiling metal posts had two purposes, one would support the ceiling of the building, as well as the control tower. The second purpose of the metal posts became the metal frame posts for the jail cell doors. Electrical outlets and light fixtures were next on the list. Jail cell entrances were wired to be opened and closed from the computer station on the second floor. The jails included four bunk beds fastened by heavy chains to the concrete block walls, a composting toilet, and a small sink with running water.

The installation of GPS equipment and circuits for controlling lights for night airplane landings, would be the responsibility of the computer technicians. Next was the construction of walls, windows, and doors for the control tower. Flight traffic controls would soon be operational in the next three days, completed by the technical support operators. The final addition, a roof, will complete work on the control tower.

Renovations of the second floor were next, as workers nailed two-by-four wood beams in preparation for installing sheetrock walls for individual rooms. Second floor rooms would serve as conference rooms, and training classrooms. The computer equipment area began coming to life on the second floor as the computer tech guys connected their sophisticated equipment. Renovation of the first floor included personnel quarters that would house one American soldier and his African partner. Also on the first floor was the chow hall, kitchen, and recreation area. An electrified metal fence, with razor wire at the top, was constructed to enclose the open end of the U-shape building. This enclosed outdoor area, will become recreational outdoor space for prisoners.

Build Africa Together purchased three cement trucks to deliver cement to the Baledogle facility for a helicopter pad, and a concrete runway for planes. Three engineer platoon soldiers supervised the mixing of the ordered cement, from a Somali business, to assure its quality. The helicopter pad was located near the entrance of the U-shaped building. The cement mixing trucks will eventually be used, when construction starts on the African intra-continental highway later in the year.

***

Two days prior to the completion of renovations at the Baledogle terminal, Rick and Jon met with the spokesman for the ten leaders. They informed the spokesman, that the commander of Build Africa together was so pleased with the work of the laborers that he will pay the leaders their end of project bonus, during a special celebration banquet, in honor to the ten Somali leaders, who had supplied the laborers. Rick mentioned to the spokesman that the ten leaders will be the guests of honors for the banquet. Jon told the spokesman that the celebration banquet would include as guests, the following people from Build Africa Together: The Somali criminal leaders, the two commanders, their two executive officers, and an interpreter, who spoke English and Lowland Eastern Cushitic Somali language.

Military vehicles will be available at 5:30 to pick up all leaders for their ride to the Baledogle banquet. The spokesmen agreed that all the leaders would be proud to attend the banquet. Saying, "No worry, I say go to meal, all go! Get us peoples, at house on Yemeni Street, use army wagons, we like to ride in army wagons."

A specially decorated, colorful enclosed room off the main personnel chow area was the location of the celebratory banquet. As the leaders entered the decorated room, champagne was waiting for them along with a table of hors d'oeuvres beautifully arranged with a Somalia mushroom dip, crackers, and cheese. Once seated in the decorated room, the banquet started with jumbo shrimp, Somalia-style with a good helping of horseradish, and more champagne followed by a choice of filet mignon or lamb. A pierced lamb was turning on a spit over a wood-burning grill. Saffron-infused rice was included with their meal choice along with a traditional Somali salad, which included seafood, with the meal white and red wine was served. Dessert included Turkish coffee, delicate pastries with powdered sugar, expensive cognac,

Cuban cigars, and as much *khat* as they wanted. *Khat* is the narcotic of choice in Somalia.

At the end of the banquet, special operations soldiers, dressed in civilian clothes returned the musicians and dancing women to Mogadishu. Colonel McGruder invited the Somali warlord leaders to visit the prison cells that their men helped build. The warlord leaders had consumed so much alcohol mixed with *khat* that they were susceptible to any invitation. Colonel McGruder was not concerned about offending these men by mentioning the phrase "Islamic terrorists" prisoners. These warlord leaders were not at all concerned about history, allegiance, human suffering, or death. Their main interest was reigning over the people who lived in the land areas they controlled. "Islamic terrorism" was simply a phrase the warlord leaders may or may not have ever heard.

After numerous trips on the elevator all leaders, the interpreter, both commanders, and their executive officers had arrived at the third-floor prison facility, where Vice Admiral Fisher was waiting with a walkie-talkie.

They were quite impressed when they saw a large open area lined with jail cells. Commander McGruder and Lieutenant Colonials O'Keefe and Andrucki escorted the Somali warlord leaders into the jail cells, showing them the composting toilets, the beds and running water faucets. One of the leaders said to Lieutenant Colonial Andrucki, "You prison clean, nice. My prison not so nice."

Once all the leaders were in the jail cells examining the facility of the cells, Vice Admiral Fisher pressed the message button on his hand-held walky-talky, and said, "Now!"

The next moment, the doors of the jail cells began closing as the B.A.T. executive officers both took one-step backwards, then hearing the clang of the metal cell doors locking in front of them. The vice admiral had a computer specialist sitting in front of his computer for the past hour, waiting for the word *now*, which was his signal to close all prison cell doors. The leaders, still holding their drinks and cigars, still in a fog from all the *khat* and alcohol consumed, simply watched the prison doors close. After a few moments, they realized they were behind bars, they dropped their glasses and cigars, yelling for someone to open the cell doors.

The colonel and vice admiral wished them a pleasant night's sleep and headed toward the elevator.

Colonel MacGruder and Vice Admiral Fisher, their two executive officers, along with the stunned interpreter, entered the elevator with contented grins on their faces, while the ten leaders continued their shouting and shaking of the metal doors. The descending elevator doors opened on the first floor, the men from B.A.T. 1 & 2 gave the five men a brisk applause, along with hoots, howls, shouts, and whistling.

When Jon Edwards and Rick Kinsley heard of the banquet and capture, they sent the following text message to both commanders: *Great to hear of your success last night! Sorry we missed the banquet. Hope you saved a bottle of champagne for us. Rick wants to know if anyone took pictures of the leaders as the cell doors closed. If so, save them until we get to Baledogle. Sorry we had to miss all the fun. We'll be leaving tomorrow morning, expect to arrive in Baledogle, Somalia, late afternoon, in time for Saturday's B.A.T.'s organizational meeting.*

CHAPTER 33

During the renovations of the air base at Baledogle, Rick and Jon, the two intelligences B.A.T. operatives, had been working in the Central African Republic attempting to locate a base of operations for B.A.T. 2 which would be under the command of Vice Admiral Jack Fisher. It was difficult finding the combination of buildings suitable for 300 men and space for equipment, trucks, a firing range, an numerous outbuildings to house trucks, military vehicles, and office facilities. They were fortunate to locate a vacant hotel/resort, which met all requirements of a base of operations for B.A.T. 2. The facility had closed a few years ago due to the deteriorating conditions of this very poor, landlocked country. The hotel included a large basement area where a firing range could be located. Edwards and Kinsley were able to negotiate a very favorable two-year lease agreement, with an option for the following three years. The rental agreement permitted renovations to the various buildings, which would meet the needs of the men from B.A.T. 2

Local contractors worked alongside of B.A.T. 2 personnel during the renovation process, supervised by Vice Admiral Fisher. The renovations included modified rooms for two soldiers, including clothing space military gear. The existing kitchen was expanded to prepare meals for 300 men. A space directly attached to the renovated kitchen area was left untouched. This vacant area was planned to be used in three years, when it would become a second kitchen, responsible for providing breakfast for preschool children living in the yet to be built, western tropical savannas farming towns. The existing outside buildings would become garages for large equipment, various vehicles and an office for the project co-manager, along with two other offices, used in the future for expected personnel. There was sufficient outdoor space to accommodate training and conditioning of B.A.T. 2 personnel.

During the renovations for B.A.T. 2, Colonel Bruce McGruder contacted the International Criminal Court at The Hague, informing the court prosecutor of the captured and imprisoned Somali warlord leaders. The prosecutor asked the commander to delay transporting the Somali leaders to the Netherlands until she completed arrangements for their safe arrival. She also expressed her appreciation for B.A.T.'s efforts to identify prospective witnesses to appear at the Hague trials, and for transporting the Somali warlords from Africa to The Hague. She would arrange for landing permits for the C-130 plane for delivery of the Somali leaders and then later for the witnesses.

Special operations "psyops" soldiers were now on duty assignment to screen potential African witnesses. Much to their surprise, the first few individuals they spoke to who had family members killed or tortured were unwilling to act as witnesses in The Hague trials of the captured leaders. The "psyops" soldiers were initially puzzled that the abused families were unwilling to be witnesses, even though the militia groups were abandoned, after their leaders was jailed. These militia groups were mainly composed of captured teenagers, forced to work, or have their family members killed, if they escaped or did not fight and kill. B.A.T. solders became more aggressive in their witness recruiting process, and eventually discovered warlord and militia gangs had a secondary leadership level, which simply replaced the jailed leaders, thus maintaining control of their carved-out territory.

Build Africa Together had made a devasting, tactical error, caused by poor intelligence. Once the problem had been identified both special operations force commanders submitted their voluntary resignation letters to Amarie and Roscoe. They felt mortified, praising themselves for the clever way they captured the criminal leaders, while making the tragic intelligence error of not fully understanding the leadership structure of their enemy.

The African partners of the B.A.T. 1 and 2 soldiers were questioned as to why they failed to inform their American partners of this aspect of the leadership structures of the criminal groups in Africa. The surprise answer had to do with the antithetical cultural trait of the docile African partners, relative to their relationship with their white American partners. After discussions on this subject, the American soldiers finally understood that the problem was white authority figures. After many generations of Africans being punished for questioning the white man, they were reluctant to interrupt their commanders and fellow special operation forces partners, by informing them of the layers of leadership of the criminal groups. B.A.T. personnel learned a valuable lesson from this blunder.

A few days later, after much discussion, the issue of expressing opinions between the American military personnel and their African partners seemed to be resolved. The African partners knew it would be difficult, but each expressed that they would try to be more verbal with their thoughts, even if contrary to planning strategies.

In the following weeks, special operations force soldiers roamed the Somali coastal region, engaging the criminal groups, identifying captains and lieutenants, and jailing them. This time, B.A.T forces completed their task properly. The final negative result of this intelligence error, forced the humanitarian organization to reveal its military presence, causing concern on the part of the Somali clan families. Fortunately, and at least for the present, there was no overt resistance from the clan families, they too were pleased that many criminal militia groups were eliminated. However, their remained an uneasy truce with the clan families; both chose not to be involved in each other's activities, which for the time being pacified their concerns. On a positive note, B.A.T. had been able to establish a defensive base of operation in Africa, without having to battle the clan families.

After the entire leadership chain was identified, arrested, and in jail, the difficult task of rehabilitating the kidnapped teenage members of the warlord and militia gangs was the next step. These mostly teenage warlord members who were kidnapped and forced to kill fellow Africans, so their parents would not be brutally murdered, did not respond well to rehabilitation techniques.

As the debriefing of teenage militia hostages progressed, it became evident that many of them suffered from post-traumatic stress disorder, a mental illness that occurs in people who experience numerous traumatic events. The commanders called for an emergency Skype conference with Pope Francis Xavier to make him aware of this serious problem, they requested additional psychiatrists to be brought to Africa, to assist the special operations psyops units, dealing with the many young men who were experiencing this mental health disorder. The pope agreed and would immediately hire psychological specialists, to assist with this on-the-ground problem.

***

Amarie was in frequent contact with Chief Prosecutor Brigitte Beugnet during the preparations for the trials of the leadership structure of the Somali warlord and militia groups, currently held at the Baledogle prison facility.

The chief prosecutor at The Hague would wait until she heard that B.A.T. had a firm commitment those witnesses would be available for the trial, before setting a trial date for the entire leadership structure of the ten Somali coastal criminal militia groups. In the past, The Hague was frequently unable to prosecute criminals due to lack of credible witnesses willing to come forward for fear of their lives and the lives of their family members. This new humanitarian organization, Build Africa Together, seemed to understand the need for an international legal authority to adjudicate individuals suspected of crimes against humanity. The International Criminal Court at The Hague provided the legal authority to try individuals in Somalia charged with crimes against humanity.

CHAPTER 34

Now that Build Africa Together had established their presence in Africa, they were ready to begin the difficult process of removing poverty from this impoverished continent. Roscoe's office was located in the Central African Republic and attached to the B.A.T. 2 headquarters. His office was very plain; the only feature that stood out was the unusual raised desk that permitted him to stand rather than sit while attending to his various clerical tasks. He had this type of desk made for him when he was president. He found the long hours of deskwork sitting in a chair caused his ankles to swell.

A conference table was situated next to a window looking out toward a northern exposure. This exposure did not allow the hot African sun enter the window, until late in the day, making this area one of the coolest spots in an office without air conditioning.

On this November morning, a scheduled organizational meeting was about to begin at the B.A.T. 2 facility. Roscoe and Amarie would lead this meeting, in attendance were Commanders McGruder and Fisher, their executive officers O'Keefe and Andrucki, Rick Kinsley and Jon Edwards, and eight sergeant majors, four assigned to each of the two military units.

Before Amarie Maalout presented the first agenda item, African dictators, He began by saying, "In two months, it will be one year that Roscoe and I began work on the ground in Africa. It feels like we started this crazy dream only yesterday, but the calendar doesn't lie. During this time, I have met with all leaders of African countries. My military vehicle has driven many miles, and members of my security detail were good companions."

Amarie was confident and smiling; even though he knew there would be troubling agenda items ahead, and began the first agenda item. "This agenda item, African Dictators, will undoubtedly be a long and difficult task. Over the years, I have mentally filed many African Dictators under four negative categories: corrupt, evil mass murders, and destructively vain. However, one dictator Joseph-Desire Mabuto a former Congolese dictator fell into all three of these categories. He squandered the abundant rich natural resources of the Congo, rubber trees, by not properly harvesting the leaves of these trees causing them to stop producing. He enhanced his personal wealth. He killed many of his countrymen, he was a vain, corrupt leader. In 1978, he turned over control of a large land area of the Congo to a West German space rocket company to use as a launch pad to develop interstellar space travel. Mabuto watched the first launch of the space rocket travel a hundred kilometers into the African atmosphere, before it disintegrated and fell back to African soil in the Luvua Valley area of the Congo."

Roscoe, with downcast eyes and a shocking grimmest on his face, found it difficult to believe what he had just heard, but Amarie continued as though his example was far too common.

"Unfortunately, today we have African leaders who, I believe, have no interest in promoting a peaceful, orderly environment in their nations. In this category, I include Omar al-Bashir of Sudan; General Mohamed Ould Abdel Aziz, president of Mauritania; Salou Djibo, head of the military junta in Niger; and Robert Gabriel Mugabe, recently re-elected in a highly contested, and rigged, presidential election in Zimbabwe. Then, of course, we have Joseph Koney, one heck of an evil man, claiming spiritual superiority. He has been around since nineteen seventy-eight, escaping capture, and is believed to still be alive, although that belief may be misguided.

Amarie then left his seat, stood in front of a map of Africa, and used his pointer to touch the country of Sudan. "Omar al-Bashir, the leader in Sudan, is a ruthless dictator known for mass killings of his people. He was very disturbed when the United Nations forced a democratic vote of the people in South Sudan to become a new nation. Since South Sudan's independence, an infuriated al-Bashir, has been sending his soldiers on periodic raids into South Sudan, killing South Sudanese people, and making life, in general difficult for the people in this new country. He has established a pattern of maiming, killing and generally making life difficult for the South Sudanese people.

"If you want a reason for prosecuting this dictator at The Hague, look no further than his actions in the Nuba Mountains, an area in the southern part of Sudan. Sudanese rebels in this area have been attempting to destabilize al-Bashir's rule, without success, for a number of years. If you were to go to the Nuba Mountain region, you would notice foxholes next to thatch roof homes. The people of the Nuba Mountains use these foxholes for shelter, during bombing raids by al-Bashir's air force."

Amarie hesitated as he attempted to control his emotions, but quickly continued. "This frequent bombing has caused horrible deaths, but these are not merely accidents of war. The constant bombing in the Nuba Mountains reflects a deliberate Sudanese scorched-earth strategy on the civilian population, so the anti-al-Bashir rebels in the Nuba Mountains will have no one left to confront his leadership. Other nations around the world have been slow to denounce his violence. When they do, al-Bashir tends to back off his aggressive behavior toward his people, and the people of South Sudan, but he soon returns to his violent attacks."

Amarie now added a second element to the violence in South Sudan. "To confuse the violence in South Sudan, I must add one more disturbing development. Adding to al-Bashir's violent soldiers, a harsh and violent civil war has recently been occurring in the world's newest country, South Sudan. This conflict in South Sudan has erupted between two influential South Sudanese residents, the president, and the man who lost the presidential elections. This dispute between these two individuals, has resulted in burning villages, killing unarmed farmers, castrating boys, raping women, and pillaging hospitals. Unfortunately, South Sudan's new leader has recently been engaging in similar behavior. It's my assessment that we may soon be forced to act militarily in this Sudanese conflict."

Amarie then passed out a report from the activist group, Enough Project, which has a history of exposing genocidal acts in Africa.

Amarie continued, "The report includes satellite imagery of hundreds of burned huts, and it describes the attacks as a 'growing crisis,' similar to the conflict that exploded in Darfur in 2003. One final aspect of al-Bashir's rule in Sudan. He has re-constituted the notorious Janjaweed militias and made them an official state military, as reported in the Enough Project. However, before making any decisions on al-Bashir, Roscoe and I have assigned Rick and Jon to visit Sudan, for the purpose of verifying the accuracy of these reports by the Enough Project."

If Rick and Jon are satisfied with the reliability of the information we have from the Enough Project, we will bring to this committee an agenda item for the commanders to design a plan to remove al-Bashir.

Roscoe took over the next agenda item, Location of BAT 2 headquarters. "Vice Admiral Fisher will command the B.A.T. 2 operations located in the Central African Republic; a country centrally located south of the Sahara Desert. From this location, his detachment of military personnel will oversee the Western African area, while B.A.T. 1 concentrates its efforts in East Africa."

Roscoe then referred to an assignment for B.A.T. 1. "Commander McGruder, Amarie and I are asking you to bring to this committee a plan with a timeline for the capture al-Shabab leader Abdulkadir Mohammed, and his entire leadership group."

Commander McGruder responded. We will begin the development of a plan, and expect to have it finalized for our next meeting. Also, I will present to this committee a plan that our military operation team executive has been discussing for the capture of the entire leadership structure of the al-Shabab in Somalia."

Roscoe acknowledged the commander's response, and thanked him for beginning his preliminary action. "Good luck, Commander, and please, I hope we're not going to have to spend money on another champagne dinner with Cuban cigars."

Everyone had a good laugh, and when the room became quiet, the first response was from the commander.

"No, Sir. You have my guarantee there will be no champagne served, much to the displeasure of Jon and Rick."

Then with a big smile Roscoe said, "Okay, time to move on. Once the al-Shabab leader, his lieutenants, and the Seleka leadership structure in Somalia are added to our prison at Baledogle, Amarie will make arrangements for sending them to the International Criminal Court at The Hague."

Amarie remembered a point he had forgotten to mention, "Oh, I just recalled, Rick and Jon, you'll have to go back to Somalia and interview the legitimate fisherman in the Puntland area. We also will have to release the pirate leaders, since the shipping companies refused our offer to press charges. However, before they are released, try to determine if these pirate leaders caused any harm to African families or if any African citizens experienced property damage. If so, see if you can convince them to become witnesses against these leaders."

The next agenda item was the preliminary planning for the farming towns in the tropical savannas. Roscoe glanced at Amarie, who began his explanation. "I want you all to be aware of the roadblock we have hit regarding our farming towns. We are still trying to figure out an economical way of irrigating the fertile land of the tropical savannas. No point in trying to soft pedal this, the stark reality is the planning team back in Italy did not consider the savannas drought seasons. The problem of being able to provide irrigation in an economical fashion is critical to our plans of building these four hundred towns in the tropical savannas. As you know, these towns are the backbone of our efforts to build a strong middle-class African society."

Roscoe added, "Frankly, unless we come up with an answer sometime in the next six months or so, we may be facing a serious derailment of our entire project. The main reason we have not brought this problem to your attention before now, is we didn't want this problem to affect all the good work that's been done these past five and a half months and not to mention the work you have ahead of you for the next six months. Our director of water resources refuses to be discouraged. He made us promise to let him keep fighting for six more months to come up with a solution, and we agreed. So, you guys do the same, do your part of the job for six more months, and hope we somehow get lucky."

Roscoe moved to a tripod located in the front of the room. He flipped a cover page to reveal contractor drawings of a village layout. He assured his audience that B.A.T. would not face drought problems in the villages in Somália. These villages are being built along the coast, near Mogadishu, and this coastal area does not present the same drought problem.

Roscoe pointed to the drawing of a village and said, "This is the prototype drawing of the four villages we designed for Somalia. We have two villages presently under construction, and in about a week, we hope to start planning our third and fourth villages. When these villages are complete, we'll use them as working models to identify any mistakes or unforeseen problems we may have overlooked. This will prevent us from making these same mistakes in the towns planned for the tropical savannas. So, you can see we've not given up and we don't want you to give up either."

Just the mention of the phrase "towns for the tropical savannas" drew a doubtful cloud over Roscoe and Amarie; these towns had been on their minds every waking hour due to the irrigation issue.

Colonel Bruce McGruder asked, "Is it essential that an irrigation system be developed for the tropical savannas?"

Amarie asked Roscoe to wait a moment as he started to look through a bunch of manila folders he had in his briefcase.

In less than a minute, Amarie stood with paper in hand and said, "I have a few copies of a study on the science of the water limitations for this area of Africa."

He then handed the folder to Roscoe and asked him to pass the report around to those committee members who may be interested, and continued. "For those of you who may not be interested in this scientific data, here is the bottom line. First, if we can't find a way to irrigate the area that will put an end to our plans for building 400 farming towns in the tropical savannas. Second, the report being passed around, completed by the Norwegian Centre for Soil and Environmental Research, explains the serious nature of this drought area."

Amarie read a brief summary of the report. *Restoration of degraded land contagious to African deserts is the only way to hold back desertification. If Build Africa Together is unable to irrigate the tropical savannas, desertification will continue to expand. Continued soil erosion and environmental degradation will expand the Sahara Desert in a southerly direction resulting in chronic food shortages in southern Africa. The eventual dislocation of population in these grassland savannas, due to terrestrial sinks of carbon and reduced rates of enriched atmospheric CO2. Soil and organic carbon contents decrease by 0 to 63 percent following vegetation destruction due to lack of water."*

Roscoe circulated the report, as Amarie continued. "The report, in simple English, says we either find a way to irrigate the tropical savannas or this now-fertile land will become part of the Sahara moving south, and the Kalahari Desert moving north."

Lieutenant Colonel Andruki asked, "Is drilling water wells not a practical solution to the problem?"

Roscoe quickly responded, "The expense of well drilling is compounded by unreliability of successful well drilling. In a direct answer to your question, if we had an unlimited budget, perhaps that might be an answer, but unfortunately, we don't have that luxury. Well drilling alone might be affordable. However, the centuries old problem of drought to the tropical savannas means that underground water is almost non existing, therefore after drilling no water comes to the surface. drilling water wells for our 400 towns would essentially not produce water."

Sergeant Major Jackson then suggested what seemed to him to be a logical solution to the water problem.

"Africa has a great number of rivers and lakes. Why can't these waters be diverted and used for irrigation purposes?"

Amarie answered this question. "First, we have to consider the value of sites such as Victoria Falls as a valuable tourist attraction. Victoria Falls is three hundred-thirty feet tall and approximately a mile in length, allowing three million gallons of water to fall over the edge every minute and pumping this water from the falls could dramatically have a negative result on Victoria Falls. Then there is the issue of the inter connectedness of Africa's waterways. For example, there is a five-mile stretch of water near Khartoum, where the Blue Nile originates from the mountains of Ethiopia. This body of water spills into the White Nile. With the possible changing the water level of the Nile River as it flows to Egypt, I believe you can see how tampering with natural water flow could be dangerous. There is also the question of obtaining permission to use this water, from the local governments, which would be difficult, if not impossible. As of today, we can only hope, something breaks in our favor in the next eight to ten months."

Roscoe showed an unusual lack of confidence as he continued. "I'm very worried about the drinking water situation in general on this continent. We can temporarily solve the clean water problem for our villages planned for Somalia by providing each village with a fifty-five-gallon Sawyer water filter barrel with spigot and Q Beta water filters, locating them in a central location in each village. Water for irrigating farmland is a separate problem from providing disease free water for the residents of the four-hundred towns."

Roscoe paused, looked at Amarie and then said, "Well, guys, it looks like Amarie and I are starting to ramble with a problem that is not yours. Please don't let this get in the way of the important work you men and women are doing. Remember, our first goal is to restore some order and safety to this continent, and that's all you should be concentrating on for now. Amarie and I will try to resolve our other problems. I strongly urge you not to make them your problems."

Sergeant Major Joseph raised his hand. "Yeah, Sergeant Major, what's on your mind?"

"This is a minor question, but it just dawned on me, you used the word 'villages' for the towns in Somali, and 'towns' for the four-hundred living areas in the tropical savannas. Is that a simple name changes for identification, or is there another reason?"

Roscoe responded to the Sergeant Major's question. "I agree it is a minor distinction, but we use it for the simple reason that the four-hundred towns in the tropical savannas will have larger acreage per household than the villages in Somalia. In Somalia, the villages will have ten acres per household, in the tropical savannas each household will have fifteen acres, making the savanna farming towns larger."

CHAPTER 35

Directly after the organizational meeting, Amarie and Roscoe had one more task before their morning was over, the biweekly Skype conference call with Pope Francis Xavier. They reviewed the three agenda items they wished to present to the Vatican team. The co-managers were not looking forward to the third agenda item, which might spell the end to the African project. They felt horrible about the news, given the fact that the pope went out on a limb and sold the Vatican treasures, and now they would have to report that it may not be feasible to economically irrigate the tropical savannas. The pope understood that the four-hundred towns in the tropical savannas, was the backbone of creating a strong African middle-class society.

The Skype picture appeared on the monitors in Rome and Africa at the scheduled time. The pope first inquired about the health and safety of Amarie and Roscoe and then their families. The Pope was especially interested to learn how well Roscoe's girls were doing in their school work. During this early part of the conversation, Amarie noticed Budi was not in the picture on the computer screen, and he inquired about him, since he was always at the side of the pope during their conferences.

The pope informed the co-managers how Budi had become very friendly with a charismatic archbishop from New York City. The relationship flourished over a number of years, and Budi was now a part time assistant to the archbishop for half of the year and a part time secretary to the pope for the other half.

The pope explained, "Budi and the archbishop had been cultivating a genuine, mutually satisfying and challenging relationship. I realized that Budi's assignment as my secretary was not providing a sufficient challenge for him. I began to notice how Budi was flourishing in many new positive directions since his contact with the New York archbishop. It was then that I encouraged Budi to split his assignment. Initially, he declined to leave his secretarial position with me for half of the year. I continued to encourage him to take this step, and he finally agreed. At the present he is spending time away from the Vatican and is on assignment in New York City with Archbishop McCarthy."

Roscoe said, "I'm very surprised to hear of Budi's division of duties, especially given the fact you both have been together for so many years."

The pope's response was very much in character. "It wasn't easy to get him to agree to the arrangement. The more he resisted, the more I knew it was best for him to move from under my presence."

Amarie added, "I'm so pleased for Budi. I'm sure you miss him, but it was very thoughtful of you to allow your closest confidant to be able to find a new direction in his life."

The pope said, "I miss him terribly, but he deserves this gratifying experience with his new friend."

Francis Xavier, anxious to change the subject, concluded; "Now it's time to discuss our African business."

Roscoe began with a positive and very important item for discussion. "As you all know, the African Plan written in Italy indicated that electricity would be expanded using solar panels and wind turbines. After consulting with the

South African Department of Energy, our director of electric power has convinced us to change our plan from solar panels and wind turbines to produce electric power, and turn to a new source of producing electric power. Let me introduce Ms. Evelyn Armstrong, who will explain the reasons why we wish to make this change."

As Evelyn Armstrong adjusted her seat to place herself on the Skype screen, she said "Good morning Your Holiness, it's my pleasure to finally speak with you relative to African electrical energy. When Mr..., there I go again, although I was informed of the reason and history of using first names, I obviously am still a little uncomfortable addressing my superiors by their first names, rather than Mister or Sir, but allow me to continue my introductory comments on African electricity, hopefully remembering to use first names.

One of my many reasons for accepting this two-year assignment in Africa from Roscoe and Amarie was the opportunity to provide Build Africa Together with a new improved concept in the production of clean, sustainable electric power. I believe, once you are introduced to the structural works of Solar Thermal Power, you will find it is a perfect fit for Africa, with its extensive, clear, white sands of the Sahara and Kalahari deserts. The Sahara is 3.5 million square miles, and the Kalahari is 350,000 square miles. Solar Thermal Power has the potential to turn these huge uninhabited areas, into an important African natural resource. Everyone will shortly be receiving a prototype picture, facts and figures of his new and exciting concept in the production of clean, sustainable electric energy."

Ms. Armstrong, clearing her throat, continued, "Next week I am off to the South African Department of Energy, to learn as much as I can about their agreement with Eckom,

South Africa's public utility company that operates the Solar Thermal power plant, named Redstone Energy. This facility is located on a semi-desert site in the Northern Cape Province of South Africa. The Redstone plant produces 1.200 megawatt hours of clean, sustainable electric energy for up to 17 hours every clear day. The Redstone facility produces enough megawatt hours to meet the peak energy demands for the Northern Province's 200,000 homes and businesses, even though exhaust from frequent fly-overs the by Jet planes and unclear days, usually results in reduction of megawatt hours. The megawatt hours produced from the Sarah, and Kalahari deserts, Solar Thermal power plants will not be prone to this same reduction of megawatt hours from frequent jet exhausts or inclement weather."

The Vatican team, attentively listening to Evelyn's every word at the other end of the Skype conference, when Pope Francis Xavier commented, "Ms. Armstrong, your brief comments so far sound very exciting. Could you please continue by discussing how the electric energy from Solar Thermal power is produced?"

Ms. Armstrong continued. "Let me preface my comments on how electricity power is produced to say a word about the African deserts. In the past, Africa's two dominant deserts, the Kalahari and the Sahara have been viewed by Africans as unproductive land areas, except for animal habitats. However, once the Solar Thermal power plants become operational, in approximately two and a half to three years, and this new electric power is sent to the African electrical grid, the African people will see these deserts as important continental natural resources."

Ms. Armstrong began her explanation of how Solar Thermal power produces electricity. "I have factored in the reflective power of the pure white sand of these two large deserts, the extensive number of clear cloudless days, and no natural blockage of sun from mountains, business buildings, and let us not forget, the smog from jet motors of passenger airlines.

Amarie apologized for interrupting Ms. Armstrong. "Evelyn has not mentioned one other advantage of Solar Thermal electricity, and that is the storage capacity of electric energy in the steam driven turbines. This storage of our unused electricity can, sometime in the future, be sold to other countries in Europe and the Middle East, through cables at the bottom of the Mediterranean Sea and the Indian Ocean. Think of the historical implications for Africa. I never thought I would live to see the time when Africa is financially compensated for its natural resources, rather than our natural resources, which was stolen by colonial powers."

Dr. Evelyn Armstrong nodded to Amari, and continued.[1] "Solar Thermal power plants consist of a central tower, on top of which, is a huge boiler full of water. This boiler is automatically, filled with water each day. Each plant has thousands of concave photovoltaic mirrors, arranged in a circle, enclosing the tower, and the water filled boiler. The mirrors contain a mineral called molten salt. The molten salt is heated by sunlight. As the computer operated mirrors, which are following the movement of the sun, as it rises in the east and settles in the west, is continuously directing their hot sun rays, all day, on the water filled huge boiler. The now heated water from the rays of the sun in the boiler, soon creates steam. Once steam is created, it is automatically directed to turbines, which are located at the base of the central tower, the steam

---

[1] Solar thermal power plant

induced turbines begin to produce electricity, which is then sent to Africa's expanded and improved electric grid system. Finally, a Solar Thermal power plant has the ability to store its unused electric power, created by the steam from the boiler, for a much longer period than solar panels and wind turbines."

Jerome asked a question about solar thermal power plants. "Can you explain how solar thermal powered steam produces megawatts of electricity?"

Doctor Armstrong said, "I must assume you are Father Jerome, is that correct."

"Yes, and I must say you are a fast learner, using by first name without skipping a beat."

Evelyn smiled and said, "How nice of you to notice."

She then continued, "After the moving Solar Thermal mirrors have produced steam in the boiler, which is then sent to the turbines, this steam causes the turbines to begin their spinning motion, which in turn produces electricity. When the new electricity is sent to the African electric grids, they distribute their electricity to homes and businesses. When the electric grids reach full electric capacity, the turbines automatically stop spinning, allowing them to hold on to their electric power."

Doctor Armstrong now moved to the cost of Solar Thermal power plants, "Using aerial and ground maps, I have calculated the population of Africa, the expanse of the continent, the approximate number of structures and buildings. Using this information, I made an informal calculation of the electricity needed for all home and commercial use; including the four hundred farming towns to be built in the tropical savannas. With that information, I believe that Africa will require nine Solar Thermal power plants, five in the Sahara

Desert and four in the Kalahari Desert. These nine plants will provide maximum electric power for the billion citizens of Africa. The nine Solar Thermal electric plants will cost seven billion dollars. However, the seven billion dollars is slightly less than the formally projected construction of a three billion solar panels, and a five hundred and ninety-six wind turbines, which would be needed to produce a similar number of megawatts of electricity that the nine Solar Thermal power plants would generate. These plants will provide this continent with sufficient, dependable, and sustainable electricity and the bonus of longer electric storage capability, will allow other countries to purchase Africa's surplus electric power. It seems to be a win-win for Africa in all columns, assuming you agree to finance nine Solar Thermal electric plants."

Dr. Hasson asked, "Can you elaborate just a little more on how this unused, stored electric power could be sent to other countries?"

Roscoe entered the conversation. "The unused stored electricity can be sold to Western European countries, Middle Eastern Countries, as well as Turkey, Spain and Greece, assuming they choose to purchase Africa's excess electricity. Foreign countries will have to lay cables at the bottom of the Mediterranean Sea or the Red Sea depending on their location. Once these cables are in place, our surplus megawatts of electric power can move through these cables to other countries."

All at the table in the Vatican agreed with the change, but they were surprised at the high cost of supplying reliable electricity to Africa. However, it was quickly accepted, and the co-managers were encouraged to move forward with solar thermal electric power.

Roscoe took the second agenda item. He outlined the abuses of the Sudanese dictator, Omar al-Bashir, and asked for the pope's permission to have commanders of B.A.T. 1 and 2 develop a plan to capture and remove the Sudanese dictator for delivery to The Hague. Surprisingly, the Vatican team quickly and unanimously agreed to the removal of al-Bashir from power in Sudan.

Roscoe then added the final step. The Sudan Supreme Court will name a transitional head of state the evening of the coup attempt; depriving other Sudanese leaders to ferment chaos, by naming themselves, as the legitimate Sudanese President.

Once agreed upon, Amarie introduced the third agenda item.

"This next agenda item is not as positive as the electricity agenda item or the proposed incursion into Sudan. This item may have a direct bearing on the entire project. There is some bad news to report."

The pope interrupted Amarie. "Oh, I hope you're not going to tell me that some of our workers have been killed or injured."

"No, Your Holiness, no one has been killed or injured. The negative news has to do with one of our project objectives, the farm land in the tropical savannas. Our water director has researched the rain patterns of the tropical savannas, going back the last fifty years. His findings show that the tropical savannas have for the past fifty years experienced extended periods of drought. This fact was something the planning team did not foresee, when they planned the four hundred farming towns. The water director tested the feasibility of drilling water wells for the towns to use for irrigating their crops. He drilled exploratory wells in many different areas of the tropical savannas, and found that eighty-nine percent of the wells he drilled, did not produce any water. The eleven percent of the wells that did produce water, his test for water volume proved to be low in quantity, producing water for a very limited time period. He has attributed this fact to the many centuries of drought in the tropical savannas."

Roscoe chimed in, "We have been mulling over this problem for months and, sad to say, we are forced to conclude that building the four hundred towns in the tropical savannas may have to be abandoned, and with it our plans for a middle-class African Society. Without irrigation, and the long history of seasonal droughts, farmers would be unable to produce crops. The Vatican team must decide if it wishes to continue the project or terminate Build Africa Together before we waste any more resources. We here on the ground strongly urge the Vatican team to place the construction of Solar Thermal electricity on hold, especially considering the cost involved.

Amarie visualizing the atmosphere around the table at the Vatican said. "I understand what this means for Build Africa Together, and for the Pope, after selling the Vatican Treasures. We are sorry to say we let you down Sunjaya. The planning team should have looked into the reason why such rich land had never before been used for farming. Sunjaya, again I can't tell you how sorry we all are, we failed you.

The silent stillness from both ends of the Skype session lasted for close to a minute. All parties to this discussion were out of words.

The pope finally broke the quiet. "Unless either of you has something else you wish to add, let us terminate this conference. I will speak to you all in a few days. In the meantime, go about your work with the same belief you had in Opi. We at the Vatican will discuss this matter further, and I will involve Budi in our discussion. I would like you both to be available for a Skype conference next Thursday morning at nine, your time. This will give us all here at the Vatican time to discuss and reflect on the information you have shared with us today, especially your assessment of the last item."

Roscoe and Amarie agreed, and the Skype session closed on Amarie's monitor.

CHAPTER 36

On Thursday morning, Amarie and Roscoe waited silently for the little green Skype status indicator to come to life on their computer screen. Amarie clicked on the icon, and in a few seconds, a blurry picture of Pope Francis Xavier appeared on the monitor. His voice came through the computer firmly. "Good morning, gentlemen. What I wish to say may seem foolish to you both, but please be patient with me for a few minutes. There was a low sigh, as though the Pope had taken a deep breath, and immediately began. "Indonesians, by their nature and upbringing, are accepting of their fate in life, a fatalism that in this case may be ill advised, but I must briefly explain. When tiny creatures crawled out of the oceans and began a new life on land, God's great experiment began."

Amari thought. *That's strange the Catholic pope did not us the Catholic teaching of Adam and Eve to explain how life began."*

"God, with all-knowing wisdom, gave humans free will, and knowingly made humans imperfect beings. God then sent Jesus to our planet, to tell humans how the Lord wanted us to live. In God's great wisdom, we were given three simple rules: Believe in your God, forgive other human beings, and love your neighbor as you love yourself. After Jesus gave us God's three simple, but powerful messages; the lord returned Jesus to heaven so his sone could remain at his side. I believe in the Lord's plan for the human race. Therefore, I do not expect God to interfere or perhaps I should say, intervene directly in my life. Nor do I believe that God directs circumstances of certain people here on earth to do good or evil, it's all on our shoulders."

Pope Francis Xavier looked as though he might begin to cry, but he continued with only a slight hesitation. "Over these past few days, I thought that my God must be sad over the abuse Africans have had to endure for far too many centuries. He must be wondering when someone is going to help these poor Africans. Then I went for three days to Castle Gandolfo, to clear my head. During these three days, I decided God would be pleased that finally someone was making an effort to 'love African's as I love myself.' Therefore, I sold the Vatican treasures using the money to help remove poverty from Africa, and now that may be a lost dream. Gentlemen, I put you in Africa for the purpose of lifting the spirits and souls of almost a billion people. We apparently will be unable to build a middle-class society, but we can show our love for our neighbors by giving them electricity for their homes. We can show our love for our neighbors by building an intra-continental highway. Perhaps these works will inspire others to use technology to find a way to deliver water to the tropical savannas. Therefore, I am directing you both, to continue your two-year tenure and proceed with implementing your plan for the instillation of nine solar thermal electric power plants. Continue your plans for the building of Africa's intra-continental highway. Finally, continue the good work you are accomplishing making Africa a safe and secure continent. And most importantly, be accepting of the fact that we will fall short of reaching our most important goal."

This was not what Roscoe and Amarie expected. They were, for a moment, shocked into silence and disbelief. They stared at each other, shrugged their shoulders, and agreed to follow the pope's wishes, believing this holy man was using his belief in Jesus to justify continuing a project destined not to reach its most important goal. They responded to Pope Francis Xavier by assuring him they would continue to work as hard as possible for the next thirteen months. They would have preferred to have talked the pope out of wasting his money, but they knew arguing against such strong religious beliefs would be fruitless.

After the surprising Skype conference, Amarie summed up their dilemma quiet simply. "Who am I to quarrel with, or discourage this holy man, for choosing to continue?"

***

On Monday of the following week, Amarie, Roscoe, Rick Kingsley, Jon Edwards, and both military commanders met to discuss an assignment they had for Rick and Jon. Jon immediately noticed that Amarie's happy smiling face seemed to be absent this morning. This signaled to Rick and Jon that the rumors they had been hearing since they arrived at B.A.T. 2 headquarters might not be speculation.

Jon said, "Before you get into our assignment, I would like to know if the rumors about the project being dissolved are true."

Amarie said, "I know you two arrived late yesterday afternoon, and I'm sure you have been hearing the gossip going around. Sad to say, we have hit a roadblock in our irrigation attempts for the tropical savannas."

Jon interrupted Amarie, "Yeah, we heard. Are you guys calling it quits. If so, we want you to know how sorry we are. We were enjoying our work in Africa, and we hate to see it end like this."

Amarie sat up straight in his chair. "Hey, hold on, you two. You're right, the news is not encouraging, but we are not, as you say, calling it quits. Yes, we have run into a problem that has no answer, but we have firm orders from the pope to continue as planned. Remember, we all have two-year contracts, so forget about leaving Africa for the next thirteen months. It is true we have scaled back our expectations to build a strong middle-class African society. But remember, we also came to Africa to bring some order to this place and supply the continent with reliable, sustainable electric energy, along with another big job to give this continent a trans-continental highway. If we can meet our timelines on these three projects, the second two-year team will be able to finish the electricity and highway while continuing to improve the safety and order for African citizens."

Amarie continued the discussion in a new direction. "I will summarize the activities that have taken place while you both have been on the road. Our two commanders and their troops are still in the process of assessing the young soldiers from the warlord and militia groups, and they have begun interviews with some locals interested in the arrangements for the coastal villages of Somalia. The highway crew has just turned the major eastern highway section north heading to Algiers. The electricity director and her crew of Africans will be finished with the repairs and the extension of the electric grids. Their objective is to spend their final year working on bringing one Solar Thermal electric power plant online. The village contractor has one more village to survey on the coast of Somalia, and he expects to be done in about two weeks. Roscoe has a few interviews to complete and then he's off to the Sahara Desert with representatives of the Bechtel Company to identify the nine locations of the Solar Thermal power plants. I have meetings with country leaders regarding rights of way for our various projects, which will keep me on the road for the next few months. So, as you can see, we may be wounded, but we still have a pulse."

Amarie finished by adding a personal touch. "Look, you two, I didn't spend over ten years in an African jail and then two terms as leader of South Africa to, what was the phrase you used, call it quits, which brings me to the assignment for you both. Over the next three to four weeks, we have plans which I expect will put considerable mileage on your SUV, but before we get into that, I'm ready for my morning coffee. Care to join me?"

The four men followed Amarie to the coffee maker, as Amarie continued. "We plan on meeting our project time-lines so that the second two-year team can complete our work. We may not be able to build a strong African middle-class, but we can make life safer for many Africans and improve the continent's infrastructure. That's nothing to be ashamed of."

Rick Kinsley, now fifty-seven years of age, was a career intelligence operative who retired two years ago from the CIA in Langley, Virginia. Rick looked somewhat older than his age due to his bushy full head of grey hair. He remained exceptionally fit for a man his age. Rick was recruited by the CIA, after a short stint in the Federal Bureau of Investigation. He always approached his work in a deliberate, cautious manner.

Jon Edwards was fifty-five years of age. Jon entered the CIA directly out of college. During his thirty years with the CIA, Jon had always been a field operative who made it known to his handlers he would quit before accepting deskwork. Having been in the field for his entire career, Jon had to keep himself physically fit. The bald-headed, quite handsome man with chiseled facial features thrived on excitement. The probability of danger always seemed to get his blood flowing.

The men returned to Amarie's desk with coffee mugs in hand, and Amarie began to identify their next tasks. "Your job will be to gather information on targets and groups in four African countries,"

Amarie then explained. "Four special ops intelligence platoon soldiers will assist you on this mission."

Amarie, hesitated a moment before removing four folders from his desk drawer and placing them atop his desk. He went on to explain the first task. The director of Philanthropy, Ms. Mary Louise Thorp, has obtained the donation of seven fishing boats from Western and Northern European boat manufacturers. Her negotiations with the leaders of these nations included a rather frank summary of their colonial history in Africa, and that seemed to have encouraged authorities in those countries to put some muscle on their boat manufacturers, explaining how a donation of these fishing boats to B.A.T. would help the fishing industry in Africa."

Amarie then identified the specific task. "First, contact the two men identified in the folder just given to you. These two men have cleared our vetting process many months ago, and they have received new fishing boats. They may be able to help identity other former fisherman still in the area. The intelligence team was instructed to locate any of the original Somali fisherman that took matters into their own hands by driving foreign fishing vessels from Somali territorial waters. If those men can be located, we will talk with them about resuming their work. The intelligence team will also have to identify those who decline our offer of fishing boats, and attempt to determine if they are going to remain lawful or if they are planning on continuing their pirate business."

Amarie passed a second folder to Rick and Jon and began his review of this task. "This folder includes preliminary information on the situation in the Democratic Republic of Congo. Your task in the Congo is to determine the accuracy of this preliminary information and fill in as much detail as you can on the rogue criminal outfits operating in the area. The preliminary information would seem to suggest there are numerous independent rogue criminal groups who have established control of the Kahuzi-Biega area in eastern Congo. Our information suggests they can act with impunity by giving themselves fraternal sounding names such as good will, unity, family, tribe, clan, brotherhood, etcetera. B.A.T. commanders are considering an incursion into the Congo but they need some information. Identify the leadership structure of these groups, the approximate number of criminal gangs, their general location, the type of military equipment used and, if possible, identify whether their soldiers are mature and experienced or kidnapped teens. Did I go too fast? Were you able to record each of these requests?" Jon nodded in the affirmative.

Amarie plucked a third folder from his pile and began to discuss the information in this folder.

"Preliminary media information on Libya would seem to suggest this North African country may be a quick stop. You both need to verify reports suggesting that since the overthrow and killing of Muammar Gaddafi, Libya's opposition parties are hopelessly divided and unable to form a unified governmental structure. If this is accurate, determine the extent of the internal turmoil existing between the major rebel groups, and identify if they are willing to come together to identify a single legitimate candidate, or are they simply military or political organizations battling for legitimacy."

Amarie reached for the next folder. "I have saved the most volatile situation for last. We have solid information on the terror the Sudan dictator, Omar al-Bashir, has caused in both Sudan and South Sudan. That information is included in your folders. Commander McGruder and Vice Admiral Fisher are considering the capture of this ruthless dictator, and they would like a thorough intelligence report. Once that is completed, they would like you two to acquire information on the location of his compound, its defensive strength and his travel patterns."

Amarie sat back in his seat. "Well, gentlemen, you have your assignments. It may take you months, rather than weeks, and for this reason, you are not under a timeline for completion. Take as much time as you need to successfully complete your task. We prefer you to be accurate and thorough, and, if needed, we can extend the timeline we have estimated for this assignment."

Jon Edwards spoke up, somewhat surprised. "I thought for sure the al-Shabab group and their al Qaeda leader, Abdulkadir Mohammed, would be one of the groups needed for intel. gathering?"

Amarie answered. "Sorry, we do at times forget to bring you two up to date because of your extensive traveling so let me take a moment to fill you in on al-Shabab. A very successful operation under Commander McGruder, captured Abdulkadir Mohammed and his eight man al-Qaeda leadership council. They were arrested three weeks ago and have been delivered to The Hague for trial and hopefully conviction. All that remains is identifying witness for their trial."

Jon reacted to Amarie's brief explanation, and Amarie began to explain the operation. "Thanks to a great plan by our commanders, Colonel McGruder's operation went down with no casualties on our part, but I've got to tell ya, it wasn't half as much fun as the banquet with the Somali coastal militias and pirate leaders."

"Well, come on, don't keep us in suspense. How did they pull it off?" asked Rick.

Amarie began from the beginning. "A member of vice admiral's unit, Asaad Caalin, is of the Islamic faith and knows the Lowland Eastern Cushitic language. That gave the commanders an idea for the plan on Abdulkadir Mohammed's house, a plan designed to hit them from the front of the house, not the beach. Vice Admiral Fisher's Islamic man, a Delta guy, spent a couple of weeks walking one of their Belgian Malawa bomb-sniffing dogs past the front of Abdulkadir's house. He was dressed in Somali garb and made sure the dog barked as he passed the house each evening. He deliberately wanted to draw the attention of Abdulkadir's men so they would be used to him walking his dog each night. In fact, one night, one of the men came out of the house and asked Asaad what type of dog he owned."

"Asaad had to think fast of a dog breed that would be convincing, not wanting to divulge the dog as a bomb-sniffing dog. When Asaad felt the al-Shabab men in the house were used to him walking his dog each night, he made the decision one night to drop the dog's leash in front of Abdulkadir's house. The dog roamed the entire front of the house without barking telling our special ops guy that the front of the house was not booby-trapped with land mines. When three of al-Shabab's men came out to see what was going on, our guy was all apologies. He was bowing, apologizing in the Cushitic language about how his dog accidently got loose. The men in the house accepted his apologies, and off he went with the Malawah dog. The following night, five SEALS left a boat anchored about a mile from Abdulkadir's beach house. With darkness for cover and underwater tanks on their backs, they swam toward the house. Meanwhile, 30 B.A.T. 1 men were hunkered down at an intersection about an eight of a mile from the house. The five SEALS arrived at Abdulkadir's beach, and then, with only their heads out of the water, they strung a line of firecrackers they had packed in sealed plastic bags. They placed the string of firecrackers on the sand at the edge of the beach. They lit a long fuse line attached to the firecrackers, then got their asses back under water, and began swimming back to the anchored boat. When the firecrackers went off, Abdulkadir's men unloaded their long rifles at the beach. The noise made by the firecrackers and the shooting, alerted the guys in the truck at the intersection. The truck gunned it to the house, and our guys rushed the front of the house. They rammed the front door, entered the house to find Abdulkadir's men still putting all their firepower on the firecrackers going off at the beach waterline. When the firing stopped, Abdulkadir's men turned and found themselves looking down the barrels of our soldier's AK-47s. Two al-Shabab men raised their guns and were immediately taken out, which got everyone's attention. Our guys marched the remaining seven men out to a truck now parked at their front door and an hour and a half later all seven men, including Abdulkadir, were sitting in our cell block."

Jon applauded and said, "Hey great plan. I'll will have to congratulate both commanders after we get back."

Amarie turned serious. "I need to discuss one more important fact of life. You two are gathering intelligence in four countries, a long trip, so, remember, a great deal of military operations against the bad guys are needed to stabilize Africa and make it safe and secure. Your work during these first two years is only the beginning of many military conflicts to occur over the next twelve years. Our main objective is to lead the way, taking on tasks that our commanders' feel will be successful. I hope the second two-year leadership for Build Africa Together understands that the success of this goal requires them to move steadily, and in small increments, as we are doing. We hope that by year five or six, with continued success, organizations like the United Nations and other nations can help in the process of stabilizing this unruly, dangerous continent."

CHAPTER 37

Roscoe, his wife Michele, and their two girls had been in Africa for ten months. The girls had adjusted quite well to their school, and their new African friends, who, in many ways, acted so very differently than American teens. Tonight, Roscoe was upstairs having a difficult time deciding what clothes to pack for tomorrow's work day, which was to include a trip to the Sahara Desert, including one or two overnight stays. He had to prepare for devastatingly hot days and nights that felt like late autumn in Chicago.

He had chosen his clothes and was packing when the phone rang, and Michelle answered. She was pleased to hear the voice of Roscoe's old friend, Professor Tom Claffey. He was interested in knowing how things were going for the Ayala family. Michelle complained she had only recently accepted her African stay for the two-year period; she admitted she liked their home and the country of Cameroon. She mentioned to Tom that Africa is the most beautiful, interesting continent on the globe. She conceded for the first time that maybe this venture was not going to be as bad as she had expected.

"You know, Tom, I'm glad you called. Just expressing this fact has made me realize that perhaps I have been unfair to myself for taking so long to become comfortable on this gorgeous continent. Getting used to new places has always been difficult for me. Thanks Tom. Our little chat has been a big help." She then told the family friend to hold on while she called upstairs for Roscoe. "Roscoe, Tom Claffey's on the phone, pick up."

Roscoe quickly went to the phone. "Hey, Tom, so good to hear your voice, how are you, my old friend?"

I'm fine. The question is, how's my safari roaming friend doing way off in exotic Africa?"

"So far, I'm doing good. They both enjoyed a good laugh, and then Roscoe said, "No time for safaris. I'm now a common laborer like the rest of you guys."

After more laughs, Tom said, "The family and I are doing well. I decided to call to see how the Ayala family was getting by in their new country. I have to tell you I was very surprised when I heard that your first job after eight years in the White House, was with a humanitarian organization in Africa. Never did I expect that's what you'd be doing. You must have anticipated multiple opportunities here in the States, and I'm sure they would have been very lucrative."

Roscoe shrugged, and said "It's done now, but here was the situation. Pope Francis Xavier asked me, and five other government people, to develop a plan to eradicate poverty in Africa. I'm sure you have read he sold a lot of Vatican property to get the money to get this job done. Now, don't get me wrong, he's a pretty smart guy, but this little Indonesian, he's probably five foot three, and comes from a severely impoverished background. He's also not the most sophisticated man when it comes to the real world. So here was this short, unsophisticated clergyman with the guts to sell all these valuable items, knowing he was going to take a great deal of heat for his decision. I didn't want the job of project manager going to some huckster who was more interested in lining his pockets than doing the right thing. So, when Amarie Maalout, my co-manager, came to me with the proposition for the two of us to co-manage the project for the first two years, I just couldn't say no. I figure I'm still pretty young and there will be plenty of opportunities for me in America after two years in Africa, who knows, maybe even more opportunities." Dr Claffey, in responding to his friend's reasoning, said. "Well, no matter the reason, you deserve a lot of credit for giving up two years of your life, and I've got to say I'm very proud of my old friend."

Tom changed the subject. "Michelle sounded as though she has made the adjustment to Africa. How are the girls doing?"

Roscoe now laughing said, "Michelle quickly adjusting to something, never gonna happen, but I think your assessment is on target, she seems to have finally accepted that she's going to be living in Africa for another year. The girls, a much different story, there doing much better than I had expected."

"That's great, but I must say, I still can't get over the fact that you took a job in Africa. Here I was, expecting you to be in Southern California a number of times, being paid for some dumb ass speech. Or appearing at some boring function, so that Clay and I would get a chance to see more of you."

Once Roscoe heard the name Clay, he was all smiles. "How's my old friend doing? It's been years since I've seen him as well. Is he still at Cal Tech.?"

"Yeah, he's still doing his thing at Cal Tech, and he is well, we try to get together at least once a month. Besides checking up on you and Michelle, I called for another reason. When I heard you were going to be spending two years Africa, it seemed reasonable you might be doing some work with Africa's natural resources. If so, and if you don't have someone already pegged to take on that responsibility, I would like to recommend a former student who happens to presently be in Africa. He is very knowable about Africa's natural resources."

Roscoe was frank with his friend about the topic. "Tom, to be perfectly honest, we never considered doing something formal with natural resources in our original plan. Perhaps that was a mistake. Let me hear more about this candidate, especially since he's already in Africa. I may want to have a chat with him."

Tom said, "Well, there's a lot to explain, so I hope you've got some time."

Roscoe shot back, "Uh-oh, maybe I'm sorry I asked, but for you, Tom, I'm all ears."

Laughing, Tom said, "Considering the size of your ears, you should stay away from using ears as a metaphor." Tom quickly got serious. "I first contacted this kid when he was a ten-year-old prodigy, ready for college at the age of twelve. Clay and I were both after him, and I got lucky. The twelve-year-old was interested in archeology and finished his bachelor's degree in two years. Don't even ask about his I.Q, it's off the charts, and I mean literally off the chart. We were unable to determine his actual I.Q. If he is told something or reads something, that's it, the facts never leave his head, and I mean never. At the time, he received his bachelor's degree, his interest shifted from archeology to natural resources. He stayed with us for a master's degree in that area of study. After his masters, he requested to stay with us for a doctorate on the condition we would permit him to work out a pro-gram where he could do his doctorate work on-the- ground in Africa. We set up a review process where he would be required to return to California twice a year for a thorough examination of the work he was accomplishing. This was new territory for us, and at the end of his first year, I was still concerned about how this off-campus doctoral program would progress. The long and short of this experimental education program, the committee was blown away by the kid's first report and the progress he was making. Based on his performance, we agreed to a second year, with the stipulation that his orals take place on his next visit back to the States, and at the end of the second year, he would complete his written dissertation. Needless to say, he exceeded way beyond what was expected."

Tom then talked about the young man's future. "Before coming back for his finals, he was able to secure a two-year grant from an independent German mining company. The grant was quite large, but I recently heard from his mother that he and the company agreed to part company, did not hit it off, and both parties agreed to go their separate ways after one year."

Roscoe inquired, "Can you tell me a little bit more about this young man's personality and the nature of the conflict that he had with the mining company?"

"Well, from his mother's explanation, the managers of the German mine felt his attitude was disrespectful and rude. And knowing Doctor Adair, I'm not surprised at their reaction, I believe they did not understand autism."

"Rude? Is he difficult to work with, asked Roscoe?"

Tom emphatically replied, "Oh, don't worry; I haven't even started to explain this young man. Our generation would have referred to him as an idiot savant, but today we identify individuals such as Doctor Adair, as being on the autism spectrum. He has, shall I say, unusual social mannerisms. Maybe a better word is unusual social skills. It took me a good year to understand Doctor Adair's emotional neediness and his dislike of the company of others." Tom felt the need to clarify. "These are not symptoms of autism, but the results of his autism. Today it is not proper to say, he is autistic. The accepted phrase is he is a person who has autism."

Roscoe had never heard this explanation, and thanked his friend for educating him on this topic.

Doctor Claffey continued. "His entire mental and verbal focus centers on the work he is interested in., and Africa presented him with a great deal of interests. He believes Africa not only has more natural resources than any continent in the world, but he is confident that Africa has a great deal of unidentified natural resources that have the potential to revolutionize the future of Africa and the world. Moreover, he's determined to locate all of Africa's natural resources. If you did hire him, and if he agrees, I know you would find him knowledgeable. In fact, I expect that you'd be shocked to hear some of his assertions, and perhaps even a little skeptical. Even with this summary, I still believe in the positive future of this young man. If you choose to meet with him, do not underestimate anything he alleges, and I mean anything. I had to find that out the hard way."

Roscoe was now a little more interested than when the conversation about the young doctor began.

"I've learned over the years to trust your judgment Tom, you gave me some wonderful advice on a number of questions when I was president, and I am grateful that I listened and learned. However, I have no idea at this time how I could use, what's his name?"

Tom responded, "He goes by the name Jem Adair, but his given name is James Adair, and he was born in the United Kingdom"

Doctor Claffey, knowing he would be talking about the most complex individual he had ever met, was not sure how to continue. He hesitated, wondering for a moment, deciding which side of Jem Adair's genius to present first. "I'll start by giving you the positive side of this young man." Roscoe interrupted, "Positive side? You mean there is a negative side?"

Tom continued, "Well, that's for you to decide. First, he's the most brilliant person I have ever worked with. Second, unlike many of these prodigies, Doctor Adair's thinking is practical, analytical, unique, and almost often, correct. I don't usually use the word unique, because it means one-of-a-kind, and there are few one-of-a-kind people in this world. However, when explaining Dr. Adair, I do use the word unique. He's the first person I've ever known who has the extraordinary ability to listen to an unsolved hypothesis, where everyone agrees that the conclusion is flawed, and therefore the thesis must be incorrect. Then he shows up the following morning, usually arriving in my outer office by 5:00 a.m., having redesigned the problem so our presumed flawed solution is no longer flawed. He's almost, kind of scary, in the sense that he reconfigured the information within the other professor's hypothesis, and then watch the older, knowledgeable group of experts, agree with his conclusions. I've yet to see anything like him before."

Tom once again hesitated, and then decided he had made his point about the intelligence of his boy genius, and told Roscoe it was his decision to meet the doctor, or simply forget the most recent conversation.

Roscoe surprised Tom by inquired about Doctor Adair's background.

Tom began to answer Roscoe inquiry. "He was born and raised for twelve years in Wales, United Kingdom.

His parents, a British father and an American mother, were both concerned that universities in the United Kingdom would not be able to supply the services their son required."

"What do you mean by services?" asked Roscoe. Doctor Claffey said, "Well now his downside, his social behavior skills simply don't exist. He has no social behavioral skills whatsoever."

Roscoe interrupted, "I should have known, he was beginning to sound too good to be true."

Tom immediately retorted, "No, Roscoe, trust me. His upside is so strong that I would forcefully urge you to ignore his lack of social skills. If you decide to meet him, remember his sociability is only a downside if you are not prepared to accept him as he is, socially dysfunctional, but intellectually in a class all his own. For example, if during a conversation, a new thought enters in his head, it simply comes out of his mouth. No context or previous discussion, just the simple abstract thought that most often has nothing to do with the subject of the conversation. Frequently, he may suddenly become so distracted that his body may be present in a room, but his mind is millions of miles away. Physically, he begins to demonstrate, through bodily actions, how he is solving the issue that entered his mind. Most of his time is spent alone, but don't feel sorry for him, that's what he prefers. If you properly prepare people, things usually are okay, and you find your unsolvable problems had a simple answer. Understand that his social peculiarities, no matter how you may explain them away, can be hard for many people to accept. But once a person accepts that Doctor Jem Adair is in a different cosmos, things usually flow pretty well."

Roscoe was not discouraged; his only question was that he and the planning team had never discussed the matter of

Africa's natural resources, and he wasn't sure how the doctor's expertise could benefit Build Africa Together.

"Tom, I've got something on my plate right now, but in another month, I'd be very interested in meeting this young man."

Professor Claffey gave Roscoe Jem Adair's contact information in Africa and encouraged Roscoe to meet the young genius and come to his own conclusions. Professor Claffey wished Roscoe good luck in his African project and they each bid the other farewell.

Roscoe, for the first time, began to consider this question of Africa's abundance of natural resources.

He seemed to be talking himself into thinking more about the topic, wondering why the planning team never discussed this issue. Was it something they had overlooked, or was this not an important part of B.A.T.'s mission?

Roscoe thought, *If this kid is such a genius, perhaps he might be able to help. Hmm…this may be interesting. Tom's information about the kid seemed to imply he has special needs, and we have no one on board to advise us on how to deal with his personality. I think I will contact this complicated individual, that's the only way to decide if we should get involved with him.*

CHAPTER 38

Preliminary work on the intra-continental highway had begun in January 2012. Amarie Maalout, in his role as roving ambassador, was beginning his visits to African leaders of countries the highway would traverse. His second visit was to the Egyptian President Kiya Pedi Bastet, who recently took office after winning a run-off election, replacing the religious leader deposed by the Egyptian military.

The Egyptian President came out of his office to greet Amarie Maalout. Within a few minutes an aid to the Egyptian president poured a cool drink for the two men, who had taken seats facing each other.

The Egyptian president said, "Amarie Maalout, the most respected and admired man in Africa, will always be promptly welcomed into my office! How may I be of service to the greatest of all African citizens?"

Amarie explained his role with Build Africa Together and then quickly moved to discussing plans for the African intra-continental highway.

Amarie opened his explanation by identifying the seaport locations. "Ports in North Africa will be located in Algiers, Algeria, and Alexandria, Egypt. The west coast seaport will be located in Dakar, Senegal, and the seaport in eastern Africa on the Indian Ocean will be located in Somalia at Kismayu. The southwestern leg of the intra-continental highway will meet the northwestern leg, in the country of South Sudan, and it will end at the Port Elizabeth seaport in South Africa. Build Africa Together will dredge each of these seaports so they will be capable of accepting container ships loaded with African products and African agriculture products for distribution to a global market."

Amarie then spoke of contract regulations for the distribution centers. "The individual companies that win the bids for these seaport distribution centers will be required to follow pricing guidelines for goods received. The purpose of the pricing stipulations is to ensure that local farmers, meat producers, coffee bean growers and coffee producers, craft makers, and other producers of goods to be sold globally are paid a fair price for their products."

Amarie enthusiastically mentioned some examples to support his previous statement. "The many and varied advantages and limitless possibilities that result from an intra-continental highway system that travels through many African countries will be important not only for that particular country, but for all Africans."

He mentioned agricultural productivity, housing, public health facilities, new export opportunities, and an ambitious range of other profitable industrial possibilities that only an intra-continental highway could provide. Amarie then focused the discussion on the direct advantages the highway would have for Egypt. "We envision the Alexandria seaport to be an important shipping center. A great deal of cooperation between Build Africa Together and your representatives will need to occur prior to highway construction in Egypt, along with seaport improvements. The intra-continental highway director would need to meet with the appropriate Egyptian engineers to plan the pathway of the northwestern highway that will go through Egypt and end at the Alexandria seaport. We are sensitive to the fact that Egypt's existing urban traffic is heavy. We don't want highway construction to interfere with traffic movement, so planning with Egyptian authorities will be important. Much of the Egyptian path of the intra-continental highway may have to be a raised highway, so as not to interfere with local streets. Be assured all of this construction must be approved by Egyptian authorities."

"Mr. Maalout, may I interrupt you for a moment?" asked the Egyptian president."

"Please do, Mr. President, and I would appreciate if you would call me Amarie."

The Egyptian president smiled warmly. "Amarie, I am grateful this highway is planned to run through my country. I feel as you do, a highway will be an important commercial step forward for Egypt and for our continent. Permit me to ask a question pertaining to this highway's rest stops. First, I'm assuming this highway will include petrol stations along its route."

Amarie quickly responded, "Yes, Mr. President."

President Pedibastet said, "Is it the policy of Build Africa Together to operate these petrol stations as
a profitable business?"

Amarie again answered quickly, "No, we do not have plans to operate the petrol stations along the highway. We would prefer the countries where the petrol facilities are located will operate these businesses or if they choose to hire companies or individuals to operate each of their petrol stations."

President Pedibastet replied, "That is wonderful. As I'm certain you are aware, the former Egyptian president was removed from office by our military due to unrest among the Egyptian people. As you might imagine, the result is that my party and his, the Muslim Brotherhood, are currently in an adversarial position which I would very much like to resolve. I have been looking for ways to build a cooperative relationship with the Muslim Brotherhood with the hope that in time, the tensions that now exist between us will improve. With that in mind, I would like to offer the Muslim Brotherhood the opportunity to operate all petrol and rest stop stations located on the highway that runs through Egypt. Perhaps this gesture might be a starting point to bring our parties back to the negotiating table, rather than continuing as enemies which is now the situation."

"Mr. President, I believe that's an excellent idea. The highway director will be designating various places along the highway for these rest stops and petrol stations and I am sure Egypt will have petrol stations located within its borders. However, I'm sure you can understand these rest stops need to be appropriately placed. It would be self-defeating to have them close to each other, which would ultimately benefit no one."

The president seemed satisfied and encouraged Amarie to continue with his description of the highway construction. "I would be interested to hear more specifics about the highway."

Amarie felt he needed to explain the issue of procurement of concrete for the highway construction.

"I know you understand that years under colonial rule have taught our people that bribery and corruption are an integral part of the way African businesses operate. Build Africa Together is attempting to lead by example in our business dealings. We understand changing this practice will be difficult and take time, but perhaps someday the attitude of the African people will change, and our citizens will come to understand the negative effect corruption has on their daily lives."

Amarie continued with the African problem of bribery and corruption in purchasing construction materials for the intra-continental highway. "The beginning construction point and the path of the highway are directly related to this question of corruption and bribery. The first and most important operating procedure of the highway is to hire an African concrete supplier in central Africa who will permit one of our men to regulate the concrete ingredients and amounts used to ensure the road surfaces are able to absorb traffic flow while maintaining the highway's structural integrity. We want the highway's infrastructure to last long after you and I are gone. We first thought of importing our concrete from reputable dealers outside of Africa, but we found this would be much too expensive due to shipping costs."

President Pedibastet did not understand why the location of the concrete manufacturers needed to be located in central Africa. "Shouldn't an Egyptian concrete manufacturer also have the opportunity to be part of the bidding process?"

Amarie said, "That's a legitimate question, and one that demonstrates that as president of Egypt, it is your responsibility to lobby for your citizens. However, we do have a specific reason for this procedure. Let me to explain?"

Amarie was pleased by the president's question as it gave him an opportunity to explain the expertise needed to build a highway through dirt roads and deserts. "Constructing an intra-continental highway in Africa must provide concrete mixing trucks a hard road surface path to their various destinations. Perhaps this seemingly minor point is the reason that Africa is the only continent not to have such a highway running through its borders. To solve this problem, B.A.T.'s highway director chose a concrete manufacturer in the Central African Republic who accepted a quality control person from B.A.T. to monitor all concrete leaving the manufacturer's facility. The Central African Republic's location is critically important. The first concrete truck that leaves the concrete supplier will deposit its load at the front door of the manufacturer and when the first load of concrete has hardened, the second concrete truck will have a hard surfaced road to deliver its payload of concrete at the spot where the first load of concrete ended. This systematic delivery method through the entire continent will ensure that concrete trucks never have to travel on muddy dirt roads and desert sand. Traveling on these surfaces would result in the heavy cement trucks being unable to reach their destination."

When Amarie finished with his explanation, he spread an engineer's drawing of the proposed African intra-continental highway on the tabletop. Then Amarie removed a metal telescoping hand-held pointer from his briefcase and placed it on the mid-highway connector, running through the Central African Republic, which will eventually connect the eastern north/south highway to the long western north/south highway. Amarie's pointer moved to the second connecting highway running through Niger and Chad in northern Africa, connecting the eastern north/south highway to the long north/south western highway, on its way to South Africa.

Amarie then placed his pointer on the port city of Alexandria's deep seaport and ran it in a southerly path through western Sudan. He moved the pointer through western Congo down to the eastern tip of Tanzania, through central Zambia, and then slowly to the eastern tip of Zimbabwe. Finally, his pointer landed on the western tip of Botswana and then moved through east central South Africa, terminating at the deep seaport of Port Elizabeth in South Africa.[2]

Amarie placed his pointer on the mid-eastern spur off the eastern north/south highway at the Indian Ocean shore in Mozambique to Madagascar, and explained. "At this spot we have plans to build a bridge, connected to the highway to Madagascar. The estimated date for bridge construction would be in twenty twenty-four or five."

Amarie finished his explanation by placing his pointer on the four spurs off the eastern north/south highway all traveling to the east shore of Africa and the Indian Ocean. He then moved his pointer to the four connecting highways, giving motorists a roadway to both north/south highways. Finally, he placed his pointer on the two spurs off the western north/south highways that ran to the north eastern shore of Africa at the Atlantic Ocean.

"I fear I have taken too much time of your time explaining the intra-continental highway route. I will not bother you with the specific details pertaining to the construction procedures needed to build a highway through the deep sand of a desert. I will only say the construction process requires special procedures."

The Egyptian president responded to Amarie's suggestion. "Amarie this is such an exciting development for my country, I want to hear how your organization will construct a road through sand."

"I'll try to keep it short. Constructing a highway in a desert requires a precise method of preparation of the highway bed. First, a specific length and width of sand, five feet deep is removed for a distance of approximately fifty yards. This

---

[2] Intra Continental Highway

stretch of dug out sand is then enclosed by the placement of temporary wood borders on each side of the dugout sand. Then nine inches of graveled stones is placed in the dugout section. On top of the nine inches of graveled stones is placed a three-dimensional web-like plastic mat known as a 'cellular confinement system,' developed by the United States Army Corps of Engineers. The 'cellular confinement system' resting on the graveled stones is fastened to the next system by 'hog clamps', which are pounded through the graveled stones until the bottom stake of the 'hog clamp' is buried deep into the sand under the graveled stones. This connection enables the web-like pockets in the plastic cellular mats to remain open.

Concrete is then poured onto the cellular mats filling the web-like pockets and seeping down into the minute spaces between the gravel that the web mat sits on. After the cement in the web-like pockets has settled into the gravel a second level of concrete is placed on the "cellular confinement system" making all web-like pockets level. Once the web-like pockets are level, concrete is poured into the fifty-yard strip, still enclosed by the temporary wood sides, the cement is leveled, to the top of the temporary wood sides. When this top level of concrete has hardened, it becomes an approximately fifty-yard non-movable section of the intra-continental African highway. Workers then proceed to build the next fifty-yard section until the entire highway is completed. This method of roadway construction provides a strong, rigid, stable highway surface for all vehicular traffic.

"The highway running through the Sahara Desert requires a Kevlar-infused, glass semi-circular tunnel structure built over the highway path, protecting vehicles from damage during desert sandstorms."

At the conclusion of Amarie Maalout's visit he stood and thanked President Pedibastet for his cooperation and support of the intra-continental highway. President Pedibastet walked Amarie to the door of his office and asked a question. "Mr. Maalout, I do not understand why so many leaders of African countries have branded you a traitor to Africa and its people. Many accuse you of collaborating with the Catholic Church against our people. Why is this charge being circulated against a man who has proven his loyalty to our continent and its people?"

"Mr. President, some African leaders are threatened by the type of progress B. A. T. represents. This resistance comes from those who believe change will disrupt their ability to maintain their power."

CHAPTER 39

Jon Edwards, Rick Kinsley, and the three sergeant majors returned safely from their five-day intelligence missions and were prepared to meet with the B.A.T. commanders, their executive officers, and Amarie and Roscoe for their intelligence briefing.

The first item on the agenda was a report from the Puntland area of Somalia. Rick and Jon had eight credible names of fishermen who expressed an interest in returning to their fishing jobs.

The next item was Libya. Jon Edwards summarized the current Libyan situation. "A provisional government has been established to maintain some form of stability until the political groups are able to agree on an election process. The lack of cooperation between the numerous groups in Libya has caused a destabilization of the country. There does not seem to be strong support for any official who might be able to unify the splintered groups. Libya remains fragmented. There is no one in Libya able to form a major alliance of Libyans who agree on the formation of political parties. The situation remains the same as it was immediately after the assassination of former president Muammar Gaddafi. The intelligence team strongly recommended B.A.T. not make a move into Libya. Intervention at this time could only serve to add to the confusion that already exists. The intelligence team's recommendation for moving forward in Libya is to contact western nations who might be willing to provide mediation services for the numerous minor groups, who might be interested in some form of collaboration, leading to a vote by the people of Libya.

Rick and Jon moved on to the third agenda item, the Congo, which they painted as a very dangerous place.

Rick explained further, "There are many arbitrary clusters of gangs controlling relatively small areas of the country. A military operation against one gang would automatically threaten neighboring gangs. This would place our offensive units in danger of becoming isolated by the secondary gangs, who could prevent supplies and food reaching our men."

Jon entered the conversation. "These criminal gangs in the Congo consist mostly of kidnapped young

boys and men. The gangs control the people in their area through intimidation, mayhem, and killing whoever resists. They roam their area of control, taking food, forcing other young men to join their crime raids, and creating a great deal of destruction. The land area where these marauders operate covers many kilometers. It's important to note, the vast majority of criminal militia groups do not seem to be cooperating militarily with the M-Twenty-three rebel group. They are the largest militia group in the Congo, but they also have limited support among the people."

Vice Admiral Fisher asked, "Do the Congo military forces perform offensive operations against these roving criminal gangs?"

Rick replied. "We saw very little effort on the part of Congo military units attempting to eliminate this problem, we have to assume the Congo military force is faced with the same problem our troops would encounter; and finally, the Congo area where these groups operate is very large."

The two commanders were grateful for this information and agreed with the intelligence information.

The next item had to do with the intelligence data collected by Rick, Jon, on the Sudan dictator, Omar al-Bashir. Members of the B.A.T. Intelligence team confirmed his brutal attacks against his own people.

Al-Bashir's air force frequently bombs the country of South Sudan, which recently gained their independence from Sudan. Sudanese soldiers arbitrarily murder South Sudanese people.

Jon gave some statistics collected on their visit to South Sudan. "More than two million citizens of the world's newest country have been displaced, and food is scares for approximately three million people. Although al-Bashir is responsible for many of these deaths, not all the blame rests on his shoulders. The catastrophe in South Sudan is partly the fault of South Sudan's new president, who was considered a moderate leader who would bring peace to his people. However, president Salva Kiir, with help from rebels, has recently cracked down on the people of South Sudan." Jon finished the Sudan report by saying, "South Sudan President Salva Kiir is suspected of instigating civil war in South Sudan. The tragedy in Sudan and South Sudan is the failure of both leaders."

Master Sergeant Wilkinson, a member of the intelligence team, asked if he could add to the al-Bashir report. Amarie encouraged him to continue. "The ruler of Sudan has proven to be one blood thirsty bastard who rules by fear and intimidation, murdering anyone who he thinks has spoken out against him. I believe I can speak for the other members of the intelligence team in saying that if this character is allowed to remain in power, he will simply continue the brutal murder of his people and the people of South Sudan."

Amarie suggested, "It might be useful if we were to secure the legal authority to act against al-Bashir. I have contacts in the Sudanese judicial system who feel intimidated by al Bashir. I believe I would be able to obtain this authority, from the Sudanese Supreme Court, and I am sure it would make The Hague trial that much stronger."

Roscoe took control of the meeting. "Gentlemen, we have a good deal of intelligence on Sudan and South Sudan. I suggest we ask our two B.A.T. commanders to confer on this matter and determine if they need further intelligence. If so, Rick and Jon may have to return to South Sudan. Now, if there are no further comments, Roscoe glanced at the members around the table, and seeing no raised arms. "Okay, let's get back to work."

CHAPTER 40

Both B.A.T. commanders, their executive officers, segreant majors, and Jon Edwards and Rick Kinsley met early on the morning of January 9, 2012. The twelve men had been working together in Africa for eleven months; there was one agenda item for this meeting. Approval by the co-managers of the plan to remove Omar al-Bashir as president of Sudan. Roscoe would then inform the Vatican team of the plan.

There were three important strategies included in the plan. One, eliminate a direct battle with the Sudanese military. Two, Sudan Supreme Court must agree to swear in a provisional president at precisely the same hour that dictator Omar al-Bashir had been physically removed as President of Sudan. Three, Securing the Capitol building during Omar al-Bashir removal from office. After a careful review of the Sudan plan, the co-managers approved the plan, next step, informing the Vatican team.

The plan will guarantee, that the day after al-Bashir's removal would be a normal day for the Sudanese people. The one exception to a normal day, would be an announcement informing the people of Sudan that Omar al-Bashir has been removed from his presidential position; and at 4: A.M. this morning, the Sudan Supreme Court had sworn in a provisional president of Sudan, with democratic elections to follow. The Sudanese military, has been demobilized, and all military facilities have been closed. The provisional president will run the Sudanese government from a secure, secret location until next week, when the United Nations will verify the transfer of power, to the provisional president.

The Vatican team had been previously informed, and agreed to remove the dictator, all that remained for the Vatican team, was a general explanation of the approved plan. Amarie would not be present during the explanation of the plan to the Vatican team, he would be traveling to a secret location for his meeting with the Sudan judiciary. During this secret meeting there was serious and intense discussion between Amarie and the Sudan Supreme on their role in the plan. In the event that al-Bashir had planted an operative inside the Sudan judiciary, Amarie provide the Supreme Court members with a false date of the military operation against Omar al-Bashir.

Three days after the meeting between Amarie and the Sudan Supreme Court, a selected number of judiciary will covertly travel to the southernmost section of Sudan to meet with the Nuba Mountain rebel group, the strongest anti al-Bashir group in Sudan. The Sudan judiciary and the Nuba Mountain rebel group were able to agree on the selection of a provisional Sudanese leader, a constitutional format and, once again a false date arranged by Amarie of swearing in the new provisional president.

After all details of the involvement of the Sudanese Supreme Court had been agreed to, Amarie explained an important aspect of the plan. "I want you all to know that Both of our commanders have received accurate intelligence information, which has determined the day and time of the planned removal of the Omar al-Bashir; and as the plan has emphasized. If a country suddenly finds itself without leadership, even for the shortest amount of time, history has proven, that this leads to chaos in the form of nationwide civil unrest, and others claiming the presidential seat. We don't want this to occur in Sudan after word gets out the Omar al-Bashir has been removed. For this reason, Build Africa Together's second military unit, will as part of the plan, secure the Sudanese Capitol building, as the capture of Omar al-Bashir is taking place. if Sudanese soldiers on guard at the capitol building, were informed that al-Bashir residence had been attacked, they may have standing orders take over the Capitol building, barricading entrances and exits, making the government building inaccessible."

On January 22, 2012 at precisely the 2 A.M. a B.A.T. Ranger was cutting a hole in the back fence of al-Bashir's compound. When the opening was finished, nine Rangers wearing night goggles quietly passed through the fence opening. Three Rangers moved straight ahead for approximately fifty yards and took up a position in front of the rear door exit of the compound. Four other Rangers moved quickly to the two doors of the military barracks and activated their AJ-3 audio jammer, which will block all cell phone signals, including smart phones that may have Internet capabilities. The other two Rangers moved cautiously along the side of the residence wall leading to the front of al-Bashir's home. They stopped at the corner of the house and took a quick glance to see if Sudanese military personnel were positioned at the building entrance. A covered light above the front door illuminated the area. Seeing no guards, they continued along the front side of the residence, ducking under a dark window and then positioning themselves at the double front door entrance. In forty seconds, all nine men were now in position, anticipating the sound of crashing the metal fence and gunshots. Those sounds would be their cue to go into action.

At precisely 2:12 A.M. the drivers of five 2.5-ton War Pig trucks, which had been parked a quarter of a mile down the road to the front entrance of al-Bashir's compound, started their motors. The lead truck driver put his vehicle in gear and sped toward the front gate of the dictator's compound, making a sharp left-hand turn, and aimed the front of the truck directly at the locked gates. The first three War Pig trucks held twenty-two men who had hunkered down in the beds of the trucks. The fourth War Pig truck was empty, except for three Rangers prone on their stomachs, peering out of three-square holes that had been cut out of the swing-down rear metal gate of the truck, so their AK47s could bring down any guards from the gatehouse that fired on the speeding trucks after they had passed through the open compound gate.

The first truck drove immediately to the military barracks to support the four Rangers stationed at the two doors of the barracks. Metal door busters flattened both doors. Most of the Sudanese soldiers were sitting up in bed, rubbing the sleep from their eyes. A few men from the lower bunk beds were scrambling for their pants. With fifteen AK-47s pointed in their faces, they got down from their beds and stood in the center aisle with hands raised. Several the Sudanese military pressed the distress signal from their cell phones as they slowly got out of their beds but the audio jammers, with their small antennas, worked perfectly.

When the three men stationed at the bedroom exits heard the first War Pig truck crashing through the front gates, they broke down the back doors and dashed up the exit stairs to the three-bedroom doors. A whooping sound of helicopter blades could be heard as a B.A.T. helicopter was landing in front of the rear doors to the building. One Ranger entered each bedroom of the residence. The Ranger in the far-right bedroom, found Omar al-Bashir slowly wakening from a deep sleep, brought on by too much alcohol at the earlier state dinner, and a woman sitting erect with the bed covers at her shoulders. The Ranger soldier grabbed the Sudanese dictator, pressed his weapon into the back of the dictator's head, and ran him down the back exit stairs.

The truck carrying the three prone Rangers stopped abruptly in front of the double door entrance to the main compound building. The three Rangers jumped out of the truck to support the posted Ranger at al-Bashir's front entrance doors. The posted Ranger peppered the door lock mechanism with his AK-47 and kicked the doors open. The four Rangers stood in a row pointing their weapons at three Sudanese soldiers that were about to run down the steps of the compound. They immediately came to a stop when they saw the rangers, raised their hands high above their heads, and slowly moved down the curved stairs.

Meanwhile, the three rangers pushed al-Bashir into the back seat of the helicopter and jumped into the seats on either side of him. The noise of the rotating helicopter blades was deafening as the helicopter left the ground some fifty-five seconds after it had landed and started on its way to the prison facility at B.A.T. 1. The sound of the helicopter blades in full throttle rising from the grounds of the dictator's compound was the signal for all B.A.T. soldiers to begin loading the off-duty Sudanese prisoners from the military barracks, along with the other Sudanese military that had been on duty, in the front of the residence. All three soldiers were being pushed into the five War Pig trucks. Each sergeant major in the trucks took a head count of B.A.T. soldiers. The sergeant major in the first truck, after receiving a signal from the sergeant major in the second truck, to move out, immediately slapped the top of the truck cab, and the five trucks were on the road heading back to Baledogle.

At 5:00 a.m., Vice Admiral Fisher and the three hundred men of B.A.T. 2 arrived at the Sudan Capitol building. They quickly took defensive positions behind the concrete Jersey barriers, circling the building, placed they're for protection against car bombs.

At the end of the first day of the al-Bashir's removal, Sudan had remained calm. A provisional president had assumed a peaceful transition of power. B.A.T. 2 forces, with their newly painted blue United Nations helmets, remained at their defensive positions for two days along with a contingent of United Nation soldiers. A military unit from B.A.T. 1 joined the B.A.T. 2 personnel during the morning of the second of the provisional government. If the streets of Sudan remained as calm as the first two days of the transfer of leadership, a smaller contingent of B.A.T. special operation soldiers would remain on duty at the capitol building for the remainder of the week.

Operation Omar al-Bashir was successful, and Amarie had used the past ten days encouraging a team of United Nations representatives to supervise Khartoum, the capitol city of Sudan. The United Nations chose not to challenge the charade B.A.T. used in the operation. There were two negative aspects to the removal of al-Bashir. One was the resistance of quite a few African countries at the United Nations Assembly, protesting the action and deception of the so-called humanitarian organization. The other was that the curtain had been completely pulled back, exposing the long-rumored military might of the Vatican's humanitarian organization in Africa.

CHAPTER 41

Roscoe picked up the phone and called his friend, Dr. Tom Claffey in California. Tom answered on the third ring. The friends exchanged greetings and caught up on each other's most recent activities before getting down to the reason for the call.

"Tom, I'm ready to meet with your Doctor Adair. I've called Clay, we had a wonderful conversation, catching up. I mentioned I was considering to hire Doctor Adair, asked if he had anything to add. He told me all he had on Adair was paperwork. He's never met him, so he was unable to add anything further, and he suggested I get back to you. I was glad I called, as we had not seen each other for eight or nine years, we had a few laughs, talking about old times. Tom, do you have a few minutes to add anything to your earlier comments?"

"I believe I gave you the essence of Doctor Adair. I could go on with accomplishments and awards, but I feel all of that would have no bearing on your decision. You really need to meet him. It's the only way for you to decide if you and your crew can put up with him. Let me repeat one important point I made during our last phone conversation, don't underestimate or disregard anything he has to say. I can certainly understand if you were to decide he is too much of a bother, but I guarantee that his mind and work ethic will never let you down. I just thought of something else that you may find useful, and knowing you, this may be too 'loosey-goosey' for you, but here goes. If you decide to take a shot with the young man, all you need to do is outline what you expect. Don't get caught up with details. All he needs to know is a sketch of the details, and then stay out of his way. I believe whatever you decide to pay him will be money well spent."

When Roscoe hung up the phone, he was still unsure how to conduct the interview, and was somewhat surprised at Tom's laissez-faire approach to Dr. Adair. Roscoe knew Tom to be very task orientated when dealing with employees. He sat staring into space for a few moments thinking.

It's very out of character for Tom to be this informal. He usually is rather specific when it comes to employment candidates. It's also odd that he would not be more precise on how best to respond to Dr. Adair, that's not like Tom. I was expecting some direction on dealing with a candidate who was afflicted with autism.

Not five minutes had passed when Roscoe's phone rang, it was Tom Claffey again.

"Tom, I'm glad you called back. I was somewhat confused by your evaluation of Doctor Adair, perhaps you could give me more details on the young doctor?"

"I called you back to give you some information on his parents, so let's start with them. I don't think I ever mentioned his father. He's a pretty interesting character. Back in the seventies, his father, whose name is William, was considered one of the boy wonders of those new things we now call personal computers. As a young man living in England, Wang International, a Massachusetts computer company that in the seventies was one of the major players in the computer industry, recruited Doctor Adair's father and brought him to the states. When they went out of business some years later, William Adair returned to, let's see, it says here he went to Sheffield, England, with an American wife. They had a child named Matilda. His father began to do some individual contract work, until he was offered a job with a tech start up in Sheffield. He quickly earned a reputation for knowing his way around computer security, specializing in building firewalls. A few years later, the Adair's bought a farm in Wales with grazing land and horse stables that his wife rented out, and Jem's father quit his job, and began consulting work on computer security.

Roscoe changed the subject, back to the boy wonder. "Why would a university like UCLA spend the time and effort on a candidate with such unusual personality issues?"

Doctor Claffey explained. "It's not unusual for a prestigious university to seek out and track child geniuses, especially a youngster like Jem, who had been evaluated and certified by credible sources. At four years of age, he was identified as being on the autism spectrum, but that would not scare off a university. Schools are willing to provide specialists to assist with this type of candidate in the hope that the prodigy would be able to design something unique or present a new theory for study. With the chance of a breakthrough accomplishment, the school benefits greatly by the publicity and productivity."

Tom then gave Roscoe a brief history of the young candidate. "Before his first birthday, Jem Adair was teaching himself to read. He progressed rapidly, at an early age, he resisted most social interaction with other children. In school, he acted very awkwardly during the school's recess periods. Jem would frequently be found bouncing with an open hand along the ridges of the school yard fence, talking in low tones as if he were telling himself an imaginary story. When he wasn't walking along the fence, he was often seen alone on the grass, walking in a circle, with his hands and arms flying about. There is a handwritten note. I suspect it came from a high school psychologist. It reads: *James Adair is unable or refuses to, discuss his abnormal social skills or brain activity that often dominates his demeanor."*

Roscoe then asked Tom. "What happened after high school?"

Tom said, "His parents, especially his mother, were concerned the university systems in the United Kingdom and Western Europe were not equipped to deal with their child. They were pleased with the services we were prepared to offer. It was a hard decision, sending such a young child to the United States for a higher education experience, but they eventually thought UCLA offered the proper services for their son's continued growth. What tipped the scales was when we offered to pay for an apartment on campus for his mother, allowing her to be with him during his first year at UCLA. So, at age twelve he entered UCLA. He matriculated in our geology studies program, and finished his undergraduate requirements in two and a half years. He was then accepted into the master's degree program studying natural resources, and completing all requirements in one year. He then was accepted into our doctoral program, again studying natural resources. Now comes the 'kicker.' He requested to study for his Doctorate, not in California, but in Africa. The faculty accept his application, and also provided his traveling expenses to and from the African continent. His parents were concerned that a boy his age should not be on his own, moving around western Africa, the compromise was that his mother would spend the first six months with him in Africa, she was concerned for his safety. She left Africa after six months later, encouraged by how comfortable her son seemed to be with Africans and most importantly, how the African people accepted and protected him. His father,

William, told me that Africans have successfully integrated my son in their lives, much more effectively than the British or Americans. The African people refer to my son as, 'the bare footed white man, who protects our continent's natural beauty."

Roscoe was surprised to hear about the change in his social skills among the African people.

Tom said, "Well, I think they African's knew immediately they were dealing with a special white child, and his mother felt confident that living with Africans would improve his social skills."

Tom added, "The specialized doctoral program I set up for him required that he return to UCLA after one year in Africa, to deliver a mid-term report on his African studies. The doctoral committee was quite impressed. At the end of his second year in the Ph.D. program, he returned to UCLA to present his orals and complete his written dissertation, and was granted his doctor's degree in June, 2009 at the age of seventeen. I believe he was more excited to be going back to Africa than receiving his doctorate degree.

CHAPTER 42

Roscoe called his friend Doctor Tom Claffey and informed him he had contacted Doctor Adair and was meeting with him the following day. Tom hoped their meeting would go well, and he reminded Roscoe to be prepared for Doctor Adair's unusual social interaction and not to take any of his abnormal social quirks personally.

Roscoe was not focusing on his meeting with Doctor Adair. The thought lingering in his mind was the failure to find a solution to the irrigation of the tropical savannas. He kept wondering if he, Amarie, and the water director had exhausted every possible solution.

Still, Roscoe promised his friend that he would meet with Doctor Adair, even though he didn't know how he could use him, and how to deal with his social mannerisms.

When Doctor Adair entered Roscoe's outer office, a man in military fatigues greeted him.

"Good morning, sir. How may I help you?"

Doctor Adair remained standing at the open door, staring at the floor, frozen in place, thinking, *if I move toward the soldier, he may want to shake my hand. I don't like soldiers, they hurt people.*

The man in military fatigues waited for the ragged, barefoot young man to respond.

Doctor Adair remained stoic and silent standing rigid at the open door. The soldier, confused, repeated his question one more time.

Eventually, the ragged looking man, still standing erect in the open doorway, with the screen door resting against his back, whispered, "Mr. Ayala."

The soldier said, "Pardon me, sir, I could not make out what you said."

The young man at the door suddenly blurted, in a loud voice, "Roscoe Ayala!"

The B.A.T. soldier assigned to Roscoe's office said, "Oh, yes, you must be Doctor Adair. Mr. Ayala is expecting you."

Doctor Adair remained in the open doorway, seemingly ignoring the military soldier's invitation into the office.

The soldier didn't know if he had said something to upset the man with a British accent. The soldier couldn't help but take a closer look at the man standing at the open front door. The bright African sun at Doctor Adair's back caused his body to be silhouetted for a moment making it difficult for the soldier to clearly see the visitor.

The soldier could only recognize that the man in the doorway was tall, thin, and had bare feet. With the soldier's eyes now in focus, he saw the young man was wearing shredded pants that came down to his lower calf. Jem's shirt was tucked into his pants on one side, the worn shirt hung over a colorful cloth belt on the other side. The spotted shirt looked as though he had worn it far too long between washings. Attached to his colorful belt hung a flashlight and an attractive pearl handle knife in a scabbard. Doctor Adair had a handsome face that looked as though it needed a washing. A four-day crop of stubble covered his long face.

The soldier decided to alert Roscoe and knocked on his office door.

Upon hearing the knock, Roscoe said, "Come in," expecting it to be Doctor Adair.

The soldier entered Roscoe's office and said, "There is a man standing at the open door to the outer office. I believe he wants to speak with you." Roscoe moved quickly into the outer office and saw the ragged looking young man standing perfectly still in the doorway. Doctor Adair's gaze fixed on the floor somewhere past his feet. The young man thought, *I don't want to look up, sometimes I get frightened looking into the eyes of strangers.*

Roscoe walked up to him slowly and greeted the young doctor. "Hello, Doctor Adair. Why don't you come with me so we can sit in my office and talk?"

The Welsh doctor cautiously followed Roscoe, his eyes still staring at the floor. After both men had entered Roscoe's office, he closed the door, and encouraged Doctor Adair to sit in the chair in front of his desk. The young Ph.D. moved toward the chair thinking, *Good, now I won't have to shake his hand.* After sitting, Jem Adair glanced over his shoulder toward the entrance door, and said to himself. *I'm glad the soldier has left the room.*

The military receptionist had returning to the outer office thinking. *I wonder what kind of a doctor that character is. He looks like he's been rolling around in the African brown dirt.*

Roscoe said. "I hope you don't mind if I remain standing, sitting behind my desk, causes my ankles to swell, so I prefer to stand. Doctor Adair decided not to comment, but was quite interested in Roscoe's very high desk, and the big wall map of Africa, behind Mr. Ayala. Suddenly Doctor Adair stood, and moving past Roscoe, he was now close to, and remained staring at the wall map of Africa for approximately twenty seconds. Doctor Adair quickly returned to the chair in front of Roscoe's desk and sat quietly. The moments of

340

silence made Roscoe uncomfortable. So, he said, "I see you find my map of Africa interesting."

The Welsh Doctor's first words were, "You have to get a new map, because yours has two mistakes."

Roscoe thought, *oh, this is going to be an interesting interview!* Roscoe then said, "I'm glad you noticed the errors. Can you point them out to me?" Doctor Adair, pleased that this man had agreed and did not debate his comment, said, "The Tropic of Capricorn runs through the lower part of Mozambique and Madagascar. Your map has the Tropic of Capricorn running higher than it should be in those two countries."

Roscoe, trying to be as encouraging as possible, said, "Well, then you're right, I'll have to get a new map. I'm certainly glad you noticed, and pointed out the error. If not for you, I never would have noticed that mistake. Thank you, Doctor. I'm pleased you brought that to my attention."

Jem Adair did not answer, but his mind was very engaged. *Roscoe seems like a nice man. He respects my knowledge. Not like others, who would disagree when I told them their map had errors.* Once again Roscoe was painfully aware of the silence after his comment, but he did not understand that the young doctor's mind was actively working, even if he was not speaking. Roscoe broke the moments of silence once again, and asked the doctor a question "Why don't you tell me about yourself?"

With that comment from Roscoe, the doctor's mind went on a new tangent. *Wish he hadn't asked that question. I don't know what he is expecting.* Not hearing an immediate response to his question, Roscoe continued, "For instance, what made you come to Africa, and what do you like about the continent?"

Doctor Adair continued looking at the floor. *I wish I knew how he expects me to answer his question.*

Roscoe now accepted there would be periods of silence when speaking with the doctor, so he remained quiet until the young man responded.

Jem Adair quietly responded, "I like Africa. The people are nice. I'm interested in learning all the things in the African ground."

Roscoe thought, *this topic of natural resources is a good topic to get the young man responding.* So, he continued with this line of questions. "What are some of the things in the African ground that you explore?" Doctor Adair looked up from the floor, meeting the eyes of Roscoe for the first time. Doctor Adair thought, *His eyes are not as scary as I thought they would be. I guess it's okay to tell him. He seems like a nice man.*

Jem Adair then responded, "Diamonds in Sierra Leone, Angola, and Botswana. Also, there is a good deal of iron, cobalt, uranium, bauxite, silver, gold, oil, and water, in those African countries. There is something important in every country in Africa. That's what I like most about Africa."

The doctor rose from his chair and walked over to the map on the wall behind Roscoe's desk. First, Jem pointed to the country of Zambia. "I tried to tell the mining people this country had the most copper ore in Africa."

Looking at his finger still resting on the map over Zambia, he Frowned, and said, "I don't know why those mining engineers didn't want the copper. I told them, all they had to do was dig, and then they would believe me. Other men got mad at me and told me I no longer worked for them. I still don't understand why they didn't want me to work with them"

Doctor Adair suddenly had a surprised look on his face, as though he had said something he should not have mentioned. He quickly returned his eyes to the map and began to rapidly point and call out countries and their natural resources. "Katanga, more copper. Nigeria, oil. Central African Republic, bauxite and silver. Congo, ecosystems and chemicals to take away disease." Doctor Adair moved his finger to another country. Now roscoe became impatient, and thought. *He might go on for the next hour pointing and naming natural resources.* The former president tried to find a place to ask him a question, but Doctor Adair was continuing at a brisk pace. Pointing to Sudan, he said, "Cobalt." Pointing to the Sahara Desert, he said, "salt and water." pointing to Kenya..." Roscoe interrupted as the doctor was about to continue.

"I apologize for interrupting you, but you said, salt and water when you pointed to the Sahara Desert. I wonder if that was just an error, because you were going so fast. Obviously, there is no water in the Sahara Desert, only sand.

Doctor Adair paused for a three-second quick thought. *Oh, now I'm going to have to tell him he's wrong.*

After this hesitation, Jem Adair added, matter-of-factly, "When I walk in the Sahara Desert, there are places where my feet tingle, sometimes for a mile or more. That's how I know there is water deep under the sand in the Sahara Desert. Even though the water is deep in the ground, my bare feet can feel the movement of the water."

Jem looked down at his feet. "My feet feel the very little movement of sand, like the sand has waves where there is underground water, and that's why I feel a tingling sensation on my feet. My feet are sensitive. They seem connected to things under-ground. That's why I walk with no shoes in Africa, and this helps me to know what is in the ground. Isn't this an amazing continent?"

Doctor Adair looked up from his bare feet, past Roscoe, and stared directly at the map of Africa, looking towards Kenya. Roscoe quickly asked a question. "You said your feet tingle when you walk a mile or more. Does that mean you're telling me there is a mile-long area of water under the ground in the Sahara?"

Doctor Adair, continuing to stare at the map, did not answer Roscoe's question immediately. To fill

the silent period Roscoe asked a second question. "Was it difficult to walk a mile in the sand with your feet tingling? Does the tingling hurt your feet?" The young doctor quiet for a few moments, thinking, *this man askes a lot of questions,* then answered, "Oh no, it doesn't hurt my feet, but I don't know how wide or deep the water is. My feet don't tell me that.

Roscoe was discouraged. *This young man may be smart, but he may also be a little off-center in that autistic head of his.*

Roscoe, then stammered out, "Uh, I, I may not know, as much as you seem to know about Africa's natural resources but claiming there is a large water deposit under the sands of the Sahara is rather more than I can believe. For instance, if there is water in the Sahara, where did the water come from? It doesn't rain in the Sahara."

Doctor Adair looked at Roscoe and said, "In the first millennium, part of the Sahara Desert was the ocean we now call the North Atlantic Ocean, and the Mediterranean Sea."

Roscoe made an effort to remain interested, even though he could not believe the young man. *The young doctor is fantasizing, or perhaps trying to impress me, about tingling feet and underground water in the Sahara Desert. I wonder how he knew we need water for the tropical savannas!*

With a disapproving look, Roscoe once again chose to break the silence. "When you realized there was water in the Sahara did you attempt to dig a well to use for drinking water?"

Doctor Adair was a young man whose thinking process was very literal. His response was stoic and honest. "Oh, no, I don't have the proper drilling equipment to do that, but there's a university in London that could do that for you."

At his point, Roscoe mentally debating how to end the interview, he was certain he would have no use for a young man with tingling feet.

Then suddenly Roscoe remembered what Tom Claffey said: *"Don't underestimate or disregard anything he has to say. I learned that the hard way."*

The silent seconds ticked away as Roscoe was now conflicted. *Should I quickly end this interview, or be patient a little while longer, I don't want to discourage this poor young man.* During this brief interlude, Jem Adair was thinking, *Mr. Ayala seems like a smart man. Why would he think I could dig a well that deep? He must be smart to have been an American president. However, he doesn't know much about underground water.*

As Roscoe tried gathering his thoughts, the young doctor spoke, repeating, "Whenever I walk over a piece of land that has underground water, my feet get the same tingling feeling. That happens a lot in Africa. There is a good deal of underground water in Africa. I said the Sahara Desert because my feet tell me, that is the place having the most water under the ground. Kenya probably has the next largest amount of water under the ground."

Before Roscoe had a chance to respond, Doctor Adair changed the subject. "Why do you have a soldier in your building? Do you also have an army like the African dictators? I don't like soldiers.

They kill people."

Roscoe realized military personnel was on Doctor Adair's mind and that it might be wise to explain why Build Africa

Together has a military force. "Our military men are here to protect the African people against some of the dictators and warlords who harm and kill the good African people."

Doctor Adair was listening intently, and Roscoe noticed that during his explanation of how B.A.T. used their military, the young doctor suddenly seemed much more relaxed.

Roscoe was anxious to get back to the water, trying his best to be non-confrontational in his questioning. "Doctor Adair, I respect your background and knowledge in this area. I hope you can understand if I wish to verify your belief of a large underground water reserve in the Sahara, I will need a specific area if I decided to drill a well. I'm assuming when you say underground water, you're suggesting it can be reached? If that's true, could you be more specific where this water is located."

Again, a look of frustration crossed Doctor Adair's face and he remained silent, much to the chagrin of the former president. This silence allowed the doctor to listen to his brain. *Just like Americans and Germans, he doesn't trust the things I say. Not like the African people, who accept me and my knowledge of their continent. African people believe me, but Germans and Americans, I guess, are untrusting people.*

Suddenly, Doctor Adair rose from his chair. He looked at Roscoe's desktop and noticed an unopened stack of mail in a small wire basket. Without saying a word, he scooped up the top envelope that was in the basket, one that was unopened. Doctor Adair removed a pen from Roscoe's desk blotter. Turned the envelope over, and on the unwritten side of the envelope, began to write.

Roscoe was surprised and a bit annoyed, when Jem Adair took the unopened envelope and pen from his desk, but decided not mention his annoyance. Doctor Adair was continuing to write on the back of the envelope. *If this young man is intent on writing something, I'll just let him finish his writing. Tom Claffey was right. Boy, this character is very unusual.* After a few moments of writing, the young doctor handed

the unopened envelope to Roscoe. He had written longitude and latitude coordinates and spoke. "The coordinates I wrote on the paper are in the country of Libya. Roscoe noticed a brief written text under the last latitude and longitude coordinates. It read, *there are two other countries that have water under the sand of the Sahara Desert, but Libya has the largest amount of water under the Sahara Desert.*

Roscoe was impressed that Doctor Adair was able to record coordinates without referring to a map but then thought, *they're only numbers on an envelope. How do I know he didn't just scribble down latitude and longitude numbers, trying to impress me for a job? Who knows what he is thinking?*

Roscoe knew very little about the condition called autism that made some individuals act unusual. Many individuals on the autism spectrum have minds that function differently than non-autistic people; People who have this condition often have the rare ability to focus intensely on a specific topic, and frequently have above average intelligence.

Roscoe found it difficult to accept what the young doctor had said about the underground water in the Sahara and his tingling feet. *Is this young man authentic? I'll bet he is trying to play me for a job?*

Roscoe believed the young doctor was intelligent, but how could tingling feet detect water, and under the Sahara, no less. Roscoe decided it was necessary to confront the doctor directly while trying to remain non-confrontational.

Jem Adair stood erect, his fingers tapping lightly next to the wire basket on Roscoe's desk during this long minute of silence.

Roscoe broke the silence.

"Please forgive me if I'm not speaking properly to you, but in the short period of time you have been in my office, it is clear to me you are very intelligent and you are very knowledgeable about natural resources. However, you seem nervous, or perhaps you're uncomfortable with me."

Roscoe continued trying to be as diplomatic as possible. "I'm not challenging or trying to test you. Doctor Claffey has told me of your brilliant mind, so it's not necessary to impress me by saying your feet tingle when you walk over underground water. If I'm the cause of your statement about water in the Sahara Desert, I apologize. Perhaps we should start over and you can tell me how you can be of assistance to us.

CHAPTER 43

Doctor Adair did not answer but remained silent, not allowing anyone or anything that he found confusing to enter his mind.

I wonder what he means by saying I'm trying to impress him. Why do I need to impress him?

Standing rigid, Doctor Adair continued his thought process, *I don't understand. He talks pleasantly, but sometimes he can be troubling.*

During this short period of silence, the young doctor continued standing next to Roscoe's desk, gazing at the floor rather than at Roscoe.

Soon Roscoe could take the silence no longer. "I'm very sorry if I offended you. It's just that I'm wondering how your skills can be of value to our organization."

While still gazing intently at the floor, Doctor Adair spoke, "I can't be of any value to you if you don't believe what I say."

Roscoe choose to respond with a question. "Are you referring to the tingling feet and water in the Sahara?"

Doctor Adair finally looked at Roscoe. "Yes. all you have to do is go to the longitude and latitude numbers I gave you and see for yourself. That's why I wrote them down, so you would know I'm correct in saying there is a great amount of underground water in Africa. I know you don't want me to work for you, so I'll just leave."

The doctor turned, arms moving in animated gestures, and walked away from Roscoe's desk. It was as though someone threw a switch in his body, causing the silent, erect young doctor to become a different person. With his back to Roscoe and walking away from the desk, he started mumbling.

"I'm happy when I'm with African people. They are so honest about how they feel. They speak with few words and believe what they say. They don't get angry with me when I want to be alone to think. I know they will still like me the next day. I never met people like Africans; I wish everyone would be like them!"

Roscoe understood the mumbling, raising his voice saying, "Thank you, Doctor Adair, I understand how you feel. I also like people who never get angry with me."

This last statement made Doctor Adair more relaxed, and he turned to Roscoe. "Then you know how I feel when you obviously don't believe what I am saying. Doctor Claffey would believe me if he was here with us." In the next thirty seconds of silence in the office Roscoe was pondering, how *do I tell this young man that he could not be of any use to B.A.T.*

Roscoe was drawing a blank, so he suggested, "Doctor Adair, I would love to have you as my guest for lunch. Perhaps we can talk more about the natural resources of Africa." Doctor Adair nodded his head yes, and both men leisurely walked to the cafeteria at B.A.T 2 headquarters. During lunch in the large cafeteria, with many soldiers enjoying their meals, Jem told Roscoe he did not want to sit with the soldiers, and he asked Roscoe if they could sit at that small empty table located by the window. Roscoe agreed and as the two passed through the lunch line, Roscoe asked one of the servers about a food item as the young doctor continued walking, not realizing Roscoe had hesitated. Roscoe whispered to the server, "Pass the word, no one is to sit at our table."

Roscoe found it difficult to maintain a conversation during their lunch, feeling guilty, knowing he would eventually have to tell Doctor Adair, that he could be of no help to their project. After approximately fifteen minutes of Doctor Adair enjoying his large portions of food, Roscoe said, "I'm confident in your skills and knowledge, but the question still remains unclear to me regarding how you can add to our efforts in Africa. If I were to hire you, the salary would be sixty thousand American dollars per year plus room and board. However, let me say, before either of us agrees to this employment, you are most welcome to be my guest at our quarters for as long as you like. Perhaps we can continue to talk after you had a chance to enjoy a hot shower and a comfortable night's sleep?"

The young doctor looked at Roscoe with a surprised frown. "That's a lot of money to pay someone because they know about natural resources. I know everything there is to know about the natural resources of Africa. If you have a question about the natural resources in Africa, just ask me now. You don't have to pay me to tell you what Africa has in its ground."

Roscoe tried to appeal to Jem's practical nature. "If you were to become a member of our project, I would feel obliged to pay you a salary."

"I'm willing to be part of your project, but before I agree, you must do one thing. I can tell you don't believe there is a great amount of water underground in the Sahara Desert and I can only work for you if you believe that what I tell you is true."

Roscoe cringed and thought, *Oh great. He thinks I've offered him a job. Now what? How can I possibly say I don't need him?*

After lunch, Roscoe made an excuse that he was busy, and suggested once again that he wanted the young doctor to remain. Roscoe needed time to put in a call to Tom Claffey and get his advice. Roscoe invited the doctor to stay overnight and told him this would give me time to think about drilling for water in the Sahara Desert.

Doctor Adair agreed, saying, "It would feel good to be able to take a shower. I have not found a place to take a shower for about three weeks."

Before Roscoe entered the barracks hallway, he cracked the door open to see if any men in military fatigues were visible. The two men quickly scooted to the second door. Roscoe opened the door, looking again for anyone in military fatigues. Seeing no one, Roscoe moved quickly, followed by Doctor Adair who was thinking. *This man walks very fast, I guess it's similar to not wanting his ankles to get big. I must go fast if I wish to remain by his side, I hope the room is not far away.*

Roscoe opened a hallway door to a room and told the young doctor this could be his room for as long as he wanted, and he is welcomed in the cafeteria, for as long as you stay with us.

Roscoe returned to his office after he had settled the young man in the empty room. He immediately called Tom Claffey and got his voice mail. Roscoe explained he had a meeting with Doctor Adair and needed advice. Tom got back to his friend later that afternoon, Africa time. Roscoe and Tom Claffey had a long talk on the subject of the young doctor.

Tom Claffey finished the conversation by saying. "I mentioned once before, don't disregard anything Doctor Adair has to say. Water underneath the Sahara also sounds crazy to me, but if it were me, in your situation, I would drill in the Sahara, drilling won't cost you a fortune?"

Doctor Adair enjoyed his overnight stay at the B.A.T. 2 facility, especially the hot shower and the comfortable mattress. The following morning Doctor Adair went straight to Roscoe's office to wait until he arrived. It was ten after nine when Roscoe entered the room, the Welshman stood erect and asked if he could speak with him for a few minutes, promising Roscoe he would not take long. Roscoe and Jem Adair entered Roscoe's inner office, and the autistic doctor followed Roscoe and sat at the seat in front of Roscoe's desk.

Roscoe was interested to see if Doctor Adair had a sense of humor, so the first thing he said was, "I haven't had time to buy a new map, but I do intend to get a new one this week."

Doctor Adair simply replied, "You won't be sorry. Do it as soon as you can."

Roscoe smiled and cleared his throat.

Jem Adair said, "I know you feel both sorry and bothered at the same time by the way I act with people."

There was a surprised look on Roscoe's face; he was momentarily embarrassed by the doctor's comment. He thought for a moment, noticing the young doctor was shoeless and wearing the same disheveled clothes as yesterday.

The kid hit it right on the head. He even used the same words I had said to myself, sorry and bothered.

Roscoe recovered quickly, and said, "You're not only a very bright young man, but you're very observant."

A very small smile creased the corner of the doctor's lips, the second time this had occurred over these two days. Roscoe thought this to be a positive sign. He also noticed Jem Adair no longer looked down at the floor when talking to him, another good sign. Perhaps the young man was beginning to feel more comfortable.

Roscoe was about to say, *"You should laugh more often,"* but at the last minute he held back for fear his comment might be misinterpreted by the young doctor. He then changed the subject. "I have been thinking about drilling for water in the Sahara Desert. Is there some tangible evidence, no matter how small, to support your belief that there is underground water there?"

Roscoe went on to explain the problem he faced with irrigating the fertile land of the tropical savannas. He asked the young doctor if the underground water could irrigate crops. Doctor Adair assured Roscoe that these African underground water aquifers have probably been there for millions of years, resulting in the water being uncontaminated. The Welsh doctor felt comfortable enough to respond. "I hope you know that Africa has sixty-percent of the world's uncultivated, arable farmland?"

Looking at Roscoe across his desk, Doctor Adair then said, "You have an important reason to believe me when I gave you the coordinates. My feet are always uncomfortable, but they only hurt when I walk in the African country of Mozambique. That means there is a great amount of something dangerous in that ground that others don't know about. It could be some type of gas. It's not the same tingling feeling when I walk over water, but in Mozambique the bottom of my feet hurt"

Roscoe stared at the young doctor for a few moments before speaking. "If only you could show me something more tangible than tingling feet, I would drill tomorrow."

In frustration, Jem Adair hesitated slightly, thinking, *Oh, I should not have used the word tingle, he's right, tingling sounds childish.* "Jem Adair continued, "Tingle is the wrong word. My feet have a prickling sensation, like a tremor or pulsation

354

when I walk over the coordinates I wrote yesterday. I think it is the moving water that my feet feel."

Doctor Adair recalled every word Roscoe had mentioned over the past two days. "Mr. Roscoe, what I know is correct. You say you need something more tangible than my feet feeling the water. Read a good history book, and you will read that millions of years ago, the Sahara Desert was part of the Atlantic Ocean and the Mediterranean Sea. Many years ago, I read a story about an archeologist who was digging in the Sahara Desert, and found a human skeleton. On the skeleton's wrist was a rhinoceros bone, kingdom Animal, class Mammalia that had been shaped into a wrist band. The rhinoceros animal needs water to survive. That should tell you that there once was water covering the area of the Sahara Desert."

Roscoe was now transfixed with this young man who yesterday would talk to him while looking down at the floor but now looked him directly in the eyes, so sure and confident in his prediction.

Doctor Adair, now seeming more comfortable in the presence of Roscoe said, "I don't understand why you want to give me sixty thousand dollars. Don't give me that money, but instead call the people at London College in the United Kingdom. They will drill and find plenty of water for less than sixty thousand dollars." Jem, now proud of himself for standing up to this important man, thought, *if he doesn't believe me now, he never will.*

Jem Adair stood erect, even looking defiant after his suggestion to call the University College of London in the United Kingdom, while continuing to look into Roscoe's eyes.

Roscoe could see the man before him now was not the same ragged, disheveled man he felt sorry for yesterday.

Doctor Adair broke the long silent moment by saying, "I'm really disappointed you don't believe me." Jem Adair started to walk towards the office door, and was about to reach for the doorknob when he heard Roscoe say. "Doctor Adair, wait. You've convinced me. Do you know how I can contact the London College?"

The Welsh doctor turned, smiling broadly for the first time in two days. Then said, "I would like to stay and watch the drilling. That would be very exciting for me. Once you see the water, if you still want me to work for you, I will. But you don't have to pay me so much money. Having a bed to sleep on, your good food, and a shower would be enough for me."

"Let's worry about a position with Build Africa Together after the results of the drilling," Roscoe said, smiling.

Jem replied, "I think I could work for you, as long as I don't have to work with your soldiers."

CHAPTER 44

Jon Edward's mobile phone rang as he and Rick Kinsley were traveling from their last assignment in Southern Sudan. He Checked his phone screen for a name, there was no name on his phone. Odd, he thought; he let it ring a few more times, allowing the call to go to his voice mail. *"Hi, Jon, hope you remember me, this is Mullah Fazullah, we worked for the company at Langley after nine-eleven. I'm pretty sure you also know my partner Asmatullah Shaheen."* As soon as Jon heard the name Fazullah, he remembered working with him as a CIA operative. As they drove the vehicle along a dusty bumpy road, Rick immediately put the message on speaker mode so Rick could hear the entire message

The message continued, *"I know it's been a while since we both mysteriously disappeared from the agency back in 2002. Our handler at Langley, Gus Malone, happened to mention you and Rick Kinsley have retired to Africa and are working for the humanitarian agency called Build Africa Together, led by ex-President Ayala. When we heard you two were in Africa, my partner Asmatullah Shaheen got a great idea. Asmatullah never worked with you, but he believes you both have met. He's ugly as hell, but I can vouch...hey Asma, stop hitting me, I'm speaking on the phone, ready to drop our plan on Rick and Jon! So, as I was saying, we have an idea for a plan we believe you guys might buy into. The only problem is time, if Asmatullah's idea is gonna happen it's got to be now, I'm talking the next ten days. I'll explain the rush on this project hopefully if we can meet. Please get back to me ASAP, I think you guys will like what you hear. Make sure you use my secure phone number. We also want you to know, we are still good guys, and we still work for the company at Langley, and can only now explain everything. We've been under for a long time, maybe too long. I know this call is gonna sound suspicious due to the mysterious way we disappeared from Virginia. If you have any doubts, give our contact at the agency a call to verify this is legit. Gus Malone, our agency contact, is heads up on what we have in mind. I'm sure you know him, and he can now talk about our full story. I hope you two are not anxious about this mysterious call, get back to us after verifying what I just said with Gus Malone. What we have in mind doesn't usually come along so nicely wrapped up as this one might. It's important we have a face to face, we expect to be in Africa until Thursday, and would like to meet with you both. If you guys prefer to pick the meet spot, we understand. It would be nice if you could bring your boss to the face-to-face, we would love to meet him, but we understand why this would be unlikely."*

Jon slapped closed his phone, and looked at Rick, who was driving. "Can you believe what you just heard?"

Rick answered, "I thought for sure he had gone rogue or had been killed. I never in a million years expected to hear Mullah's voice again."

Jon replied, "Well, it's still possible they did go rogue, and may be looking to get something from us, or perhaps they plan to use us, but no harm in looking them over. I'm ok with an initial call to see where they want to meet us, how about you?"

"Yeah, I think we can take the gamble, but let's get to Malone first."

Gus Malone had been with the CIA for some twenty-nine years. Due to his age and a serious injury, he now had a desk job. He was a good operative, had a few skirmishes during his time in the field. Since his desk job, he had put on some weight, and has a growing stomach to prove it. He enjoyed fieldwork and would still be out on the streets if it weren't for being hit twice with gun fire to the chest. Bullet protection vests were not a requirement during his time in the field, and he never did get used to wearing the bulky uncomfortable protection vests that were used toward the end of the nineteenth century. He was touch-and-go for two days, before pulling through.

On speakerphone, in conversation with Gus Malone back at Langley, Rick and Jon were told of the lives of Mullah and Asmatullah for the past nine years. They had gone deep undercover in Pakistan, which was where they were born. They first needed time to establish a Pakistani life, which included living with their parents, and an added advantage was the fact they could hook up with two women they dated, providing they were still available. They had been forced to leave Pakistan for speaking out publicly against the government. Gus Malone said, "They had a perfect profile for this undercover job in Pakistan."

Jon and Rick were now interested, and asked Gus Malone to continue. "We originally figured the operation to go for approximately two years. As you know the Pakistan Taliban do not trust newcomers.

We asked Mullah and Asmatullah if they were willing to go under deep and long in Pakistan. We all figured they would be under for a coupl'a years, but nine years was never expected. We now have the information we were looking for but pulling out of Taliban can be hazardous and life threating. Therefore, both of us had to wait for the right time and reason to pull them out safely. An opportunity for this to happen occurred three weeks ago. And now we have this small window of time for them to be away from the Taliban cell, during which our special ops guys will capture the entire cell."

Gus Malone continued. They have a plan to involve your agency in an opportunity to take the Taliban down. I agreed to their idea, and asked them to contact you both. I would appreciate if you would listen to their idea. After that, the deal is up to you guys, and the leadership of Build Africa Together."

Rick and Jon told Gus they would be happy to listen. After hanging up with Gus, Jon immediately dialed the number given to them by Mullah, Mullah answered, "Thanks for getting back Jon, have you spoken with Gus."

Jon replied, "Yes"

Mullah then said. "Were you satisfied with his description of our past years."

"Yes, Gus covered your time pretty well."

Mullah asked. "Are you willing to meet with us to discuss the matter?"

Jon responded, "Affirmative," and then asked where they were.

"Right now, we're in Burundi, on our way to Kenya to catch a flight day after tomorrow to America," said Mullah

"We've just left Sudan; we're following the Bahr el Jebel River to Uganda. If you could find your way to the Bahr el Jebel River in Uganda near Kampala, there's a coffee shop, named Africana coffee and smoke, on the bank of the Bahr el Jebel River. From Burundi you could make it to the coffee shop, which is about halfway for both of us. We'll meet you at the coffee shop around 2 P.M. tomorrow."

"Sounds like a plan," said Mullah. Jon gave Mullah the address of the coffee shop for their GPS.

At two forty-five the following afternoon, the four men greeted each other by a look in the eye and a nod in the coffee and smoke shop. Jon had worked with the two men previously and a big hug after twelve years would have been nice, but that would cause far too much attention. Rick and Jon slowly left their table and paid their tab, a left the coffee shop. an ordered take-away coffee, picked up their cups, and left the coffee shop. Mullah and Asmatullah were in line behind Rick and Jon, waiting to get two coffees to go. Meanwhile, Jon and Rick had paused about fifty yards from the shop waiting for Mullah and Asmatullah to leave the shop with their coffees. As soon as they saw Mullah and Asmatullah hit the sidewalk. The four men moved casually moved, keeping the fifty-yard separation. Rick and Jon stopped at their black SUV and made their way into the front seats. When Mullah and Asmatullah reached the car, the rear door was unlocked. When Mullah and Asmatullah arrived at the vehicle, the motor was running, and they moved swiftly into the rear seats. The air conditioning ran on high as the black SUV moved in the middle of traffic, and the four men were now all smiles, shaking hands and conversing.

Mullah immediately got down to business. "We were able to infiltrate the Taliban organization in Pakistan. After about seven or eight years, we were moved up into their hierarchy. We had done a lot of their dirty work, fortunately we had only one killing job of a rival gang, but many jobs making many people uncomfortable."

"What was your interest in going under for such a long time? Or did Langley up your pay grade for the assignment?" Rick asked.

Mullah spoke first, "It was a combination of things. Langley wanted to use our heritage for this assignment, and we were disgusted during the Taliban reign in Afghanistan, especially after they destroyed the largest Buddha statue in the world. We both knew that we would be perfect for this operation, and, yes, we did get a pay-grade raise. The Taliban in Pakistan is well established in what was then a lot friendlier Pakistan than it is today."

As they continued to drive around, the two undercover operatives were asked to explain their idea. Mullah began. "We've been sent to Africa to inform Abu-Bakr Shaku, the African Nigerian leader of Boko Haram, if he would be interested in an affiliation arrangement with the Pakistani Taliban.

Mullah then interjected what he thought to be an important point. "The Taliban have been looking for a way into Africa ever since Build Africa Together broke up al-Shaba by sending Abdulkadir Mohammed and his al-Shaba group to The Hague. The Taliban chose me to represent them to Boko Haram, convincing the Boko Haram leader to take on Taliban status, Boko Haram would gain status, supplies, and a one-time cash payment. Taliban would get their foot into the African continent, a win-win for both groups."

Mullah then handed the conversation over to Asmatullah. "On the plane trip to Africa, while Mullah was snoozing, an idea popped into my head. When Mullah opened his eyes I bounced the idea off Mullah, he liked what I had come up with, so when we landed, we immediately contacted Gus. I explained the idea to him, he approved and asked us to contact you both."

Rick, unlike Jon, had never worked directly with either Mullah or Asmatullah. Rick was a little concerned about what he had just heard. It's not unusual for someone who has been under for such a long time to either crack and turn or go rouge, or simply never be heard from again. Rick was suspicious, there story so far, was simply too convenient.

He interrupted Asmatullah. "Hang on a minute, tell us why you two were chosen to conveniently be named as lead negotiator with Boko Haram, and if it's so hard to get away, how come they had no problem with you taking Asmatullah along on your trip to Africa? Another thing that bothers me, why the need to be away when the Taliban is captured? If your story is legit, when the Taliban group gets scooped-up, all Gus had to do was pull you two out."

Mullah replied, "Years ago, oh, maybe the fourth or fifth year that we were under, I had been giving one of the leaders a bullshit story to make me look informed and dedicated to their cause. I told him I had been in Yemen during the time Clinton sent the marines into Somalia. I told him how angry I was by the American invasion, and that I joined the Somali clan families, helping to fight off the American marines landing in Somalia. I had all the facts to back up this story because I was a member of a planning committee with the marine brass working out the plans of that operation, and my story matched what this Taliban leader knew about the Somali invasion. I could see in his eyes what I was saying matched what he knew, so I decided to lay it on even thicker. I was able to embellish tactics, dates, number of ships, the landing, and the Somali pushback. I could see he was impressed. At the time, I was simply trying to build my resume, and forgot about it. Well, some seven years later, this leader described my involvement in Somalia and nominated me, telling the others of my brave action in Somalia would help me with the Boko Haram assignment."

Rick said, "Okay, I can buy that, but tell me, why the Taliban let you pick Asmatullah to hitch this ride to Africa. To tell you the truth, that sounds a little staged to me."

Mullah responded, "I understand your caution, I would also be anxious about taking a story from two guys who have been under for as long. I can assure you we have not turned. If you still have doubts, call Gus again and ask him about the Somali story. But getting back to your question, it's customary for a man sent on a mission to pick a partner. As soon as I was asked to go to Africa, I knew this was our opportunity to come out, and I picked Asma to be my second in Africa."

Rick again asked, "Okay, but that doesn't tell me why you had to be away during the capture operation. As I said before, why couldn't Gus just pull you two guys out?"

Mullah was not frustrated with Rick's suspicions. "Good question, Rick, allow me to explain. Suspicion consumes the Taliban and they constantly fear a plant. We saw this in action numerous times, usually during discussion of new plans, someone jumps up pistol in his hands and kills the person to be involved. The killer shouts out he is not Taliban and I did not trust him. No one objects to the killing, the killer simply sits back down; the dead body removed, no one questions the shooter about why he put a bullet in the guy's head. I would not be surprised if, when our guys break down the door, one or more of the Taliban takes out a gun and simply blows a hole in my head. Paranoia was a very common trait with these guys, we just didn't want to take the chance."

Rick said, "Ok for now, go on with the explanation of your plan." Asmatullah was about to continue when he was interrupted by Mullah. "Rick, Jon, if you guys are not satisfied so far, I fully understand, we don't have to get this done, we just thought that the pieces were available, and we wanted to share the idea with you both."

Jon said, "Rick, are you satisfied?"

"Well let's hear what you have in mind first, that might help us to decide."

Asmatullah leaned forward in the back seat of the car and began his explanation. He explained how the Taliban had been following the progress of Build Africa Together over the past seven or eight months on Google. "They were up to date on the structure and organization of the project, especially after what you guys did in Sudan."

Mullah entered the explanation, "Almost immediately after we had begun our discussion with the Boko Haram leader, he needed no encouragement to contact the Pakistani Taliban, confirming our story. Once that was out of the way we began explaining our plan. We began by telling the Boko Haram leader that Build Africa Together, is an organization secretly run by the Taliban. After eight months of work on the continent, Build Africa Together feels they have gained the confidence of the African people, and are now ready to come out of the shadows, and begin the earth-shattering plan to turn the entire continent over to Taliban rule instituting Islamic Sharia Law in Africa, one country at a time."

Asmatullah continued. "When the Boko Haram leader hears that he is being tapped to lead Build Africa Together out of its cover, he will be so thrilled he will never become suspicious. Asmatullah foresees one difficult requirement for the plan to work. It would have to come together in the next two days, because the Pakistan cell is scheduled to be taken down three days from now."

Asmatullah then asked Jon and Rick, "If this timeline cannot be met by Build Africa Together that would be the killer for the operation we have in mind?"

Rick said. "Before crossing that bridge, give us a complete description of how you plan to implement this bluff."

"As I mentioned before, we Googled Build Africa Together, and we have a simple outline of your operation. We know your Special Ops guys have African Buddies. We think you two will agree that if Boko Haram sees white guys that will tip them off that they are being had. Therefore, the first step would be to move your African Special Ops troops from your Somalia site to The Central African Republican site, and do the same with the American Special Ops, from the Central African Republic headquarters to the headquarters in Somalia. We would have told them that African Taliban troops will be there to meet and greet."

Jon agreed. "That should not be a problem."

Asmatullah added, "You know what might be a nice touch? When Boko Haram finishes reviewing the African soldiers and the equipment you guys have. How about you guys treat them to a good meal?"

Rick Kinsley was slightly annoyed at the two undercover operatives, as they seemed to be too self-pleased as they were explaining their plan, but he chose not to interject this at this time in the conversation.

"When they finish their meal, have an African soldier drive a military vehicle carrying the Boko Haram's leader to lead a caravan of pick-up trucks, dirty, scratched and dented older Boko Haram cars to your Somali base with the expectation of meeting another three hundred men and similar military equipment."

Mullah added, "As the Boko Haram leader is traveling to your site in Somalia, in the lead vehicle, I would expect him to be counting the number of Taliban fighters that will be placed under his command. Six-hundred Taliban African soldiers ready to join his existing soldiers that will give him just under a thousand men," Asmatullah mused, "then...when the Boko Haram crew arrive at your Somalia site, they will be greeted by the three hundred American Special Operations soldiers with long rifles pointed at them."

Rick chimed in, "Hold on guys I think you have gotten ahead of yourselves. When the Boko Haram caravan arrives at our Somalia site looking at three hundred American soldiers, I'm not that confident they will drop their weapons and raise their hands. I suspect that our commanders are going to raise a concerned that this could become a blood bath"

Mullah said, "Hey, Rick, Jon, perhaps we owe you guys an apology. I guess we both came across a bit smug about this idea. Perhaps our long time away from operations made us forget the reality of the situation. Rick, your assessment is well taken. Look, we just wanted to make this last big score."

Asmatullah said, "Same goes for me, I guess I also got a little carried away. All we can ask is that you two get the idea to your commanders. If they decide it's not operational, simply let us know by tomorrow, and that's the end of the idea."

Jon looked at Rick and said, "Are you ok with sharing the idea with our commanders?"

Rick responded, "Even if our commanders think of some way to reduce the bloodshed, we still have the hurdle of getting the pope to agree."

Rick added. "Jon, let's get these two guys back to their vehicle, then we can hustle back to the Central African

Republic and spring the idea on our commanders, perhaps they may figure out a way to stop any bloodshed."

Mullah and Asmatullah thanked Rick and Jon one more time before getting out of the SUV. Rick and Jon were on their way to Central African Republic. Upon their arrival at B.A.T. 2 headquarters Rick and Jon met with both commanders via Skype, and explained what they had heard from Mullah and Asmatullah. The commanders immediately contacted the pope and explained the procedures of the plan. The commander's characterized the plan as well designed but warned that loss of life on both sides would probably be high.

The pope reacted immediately. "If the plan is well designed, why would casualties be high?"

Colonel McGruder answered this obvious question. When the Boko Haram soldiers arrive at B.A.T.1 and are greeted by American soldiers pointing guns at them, Boko Haram's history has been to fight until the last man is killed. We expect to win the fight, but if Boko Haram reacts as they have in the past, many deaths on both sides are inevitable.

The pope remained silent for a long moment, simply staring into the Skype screen. Finally, he said.

"I'm sorry commanders; I believe life to be sacred. I believe it would be immoral for us to enter into a plan knowing that so many on both sides will die. I would react the same way, even if you were to tell me that Boko Haram were a direct threat to our plan's objectives."

Jon contacted Mullah and Asmatullah and gave them the news. Jon felt a twinge of guilt, understanding his fellow operatives would be disappointed, especially after giving up so many years of their lives to their undercover operation.

CHAPTER 45

Amarie was skeptical and not in favor of drilling for underground water in the Sahara, his concern was that no scientific data exists supporting drilling. Amarie understood Roscoe's decision to drill, was made out of desperation, and for this reason, he eventually chose not to stand in the way of the drilling.

Roscoe was also skeptical, about going against the opinion of Amarie, as well as his director of water use, but he ultimately felt the gamble was worth the effort; far too much was at stake. Tom Claffey's endorsement reverberated in Roscoe's mind: *I'm not sure how he can assist you, but I will tell you this, whatever he does or says will, in some way, be beneficial to your project.*

Roscoe was aware of the jokes that were spreading among the B.A.T soldiers, regarding the ragged young man, his tingling feet, and Roscoe's decision to drill for water in the Sahara Desert. It got to the point that he was embarrassed when he went to the cafeteria, having to listen to the good-natured ribbing from others. Roscoe didn't know if Doctor Adair was perceptive enough to fully comprehend the ridicule surrounding his tingling feet and chose not to bring up the subject to him.

Dr. Adair's Sahara Desert longitude and latitude coordinates were located within the boundaries of Libya. Since the rebellion and killing of Libya's long-time ruler Muammar Gaddafi, the Libyan caretaker government had the same doubts as everyone else when it came to the issue of underground water in the Sahara Desert. They were dealing with problems of national stability, not underground water. Subsequently, Amarie easily obtained written permission from Libya to drill within their border, and if water was found, B.A.T had title to its use.

Fifteen days after the arrival of Doctor Adair at the B.A.T. 1 facilities, the British geological survey team from the University College in London was loading unfamiliar metal equipment into a B.A.T. War Pig military truck headed to the Sahara. Followed by a military vehicle carrying Roscoe, Amarie, B.A.T.'s water director, and Doctor Adair. Two military personnel from B.A.T. 1 joined the caravan as security, riding in a separate vehicle, furthest away from the truck carrying Doctor Adair.

The War Pig military truck, carrying the British geological survey team members and their drilling equipment, arrived at Doctor Adair's first underground water coordinate.

The British survey team began their work by setting up a canvas tent, held in place by aluminum poles and rope anchors, driven deep into the sand with wood mallets. The square canvas tent top had an opening in its center. The British team set up a tripod with a motor attached, inside of the tent floor. A heavy-duty generator on a stretcher like platform, was carried by two London College employees, and place outside the tent. As these preparations were taking place two employees of the British team began attaching what looked like individually bent aluminum ladders, until the ladders formed a large semi-circle over the top of the square tent. The strange looking aluminum structure was then carefully lifted by six British survey men, until the middle of the semi-circular structure was directly over the hole, in the top of the ten.

The four aluminum ladder legs of the structure touching the sand were driven securely into the sand, until the top of the semi-circular devise was inches from the tent's opening at the top of the canvas tent. After the placement of the aluminum structure was completed two London College employee climbed the left and right side of the side of the semi-circular aluminum structure, both carefully carrying a long thin metal pipe. The two employees met at the opening on top of the tent, and began attaching the two thirty-foot metal pipes. When completed the 60-foot metal rod was lowered into the tent. The team members inside the tent then maneuvered the tip of the pipe, enabling them to attach a 12-inch bit onto the lead pipe going into the sand. The two geological team members in the tent yelled out to the employee operating the generator, to crank it up.

The generator was supplying electricity to the motor on the tripod, inside the tent. The motor was turned on and slowly the sixty-foot metal pipe began its dive into the sand, producing a harsh buzzing sound. A container attached to the sixty-foot metal rod just above the drill bit was slowly releasing cool water on the bit's surface as it continued its descent into the sand. This slow drilling process had been going on for approximately twenty minutes when it suddenly stopped. This time only one British team member, carrying a thirty-foot long extension pipe, once again climbed the aluminum semi-circular structure over the tent. The thirty-foot pipe was lowered through the hole in the roof of the tent. The two people inside the tent threaded the lowered pipe onto the top of the sixty-foot pipe holding the drill bit, which had penetrated approximately fifty yards of sand. This threading procedure would repeat itself three more times, attaching thirty more feet onto the pipe going into the sand.

After each extension was added, the motor would be turned on, which continued the long pipes descent into the Sarah sand, including the harsh buzzing sound.

After a period of time the drilling, stopped for no apparent reason. Roscoe entered the tent eager to know why the drilling had stopped.

The operator said, "Our computer is telling us our drill will soon come into contact with a very large, unknown object. We wish to know if you want us to continue drilling, but before you decide you should know that the large mass our computer has identified, is probably not a water aquifer. I've never known an aquifer to be as large as the mass being shown on our computer; and I've never known an aquifer to be three hundred yards deep underground. When you factor in the size of the mass, and its deep location under the sand, we have to conclude the mass we see on our computer, is most likely to be a hard mass of coal, or perhaps a mass of iron ore, or simply a hard rock like mass. You're paying the bill, so we have no problem if you choose to stop drilling, which is what we would strongly recommend.

Roscoe was not about to have the drilling terminated; not knowing would haunt him the rest of his life. "I want you to continue your drilling, until you penetrate whatever is down there, if it's not water only then you can stop."

"In that case, we will have to pull the pipe completely out of the sand and change the 12-inch drill bit to a one-inch bit."

A surprised Roscoe, questioned the drillers. "I don't understand, why would you change the size of the drill bit? I'm concerned that if you bring the drilling pipes to the surface, when you go back down with the one-inch bit, you may never locate the large mass a second time."

"Mister Ayala, on the outside chance that the mass under the sand is an aquifer, and we penetrate it with a 12-inch bit, an aquafer that size will collapse, resulting in one hell of a huge sinkhole, with us in it. If the mass down their turns out to be an aquifer, penetrating it with a one-inch drill bit will prevent the aquifer from collapsing."

A nervous Roscoe agreed to have the dill pipes brought to the sandy surface. The team working in the hot sun of the Sahara slowly removed one drill pipe at a time, until the first drill pipe, with the twelve-inch bit reaches the surface of the sand. After forty minutes a one-inch bit on the drill pipe, began re-drilling for the second time.

After an hour and twenty minutes, which seemed like an eternity to Roscoe, the drilling stopped. The team leader came out of the tent and called for Roscoe to join him in the tent. At the entrance to the tent, Roscoe pulled back the tent flap and entered. The British survey team was beaming as they pointed to a shallow puddle of water on a plastic pad sitting on the sand inside the tent.

The team leader said, "I was wrong, the object under the sand is an aquifer, and the amount of the water in this aquifer is so large, our water meter does not have the capacity to calculate the exact amount. I must apologize for not bringing the proper water meter, but to be perfectly frank, we never expected to find water, let alone the quantity that is down there. There will be no charge to bring us the new meter to Africa, that was our error."

Roscoe had tears in his eyes; Amarie had a startled look on his face. Roscoe walked over to Dr. Adair, and with his still moist eyes he said. "I will never again doubt a word you tell me. You may have single-handedly saved our African project. I hope you will consider being a permanent member of our staff."

The young doctor did not immediately respond to Roscoe's offer. Jem Adair was deep in his head. *I can tell Mom, Dad, and Matilda I have a job with Roscoe Ayala and Amarie Maalout, making sixty thousand a year, with a room, a shower, and meals. All for doing what I would have done for nothing. I can tell Mom she doesn't have to worry about me getting hurt anymore. I can stay in Africa for as long as I want.*

Now the people from London University College were anxiously questioning the Welsh doctor on his background, his studies, how he knew the precise location of the aquifer, the role his feet played in this find, Doctor Adair was not able to deal with these men and the noise they were making; he simply blocked the noise mentally, while remaining where he was standing. While a gaggle of men and women from London University College were continuing their silly questioning of Doctor Adair, then his brain immediately envisioned the tropical savannas, and he no longer hear their questions, only noise. His brain would often remove noise coming into his ears. With the noise gone his mind began to concentrate on the appearance of the *tropical savannas land area, soon he was visualizing the formation of the farming towns, moving his hands to simulate the house and the stone wall around the town. Then his mind formed the picture of crops growing on the fifteen acers of land, the vegetation sprouting from seed; his arms began to move as though they were lifting objects, and then his arms were performing tasks needed to preserve and manage the savannas. He then decided that was enough for now. I'll find Roscoe and Amarie, I am now working with them.* He turned and walked away from the people attempting to receive answers to their questions

Roscoe had put a call in to the commander of B.A.T. 2, requesting a team from Bravo platoon to come as soon as possible to the longitude and latitude coordinates he was about to give him. Everyone would wait until the temporary guard platoon arrived. Roscoe ended the phone conversation with an order for each commander to organize an around-the-clock guard patrol of the underground water pipes. Amarie made a second call to the Vatican to congratulate the Pope on the good news. The water technicians began their work at the desert site of the aquifer, structuring three pipes, which were carefully being secured to the aquifer, by a machine that was controlled in the tent. The next day a skilled technician from London University College would arrive in Africa. During her stay in African the technician would permanently install heads to the pipes above the sand, allowing for the safe removal of water from the aquifer.[3]

---

[3] Aquifers in Africa

CHAPTER 46

Dean Helen Bonnser from London University College informed her team leader in Africa that Doctor Grace McDougal would arrive in Africa tomorrow to prepare the site in the Sahara Desert, for pumping water from the Sahara Desert aquifer.

The next day Doctor McDougal arrived in Africa, and met with Roscoe, Amarie, the B.A.T. water director, Doctor Adair and the two military men from B.A.T. 1. She briefly explained the process of allowing water from the aquifer to irrigate the three zones of the tropical savanna. She intends to place three small circumference pipes through the sand and permanently attach them to the Sarah Desert aquifer. These three pipes, after being permanently attached to the aquifer, will extend five feet from the surface of the African sand, and positioned twenty yards apart from each other. Next the engineering corps of B.A.T 1, using a front-end digging vehicle, will dig a forty-foot deep, three-foot wide, hundred-foot-long moat, going in a southerly direction from the three pipes in the sand. Placed into the forty-foot-deep moat would be a hundred-foot pipe, the same circumference as the three pipes above the surface of the sand.

Doctor McDougal will then permanently attach the hundred-foot-long pipe going in a southerly direction to the three pipes extending from the surface of the Sahara sand. She will then use a cap on the threaded end of each hundred-foot pipe. When the hundred-foot pipe extension is capped, Doctor McDougal will then attach a computer-controlled device attached to the top of the three five-foot pipes from the sand surface, which will allow water to flow from the aquifer. The engineering corps of B.A.T. will then have the long tedious job of digging the next forty-foot deep, three-foot wide, hundred-foot-long moat always in a southerly direction, and continue this same process until they reach the three tropical savanna zones. When this laborious task is completed, Build Africa Together will be able to provide irrigation to the four-hundred farming towns in the tropical savannas.

On the return trip from the Sahara Desert, Roscoe had a question for Doctor Mc Dougal. "You mentioned earlier the phrase water table, I have always found it difficult to visualize, and understand the phrase, water table. Can you take a moment and clarify this phase for me?"

Doctor McDougal replied, "Well, you're an American, and, as we all know, America has many wonderful, sandy beaches. We in the United Kingdom are not so fortunate. Our beaches are mostly rocky areas. Have you ever been to an American sandy beach?"

"Yes, many times," said Roscoe.

"Well Then, imagine yourself at a sandy beach, you're digging a hole in the sand. Let's say you're thirty feet from the water line, and as you are digging, you may suddenly be surprised to see water coming up in the hole you've dug. Well, the spot when you first saw water in the hole you dug is known as the water table; and if you were to measure that spot where you first saw water, that spot would be at the same level as the ocean water. Now, at different depths, rainwater soaks down below the water table and is absorbed by rocks, mud, and soil, and years later, due to the contour of a certain spots, if drilled properly, that spot can become a water well.

"That's correct. That is also where the water in natural springs come from. You must also understand that the rate of rainfall, what we call recharging, is not the same for all areas and aquifers, and that's the reason for the various pumping restrictions my report will places on the amount of water that can be safely pumped for irrigation purposes. I'm pleased that you asked this question, this will allow me to emphasize this critical pumping procedure from an aquifer. It is crucial that your water director have absolute control over the pumping of water from any aquifer for use on land. Do not, under any circumstance, allow irrigation to be controlled by each individual farmer or livestock producer. Allowing indiscriminate use of water being pumped from aquifers is very dangerous. If an aquifer is drained of water, it will be destroyed, and result in a sink holes on the surface of the earth. For this reason, I will not strongly urge, but rather I demand that you to take the following steps. Purchase underground water sensors for each of your homeowners. Do not allow the homeowner to insert the sensor on his or her property. You must be positive that each home has a water sensor property installed. This will allow for centrally controlled water distribution by your water director. The water sensors will provide your director with accurate information relative to ground moisture at each farm. The sensor reading will determine the proper amount of water to be used on each acer of land, for proper plant growth."

Amarie asked. "How much will four hundred moisture sensors cost?"

Doctor Mc Dougal said. "This may sound like overkill, but it's the only way to protect each aquifer, and given the fact that you will need four hundred sensors I would estimate the cost will be many. thousands of American dollars."

CHAPTER 47

In February of 2012, twelve months after Build Africa Together officially began its operations in Africa, Roscoe and Amarie prepared for their first-year summary report with the Vatican team on their Skype line. Present at this meeting would be Pope Francis Xavier; his secretary, Father Budi Susanto; Dr. Mohammad Hasson, director of the Vatican Bank; and Jerome O'Bannon, now site director for the remodeling of the Vatican Museum, Library, and Saint Peter's Cathedral.

The four men greeted the co-managers with bright smiling faces. After a few minutes of inquiry about families in Africa, and happenings at the Vatican, the four men were anxious to receive their first end-of-year report from the co-managers, especially now that the drought issue in the tropical savannas had been resolved.

Roscoe began. "There are always information gaps when communicating by phone or e-mail. This is why we felt it necessary to have all of you together this morning for our review."

The tone in Roscoe's voice was part question, part surprise, and part disbelief. He sounded like a man who had offered to take an assignment with a pre-determination of failure but was now pleased to note unexpected success. "With a lot of luck, and the wind at our backs, this bizarre, improbable endeavor might someday conclude successfully. Yes, we did make mistakes in Somalia by not capturing the full leadership structure of the coastal warlord and militia gangs. But after learning from our mistake, we made slow, but steady progress. The four villages in and around the coastal area of Somalia have been completed and all homesteads are now occupied. These four villages have become working models for improving the four-hundred towns planned for the tropical savannas."

Roscoe shared a second Somali victory. Through the efforts of the young lady who has been hounding plutocrats, and European countries for donations to our project, we have received a sufficient number of fishing boats, allowing a number of fishermen to resume peaceful fishing in Somali waters."

"We have Sunjaya to thank for the next achievement. The recruiting of psychists to assist our psy-op military units providing treatment for PTSD to the kidnapped teenagers, forced to kill other Africans, as members of militia and warlord criminal gangs."

At this point in the presentation, Roscoe turned the meeting over to Amarie. "We have a great deal of work ahead of us for our final year in Africa. The on-going work on the intra-continental highway, with its distribution centers at Africa's five sea ports. We are now in the process dredging those ports so they can someday in the future, accept container ships. It now seems possible, thanks to our Doctor Adair, before our tenure is up, we will see a number of African farmers and livestock meat producers beginning their work in the tropical savannas. Let us not skip over those entrepreneurs that will not, be operating in the tropical savannas. Coffee and tea producers, crafts people, those growers of specialty agricultural items, and others who will be motivated to create products, knowing that soon this continent will have the ability to ship their products to a worldwide market, enabling those entrepreneurs to receive a fair price for their products. Finally, a subtle, but nevertheless significant outcome, based on the theory of supply and demand, the addition of African food from our four hundred towns, being sent to global markets, may in the future, force large agriculture conglomerates to lower commodity prices to remain in business. This objective, assuming it is successful, may be another way of helping the poor on other continents."

Amarie now interjected his personal point of view. 'Sunjaya, in 2010. when you convinced us to go to that beautiful Italian mountain town and design a plan, to help millions of poverty-stricken Africans to improve the quality of their daily existence; and we chose to accomplish this by turning the African continent into an agricultural global power. I am so grateful to be a part of that dream. I wish to end my comments by making a few predictions. I predict that by the year 2050, Africans will enjoy a peaceful nonviolent existence in their home; no longer fearful of criminal militias and war lord gangs. By 2030, African children will be attending interesting public schools that will motivate them to live a more interesting, productive and financial stable life. I predict that by 2013/14 the African intra-continental highway with distribution facilities to send food to global markets, at fair market prices, will affect the stagnant price structure for food. These predictions are all based on a pope who had the courage to eliminate the poverty of a destitute continent"

When Amari finished, Jerome asked a question about a statement by Amarie. You indicated a few moments ago, that because of African agriculture, big agriculture will have to reduce the price of the products they send to market. I believe there now exists other competitors in the food industry, and the large agricultural conglomerates do not seem willing to reduce their prices, in the face of their competition. Why would African agriculture be different?"

Amarie opened the folder in front of him, removed a single piece of paper, and began to respond to Father Jerome. "The standard benchmark relative to anti-competitive behavior in an industry that controls more than 40% of the agricultural market, is referred to as "excessive consent ratio." Big agriculture is a heavily concentrated industry, controlling 82% of beef slaughter; 53% of chicken sent to market; 85% of corn and soy processing; 62% of pesticide production, and 58% of seed production. Big agriculture also controls the ingredients used for the packages used in the store food industry. The big agriculture industry is the sole producer of comities used by the fast-food chain restaurants; high-fructose syrup made from corn products used in packaged food sold commercially. Big agriculture is also the sole producer of soybean oil used for deep-frying in the fast-food industry. Big agriculture also dominates the production of salt, listed on packagers as sodium. This domination by the big agricultural industry, enables them to maintain high commodity prices for their products. However, what is most alarming, is the negative effect that high-fructose syrup, soy bean oil, for deep frying, and the use of high quantities of salt or sodium to improve the flavor of food in frozen meals, and in restaurants, all have a negative effect on the health of people, by contributing to diabetes, stroke and heart disease."

Amarie then directed his final point to the entire Vatican team. "The following information is also directed toward big agriculture. during our planning and we felt it was important to establish legal protection of the farmland in Africa's Tropical Savannas. Mr. Vecchiolla, legal counsel to the pope, provided us with an Ironclad contract for homeowners of the villages and towns. The signed contract for tenants allows them to sell their home, which is located on leased land. The Vatican will remain as the owner of the land for hundred-year segments. This essentially prevents big agriculture from purchasing privately owned farmland, so they can continue their pricing monopoly."

CHAPTER 48

The history of African coffee production began in a dilapidated town in the Karesse region of Kampala. The town of Karesse was at one time populated by the miners of a now abandoned mine. The nearby mountain range to Karesse was named for the ancient Greek geographer, Ptolemy. In 1962 a Swahili coffee bean farmer named Jabari Lela purchased a strip of land on a Ptolemy Mountain. The soil was rich, the sun and whether was desirable, and most important the high altitude of his property was just what his coffee plant desired. Mr. Lela bought the land, and produce excellent coffee beans. Word spread of the Swahili's tasty coffee. The quality of his coffee beans encouraged other coffee farmers to come to the Kampala region, to find their own mountain in the Ptolemy Mountain range, to grow their coffee bushes. By the 1980's the town of Karesse became the coffee center for African coffee farmers.

Roscoe looked at his friend and confidant, sitting in an easy chair, relaxing while reading the coffee report that Roscoe had produced titled, "*African coffee production.*"

"Amarie looked up from his reading and spoke. "Okay, it seems as though I must attend to my overachieving, task-oriented friend and discuss his report on coffee growers in Africa."

Roscoe asked, "How many times are you going to read that report? Are you stalling so you can enjoy your comfortable easy chair a little longer?"

Amarie stared at his friend. "Oh, what am I going to do with a friend who does not understand the value of relaxation?"

Amarie had come to learn Roscoe's personality trait, of always putting business before pleasure, and he knew that it was useless to ignore his needs.

Amarie continued his pose in the easy chair and said, "I found your report to be quite interesting regarding coffee production. I did not realize coffee growing and production has been gaining such fast momentum in Africa, and I am intrigued by your opinion that B.A.T. should become more involved, especially now that the intra-continental highway is progressing on schedule."

Roscoe then mentioned to Amarie, "From my phone contact with three coffee growers, I learned they have begun plans to expand their coffee bean yields when they read about the recent publicity we received on our African intra-continental highway. They have invited a representative from B.A.T. to attend their next coffee farmers meeting in March, for the purpose of explaining our highway plans. I asked our director of construction to attend the March meeting. After they hear of his plans, I'm hoping other coffee growers will be motivated to consider further expansion of their growing and production capabilities. We never did talk about African coffee growing during our planning session in Italy, and I believe we should now get more involved, especially encouraging coffee growers to refine their production efforts."

Yes, I do recall. this is a perfect example of what we discussed in Opi, relative to those on the ground remaining flexible when they confront issues that the planners had not considered."

Amarie rose from his chair, returned the African Coffee report to his dear friend, and said. "Instead of the director of construction attending the coffee farmers meeting, I feel you should represent B.A.T at their March meeting. You wrote the coffee report, I think you are the man for the job."

"Oh, thanks a lot for volunteering my services, my infamous, relaxing co-manager."

After a good chuckle, both men came to an agreement that Roscoe would join the director of construction at the coffee growers' March meeting.

CHAPTER 49

Roscoe's calendar had him in the Sahara Desert, reviewing the highway and electricity projects, and was not expected to return until Thursday. On the second evening of his Sahara visit, Roscoe was complaining to the director of electric energy about being away from his comfortable bed.

"I'm suddenly realizing this job was meant for a younger man. When you start missing the comfort of your bed, you know your body is telling you to start thinking of permanent retirement."

Amarie Maalout was also preparing for sleep that same evening in his home in the Central African Republic. His wife was still awake, waiting for her husband to join her. Amarie sat on the edge of his bed and reached for his daily mail. Quickly sifting through envelopes and putting them off to the side for attention in the morning, he suddenly paused and slowly read the return address on one particular envelope. It was from Dr. John O'Hara, Director of Doctors Without Borders. Amarie opened the letter as his wife grumbled and turned over, no longer waiting for her husband to join her.

The letter contained a message that he had been waiting for.

Dear Amarie,

I have been able to complete my recruitment of six hospital administrators for their twelve-month assignment at African hospitals, and twenty doctors for their six-month tour of duty in Africa. I will begin the doctor recruitment

for the second six-month tour next week. Touch base with
me as soon as possible.

Sincerely yours,
Doctor John O'hara

Suddenly, Amarie was wide awake. He was ready to start his important next task. As a young African attorney, Amarie Maalout chose to make difficult sacrifices in his personal struggle to end apartheid while sitting in a South African prison, unjustly separated from the woman he loved and enduring harsh treatment by the South African government. During these years of imprisonment, rejection, and abuse, he was able to endure without hate for his jailers. He believed his beloved continent would be unable to survive if this unjust regulation known as apartheid continued. During this sad period in his life, he also knew that his fellow citizens suffered from another injustice, one he felt was equal to that of Apartheid — lack of access to basic medical care.

Now in his later years, he felt grateful he would have the opportunity to change yet another unjust oppression by providing, under B.A.T.'s direction, eventual free access to proper and effective medical care. Roscoe and Pope Francis Xavier had agreed Amarie would lead this task objective to lay the foundation for bringing quality health care to the African people.

Amarie and Roscoe had no illusions regarding their limited time on the continent and reaching the goal of basic, quality health care, but Amarie was determined to start the movement of this project. Amarie considered free, quality health care a right, and not a luxury.

Africa lags behind the rest of the world, including South and Southeast Asia, in health care. Much of this gap had widened since the 1980s, due, in large part, to Acquired Immune Deficiency Syndrome (HIV/AIDS). Another major problem causing poor health is the fact that African governments require direct payment for care and do not provide any type of health insurance mechanism for its citizens, except for a few major cities. A second factor interrupting basic quality health care, is rapacious government corruption when dealing with African health budgets. A third factor is the geography of the African continent. Poverty-prone remote areas slowed the emergence of quality health care in Africa.

Adding to these major constraints is the addition of a tropical climate, which encourages germs and parasites to flourish. Resulting in untreated, unhealthy, inhabitants of a continent with a severe health crisis. Africans have the lowest life expectancy of all the continents surveyed by the World Health Organization.

With this information indelibly imprinted in Amarie's mind, he began his task of improving health care for African citizens. The next morning, he put in a call to Pope Francis Xavier's office. Budi answered, and Amarie inquired if the date of a Skype conference could be rescheduled to an earlier date. Budi assured the co-manager that his request would not be an imposition.

Amarie's next call was to France to speak with Dr. John O'Hara. Good morning, John, this is Amarie Maalout. I'm responding to your letter confirming hospital administrators and doctors for our hospitals."

"Good morning to you, Amarie. As my message indicated, I have been successful in recruiting the first installment of personnel for your African initiative. Six hospital administrators can be in Africa as early as May 1st. And the twenty doctors will be available to staff your field hospital facilities as soon as you give me the word."

"That's great news, John. I will contact my Vatican team and inform them we are ready for action. I can't thank you enough for what you are doing for Africa."

"And in return, I want you to thank the pope for his generous financial contribution to our organization."

As Amarie was helping himself to a cup of tea prior to contacting the Vatican, he felt invigorated now that he was going to start this important plan objective he was thinking. *Finally, I will be able to expose the embarrassing, often hidden truth of the very poor quality of medical care provided by the continent's public hospitals. Those aware of the deplorable state of African public hospitals understand all too well that if a person becomes ill and needs medical attention in a hospital, and cannot afford the price of a private hospital, they are just as likely to die as to be cured, by entering a public African hospital.*

Public hospitals in Africa are deficient in almost every aspect of proper medical treatment defined by world standards. They are terribly underfunded due to financial deficiencies caused by funds for improving patient care will often find its way into the pockets of corrupt government officials.

African Public hospitals are short on supplies. African public hospitals fail to meet minimum international standards for sterility and proper antiseptic procedures. Hospital staff limitations often force family members to tend to the basic needs of a family member. Important equipment needed to assess the health problems of patients, such as X-ray machines, CAT scanners, MRI, and mammographic

390

machines, are often not be available in many African public hospitals.

Africans who live in rural areas, face an even more deadly problem, using "witch doctors" to treat their health needs. It's impossible to stop this practice, because there are no medical doctors practicing in rural regions of Africa. This unfortunately is due to the fact that African public and private hospitals are non-existent in rural African.

Amarie was excited to begin the task of improving the quality of health care for all Africans. He had three months left on his two year-term in Africa, So, the word beginning was most appropriate. His only regret was that he might be dead by the time that improved, quality of health care, would reach the majority of African citizens.[4]

As the Skype screen came alive, in Rome and Africa a smiling Amarie knew he would be talking with a sympathetic proponent of his healthcare plans. "Good morning, gentleman. I want to inform you that we have everything in place, to begin our healthcare objective. As a first step towards this objective, Pope Francis Xavier had accepted the financial responsibility, by providing a generous fee to Doctors Without Borders for hospital administrators and doctors to come to Africa, to assist the medical staff in a few hospitals."

The French humanitarian agency known as Doctors without Borders is a volunteer organization of doctors who devoted a period of their time attending to the health needs of impoverished people around the globe. The involvement of Doctors without Borders was the first of many steps in this objective.

---

[4] Tent hospitals by Build Africa Together

Under a formal contract, Doctors Without Borders will assist public hospitals in the Ivory Coast Uganda, Namibia, Gabon and Sudan for a six-month period. During this time, the administrators will work with hospital staff, helping them to set up practices, which will improve their sterility standards, while working their way towards eventually meeting the World Health Organizations minimum standards for sterility and antiseptic procedures.

A second important step, which will begin immediately, our director of philanthropy, Ms. Thorp will concentrate on obtaining donations of used equipment from hospitals in developed countries. Many progressive hospitals in developed countries have been reorganizing, through the purchase of smaller neighboring facilities able to perform specific medical procedures. This consolidation effort on the part of large hospital facilities is being used to eliminates duplication of services, by provides these smaller satellite hospitals and doctor offices. This type of reorganization in the hospital services, saves valuable health resources, hopefully reducing health care costs.

Build Africa Together will also be responsible for funding ten MASH-like triage tent hospitals, being staffed by doctors from, Doctors Without Borders and African nurses.

Two days after the agreement between Build Africa Together and Doctors Without Borders was finalized, Amarie sitting at his oblong table, conducting his first meeting on improving health care for Africans. In attendance was Roscoe, both BAT commanders, their executive officers, and ex-CIA operatives, Rick Kinsley and Jon Edwards.

"Gentleman, I've called this meeting to discuss our future tent hospitals. Roscoe is here to hold my hand. Commanders, you're here to tell me what I need for security on this project.

And the other two pranksters have only been in Africa for a year and already know more about African population clusters than I do. If they weren't so damn smart, I would have fired those two months ago for all the mischief they cause around here." Everyone in the room had a good laugh at the expense of the two intelligence operatives, Rick Kinsley and Jon Edwards.

B.A.T. personnel were no longer surprised at the good humor and gracious manner of Amarie Maalout. One would think with what he had to endure in his life as a prisoner in South Africa that he would be ill-humored and less gracious, but with Amarie it was just the opposite.

Amarie introduced his concept of field hospitals, replicating the MASH-type triage field hospitals established during the Korean and Vietnam wars in Africa. Amarie explained he had enough financing to establish ten of these facilities around ten rural African areas — not nearly enough, but a start.

Amarie then said, "An important goal to improve the African healthcare system will be the consistent electric power, as soon as our Solar Thermal power plants are operational, in the meantime power for these facilities will come from a 1.4-megawatt fuel cell battery powered by hydrogen and obtained from an America company in Danbury, Connecticut. These batteries will also be used to provide electricity to our ten tent hospitals. These same batteries will be given to all public hospitals, to us during electricity disruption. Once Africa has full electricity, these batteries can be used to provide electricity during accidental electric outages."

Amarie concluded, "The battery in each MASH-triage tent hospital is indebted to our director of natural resources, Dr. Adair, who identified the huge natural gas deposits, this time not using his tingling feet, but his painful feet as he strolled through Mozambique. Although I no longer have doubts about the good doctor, I still feel foolish explaining his gift to others, but we've discussed that enough. Let's get back to our field hospitals."

"What do you hope to accomplish with the field hospital units?" asked Jon Edwards. "First, it's important to mention we can only afford ten field hospitals, which is not an adequate number for this continent, but as I said ten is better than zero. I am banking heavily on word-of-mouth to encourage African citizens to visit."

Jon Edwards interrupted, "My first question a moment ago was poorly stated. When I asked what you hoped to accomplish, I should have asked what type of treatments will be offered at these facilities."

Amarie said, "Ah, of course, an important question. In the beginning, I expect many people will simply be curious and others distrusting. Therefore, my guess is, early in the process, we will be dealing with basic injuries. Once the people in each sector gain confidence in our ability to heal their illnesses, it is my hope they will come to us rather than visiting their witch doctors."

Amarie hesitated as though he forgot an important point. "If this plan is successful, we will be encouraging people to visit the field tent hospitals for preventive care, but I understand that will take time. Along with attending to emergency and general medical needs of Africans, these field tent units will, hopefully sooner rather than later, begin to assist people with critical medical conditions. It is my intention for these tent facilities to become the location for dispensing, free of charge, AIDS cocktails to any African diagnosed with the HIV virus or AIDS. In addition, I know you are aware of the high-volume distribution of out-of-date and fake medicine on the African continent. Our tent facilities will also distribute properly dated, clinically approved, and tested medicine."

Amarie mentioned another important medical procedure that can be accomplished in a medical tent facility. "A field hospital would also be an ideal place for young women to receive the vaccine for human papillomavirus, a sexually transmitted infection that can cause cervical cancer. The inoculation of this vaccine has proven to be successful for a generation of girls around the world, preventing and reducing incidents of cervical cancer by fifty-six percent among girls ages fourteen to nineteen since the vaccine was

first introduced in 2006. Unfortunately, this treatment has not been reaching young African girls."

Amarie added a third treatment where tent medical facilities would be very helpful to young girls. "The tent medical facilities would also be an ideal setting for treating a medical condition referred to as fistula, which is not difficult to medically repair by a qualified doctor. This is a particular problem in Africa and Middle Eastern countries, so much so that I fear it is close to reaching epidemic proportions."

Before going further in his explanation, Amarie looked at the two commanders. "I'm sorry to have to burden you two with another assignment, but this fistula treatment may need the intervention of your men in some cases."

Amarie then expanded on his explanation of fistula. "Due to custom, tradition, and religion, young girls are frequently forced into family or tribal ordered marriages at a very young age. These relatively immature girls, often at preteen age levels, may not have reached physical maturity. If they are to give birth to a child at a young age, then soon after the birthing process; if they are required by their husband to engage in sexual activity, this forced sex will almost always cause the fistula to open. This condition damages their uterus and may result in an internal hole, or fistula, which is located between their bladder and vagina, causing uncontrollable leakage of urine. The urination problem results in banishment from the home, because the husband now considers his wife unclean. The tent unit doctors would be able to perform an uncomplicated medical procedure to surgically close the fistula under anesthesia."

Amarie now gazed toward the two B.A.T. commanders. "And now, commanders, this is where your security detail at each tent facility may have to intervene. For these young girls, it is critical they do not have sex for a period of six months after the fistula procedure. If a young girl is forced into sex with her husband before the six-month abstinence period, the fistula does not have time to heal and will reopen. Unfortunately, many husbands will not follow this restriction. Therefore, I am suggesting a young girl who has the fistula medical procedure be held at either of our B.A.T. facilities for six months, allowing her to properly heal."

Amarie than added. "Unfortunately releasing these young girls to their maternal family has not been successful, arranged marriages have family connections so strong that the husband's wishes come before their daughter's health. What I am asking is that your men at each site, prevent the husband from taking his wife home during the six-month healing process. Commanders, would you both have your men protect a young girl in this situation, your men will likely have to confront her husband, and either convince the husband, perhaps with rifles in hand that he cannot take his wife home for the six-month time period."

Vice Admiral Fisher responded, "It would normally go against my personal instincts to interfere in personal matters, but given what you just explained, I'd be happy to prevent these selfish bastards from prematurely damaging their wives. As for our men, confronting the husband, my guess is that once our men are informed of the protective reason for their duty at the tent, they will be arguing with their buddies, so they can be assigned to the tent. Can you imagine? They can't keep it in their pants for six months. Gimme a break!"

Commander McGruder was much more succinct he simply said. "Agreed."

Amarie identified another medical benefit of a field hospital that could save many thousands of lives each year. "A septic throat, which is commonly called strep throat, is caused by a streptococcal infection, and when left untreated, it most often results in rheumatic heart disease in young adults. Thousands of African youngsters, who now remain untreated for septic throat, often die in their late teens or early twenties from heart disease. If children with strep throat are brought to a tent hospital as soon as the infection enters the body and receives free antibiotic medicine, the rate of young twenty-something deaths from heart failure could be completely eliminated. This infers that along with our tent hospital, a public relations effort is very important to convince parents to bring any children with strep throat to a public African hospital or one of our field hospitals for the free antibiotic treatment.

"And finally, the field units may be able to stop an outbreak of Ebola before it spreads and becomes a serious health problem, killing many before it has been identified. The disease has typically surfaced in remote, forest villages, and has the potential to kill those come in contact with an Ebola victim."

Amarie took a moment to have a sip of his tea, and then continued. "In the case of Ebola, the final step is simple, but the detective work, determining who had contact with the victim, that can be difficult."

The two commanders sitting next to each other leaned sideways and began a muted conversation, sharing ideas. Amarie was able to finish his tea. Others at the table could make out the gist of their conversation, but some of the military terms were confusing. After only a few minutes, Vice Admiral Fisher deferred to Colonel McGruder.

"We both agree we can provide effective protection of the tent medical facilities. We would use our sixteen-ton, four-man Oshkosh defense vehicles, for this type of security detail. It's a mine-resistant, ambush-protected, all-terrain vehicle. It can sit in an open space without concern of a successful attack."

Colonel MacGruder then explained that the vehicles have a weapon systems platform that includes an M 240 turret machine gun, MK grenade launcher, two Browning machine gun positions inside the vehicle, and a quick firing anti-tank missile launcher. He then mentioned to Amarie that between the two military units there are sufficient personnel working in shifts to be able to provide 24-hour security protection, 365 days a year.

CHAPTER 50

Roscoe was going through the afternoon mail delivery when he noticed a certified mailing from the World Bank. Roscoe, interested to see why the World Bank would send a certified letter, addressed to both co-managers of Build Africa Together. Curious, as to what the World Bank wanted from both co-managers of B.A.T. Roscoe opened the letter. After reading the letter, Roscoe was dismissive of its content. The World Bank was inviting the co-managers to testify before the World Bank's health sub-committee on the topic of Africa's public hospitals.

Roscoe called Amari, whose office was at the B.A.t. 2 facility. "Hello Amarie, it's your unrelaxed, worry some partner. I have a certified letter from the World Bank, addressed to both of us, regarding a World Bank health sub-committee interested in Africa's public hospitals. I want no part of traveling to Kenya to listen to the World Bank tell me what's wrong with African hospitals, and then never hear from them again. This one is all yours. I'll send you the letter in our daily mail packet. You can take care of responding, tell them we are both too busy, or if you want to attend the meeting, then sign-up, but remember to tell them, I'm not going to be there, because I'm too busy saving this continent."

When Amarie received the certified letter the following day. After reading the letter, and noticing that Doctor John O'Hara, from Doctors Without borders, was also going to be a witness he thought. *Ah-ha, so that's why we received an invitation to testify! This must be the work of Dr. John O'Hara.*

Amarie decided it would be best for him to testify before the committee.

When Amarie noticed the location chosen by the World Bank, Kakamega Provencal General Hospital, Kenya, Africa, he understood why this location was chosen for the sub-committee meeting. The hospital in Kenya, earlier had an outbreak of violently ill patients, after drinking disease contaminated drinking water.

Amarie returned the invitation that afternoon with a note saying, I will be pleased to testify before the health sub-committee in Kenya.

On the morning of 21 June, 2012, after a pleasant breakfast, the World Bank health sub-committee and their invited witnesses used a hospital conference room for their meeting. The chairperson of the health sub-committee called the meeting to order promptly at 10:00 a.m. The chairperson explained the role of witnesses at this meeting was to testify on the subject of public hospitals in Africa, and both health sub-committee members and other witnesses could ask questions of each witness.

Amarie was surprised to be named the first witness to comment. He planned his time delicately but spoke with passion, so the members of the health sub-committee would understand the very poor conditions of Africa's public hospitals. Amarie spoke of the practice of corruption on his continent as a major factor in the poor quality of health service administered at public hospitals. Amarie finished his testimony by informing the committee of the recent steps taken by Build Africa Together, with the cooperation of Doctors Without Borders, to provide hospital administrators with supervision responsibilities in a number of public hospitals; and the construction of ten tent hospitals by the Italian humanitarian organization named Build Africa Together in rural Africa, where there are no hospitals or doctors. Sub-committee members and a few of the medical witnesses waiting their turn to testify had a considerable number of questions for Amarie Maalout regarding the cooperative efforts of Build Africa Together and Doctors Without Borders.

The second witness to speak was the African heart specialist, Abioye Aguda, from Niger. His comments were quite alarming. "A person who becomes ill in Africa and is not wealthy enough to afford a private medical facility should only enter a Public African hospital if the illness has the possibility of being fatal or if an injury has incapacitated the individual. To enter one of Africa's public hospitals only invites new negative health symptoms."

After numerous questions by committee members Dr. Aguda returned to his seat.

The third witness was Dr. Mosi Kalijayie from Angola. "Africa's public hospitals are in desperate need of funds to hire properly trained staff and to acquire the necessary supplies to provide a sanitary hospital environment. There are also practices in public hospitals that need to be changed. For example, many women I treat prefer not to go to a public hospital for delivery of their child. First, they are concerned about poor hospital sanitation and indifferent treatment. Secondly, African public hospitals require patient testing for the HIV/AIDS virus, and many women refuse the stigmatization associated with this mandatory test. I understand the reason for the test, but the fact remains that infected pregnant women, most often choose to give birth to a child in their home, rather than being tested for, HIV/AIDS."

She completed her testimony by suggesting that health committee members visit the website healthlinkafrica.com, where they could confirm her pessimistic view, expressed today. The committee members questioned Dr. Kalijayie on the contents of this website and were interested in hearing in more detail about the lack of training for hospital staff members.

When Dr. Kalijayie finished her summary, the fourth witness to testify was Dr. Donald Dimka from Kenya. His comments centered on a comparison of the care given to wealthy patients in private hospitals, versus the care given to Africans unable to afford a private hospital. He also talked about the need for proper diagnostic equipment unavailable in most African public hospitals.

The fifth witness to give testimony was Dr. Imani Egwn. His comments related to the lack of competent medical doctors. "All too often, competent Africans travel to other countries to obtain their medical schooling. When they leave Africa, many students have plans to return to their home country to serve the African people. However, the recruiting process, outside of Africa, with its inviting salaries, and working conditions, are frequently too promising for graduates to turn down. This results in far too many African born doctors choosing to practice in foreign countries. A second problem has to do with the salaries of competent African doctors who work in public hospitals. Their compensation is so poor that many physicians find they are unable to afford their continuing to work in Africa."

When finished with his testimony, Dr. Imani Egwn stood, moving from his seat, and rested his hands on the back of his chair, momentarily hesitating before continuing, ensuring his hesitation would get every member of the health sub-committee's attention. He spoke in a forceful manner, hoping to emphasize the point he wished to share with sub-committee members. "I wish to mention the environment that I see in the

African public hospitals. They are crowded, noisy, unsanitary health facilities. They are understaffed, short on medicine. They lack the basic, and necessary supplies, to maintain a sterile facility. Public hospitals often experience electricity failure. Public hospitals are breeding grounds for many diseases that find their way into the sick bodies of patients. There are just under a billion people on our continent. The vast majority of these billion people cannot afford to enter a private health institution. They frequently will not enter a public hospital when they are ill because they know their chances of attracting worse ailments is very likely. In summary, the African public find they are left with two options: consult their local witch doctor or enter a public hospital that they fear is not safe. In a public hospital, they encounter an unsterile, septic, bacteria-growing environment resulting in both children, and adults may often experience diarrhea, cholera, and other easily transmitted diseases, before being released by the hospital. The sad truth is that these public hospitals are some of the most dangerous places on our continent."

Dr. Egwn then referred to a shocking statistic: "Two million children under the age of five, which is when they are most susceptible to an infection, die from contagious infectious diseases during visits to Africa's public hospitals."

When Dr. Egwn finished, there were no questions from the sub-committee. He had graphically but accurately described a failing public health system. The atmosphere in the brightly colored room was heavy with disbelief and discouragement. Two committee members leaned sideways to speak to the committee member next to them. The witnesses were not sure if this would conclude the committee meeting. Committee members seemed confused by the brief but powerful testimony.

After a moment of further silence, the chairperson of the health sub-committee asked an open question to the witnesses.

"Your testimony, though brief, is quite disturbing. One can hardly believe the picture you have painted. Will you help our committee members to understand the reason or reasons why these conditions exist? Would you also explain how an organization such as the World Bank could help Africa improve its healthcare, for the average African citizen?"

Dr. Mosi Kalijayie, a female physician from Angola specializing in primary care, stood at her chair and responded. "There are many ways in which your organization could be of great value to the overall health care of our people. The donation of sterile supplies would be valued and most welcome. As would a donation of a water purification device similar to the water purification device that Build Africa Together provides to their farming villages in Somalia. These water purification devices would be of immense value.

Allow me to interject at this point the importance of what Amarie Maalout mentioned earlier regarding corruption. If you choose to provide financial or other support to our public hospitals, I would urge you to allocate this assistance directly to each hospital administrator. If your donations are routed through local government departments, this money will surely never reach its intended destination."

Doctor Kalijayie then explained, "The four medical personnel you have invited this morning have asked me to express the view of all four of us. Our great African citizen Amarie Maalout, in cooperation with the Vatican and Doctors without Borders is, as we speak, bringing proper health care to many Africans who live in rural regions of Africa through his ten tent field hospitals."

She then hesitated, looked toward Amarie, and asked, "Mr. Maalout would you inform the health sub-committee of the medical services your triage field hospitals provide? And please repeat the number of tent facilities offering free quality medical care to African citizens."

Amarie was surprised that Dr. Kalijayie asked him to expand in more detail on the medical tent facilities. Before standing, Amarie's eyes shifted to Dr. John O'Hara, director of Doctors Without Borders, looking for agreement to share the information. Dr. O'Hara, with a broad smile, nodded in the affirmative. Amarie wondered if Dr. O'Hara and the other doctors present at today's hearing, were responsible for his invitation to this morning's gathering, as the only non-medical doctor to testify.

Amarie stood erect before the committee. "The Italian humanitarian agency I co-manage in Africa is currently in the process of constructing and supplying ten tent hospitals in the areas of Africa that have clusters of people, located in rural African that have no local public hospitals or doctors.

The French agency, Doctors Without Borders, has agreed, provide medically trained doctors to staff these tent facilities. Pope Francis Xavier, through his humanitarian agency Build Africa Together, has agreed to make a substantial yearly donation, each year for the medical services they provide.

Amarie Maalout concluded his remarks. "We hope these ten tent hospitals will encourage Africans who need medical attention to use our informal tent facilities for treatment. We understand ten triage tent facilities are inadequate to meet the medical needs of a billion Africans. If this innovative approach to health care proves to be successful in terms of meeting the medical needs of Africans, it is our hope that citizens, will in time, come to see our tent facilities as a positive and safe alternative to Africa's public hospitals."

Dr. Kalijayie sported a slight grin on her face, knowing the four doctors pulled a surprise on Amarie. When Amarie returned to his seat, the five doctors stood and applauded Amarie Maalout. The look on the faces of the World Bank's health sub-committee members suggested they also had not expected this unusual behavior by their medical witnesses. Amarie continued to remain seated with a surprised, embarrassed look on his face.

Six months had passed since the World Bank's health sub-committee met in Kenya, Africa. On a Tuesday afternoon, late in the day, Amarie was relaxing after a long day's work, sitting at his desk, and opening his usually boring mail, with many letters offering for sale some type of useless product or advertisements from a strange-sounding company name. In the middle of the envelopes was a certified letter from the World Bank. Amarie believing this letter contained a thank note for his recent appearance before the health sub-committee. He was surprised that the World Bank they would send a thank you response by certified mail. He thought, *World Bank people must believe Africa's postal system is so poor that letters must be sent certified to reach their destination.* He ripped the end of one side of the envelope, then, holding the open end in front of his mouth, blew a short burst of air, separating the open end of the envelope. He tilted the envelope toward his desk, the contents fell onto his desk blotter. He opened the letter and noticed what looked like a check. Now more interested, he scanned the check. His eyes grew wide and his jaw dropped as he looked down at a certified World Bank check that indicated a number 1 and a long series of zeroes. He didn't bother counting the zeroes, but he looked at the written amount in the middle of the check. Typed along the line were the words "One billion dollars and zero cents." The check was made out to Build Africa Together, the message in the letter instructed Amarie to use this donation only for the construction, maintenance, and supplies needed to add thirty-seven tent triage hospital sites on the African continent.[5] Amarie brought the check close to his face, and kissed it.

---

[5] Tent hospitals funded by The World Bank

CHAPTER 51

It was time for the Vatican's six-month site visit to Africa. Normally, this responsibility fell on the shoulders of Father Budi Susanto, but with his new-half year status as the pope's secretary, Father Susanto was in New York City, assisting Archbishop MacCarthy's ministry. The Jesuit priest responsible for overseeing the recently completed renovation of the Vatican Museum, Library. The renovation of Saint Peter's Cathedral was scheduled to begin in ten days. Father Jerome O'Bannon being free for ten days, volunteered to pinch hit for Budi, and be responsible for the six-month African site visit.

Jerome O'Bannon grew up in the borough of Queens, New York City. His parents, second-generation Irish Catholic immigrants, remained close to their cultural roots. His older sister participated in Irish dance competitions. Jerome found the religious eulogies of the diocesan priest at his Mineola parish church, to be boring and dogmatic. He regularly attended Sunday Mass with his parents, despite his less than enthusiastic attitude. He attended Chaminade High School in Mineola, New York. It was at Chaminade, under the tutelage of a Jesuit teachers, that he excelled academically. In his sophomore year at Chaminade, the Jesuit teacher encouraged him to consider a vocation as a Jesuit priest; he politely turned down the offer, explaining that upon graduating from high school, he expected to attend Hofstra University, located close to his home, in Hempstead, New York, which was a bus ride from his home in Mineola. Living at home, would save his parents the cost of room and board during his higher education experience. However, early in his senior year at Chaminade High School, he began to realize the tuition cost at Hofstra, for four years may no longer be an option. He conferred with his Jesuit confessor at Chaminade for the remainder of his senior year, and upon graduation from high school, he accepted the option of attending a Jesuit seminary on a trial basis in Calacoon, New York. The rest is history.

Jerome arrived in Africa late in the afternoon and was picked up at the Kenya airport by B.A.T. military personnel, and driven to B.A.T. 2 headquarters. He arrived ten minutes after five, just in time for a welcoming drink and finger food prior to dinner in the B.A.T. 2 cafeteria. Roscoe greeted Jerome and was interested in learning about the renovation changes, made at the Vatican. Roscoe was discouraged to hear Pope Francis Xavier was still dealing with internal protests regarding the many changes being implemented at the Vatican, and the continuing lack of enthusiasm for the pope's underwriting of his African program, from the laity and a significant number of the church hierarchy, and even priests. During dinner, Jerome asked if he could meet Doctor Adair. Roscoe agreed to set up the visit.

Jerome said, "Roscoe, this may sound as if I'm being critical of your judgment, and I hope you won't take it that way, but to be quite frank, I found the story about Dr. Adair and his tingling feet to be nothing but a hoax. Were you ever able to determine if he had prior knowledge of the underground water and was using his tingling feet to either influence you or perhaps amuse you?"

All the participants of the dinner stopped eating for a moment and looked up at Jerome; this seemed a harsh way to express doubt, especially since Jerome had not yet met the young Welsh doctor.

Observing the reaction of the others at the table, Jerome apologized. "Sorry, Roscoe. Now that I've expressed my opinion out loud, I can understand that, in fact, it came out as a criticism. I really have gotten off on the wrong foot here in Africa, so please accept my sincere apology."

Jerome respected Roscoe and the work he had accomplished during his first year in Africa, but he found it difficult to understand why Roscoe went along with what he considered the young doctor's foolish deception. What was most troubling to Jerome was that the young man chose to play a foolish game with something so very serious. Jerome was surprised that a man of Roscoe's stature would be so accepting of this charlatan.

Amarie, noticing how uncomfortable Jerome was for speaking his mind, tried to make light of the comment. "Oh, Jerome, try not to feel so negative until you have met the young man. It's true, those who meet Doctor Adair for the first time or hear stories about him tend to be skeptical, but we have come to respect our young genius, warts and all. His social interaction will no doubt strike you as rude. I feel his actions are simply a manifestation of his condition, autism. If you're willing to accept him as he is, you'll have an interesting time. If not, I'm afraid you will be disappointed."

Roscoe interjected himself in the conversation. "As I have said too many others, the truth is, I was one hell of a desperate man when he casually explained his tingling feet and water under the Sahara. If he had said there was water available on Mars, I may have asked him how we could get it."

Jerome still felt confused and skeptical, but he was much too embarrassed to continue the conversation, but from the look on Jerome's face, it was clear to all that Roscoe's and Amarie's attempt to explain the unusual behavior of Doctor Adair had not satisfied Jerome.

Amarie once again entered the conversation by speaking directly to Jerome. "I understand your skepticism, you're not the first person to doubt the sincerity of Doctor Adair. However, we have come to accept that his brain function, somehow connects his body to the earth. My reading on autism since hiring the young doctor, has indicated that even medical experts do not yet, have an explanation of the workings of the autistic mind. There are some theories, but no definitive theory of how the autistic mind works. All we know is the young man has been a sensational find for our project. By the way, he was invited to your welcoming dinner this evening, but he declined because, as he said, 'I'm in the middle of a project and have no time for a long boring dinner!'" Now for you and I to respond in that fashion, I agree is rude, but Doctor Adair simply blurts out loud, every intimate thought or feeling that enters his mind."

Jerome, like so many others, have no clear understanding of the cause of autism. The only confirmed understanding is that the wiring of the brain of a person with autism, is different from the wiring, of what we believe to be a normal brain.

Jerome then inquired, "Before I leave, I would love the opportunity to spend some time with him. I have a million questions relating to his so-called special gifts. I'm interested to see if he attempts similar tactics when I speak with him."

Roscoe and Amarie rolled their eyes at each other, Amarie was the first to speak. "Regarding asking him questions. Allow me to share a recommendation, don't! He will interpret your questions as challenging his thoughts; now for you and I, we would usually have a challenging conversation attempting to politely explaining our thoughts and/or theories. The best piece of advice I can give you when you meet with the young doctor, is that he is the most intuitive person I have ever met. The minute you offer your hand to shake his, he'll know you have negative thoughts about him; so, don't expect you will be able to hide your skepticism. And, by the way, he doesn't shake hands with people who he meets for the first time, so I suggest you not get worked up if you decide to offer him your hand and he doesn't take it."

Roscoe said, "I fully agree with Amarie. Don't start by asking him questions about his behavior, his social interactions, or his mind. We have come to understand those types of questions shut him down completely. We have a theory that he interprets general, unintrusive questions as analytical people, who are trying to challenge his brain. Your conversation will be much more productive if you become interested in his work and prepare yourself for him to initially become unresponsive. Frankly, we still don't know if this unresponsive characteristic is a mood change or if he feels people are interfering with his work."

Roscoe encouragingly added, "I'm confident he'll meet with you once I explain who you are. However, expect him to know immediately if you're only interested in disagreeing with his actions and behavior."

Jerome suddenly thought to himself for a moment, *I wonder how I should dress when I meet with him. Might he be more receptive if I dress in civilian clothes or wear my priestly robe?*

Jerome appreciated the advice, but still not completely convinced of the motives of Dr. Adair, said, "So, a visitor to Doctor Adair has to expect the unexpected when it comes to his general attitude. I'm willing to try my best, but I hope I can remember all the rules."

The day before Jerome was to leave Africa and return to the Vatican, a time was set aside for him to meet with Doctor Adair. Roscoe and Jerome left Roscoe's office, taking a shortcut through a garage that housed three War Pig military trucks. They headed for the back door exit, which led them to an outside grass area with a concrete platform for a helicopter landing where once a pool had been located. This property was once a tropical resort hotel for tourists from the United Kingdom. Dirt and construction debris had previously filled the pool once used by tourists, and we built a concrete helicopter-landing site on top of the debris. Past the heliport pad, the two men walked along a path. Wild colorful flowers enclosed the pathway on both sides. This parcel of land had been the recreation area of the former hotel. The pathway ended at a series of smaller out buildings; one of the small buildings was Dr. Adair's laboratory. Roscoe escorted Jerome into Doctor Adair's laboratory. They found Jem squatting next to a film projector, his knees bent up to his chest, the heels of his bare feet touching his rear-end. This position was his serious working position. On a blank white wall was a large image of an insect walking slowly over a pure white background. Doctor Adair remained focused on the white wall and was not distracted as the two men approached, nor did he seem to be disturbed at the sound of the metal door of his laboratory opening, and then closing. He remained watching the slow movement of the colorful insect, occasionally jotting down information on a yellow pad of lined paper.

Roscoe attempted an introduction and said, "Doctor Adair, I'd like you to meet Father Jerome. He is..." Jem Adair interrupted Roscoe and said, "I'll work while we talk."

"Of course," Jerome said, approaching the doctor cautiously. "I'm so pleased to meet you. Pope Francis Xavier wanted me to pass on to you, his regards."

Doctor Adair, remaining in his unusual squatting position, and without raising his head said. "You can talk while I work." The doctor ignored Jerome's outstretched hand.

Glancing at Roscoe, Jerome slowly retracted his hand and slipped it into his vestment pocket.

"Well, I'll leave you two to get acquainted," said Roscoe.

There was a brief nod from the doctor and a mumbled statement in a low hushed voice, something to the effect that he was going to continue his work. Roscoe did not respond and took his leave.

During this incoherent statement, Doctor Adair was, at the same time, placing a different slide into his film projector.

Jerome felt rather helpless standing beside Jem, who had not offered a chair for him to sit on. In fact, Doctor Adair had not yet offered Jerome a sideways glance.

Jerome looked around the cluttered room, and his eyes focused for a moment on a desk located toward the back wall. The top of the desk looked as though someone had emptied a wastebasket on it. There were scattered pieces of paper, open file folders at one end and stacks of papers at the other end. A small place in the center of the desk was clear of clutter. Jerome's eyes moved toward the center of the room, where he saw a black marble top laboratory table with a small sink at one end. There were beakers, some containing liquids, and a series of large jars filled with a brownish liquid, holding what looked to be human or animal parts, Scrap paper, folders, a cardboard box of rubber bands, and unidentified instruments, littered the floor of the laboratory. There were three file cabinets; one of the cabinets had a drawer pulled out, and file folders on the top of each cabinet. The appearance of the room was discouraging to the organized Jesuit priest.

After this quick observation, Jerome decided to accept Roscoe's and Amarie's suggestion to become interested in his work. "The animals you are viewing are very strange looking. Do they live on the African continent?"

The young genius simply replied. "Not animals, insects. "Class Insecta, may also be known as Hexapoda."

Jerome said, "Oh yes, you are correct. I do apologize for using the incorrect name."

With the projector still displaying an enlarged invertebrate, Dr. Adair said, "Roscoe told me you're a nice man, who helps poor people in Indonesia. You don't look anything like the fat, sloppy, old priests that drink alcohol, smoke cigarettes, and hurt young children. I'm glad you're not like them."

Jerome stood silently with an open mouth, not expecting such a comment but in a moment, he conquered his urge to respond defensively, and decided to change the subject. "Are you especially interested in small insects?"

Doctor Adair said. "These are important insects that live in the Gorongosa National Park. I must record each species as part of my plan to survey all living animals in this park, destroyed by men fighting with guns and knives. I want to make this national park important again, just like it was before the fighting between soldiers."

Jerome could not help but be intrigued by such a contrast, the clearness and cleanliness of the insect picture, juxtaposed with a laboratory that resembled a landfill site. Jerome thought, *how odd*. He concluded that the pictures shown on the wall must had been purchased, perhaps over the internet.

"Were these sound slides purchased in Africa or from outside of this continent?"

Doctor Adair continued to write short notes on his yellow pad, remaining in his squatting position. A moment later he said to the priest "No. I spent six weeks, night and day, photographing these species of insects that lived in the Gorongosa National Park in Mozambique." Jerome was now becoming interested in the doctor's work and less concerned about being manipulated. The Welsh doctor's intense attention was completely directed at listening to the sounds the insects, as they moved their bright multi-colored bodies across the pure white surface. Jerome still had his doubts about the sincerity of Doctor Adair. *I can't understand a person who keeps his laboratory looking like a heap junk, and this same person is able to take sound slides of such high quality. Is he playing me as he did with Roscoe?*

Jerome thought. *The answer to these questions, will be able tell me if he was the originator of these slides.* "Would you kindly tell me, how you were able to capture the essence of these beautiful insects on film? The results of the film you made, clearly has captured the intriguing eyes, face, legs, the brilliant body color of the insects."

Doctor Adair was pleased to explain to this encouraging priest, how he was able to produce such perfect slides "I first staked out the entire park into six square subtending areas by measuring a central angle of degrees. I then bounded each subtending area by two perpendicular radii, which allowed me to subtend each of the six areas into smaller measurable sizes. This insured that I would cover every quadrant foot of the national park."

Jerome was surprised, hearing such technical words that he did not comprehend. The best he could deduce by the young man's explanation was he had measured an area of land.

Jem Adair had a look of accomplishment on his face, but he was not yet finished with his measurement explanation.

"Then I had to stake out my first quadrant area into thirty-by-thirty-yard squares. I brought along a white canvas measuring this same yardage. The white canvas had eight metal grommets to secure it tightly to the ground. This allowed me to know I was working in an area measuring thirty-by-thirty yards. Then I sat, fully camouflaged, so I could blend in with the surroundings, and waited until an insect or sometimes a pack of insects walked across the canvas. I was ready, waiting on my knees with my special power lens camera, with the attached microphone inches away from the moving insect. For the next two weeks, I moved the thirty-by-thirty-yard canvas, making sure I kept it free of dirt or spots by washing the canvas before I slept each night. That is basically how I was able to record these insects."

Jerome now had a mental picture of how the young Welsh doctor recorded such fascinating sound slides. He glanced at the disaster and mess of the laboratory, then returned his confused eyes to Jem.

Doctor Adair finished his task of filming the entire national park. "It was many days in the park, but it was worth it. Because I was able to finished filming every thirty yards by thirty yards of the park grounds, I had pictures of every invertebrate living in the Gorongosa National Park., allowing me to determine the eating habits of every invertebrate that live in this park, permitting to understand the food chain process of the park's invertebrates. Now I can begin to reconstruct the ecosystem that existed before the soldiers destroyed everything."

"My next visit to the park will allow me to observe the next classification of creatures that live in the park. I will follow the same process as I have done with these invertebrates and continue until I have moved to each animal class. When I have finished recording all animals I will write my findings, and send it to various magazines who are interested in ecosystems.

Jerome was speechless, not knowing how to respond, but soon recovered, and asked Doctor Adair if the Pope could receive a copy of his magazine article? Doctor Adair responded. "Will the pope read a copy of my report when I'm finished?" Jerome was certain that both he and the Pope would enjoy his magazine article

Jerome was due to leave Africa at three in the afternoon. He spent the morning in Amarie's office, huddled together with both co-managers, reviewing notes he had made regarding the progress of Build Africa Together. Jerome was unclear about the location of the African tropical savannas and asked Amarie if he would clarify their locations in case Pope Francis Xavier has any questions. Amarie rose from his chair and went behind his desk to a file cabinet and removed a map of Africa, which detailed the three tropical savannas, to take back to the Vatican[6]

---

[6] A map of Africa's tropic savannas

CHAPTER 52

When Build Africa Together began its operations in Africa in February of 2011, one of their first tasks was to establish an Executive Council which was scheduled to meet monthly. There were three purposes of these council meetings. One was to review the progress of each objective and the functioning of each support unit to that objective. Second, to review all new scheduled objectives before they became operational, assigning the appropriate support units needed to complete the objective. Third, to offer Executive Council members the opportunity to include agenda items that they felt important.

The members of the Executive Council were the two co-managers, Amarie Maalout and Roscoe Ayala, Special Operations Forces Commanders, Colonel Bruce McGruder and Vice Admiral Jack Fisher, Rick Kinsley and Jon Edwards, all project directors, and sergeant major Louise Manual. These meetings were to take place at B.A.T. 1 & 2 headquarters, on a rotating basis

At the June 2012 monthly meeting in the conference room at B.A.T, 1 the co-managers called the meeting to order. The first item on the agenda had been submitted by Commander McGruder and was titled financial accountability.

Colonel McGruder explained. "For the past year, I have had this little whisper in the back of my head telling me we've been missing something in our operations. I believe we are all honorable men and women, and I, for one, feel it has been my honor to serve with each of you over these past eighteen months. I hope some of you will not find my suggestion an insult or an attempt on my part to imply we have someone in our operation who is dishonest. My proposal is not meant to be punitive, but rather meant for the welfare and protection of each of us around this table, and that would include Sergeant Major Manuel, and all other sergeant majors, who have operational command, once a military operation is in progress."

There were no comments from members at the table. However, each council member did wonder what Commander McGruder had in mind.

The colonel continued, "I have been thinking over the past month or so that the financial accountability of the people sitting at this table is rather fragile. We are all, in one way or another, responsible for spending significant amounts of money on individual projects. Pope Francis Xavier has turned over responsibility for spending to our co-managers. I have to admit I'm grateful that our system reduces paperwork. On the other hand, I feel somewhat vulnerable. What is stopping any one of us from personally benefiting financially from this project? He hesitated momentarily, took a sip of water, wondering if others might resent his last comment, and continued.

"I would like to suggest that our co-managers name a sub-committee to design specific financial accountability procedures, for all of us around this table; and perhaps Dr. Hasson, at the Vatican, can review these procedures ensuring that our procedures, protect us, and the project. Dr. Hasson might even identify other personnel who may also need financial protection."

Roscoe sat with a painful expression on his face. Commander McGruder had a valid concern, one that the co-managers should have considered eighteen months ago.

Amarie inquired if the Executive Council members wished to proceed with Colonel McGruder's suggestion. Each member voted in the affirmative.

As Amarie was speaking, Roscoe decided that this idea was too important to wait until next month's meeting, to name members of a sub-committee to consider the particulars the Colonel's suggestion.

When Amarie had finished speaking Roscoe added to the discussion. "I wish to suggest that we move forward on this idea now, rather than wait until next month's meeting to propose names to this sub-committee, that is unless any one has an objection."

Amarie responded. "I have no objection to naming sub-committee members explore this matter at this meeting. Does any member disagree with my suggestion? A moment later Amarie said. Hearing no objection lets proceed with naming the sub-committee now. Roscoe agreed, and began the selection process by saying, "If anyone has an objection to the individuals suggested, let us hear your reasoning and move forward on this matter."

Roscoe, hesitated for a long moment, and hearing no suggestions; sat up in his chair and said. "In that case, how about the following for this committee: Commander McGruder, intelligence operative Rick Kinsley, computer operations director Joe Thomas, director of electricity, Ms. Evelyn Armstrong, and Sergeant Major Louise Manual, and I would further suggest Colonel McGruder as chairperson of this sub-committee. If there is any objection to the suggested names, now would be the time to speak up?"

There were no hands raised, and no verbal objections. Roscoe looked directly towards Colonel McGruder, "Colonel I suggest you waste no time getting this sub-committee down to business. I would like a report from your committee, at next month's Executive Council meeting."

Colonel McGruder agreed, and asked for all Executive Council members who were nominated to remain for a brief organizational meeting.

At the following months meeting of the Executive Council, Colonel McGruder reported. "A number of steps were recommended by the sub-committee to support the purpose of financial accountability. Number one, all purchase orders will include a statement informing vendors if a bribe and/or kickback was implied or suggested, the purchase order would be automatically canceled. Number two, all employees of Build Africa Together would be required to submit the name of all banks where they held accounts. Number three, all personnel would be required to sign a waiver allowing the computer technology team to examine their bank accounts. Number four, Dr. Hasson would be responsible for reviewing the bank accounts of the five-member sub-committee members. The Executive Council voted unanimously to accept the sub-committee's procedures on financial accountability.

***

Two days after the June 2012 Executive Council meeting, Roscoe was still mentally beating himself up for failing to put into place similar financial safeguards. Interrupting Roscoe's thoughts was an incoming phone call. Roscoe picked up the receiver and heard the voice of Pope Francis Xavier.

"How are you Roscoe?"

"I'm just fine, Sunjaya. You know, after all these months of referring to you by your first name, I have to admit, I'm still a bit uncomfortable.

The pope, after laughing said. "If it makes you feel any better, I also feel somewhat uncomfortable, but as you American say, 'join the club.'

The pope then inquired. "I do hope everyone in Africa is safe and sound."

"Yes, we are all just fine." The pope then explained the reason for his call.

"Roscoe I have a small break in my schedule, and I am dying to visit with the families in the Somali villages, and hear how they are progressing. I hope it will not be inconvenient for you to arrange my visit."

Roscoe responded, "Sanjaya, let me know in advance when you wisht to visit, and I would be happy to lead your tour of our Somali villages."

"Oh, that's wonderful said the pope." I will call you in a few days as soon my schedule has been arranged."

CHAPTER 53

Roscoe Ayala was finishing some paper work relative to the electric grids, when he received a call from Father Susanto. Picking up the receiver, Roscoe said, "Hello, Budi, we missed you a few months ago at our site visit. I hear you are doing double duty in Rome and New York City."

"Yeah, Roscoe. Pope Francis Xavier got tired of me pestering him for twelve months of the year and made me go to New York City for six months so he could get some rest."

Roscoe answered, "You're still a rascal, Father Sus... excuse me, I mean Budi. After a year and a half in Africa, I'm out of the habit of first names. Nice to hear from you. Can I be of some help?"

Budi said, "Well, you have the right question. You can be of help to me. A good friend of mine, Archbishop Benedict McCarthy, a powerful member of the clergy from New York City, is going to be in Africa the first week in November. I've been raving about your work in Africa, and he would be interested in visiting overnight and hopefully getting a tour of the project the following day. It would be big favor if you and Michelle could put him up overnight at your place in Cameroon, and perhaps one of your guys could give him the grand tour the next day? I hope this request is not an imposition, but he's such a big deal in the New York area, and I thought it might be wise to maintain good relations with him. The archbishop has become a valued and admired friend who recently entered my life, and I would also personally appreciate if you could accommodate this request."

"Budi, say no more. I would be happy to put him up at my place. It's a big house and we have spare rooms. After all the church is doing for Africa, how could I say no to an archbishop for a grand tour of the Vatican's project?"

"Thanks, Roscoe, I'll be in touch once I confirm the dates. Stay well, and thanks for all you do for us in Africa."

Roscoe's house in Cameroon was a half hour car ride to B.A.T. 2 headquarters in the Central African Republic and situated on a half-acre plot of land. The four-bedroom house had a large front porch, which was the favorite place for the Ayala family. It had a small kitchen, living room, and a spare room off the kitchen, used by Roscoe's family as their eating area.

On 3 August 2012, Archbishop Mac MacCarthy arrived at Roscoe's house, by rental car, with an African driver. Michelle and Roscoe greeted the archbishop; they were both surprised that on this warm day he was dressed in his formal robes. Of course, they were not aware of the nature and pride the archbishop had for his position in the church. A large part of what made people take notice of the tall handsome man was his deep baritone voice that one would expect of an opera singer.

His archbishop attire, which he always wore, accentuated his imposing figure as he walked up the front steps of the Ayala home in Cameroon. Resting upon his thick, wavy, light brown hair was a distinctive satin six-point cap. He wore his priestly white-collar, with a decretive cassock, buttoned at his neck, and extending down to the light blue satin bottom trim of the lower part of his cassock.

He wore a beautiful jeweled crucifix suspended in the center of his chest by a gold chain. Around his waist was an 18-inch bright red waistband, which blended perfectly with the light blue satin strips. A dark blue satin cape, attached to the rear of his cassock, was held in place by sewn-in garment hooks located in his rear shoulder area.

As the archbishop was climbing the front steps, Roscoe thought *Budi was right when he said the archbishop is a formidable figure of a man.*

November in Africa was warm, but it was also a beautiful month, many flowers around the house were at their peak of beauty. After formal greetings, they were about to enter the house when Roscoe noticed the driver was still seated behind the wheel of the rental car.

"Archbishop, we have two spare bedrooms and would be happy to put up your driver as well. It would not be an inconvenience. We have plenty of food."

Archbishop MacCarthy informed Roscoe that his African driver was responsible for making his own arrangements. "I would not think of inconveniencing you any further by inviting my driver to stay at your house."

Michelle, an attractive, slender, African-American woman with short black hair pushed back off her face, was conservatively dressed in an attractive pantsuit, and repeated Roscoe's invitation. "I assure you we have plenty of room and food for you both."

The archbishop responded to Michelle, "Mrs. Ayala, I will not hear any more of your kind offer for my African driver. He is capable of making his own arrangements, and that's the way I would like it to be."

"Well, okay, if that's your preference." Michelle thought the archbishop's response was unusually cold but gave it no further thought.

The archbishop enjoyed his African-style evening meal and then the three adults viewed the sunset on the porch with coffee and dessert. With the top of the sun still visible and the white clouds sitting against a blue-sky background the sky began turning a bright yellow, as the sun disappeared in the west, and for the next twenty minutes, the bright yellow sky began slowly turning to an orange hue, and soon the yellow-orange hue began slowly turning into shades of pink. While the pink tones slowly changed into an inferno of splashy red. The cloud formations, which were different from evening to evening, would determine the intensity and shapes of the rainbow shower of colors. When the color show faded, night gradually darkened as the continent fell into its usual pitch-black evening. This was a cue for Roscoe and Michelle's two girls to say goodnight and prepare for school the following day. The three adults remained on the porch, the archbishop enjoying his port wine and dominating the conversation until almost 10:30 before all retired to their bedrooms.

The archbishop had planned to stay with the Ayala's over-night and then be escorted for his tour of B.A.T.'s projects. His African driver had instructions to pick him up at 5:00 p.m. at the Ayala's residence in Cameroon for his flight to New York City. Roscoe informed the archbishop that a helicopter would pick him up at 9:30 a.m. for a thrilling helicopter ride to view their various projects and facilities.

That morning, after a pleasant breakfast on the front porch, Michelle apologized to the archbishop for leaving him alone and excused herself at 8:55 to take her two girls to school. Roscoe had a previously scheduled early morning meeting with the district governor of Cameroon. He left the house at seven in the morning. The archbishop was very accommo-dating, informing his host that the lovely African morning atmosphere and sweet smell of the flowers would keep him company while she was away.

Then promptly at 9:30, the archbishop could hear the "whop, whop, whop" of the slow, gentle helicopter blades as it landed in the front yard of the Ayala residence. The archbishop, dressed in his full regal attire, dashed toward the passenger seat of the helicopter with note pad and pen in hand, looking forward to the day's events. Sitting next to the pilot, the archbishop securely strapped himself into his seat. The big bird's motor began to rev up as the large helicopter blades whirled powerfully, causing all vegetation within a 50-yard circumference to be vigorously propelled back and forth. The helicopter slowly left the ground, picked up speed, and headed west for an aerial view of the tropical savanna farming towns, which were being constructed.

The aerial view of large herds of animals moving swiftly to avoid the noise of the helicopter blades was a thrilling sight for the archbishop. The chopper headed north to the Sahara Desert for a panoramic picture of the highway and solar thermal power plants under construction. As the helicopter was about to leave the Sahara for B.A.T. 1 headquarters, the archbishop asked the pilot to fly over the irrigation sites of the underground water facility. The pilot shouted back there was little to see at this site, only a fenced in area and some pipes coming out of the sand.

The archbishop suggested that since this site was so important to the entire project, he would like to say he saw the irrigation pipes in the Sahara. The pilot contacted B.A.T. 2 headquarters and requested the coordinates of the underground water pipe facility. Twenty seconds later, she received the coordinates, and, as is customary, verbally repeated the coordinates back to headquarters for confirmation. After the successful confirmation of the coordinates, the pilot immediately banked her chopper to the left, and in seven minutes, the bird was over the underground water site, which, as predicted, were five small pipes jutting from bright sand, enclosed by a metal fence topped with razor wire, along with a twenty-four-hour security detail. The helicopter's next stop was a visit to the B.A.T. 1 facility to meet the commander, Colonel Bruce McGruder, who took the prelate on a tour of the military facility and the prison before enjoying a light lunch.

After lunch, the helicopter flew toward its last visit, the Central African Republic, for touchdown at the B.A.T. 2 facility, and a meet and greet session with Commander Vice Admiral Jack Fisher.

The archbishop returned to the Ayala's residence by helicopter at 4:20 p.m. He had packed in the morning and was ready for the return flight to America. The archbishop shook the hand of the helicopter pilot and thanked her for a wonderful day.

The archbishop went to his room, briefly refreshed himself, returning to his host's living room. He thanked Roscoe for a very exciting visit to the various sites; he then turned to Michelle and thanked her for her hospitality.

"I'll never forget the magnificent African sunset and the company you and your husband provided yesterday evening. It, and the helicopter ride, were the highlights of my trip."

The archbishop turned and sauntered out of the house to his rental car. The driver quickly left his seat behind the steering wheel and was told to go to the archbishop's bedroom and bring his luggage to the car. A few minutes later, the driver was placing luggage in the boot of the vehicle, and off they went for the archbishop's return trip back to New York City.

CHAPTER 54

The last four months of Roscoe Ayala and Amarie Maalout's tour of duty in Africa were turning out to be very challenging. Roscoe's priorities were to assess the beginning of the southwest highway, which had recently entered Chad from the Egyptian border. This western leg of the highway construction had begun its long route from Egypt to Port Elizabeth in South Africa. Amarie's final months of service to Pope Francis Xavier centered more and more on the procedures to strengthen the delivery of healthcare for African citizens.

Then in late September 2012, the co-managers of Build Africa Together received a telegram from the United Nations observer's office. The telegram informed Roscoe and Amari that a United Nations observer team was requesting a site visit of undetermined length to inspect the military operations of Build Africa Together. The request included a statement that read: *Build Africa Together will be required to make available all military supplies and equipment for inspection, without exception. All military personnel of Build Africa Together must be available for this inspection, also without exception. Build Africa Together's military facilities in Somalia and in the Central African Republic will be inspected on 15 October 2012.*

This request came as a complete surprise to the co-managers. The moment Roscoe got word of the United Nations inspection team's request, the first thing he did was to put in a call to Josh Feely, the campaign manager for his two presidential runs in America. Josh was now working in public relations at the United Nations. When Roscoe called, Josh was not at his desk, and Roscoe decided not to reveal the reason for his call. He simply asked Josh to call him back, indicating the matter was urgent, and he left his African number, which was on a secure, dedicated landline phone. Josh returned the call two hours later. Roscoe had not seen or spoken to Josh during his time in Africa. The two colleagues had much to catch up on in their lives, but soon the call turned to the question of the United Nations visit to Build Africa Together.

After explaining the United Nations inspection notice, Roscoe said, "I'm puzzled by the request since Build Africa Together is officially listed as a humanitarian agency, which normally wouldn't be under the jurisdiction of a United Nations inspection team. Furthermore, they are interested in inspecting our two military facilities and personnel. I need a favor, could you casually snoop around and try to find out the origin of this authorization for inspection? I'd like to know who at the United Nations may have a problem with what we are doing militarily."

Josh agreed to help his former boss, pleased he could be of assistance. Josh returned his former boss's phone call two days later; Roscoe was surprised at the quick turnaround of information. He expected Josh would have had to jump some hurdles to get the information he had requested. The United Nations was famous for its bureaucratic intrigue and roadblocks.

Josh said, "Roscoe, I got the information you wanted. The U.N. delegation from Mozambique and Zimbabwe made a formal request to the U.N. observer's office requesting an on the ground inspection of all Build Africa Together's military equipment and facilities. The reason for this inspection came from complaints that Build Africa Together had over-stepped its authority as a humanitarian agency by using military force to remove the Sudanese African president. The other part of the complaint was that Build Africa Together was not treating prisoners humanely."

Roscoe, not surprised by Josh's findings, said, "Interesting Josh, thanks, I hope you have some cover for my request." Josh responded. "That's not going to be a problem for me. I guess you rubbed someone the wrong way." Josh then added, "Something else bothers me about this. The observer's office was far too accommodating and forthcoming with this information. They usually hold things close to their chest, especially when it comes to a public relations issue. Another thing that was unusual was that about two hours after my initial request, who walks into my office but the leaders of the Mozambique and Zimbabwe delegations. They seemed suspicious about my interest in the matter. I gave them the best bullshit reason I could come up with after being surprised by their questions. I'm not sure how convincing I was. Then they said another surprising thing. They made a point of sharing that the observer team would be demanding to see every piece of military equipment and every number of military personnel listed on your application for humanitarian status. Why they chose to share that information with me was very questionable, since I had only asked who requested the humanitarian review."

Roscoe thanked Josh for the information and especially for the extra details. Roscoe was going to call a meeting of the Executive Council, but after thinking for a minute, he decided against it. He hated to call them away from their tasks for information they may feel had no relevance to their work. Besides, the fact that other African leaders would be concerned over B.A.T.'s interference in country matters was expected, and thoroughly discussed. Roscoe or Amarie had not received any personal complaints from other African leaders after capturing the Sudanese dictator but obviously some rumblings had been taking place at the United Nations regarding our actions in Sudan.

On 22 September, 2012 a meeting to review procedures, and prepare for the October 2012 United Nations observer team inspection of Build Africa Together's military operations, was held at the B.AT. 2 facility, consisting of Roscoe, Amarie, Colonel McGruder, Vice Admiral Fisher, Majors O'Keeffe and Andrucki, along with Rick and John. Roscoe shared The U.N.'s comprehensive packet of schedules and instructions was discussed in detail. The procedures for the inspection proceeded without problems until Roscoe mentioned that the United Nations gave written instructions that all personnel, along with supplies, were to be available to the U.N. Observer team. Vice Admiral Fisher Interrupted Roscoe's explanation.

"I have to assume you are going to exclude from this inspection, the helicopter gun ship and the personnel scheduled for the day and evening guard duty patrols at our project sites, and I'm thinking especially of our Sahara Desert projects. We have Islamic radicals frequently approaching some of our more delicate projects, ready to do some destruction until they see the fire power of our security squads."

Roscoe continued, "I'm afraid that's not going to be possible. I called the inspection team leader after receiving their information packet and inquired if the guard duty assignments at our hospital tent facilities and our Sahara Desert projects could be excluded from the inspection along with their vehicles, and the answer was no. The inspection team will be using our humanitarian application, which lists the number of Special Operations Forces and all our military equipment. Their communication to us emphasized they expect all men and equipment listed on our humanitarian application to be available for inspection. Sorry, Commander, but I'm not willing to jeopardize our license as a humanitarian agency by not following their guidelines. I know this is a deviation from our protocol, and I'm aware of the possible danger leaving our projects unprotected but we just don't have an option. I suspect they're looking for any pretense to ground our operations and kick us out of Africa. We're going to have to leave the solar thermal mirrors, the irrigation pipes, the highway sites, and our medical tent hospitals unprotected during this inspection."

Vice Admiral Fisher disagreed, saying "I fully understand what the U.N. directives indicate, but they must understand that following their directive will compromise our security operations. I think this is a gamble we should not take. At the very least, can we have our Triton drone flying over the sites, looking for unusual activity?"

"I understand your position, Jack. I too thought of using of the drone. I mentioned to the U.N. team leader that we expected to use the drone during the inspection for security reasons. His response was their packet of information specifically mentioned an inspection of the drone to determine if it complied with our application, stating it was for intelligence purposes only and did not have warhead capabilities. I'm concerned that our humanitarian status would be placed in jeopardy if the drone was not available for inspection."

"Okay, Roscoe. Your position is clear, but I would like my protest noted to the United Nations team." Colonel McGruder spoke on this matter for the first time. "Jack, your concern is well advised, but I can also understand where

Roscoe is coming from. They are clearly suspicious of our military operations, and not having a drone available will only set off red lights. I'm not as worked up over your security concerns as you seem to be, remember no one has the coordinates of the sites in question, and the Sahara is one hell of a big desert."

Vice Admiral Fisher finally agreed to go along, but he was not at all happy about the final decision. With this concern seeming to be resolve, Roscoe ended the orientation meeting. Everyone understood his or her role during the inspections, which would take place over the next two days.

Vice admiral Fisher, now back in his room, and still disturbed about the lack of security, especially at the Sahara Desert sites. Jack was worried, only he and his men, who protected the Sahara sites daily, understood the danger of leaving these sites unguarded. However, disobeying a direct order was contrary to everything military life had taught Jack. He paced up and down in his room, uneasy about the risk Roscoe was willing to take. *The camel caravans that have crossed the Sahara for centuries, when they see change in their desert, it becomes a threat to their way of like and traditions; and the criminal militia gangs, for them progress threatens their power. I cannot let one night, destroy eighteen months of progress.*

After a great deal of personal conflict, Vice Admiral Fisher decided to take matters into his own hands it would mean disobeying a direct order, but he decided he had no option. He began to mentally calculate how he could provide security for the sites and still have every piece of military equipment and personnel available for the inspection team. After a good deal of thought about time and distances, he concluded that he might be able to work out a plan to have the Sarah sites covered but the tent hospitals would have to remain unprotected. The answer to his dilemma was the time sequence for inspecting each military section at both of B.A.T.'s headquarters. He began by accounting for every minute of the inspection procedures, then carefully calculating travel time to each site, speed of vehicles, and distance between each site. The rotation of personnel to match inspection times at the B.A.T. 2 facility, vehicle departure time, and vehicle cleaning time also had to be considered, after traveling to and from the desert sites. At two A.M. in the morning, he put his stopwatch, paper, and pencils away. The one weakness in his plan, which he could not resolve, was that the three Sahara sites would not have security for two daylight hours.

He printed out detail schedules for both men and vehicles. He was confident that his plan, at least on paper would work, but specific details were calculated to the minute, and in some cases less than a minute. One slight delay or misstep and it would not work. As he was trying to get a few hours of sleep that evening, the was kept awake by the thought of disobeying a direct order from a superior, he had never before broken military command procedure. He also understood his independent actions, threated his job with Build Africa Together. The first day of inspection would begin at the B.A.T. 1 facility at 8:30 a.m., and finish at 3:00 p.m. The inspection at B.A.T. 1 proceeded on schedule and the United Nations team boarded a bus for their trip to the B.A.T. 2 facility arriving a few minutes after 4:30 p.m. The first item for inspection at B.A.T. 2 involved a personnel head count. After completing the head count, three six-man security teams from B.A.T. 2 walked two hundred yards away from the facility in full gear. They boarded three Oshkosh military vehicles that had been earlier driven off the facility, so the observer team would not hear them leaving. The Oshkosh vehicles carrying the evening guard patrols for the Sahara Desert projects left the B.A.T. 2 facility without any notice. These three-security military teams provided security at the highway construction site, the water pipes, and the solar thermal power plants. The Vice Admiral's plan had the three security teams returning to the B.A.T. 2 facility as soon as the blush of morning sun rose in the desert, and the three Oshkosh vehicles would be cleaned and ready for inspection, promptly at 8:30 a.m.

The Sahara Desert, after sundown, was the blackest black that could ever be imagined. The Oshkosh vehicle carrying the security patrol for the Sahara water pipes was soon to arrive for protection duty. Their time of departure from B.A.T. 2 based on the U. N. inspection team's schedule would force them to arrive at the water pipes after sundown. The security patrol was approximately a hundred yards from the sand ridge leading down to the underground water pipes when the driver suddenly hit the brakes and stopped. He called out to Sergeant Major Trent, to come forward. As the sergeant major slid into the front seat, he saw lights in a completely dark desert beyond the ridge. Something unusual was happening. He called to Corporal Jenkins to accompany him on a re-con mission to the top of the sand ridge to determine what was causing the appearance of lights in an otherwise pitch-black desert. When the two men arrived at the edge of the sand ridge, they were surprised to see a spotlight coming from a Chinook helicopter illumining the fenced-in water pipe area. Men were unloading barrels from the helicopter and stacking them at the fence enclosing the underground water pipes. A makeshift path of plywood on the sand enabled men to roll the barrels easily from the helicopter to the fenced-in water pipes. Sargent Major Trent had all the information he needed, and the two men quickly returned to their Oshkosh vehicle, and a plan was hastily agreed to.

The Chinook helicopter motor was in neutral as the ten men were unloading the metal drums. The helicopter motor noise drowned out the noise of the Oshkosh as it approached the sand ridge and stopped. At the ridge and on command, three things happened simultaneously. The Oshkosh headlights turned too bright, along with the two spotlights on either side of the vehicle's front hood. The Oshkosh vehicle immediately roared over the ridge toward the ten men and the helicopter. The vehicle's headlights and spotlights temporarily blinded the men rolling the barrels, preventing them from seeing what was coming at them. However, the pilot in the Chinook helicopter, due to the high pilot seat had not been temporarily blinded, and immediately changed gears and lifted his bird off the sand, and was airborne, leaving the men on the ground. By the time the eyes of the men rolling the barrels adjusted, they found themselves facing four men pointing AK- 47 rifles in their faces. The unarmed intruders raised their hands, not wishing to fight. Plastic cuffs were placed on their wrists and legs and ordered to sit on the sand as a group, they were guarded by two men of the security patrol. Master Sargent Trent called operations at B.A.T. 2 facility and reported the incident to Vice Admiral Fisher. The vice admiral told his master sergeant that he would call Commander MacGruder and have a helicopter sent from B.A.T. 1 to pick up the ten men, and that they should hold their position, maintaining their security assignment, until the helicopter arrived, and, then return to the B.A.T. 2 facility at the time originally planned.

Vice Admiral Fisher congratulated Sergeant Major Trent and asked him to pass on a job well done, to his men. The vice admiral instructed Sergeant Major Trent to "contact the other two Oshkosh vehicles and tell them to hold their position an also return as originally planned. The three security patrols returned to B.A.T. 2 as soon as the sun rose in the Sahara Desert, and were ready for inspection at 8:30 A.M. The Vice Admiral then gave Sergeant Major Trent his final order. "Do not concern yourselves about the dirty appearance of the three vehicles I have that covered."

Sergeant Major Trent responded. "Will do Vice Admiral, we'll be ready for the head count." Roscoe and Amarie were with the U.N. observer team when the call from the Sahara Desert came into the vice admiral. After hanging up, Vice Admiral Fisher immediately re-joined Roscoe, Amarie, and the observer team. He politely interrupted the observer team's review of the basement fire range and explained that three Oshkosh vehicles had been delayed in their damage repair and were still at the vehicle garage. He presented a revised observation schedule, which showed the vehicle observation item on the schedule moved from number 3 to the last item on their schedule.

Roscoe and Amarie gave the Vice Admiral a quizzical look, including a wrinkled frond forehead and eyes-widened look, but they choose not to question the Vice Admiral in front of the U.N. Inspectors. Amarie then quickly apologized to the observer team and assured them that the revised schedule was unavoidable. Thinking quickly, Amarie elaborated "parts for the repair of these three vehicles had arrived late, but the mechanics have assured me that all three vehicles will be finished and ready for their inspection, as the last item on the list." Amarie then questioned the Vice Admiral. "Vice Admiral Fisher am I to correctly assume that you will be able to guarantee the availability of these three vehicles during this revised vehicle inspection time."

The Vice Admiral responded in an unusual formal manner. "Yes, Mr. Co-Director, the vehicles will be available in exactly thirty-five minutes. However, the mechanics have informed me they will not have time to wash the vehicles before having them ready for inspection."

Roscoe, attempting to hide his emotions for the moment, said. "Thank you, vice admiral we will proceed as per the revised schedule.

The observer team review ended as scheduled, they had previously packed and were now being driven to the airport, for their return flight to America.

After the team had departed, Roscoe and Amarie quickly walked to the quarters of the vice admiral. Vice Admiral Fisher was expecting the loud knocking on the door to his quarters.

Closing the door behind them Roscoe said. "What the hell did you do? You know you had orders to have everything available for the observation team. Vice Admiral Fisher sheepishly informed Roscoe that he had disobeyed a direct order, and then explained what he had done and what his men found at the water pipes in the Sahara Desert. Roscoe told the vice admiral that they would discuss his actions later, but for now Commander MacGruder should lock the ten men in the prison at B.A.T. 1 and have him send a platoon of his military men for security at the water pipe site. With the U. N. Observer Team on their way to the airport, and out of B.A.T.'s hair, Roscoe, Amarie, and both commanders scheduled an inspection trip to the water pipes to assess the situation.

When the four men arrived at the water site that afternoon, they found 104 forty-two-gallon metal barrels, sitting on the plywood path leading to the water pipes. There was, at this time, no way to tell how many forty-two-gallon barrels remained on the helicopter as it took off from the Sahara sand.

The only puzzling, and unanswered question, was how the enemy Chinook helicopter carrying the ten intruders and the unknown number of barrels knew the exact location of the underground water pipes in the huge, pitch black, Sahara Desert. No one except B.A.T. personnel knew the longitude and latitude location of these pipes; they all concluded that B.A.T. may have an informer. Vice Admiral Fisher, the Colonel and co-directors, agreed from this time forward tighten information, on a need-to-know basis, and proceed with a four-man operation to investigate all personnel, but for the immediate future there would be no mention of their suspicion.

Interrogation of the ten intruders began. An unknown individual offered each man two thousand dollars and plane tickets to and from Libya. Upon landing in Libya, their instructions were to go to a specified gate number at the Libyan airport where they would each board a Chinook helicopter, which would be waiting for them. Their task would include an unloading operation and pouring the contents of the barrels into the water pipes. Their instructions upon arriving back in America was to open a website, www.chinookcarries.net, hit enter, which would cause a window to appear, for their bank account number in to which a deposit of ten thousand dollar would be made.

That evening, Jon Edwards contacted an associate he had previously used while with the CIA who was a very good computer hacker. Jon understood time was a crucial element if they were going to be able to find the people behind the website "Hey, Billy, it's Jon Edwards, your old friend from the CIA."

"Good to hear from you, Jon. What's up," asked the hacker. "I'm working with a humanitarian group in Africa, and I need a big favor."

The hacker responded, "You always need a big favor when you call me."

"I'll pay double your regular price if you get on this job done as soon as I hang up. I need to find the person or group, behind a recent website, which most likely went live in the last couple of days."

"You got it, Jon, give me the name of the web site." After Billy had the web site name, he told Jon, "This should not be too difficult. Give me a about an hour, and I'll have your answer."

Jon hung up the phone and waited by his phone. After two hours and forty minutes. Billy got back to Jon with discouraging news. "Jon, the website was taken down after being up for two hours. My forensic software is good but not that good. I was not able to retrieve anything. However, this does tell me one thing. Whoever put this site up is a skilled professional with serious computers. It's not easy to put up a site, and remove it two hours later, without leaving a trail. Sorry I was unable to deliver, Jon, but that site is gone forever."

"Thanks, Billy. I know you did your best. There is no one better. A check will be in the mail from Africa in tomorrow's mail using the same procedures we used when I was on the job. At least I know we're not dealing with some amateur, which is important information for me."

Vice Admiral Fisher was the hero of the hour. He had prevented some type of sabotage of the underground water irrigation facility. The liquid taken from one of the barrels was sent to a lab to be analyzed.

Roscoe and Vice Admiral Fisher met privately the next day. Fortunately, for the vice admiral, Roscoe does not have a defensive personality, and told the Vice admiral. "I can't argue with a man who had better judgment than I had in this situation. I guess I should be angry that you disobeyed a direct order, but I don't know what that would prove. I'd rather express my appreciation to a man who did what he thought was the right thing, and then pull it off successfully."

Four days later the toxicology report on the liquid in the large sealed metal containers unloaded and now stacked on the plywood plat form was a herbicide mixture known as 24-d, triclopyr-glyphosate. Had the herbicide mixture been poured into the various pipes and then into the Sahara aquifer the water in the aquifer would kill all vegetation within four days.

A man who disregarded orders and followed his instincts had averted disaster.

CHAPTER 55

1 November, 2012 was to become the most damaging day since Build Africa Together hit the ground twenty-three months ago. The phone rang in Roscoe's office while he was out inspecting the solar thermal construction site in the Sahara Desert. He received a message routed directly to his cell phone. Roscoe saw it was a call from Vice Admiral Fisher, and he answered immediately. "Hello, Vice Admiral, what can I do for you?"

Vice Admiral Fisher's voice was toneless and solemn. "Mr. President, Colonel McGruder and I need to speak with you immediately."

"Vice Admiral, the tone of your voice suggests something has happened. What is it?"

"Mr. President, we can't discuss this matter over the phone, but we also cannot delay meeting with you, and I mean this is ASAP urgent."

"Jack, has something happened to Michelle or the girls?"

"No, Mr. President, I can assure you your family is fine. The colonel and I are at your house, so we know they are safe."

"You're at my house? You want me to go to my home, not my office?"

"That's right, Mr. President."

"Okay, Vice Admiral, since this is something, you can't discuss over the phone, I'll head back at once. I should be there in about two hours."

"Mr. President, is there a helicopter available where you are? If so, see if you can hitch a ride and have someone else drive your Jeep back to your house."

During this brief conversation, Roscoe was turning 360 degrees, looking to see if there was a helicopter "Jack, I can't see a helicopter at this site. I'm going to have to drive back, but I will keep a foot hard on the gas. I'll get there as quickly as I can."

"No, Mr. President, I'm not suggesting you speed back and get into an accident, just don't delay leaving. If you are in the middle of something that needs to be finished, do it, but don't start something new. Get back here safe and sound."

"Okay, Vice Admiral. I should be in Cameroon in a few hours."

"We'll be waiting."

When Roscoe arrived at his home in Cameroon, he hurried from his car to the front door. Colonel MacGruder and Vice Admiral Fisher had been sitting on the porch, and rose to greet the ex-president Colonel McGruder said, "Mr. President, can we go somewhere private, this is quite personal."

"The porch is fine, please no more intrigue, what has happened."

Colonel McGruder began his explanation, "Over the past month, our computer guys have been following our new protocol regarding financial transparency. Everyone came up clean with local and American banks. They then expanded their search to foreign banks, and everyone turned up clean."

"Commanders, please stop with the introduction. Have you found the employees who is dirty?"

Vice Admiral Fischer entered the conversation for the first time. "Mr. President, our men began their search of private shady banks and found a Cayman Islands bank having an account under your name which received a deposit of two million dollars in May of this year."

Roscoe was speechless for a long moment, and then with a nervous grin he said, "There must be some mistake. I have no knowledge of an account or a deposit in a Cayman Island bank under my name. Commanders, you have to believe me. I have no bank accounts in the Cayman Islands, never mind one with two million in it. Is it possible our tech guys made a mistake?"

Colonel McGruder answered, "Mr. President, we also could not believe the information, and we told our guys to double check. They did, and once again, they came up with an account under your name, with a deposit of two million on 1 April, two thousand and twelve. We're praying you have some rational reason for this deposit. Perhaps an inheritance from a deceased member of your family? Anything, with some paperwork, to verify the legitimacy of this deposit." Roscoe Ayala was now pale faced.

"Wait, wait...anyone can open an account in the name of Roscoe Ayala and deposit two million dollars in it. I have no explanation, only to think someone must be framing me."

The two commanders wanted desperately to believe Roscoe. "Mr. President, given the situation, I'm suggesting you stay home and not return to your office until we have had a chance to report this to Amarie."

"I suppose you're right. Inform Amarie and let him take it from there. I understand."

Roscoe stood erect on the porch, watching his two commanders enter their car. He then leaned against one of the pillars holding up the porch roof, feeling lightheaded, continuing his stare as the car left his property.

Later that afternoon, the commanders informed Amarie of the Cayman Island bank deposit, emphasizing they believed Roscoe may be the victim of a slander campaign to help destroy the project. They reasoned that an American ex-president, after serving two terms in office, could probably make two million dollars in one speaking fees alone. Amarie agreed the deposit made no sense; they refused to believe Roscoe was dirty.

They surmised a guilty Roscoe would have used an off-shore bank that protected their investor's transactions from computer hacking capabilities. Cayman Island banks were recipients of a good deal of business from foreign investors for tax purposes, not for secure deposits. The tech guys wanted Amarie to immediately contact Roscoe and Michelle to obtain the names of all the people who Roscoe did business with, both in America and Africa; and names of people who Roscoe felt wanted to take him or Michelle down because of his presidential years in America. They asked Amarie for his authorization to purchase software built to trace individuals or organizations involved in bank transactions. Amarie agreed and thanked the technicians for thinking to order the new software. The new software was ordered with a one-day delivery. After receiving the new software, the following day, a comprehensive computer search began. Four days later the B.A.T. computer technicians reported that they had not found the name of anyone on the long list who had opened an account under the name of Roscoe Ayala, in the Cayman Island Bank

The following day, all B.A.T. employees received a message from Pope Francis Xavier.

"Roscoe Ayala is taking a temporarily leave of absence from his duties as co-manager of Build Africa

447

Together due to suspicion of bribery. Build Africa Together will continue its operation in Africa under the sole management of Amarie Maalout until 29 February, 2013, when the new leadership team will arrive.

CHAPTER 56

A day after the announcement of Roscoe Ayala's leave of absence and the leadership change for Build Africa Together, Amarie was far to upset to get started on his work. He stood at his office window, gazing at a grassy area with a pathway leading to a series of outbuildings where Doctor Adair had his laboratory. He thought of his dear friend, who must be confused and frightened. A disturbing thought began to enter his mind. *Have I misjudged my American friend?*

Gazing out the window he mumbled to himself, "Could leaders around the world have also misjudged Roscoe?"

A forceful knock on the door of his office shook Amarie out of his trance-like state.

After a pause, he raised his voice and said, "Come in."

Standing in the open doorway of Amarie's office was Doctor Jem Adair, dressed in a plain white tee shirt and jeans cut at his knees, his short blond hair disarrayed. On his feet were his homemade rubber sandals, a quarter-inch thick rubber base fashioned to fit his large feet. Wide black rubber straps cut in a long V shape and attached to the platform base, over his instep, and down between his first two toes. He looked down at the floor for some time without speaking. His thoughts were confused and moving rapidly.

Doctor Adair finally said, "Mr. Amarie, I want the names of people working for us. I will find the people who put money in Roscoe's name."

Doctor Adair stood in the doorway to Amarie's office. Understanding Doctor Adair's autistic characteristics,

Amarie did not suggest he sit with him at his desk, but rather Amarie moved away from the window toward his visitor at his front door. When he arrived, he reached down and gently touched the back of the Welsh doctor's hand. Both men stood silent, for a long, drawn-out moment.

Amarie was the first to speak. "My friend, I'm so pleased you want to help Roscoe. I too want to find the person who deposited so much money in a bank under his name. We have staff members that will get to the bottom of this and your friend will soon be here, sitting behind his desk."

Now agitated, Doctor Adair pulled his hand away from Amarie's and calling on all the courage he could, he fixed his stare into Amarie's eyes, which was an unusual show of courage from the young doctor with autism.

Raising his voice in anger, he said, "Why do people stop me from doing what I know is right? Mr. Amarie, you make me very angry!"

The Welsh doctor stood defiantly in front of Amarie. "If you believe in Roscoe, you must do what I want. Stop preventing me from finding the bad people who did this to my friend! I need names for my father, who can find the person who put money in a bank, under Roscoe's name"

Amarie quietly listened to the angry doctor in front of him and recalled something Roscoe had mentioned after Doctor Adair had been correct about the underground water sites in Africa. *His autism makes you feel uncomfortable when talking with him. His manner at times makes him seem childish, but I will never doubt him again.*

Amarie did not speak for a moment and thought, *what harm can this do? Let the young man have something to take his mind off the situation. He seems so lost.*

"Here is what we'll do doctor. Have a seat, and I'll make copies of the names of people who work for us, and I'll also include the list of people that may have visited Roscoe's home, that I obtained looking through his monthly desk calendar for this year."

When Amarie finished making the copies, he placed them in a folder and handed them to the Welsh doctor. Doctor Adair quickly moved to Amarie's fax machine and dialed a number, and in a moment, the fax machine was humming. He placed the papers from the folder into the fax tray, and they began their slow movement into the body of the machine.

Amarie, in a confused tone, inquired, "Doctor Adair who are you faxing that information to?"

Doctor Adair angrily said, "My father, he can prove Roscoe is innocent. Amarie protested. "Why do you want to send this information to your father? It's not necessary to bring a person from the outside into this investigation."

Doctor Adair, now even more furious than a minute ago, stood erect, raised his head, and once again stared directly into Amarie's eyes, no longer afraid of those large brown pupils, set against the cornea.

"You foolish man, why can't you understand? My father will bring Roscoe back to work."

Amarie took no offense, but he was unsure if it had been appropriate under this circumstance to give Doctor Adair the names of people who worked for B.A.T. He stood silently and thought, *but the deed has been done, let's hope this does not somehow backfire.*

Doctor Adair, with his back now against the fax machine, said, "Thank you, Mr. Amarie." And then he walked briskly out of Amarie's office without saying another word.

***

Doctor Adair's father, Bill Adair, was retired from his contracting jobs in the computer industry throughout the United Kingdom and Western Europe. He was the top man in cyber security, employing his complicated hacking skills.

Later that evening, Jem Adair called his father in Wales. The time difference between the United Kingdom and Africa meant that it was 11:20 p.m. at the Adair home in Wales, U.K. Bill Adair and his wife Cara had just settled into bed for the evening when the phone rang. Both parents looked at the time, their thoughts jumping immediately that something had happened to their young son in Africa. Bill quickly picked up the phone. Before he could say a word his son, Jem blurted out, "Da, I need your help this favor is very important, so don't argue with me."

Jem went on to describe what Build Africa Together had found in a bank called Cayman Island bank and how Roscoe was innocent. He told his father that the list of names faxed to him earlier were the names of the people who worked for Build Africa Together, and a second list of names who Roscoe knew when he was president of America and a third list of names, who were people who had been at Roscoe's home over the last two years. He wanted his father to find a person who might have recently withdrawn two million dollars from their bank account, and deposited the same amount in a bank under Roscoe's name.

Jem Adair's father could hear the panic in his son's voice and interrupted his son, asking him to slow down. He was having a difficult time grasping the issues involved. When that was resolved, Jem's father repeated back the information given to him by his son.

"Based on your information, it is my understanding there are people within your organization attempting to frame Mr. Ayala by depositing a large amount of money in a Cayman Island bank account under his name."

"Yes, Dad, and you must find out who that person is. And stop repeating what I have told you and start looking for the bad person the minute I hang up!"

Bill Adair knew his son was upset over the situation and that it would be useless to try to clarify further, or even suggest he would wait until morning to begin the process. He simply replied, "I'll get started immediately, now that I understand what you want done."

Bill put the receiver back on the phone and told his wife about their son's request. His wife Cara said, "Better get to sleep. It looks like you're going to have a few busy days, starting tomorrow."

CHAPTER 57

Jem Adair called his father later the next morning. "Da, do you have any information on the bad person?"

Jem's father replied in a calm, controlled voice. "I've been working hard and have gone through many names, but I still have many more names to search. I suggest you stay busy with your work and let me stay focused on my job. I promise to call you the minute I have identified any suspects. Jemi, try to stop worrying about things you have no control over. Just be confident that I'll be working as hard as possible to identify who may have done this to Roscoe. While I have you on the phone, let me clarify what you want done. You would like me to find the name of a person or persons who deposited two million dollars in a Cayman Island bank under Roscoe's name?"

"Yes, that's what I told you last night."

"Okay, now get back to your work."

"Thanks Da. Let me know the minute you find something."

"Okay, Jemi, I will. Now get back to your work."

Four days passed and Jem, unable to wait for news from his father, called him. Jem's father told his son once again in his calm voice. "I have not finished searching all the names on the three lists you sent me, but so far I have not found anyone who may have framed Mr. Ayala."

A dejected Jem closed his cell phone without a goodbye. Seven days passed and a frustrated Jem Adair, on the phone to his father was pleading for answers. "Da, work faster."

454

Jem's father was not upset with his son's anger. He understood his son's anxiety was the result of the dread of disappointment. Jem had never had the pleasure and anxiety of passing through adolescence; his parents and sister understood his teen years remained with him even now as a young adult. Jem, for all his rash social behavior, for giving the appearance of total independence and disdain for the feelings of others, was actually a young adult who had only felt an emotional connection to his family in Wales. However, now Jem had emotionally allowed another human being into his life. A disaster such as this caused the Welsh doctor a great deal of pain.

Meanwhile in Africa, Jem sat alone in his dark bedroom, unable to sleep.

My father went through all those names and could not find the bad person. What happens if he can't find the bad person? What is going to happen if Roscoe is the bad person?

The next morning, Jem's phone rang. "Hi, Jemi. Look, I may have a lead. A new software product sent to me by a friend in London allowed me to crack into the Swiss Bank's executive's documents."

"What's the name of the bad person?" Jem said, interrupting his father.

"Hang on, son. Listen while I give you the information I have. Two names were on the list you gave me that recently had large amounts of money deposited in banks under their name."

"Yes, yes, go on. Who are they?"

"One name had a large deposit made under his name in a Swiss bank, and a second person had one in a private bank account. Jem, I want you to write this information down so you can recite the information back to me back to me. This is important, in a manner such as this, we cannot afford a mistake."

"Okay, Da, go ahead. I have a pad and pencil ready on my desk."

"The first name is a Mr. Bruce McGruder. Do you know a man by that name?"

"Yes, he is one of the commanders of the military units. I should have guessed it would be a soldier. Da, who is the other bad person?"

"Does an Archbishop Benedict MacCarthy work for Build Africa Together?"

"No, Da. I never heard of or even met a man named Archbishop Benedict MacCarthy."

"Jemi, ask Mr. Amarie if he knows this name. It was on the list of people who visited Roscoe's home in Cameroon."

"I will, Da, I will, right after I get off the phone."

"Okay, now the important information. This may get a little complicated, so write this down, names, dates, deposits, amounts. All this information will be important for Mr. Amarie to have. Let's start with Mr. McGruder, because his involvement is easier than the archbishop's. Three agricultural companies electronically wired two million each into a Swiss bank account under Mr. McGruder's name. Mr. Amarie will need to know the names of these companies, where they are located, and the date of the $6 million deposits, so write this down. Ready?"

"Go ahead, Da."

"Agrium Agriculture and Chemicals Inc., New York City. American Allied Foods Inc., London, United Kingdom. And Goldernst Agri Inc., Dresden, Germany. They are the three companies that opened an account under Mister McGruder's name, each depositing two million dollars into his Swiss Bank account. These deposits were dated, 13 November, 2012.

Doctor Adair's father cautioned his son, "Now, don't jump to conclusions. I will admit it is a bit strange that three agricultural companies would wire an ex-military man six million dollars, but that in and of itself does not remove any guilt from Mr. Ayala. Mr. McGruder has not made any withdrawals from his account. That means he's not the one who opened a Cayman Island account in Mr. Ayala's name, and no other names on your list showed up in the Swiss Banking system. That still leaves us with the question, how did two million dollars find its way into Mr. Ayala's account in a Grand Cayman Island bank?"

Jem's father then said, "Okay, now hold onto your hat. This is going to be a long, convoluted story. Again, make sure to take notes of banks, amounts deposited, and deposit dates."

Bill Adair began his winding story. "With the new software sent to me by a friend, I was able to crack into the private shady banks that operate in countries that have limited or no bank regulations. These banks deal almost exclusively, in what we call black accounts. I searched these private banks by hacking past their password systems. As I was looking into the private banks in India, I got lucky. I found one Indian bank that had an account under the name of Archbishop Benedict MacCarthy, which also had six million dollars electronically deposited in his name. Now notice this fact, Mr. McGruder's Swiss Bank account and the archbishop's Indian Black account had the same amount of money electronically deposited under their name."

Jem's father emphasized an important point to his son. McGruder's Swiss Bank was opened on 13 November, 2012 and the archbishop's bank account in the Indian Bank was opened six days later, on 19 November, 2012.

His father said, "When I'm finished, you will see why these two different dates are important. Now, another important difference is the fact that McGruder's deposits came from the three agricultural companies as I mentioned earlier. However, the archbishop's electronic deposit came from a bank in Sa'dah, Yemen. That fact struck me as odd, so I decided to find out if the archbishop's electronic deposit had a transactional history prior to its deposit in the Yemen bank."

Doctor Adair's father then explained that the Yemen bank received an electronic deposit of six million from a United Emirates bank under the name of Archbishop Benedict MacCarthy on 13 November, 2012. I then traced the United Emirates account, thinking I would find the original deposit. However, what I found was that Arab bank account under the name of the archbishop was opened on 4 November, 2012, from an electronic money site.

Jem could hear new excitement in his father's voice.

"Now I was determined to find the original deposit. What I found next was an electronic deposit of eight million, not six million, in a Mindanao, Philippines national bank. Here comes the good news. Archbishop Benedict McCarthy's Philippines bank account shows a withdrawal of two million dollars sent to the Grand Cayman Island Bank to open a new bank account under the name of Roscoe Ayala."

"Aw, Da, you found it! Roscoe is not a bad man. He did not make me suffer."

"Yes, Jemi, Roscoe is good man."

"I've got all the information written down, and I will go to Mr. Amarie first thing in the morning. Da, I just knew you could do this for me. I love you, Da. Goodbye."

"Wait, Jem. There is one more important piece of information Mr. Amarie needs. Now, make sure you write this down. The eight million dollars used to open the archbishop's account in the Philippines came from a Chase Manhattan bank branch, in New York City. Now here is why this will be important information for Mr. Amarie. The archbishop's Chase Manhattan Bank account was opened with three electronic deposits of two million dollars from each of the three agricultural companies that opened your Mr. McGruder's Swiss bank account."

When Jem Adair got off his cell phone, it was ten to eleven in the evening. He immediately dialed another number, and six rings later a joyous Dr. Adair screamed into the phone, "Roscoe, Roscoe, you're a good man. You didn't take the bribe. Roscoe, you're a good man, do you hear me? You're a good man!"

Roscoe was bewildered at first by Dr. Adair's screaming, then suddenly it hit him. Jem Adair had brought a ray of new hope to a man who imagined his life was over at fifty-three years of age. Roscoe's pulse began to quicken. He was unsure of what had happened, but the joyous news might mean that his nightmare was finally be over.

It took the Welsh doctor a few minutes to calm down and speak to his friend. He then told what his father had been able to accomplish. Roscoe told the young doctor to tell Amarie first thing in the morning and to have Amarie call him.

When Roscoe put his phone down, he looked into the eyes of Michelle and said, "Thank God. It would seem my horror has been lifted."

He then told her how the young doctor had somehow managed to save his life.

Roscoe slumped down in his bed, his head resting on his pillow, and mumbled, "All is well. I'm going back to my office tomorrow morning with my reputation intact. The doctor did it again."

He remembered Tom Claffey's parting words many months ago, "Never doubt Doctor Adair."

CHAPTER 58

The following morning, Doctor Adair arrived unusually early at Amarie's office. He noticed that Amarie's car was there as he rushed in, bursting through the outer door of Amarie's office without knocking and screaming, "Roscoe's a good man! Roscoe's a good man!"

A startled Amarie said, "Calm down and explain what you mean. And please, stop yelling."

Jem Adair tried and in a less excited voice explained his father's information. On three crumpled pieces of scrap paper, Jem handed Amarie the information from his father. As Amarie slowly read the young doctor's handwriting, a nervous grin began to appear. Soon the nervous grin became a smile, and by the time he finished reading, he was smiling broadly, now as excited as Dr. Adair.

Amarie couldn't thank the young genius enough, but he tried, telling him how much he appreciated his work, and thanking him repeatedly. Without thinking, Amarie pulled Doctor Adair to his chest and hugged him, suddenly realizing what he had done. The young doctor's body froze and became rigid. They stood still for a moment then Amarie released the young man from his grasp. Jem Adair remained rigid, gazing at the floor and Amarie's shoes. Amarie quickly apologized.

Jem continued to glare at the wood floor. Amarie had been the first person other than his family members to make such vigorous bodily contact with him. After about ten seconds of awkward silence, Doctor said, "I was not expecting you to do that, but I think you were as happy as I am, and you just did that, am I right?"

Amarie responded, "Yes. I'm so sorry, Doctor. I lost my mind for a moment. I hope you're not angry with me for doing what I did. It's my normal reaction to good news."

Jem said, "Uh, I... I... I think I'm fine. That wasn't as bad as I would have imagined."

The two men stood in the middle of the room and cracked a grin. Jem quickly changed the subject.

"I called Roscoe late last night and gave him the good news. He said for you to call him as soon as you could. He's ready to come to his office, if you agree."

Amarie was about to pick up the landline telephone receiver, the only landline telephone in use by B.A.T. personnel, when the door to his office suddenly flew open. There stood a smiling Roscoe Ayala. After a hug from Amarie and now a firm handshake from Jem, the men began strategizing. Roscoe was a new man; his gaunt, depressed look had disappeared with his first good night's sleep in some four weeks. After a conversation that involved questions of what to do next, Roscoe decided he would call Pope Francis Xavier with the good news and express his gratitude for believing in him during these agonizing weeks of despair and confusion.

During this phone call Pope Francis Xavier and Roscoe both agreed to postpone the Skype conference, originally scheduled for that morning. The three men wanted some time to discuss how to best confront Commander McGruder and the archbishop. During that Skype conference, the decision reached was that Amarie and Roscoe would confront Colonel McGruder, and the pope would have the archbishop called to the Vatican, where he would take the lead. The pope wanted the co-managers to be present during this meeting with the archbishop, which would also include Father Susanto. The archbishop's attendance was ot in question, since the pope had the authority through a priest's vow of obedience to order the archbishop to the Vatican.

Roscoe was not in full agreement with the pope on Budi's presence at the meeting, but the pope insisted. Pope Francis Xavier believed Budi would not accept Archbishop McCarthy's actions unless Budi heard it from his mouth. Pope Francis Xavier agreed that being in the same room as the archbishop during this confrontation would be emotionally punishing for his loyal friend, but the pope was insistent.

The following day, Colonel McGruder took a chopper to B.A.T. 2 headquarters to meet with Roscoe and Amarie, completely unaware of what Roscoe and Amarie knew.

The colonel walked into Roscoe's office, and said, "Glad to see you back at work, Mr. President. I hope your presence here means good news. Good morning, Amarie."

Roscoe wasted no time, getting directly to the point. "Colonel, I want to show you a copy of a Swiss Bank account in your name. Do you have a legitimate explanation of why three agricultural firms would deposit six million dollars in a Swiss Bank account under your name?"

The colonel sat rigidly in his chair, his face turning a slight pink color, staring straight ahead, refusing to make eye contact with the two men behind Roscoe's desk. He slowly slumped in his chair as a long, awkward silence passed. The colonel then slowly looked up and stared at his co-managers with desperate eyes.

Without saying a word, he removed his military revolver from its holster, placed it on Roscoe's desk, and said, "I resign my position with Build Africa Together. I will remain in my quarters until I hear what you wish to do with me."

Without waiting for a response, he stood and left the office.

That afternoon, Roscoe sent an e-mail message to soldiers in B.A.T. 2, informing them of Colonel McGruder's resignation. The following day was a sad day, especially at B.A.T. 1 headquarters. Every man in his unit dreaded the scene of their commander entering the mess hall for breakfast but he never arrived, and his men understood why. By 11:00 a.m., the colonel had not yet left his room.

By two that afternoon, Sergeant Major O'Mara could wait no longer. He knocked on the colonel's door and waited. However, there was no response. He knocked once again; this time harder. Still no answer. This time he made a fist, and pounded harder on the door and called out, "Colonel McGruder, sir!"

Sergeant Major O'Mara then reached for the doorknob and found it was open. He opened the door an inch or so and called out once again.

"Commander McGruder, sir!" Again, nothing but dead silence.

As he opened the door, he saw Colonel McGruder slumped over on a small sofa. He was fully dressed in his old parade military uniform, his many medals pinned to the upper left portion of his jacket. His much-admired, pearl-handled pistol with a silencer attached, dangled from his right hand, held by two limp fingers. Dried blood stained his neck and shirt collar, a bullet hole in his right temple.

After a full military funeral attended by the men of B.A.T. 1 and 2, his body was returned to America in BAT's C-130 cargo plane and six days later, he was buried in a quiet funeral attended by his three children, five grandchildren, and a few childhood friends.

CHAPTER 59

Three days later, Pope Francis Xavier, Roscoe, Amarie, and Father Susanto were in the pope's office waiting for their 9:00 a.m. meeting with the archbishop. The temporary secretary immediately recognized the tall cleric who entered the pope's outer office at 9:36 a.m. The visitor's elaborate, decorated, colorful cassock could only mean Archbishop Benedict MacCarthy had arrived.

The young, temporary secretary rose quickly from his chair behind the desk, formally greeted the archbishop, and then said, "I'll call Pope Francis Xavier and let him know you have..."

Suddenly the archbishop brushed past the secretary, almost pushing him off balance, and strode directly into Pope Francis Xavier's office. With the secretary trailing behind, the archbishop, he attempted to explain.

"I tried to stop him, but he pushed me to the side," the secretary explained."

The archbishop stopped abruptly and turned to the young secretary.

"Were you taught nothing in the seminary, young man? I am Archbishop Benedict MacCarthy, and I expect to be addressed as such, I certainly do not expect to be addressed as 'him'!"

The archbishop then stepped directly in front of the pope's desk. "Father Prantata, why have I been called to Rome, interrupting my ministry in America?"

Before the pope could answer, Roscoe said, "Why did you refer to His Holiness as Father Prantata?"

The archbishop, now red-faced and furious, turned to the former president. "You sir, have no business correcting me on how I address this priest!"

Roscoe quickly responded, "I'm sure you know better than to address the pope by his priestly name."

The archbishop glared at Roscoe. "Mister Ayala, I do, know how to properly address a pope, but what you fail to understand is that this Indonesian black priest is not my pope, and therefore I have correctly addressed him."

By this time, Budi had moved himself toward the pope's secretary and said, "It's okay, Father Joseph, be concerned. Everything will be fine. Just go back to the outer office." A bewildered Father Joseph quickly left the room and quietly closed the door behind him.

Budi looked pleadingly into the eyes of his mentor. "Benedict, please don't be angry. We only want to hear your explanation, help us to understand the reason for the money in your name. I know there is a legitimate reason. I know this is all a mistake."

The archbishop looked down at the face of the much shorter Father Susanto. "Not only am I forced to deal with a false pope, I am forced to deal with yet another Indonesian fool. Get away from me, you whining, sniveling, poor excuse for a priest!"

Budi, flabbergasted and speechless, stared at the archbishop.

Pope Francis Xavier quietly but firmly said, "Archbishop, would you be good enough to sit in the chair in front of my desk?"

Not saying a word, the archbishop, in his usual pompous style, sat down, his appearance sitting upon a simple wood chair was, even in silence, artificial. The pope remained silent for a few moments, knowing people with an attitude such as the archbishop were usually uncomfortable with silence. Just as the pope was about to speak, the archbishop could stand it no longer.

"Father Prantata, I am here at the Vatican, not because you requested my presence in Rome, but because my superior, Cardinal Mac Given of New York City, asked me to come here. I demand to be told why I have been made to make this long, unnecessary trip to Rome."

The pope remained silent for a few more moments then said. "Archbishop MacCarthy, I appreciate your visit to the Vatican. I requested your presence here for the purpose of knowing more about your plan of action as it relates to my African project."

"My plan of action, as you put it, was to defend the church against your illegal and deceitful funding of the project known as Build Africa Together. You did not have the authority to sell the treasures of the Vatican and use the money, you illegally gained from that sale, to support your foolish and wasteful African project. The Catholic people, myself included, will never forgive you for your deception, secretly selling church property."

Pope Francis Xavier, still very calm and subdued, said, "Yes, I am aware that many in the church do agree with you, but for now I am more interested in learning the very clever details of how you intended to stop the project in Africa. After all, you are a very intelligent and powerful man and I am intrigued to learn from you. Father Susanto has often told me of your intelligence. Do you mind sharing with us your clever plan to terminate the African project?"

The others seated at the desk were shocked at the pope's composure, and especially the flattering words he was using, given the damning evidence against the archbishop.

The archbishop responded to the pope's last comment. "I have no desire to explain my actions to an Indonesian black priest, pretending to be pope! Did you call me to the Vatican to ask me foolish questions?"

The room was silent. The pope remained silent for a very long moment, the two men on either side of him were so confused, they also were silent.

In the brief silence, the archbishop muttered for all to hear, "I should have expected nothing less from an illegal pope. I will not cower in shame to this Indonesian or anyone else in this room. This illegal pope is the one who should be apologizing to Mother Church for auctioning off her religious possessions, which, I may add, is the view of all the hierarchy of the Catholic Church. The money already used for your foolish, illegal project, has dishonored the very roots of Catholicism. I insist, once again, to know why my superior asked me to come to the Vatican. If it is about my efforts to stop your illegal project, I will tell you that I was the only man strong enough to act, by halting the distribution of illegal money to the savages of Africa!"

The pope once again stayed calm as he spoke. "Archbishop MacCarthy, we thought the elements of your plan were rather creative. I am very interested to learn about the imaginative steps, you designed to thwart my efforts in Africa. Please, enlighten this lowly Indonesian convert."

The archbishop now seemed more relaxed as he responded to the statement.

"Well, for an Indonesian, you at least know your place and respect a man of my stature. My plan would have been effective, if the United Nations hadn't been so incompetent. They should never have allowed that vehicle out of their sight."

The pope now seemed thoroughly absorbed by the actions of the archbishop. "I do agree that had the United Nations observer team not failed you, your ingenious plan would have been successful. Tell me, Archbishop MacCarthy, I'm very interested to know how your plan began. I may be able to learn from you."

Roscoe used every muscle in his body to constrain himself at the pope's approach toward the archbishop. Roscoe wanted to confront this foolish man, but thought best to contain his anger. *Questioning the pope's approach in front of the archbishop would only embolden this outrageous man. Why is Pope Francis Xavier not interrogating the archbishop about the illegal money he received, to destroy the project?*

Roscoe was concerned that the archbishop could very well take control of this meeting, but for the moment at least, he chose to remain silent, and instead, he slowly slid a small piece of paper across the pope's desk. Written on it was the amount of money in the archbishop's Chase Manhattan bank account. The pope glanced at the paper, placed it on the right side of his blotter, and asked the archbishop to continue.

"I approached a representative of Agrium Agricultural in January, of two thousand twelve. Asking him to help me to stop the building of the towns in Africa. Termination of the African project was in the church's best interest. The agricultural company had some ideas about how to stop the building of the farms in the savannas, but I presented a better plan. I knew the foolish Indonesian priest would never suspect a collusion between the United Nations and the pollution of the underground water in the Sahara. Once the agricultural industry heard the details of my plan, they immediately agreed my plan was superior."

The archbishop sat erect in his chair and continued. "The plan began when I asked Father Susanto if he would contact Roscoe and request a site visit for me to the African project. During this visit, I saw the solar thermal electricity plants and the intra-continental highway from a helicopter. After seeing these two sites, my plan began. I asked the helicopter pilot if she would fly me over the underground water pipes, knowing that once the helicopter was in the air, the pilot would have to call back to headquarters to obtain the coordinates of the water pipes inserted in the underground aquifer."

The archbishop had been certain the pilot would automatically follow standard military procedures by verbally repeating the coordinates she received in her headphones back to headquarters for accuracy. The archbishop had brought a pen and paper to jot down the coordinates as the pilot confirmed her information. This maneuver allowed the Chinook helicopter, with its poisonous cargo, to fly directly to the underground aquifer water pipes in the Sahara Desert, in the dead of night. The next crucial step was to frame a project employee with accepting a bribe, which would have automatically branded the employee with colluding to destroy the project. I wanted this person to be Roscoe Ayala. As for McGruder, he was unable to resist six million dollars to simply plant the concept of financial transparency to others in the project, which by the way was an idea he was surprised the co-managers had never considered. As I had expected, this tactic also was successful. I then chose a bank in the Cayman Islands, knowing their casual security procedures, would allow this account to be found. The agricultural companies supplied the finances for the plan and were responsible for poisoning the underground water in the Sahara Desert. The first time that the crops were irrigated. All the crops would die, and of course the blame for the crops dying would be blamed on water from under the ground. The African project would be unable to absorb a double blow, dead crops, and a corrupt co-manager."

The archbishop sat proudly in his chair and continued. "And let me remind you the plan would have been foolproof, if all parties correctly executed their planned part. The incompetent United Nations Observer Team, allowing vehicles to escape their inspection was inexcusable."

Roscoe and Amarie were now fuming internally. The archbishop had controlled the entire meeting. They were convinced the pope had fallen back on his non-aggressive Indonesian cultural personality. The co-managers felt trapped, wrestle control of the meeting from the pope in front of the archbishop would damage the pope's position, and support the pompous ego of the archbishop. To make the situation even more frustrating, all they had to do was glance toward the pope's office alcove section, where Father Susanto remained cloistered. Budi was sitting in a fetal position, crying, no longer listening to the conversation.

The archbishop true to his outlandish behavior became personal. "Oh, you can't imagine how much fun I had using your stupid friend Budi, for almost two years, and never once did he disappoint me. Amarie and Roscoe, found it difficult to accept the pope's obvious abandonment of his boyhood friend at this terrible moment. Both men were about to rise from their chairs, ready to destroy this pompous ass sitting across the desk from them. The pope noticed slight movement from the men at his side. He put his arms forward in their direction, signaling them to remain seated. He then reached into the open left top drawer of his desk, pulled out a hand-held recording device, and placed it in front of the archbishop.

Pope Francis Xavier picked up the phone receiver on his desk phone, hit one button, and said into the receiver, "Send the five Swiss Guards into my office immediately." He quietly placed the receiver back on his landline phone. "I hope you don't mind that this Indonesian pope recorded every word you said since you entered my office. I wanted Father Susanto to hear for himself your words. If not, I feared his loyalty to you would prevent him from truly accepting your actions."

The pope rose from his seat and slowly moved around his desk until he was standing before the archbishop. In one quick move, he violently slapped the left cheek of the archbishop. The thunder-like clap of the pope's open hand against the archbishop's left cheek shook the atmosphere in the room and every person in it.

The pope then said in a slow steady voice, "That, Mr. Mac Carthy, was not for what you did in Africa; that was for the damage you did to my dearest friend. A man who loved you so much he would have gladly given his life to save yours. What you said to my friend was the most hatful thing I believe I have ever witnessed. The Swiss Guards will be here shortly to deliver you to the Italian police. The head of the Swiss Guards will then contact the American embassy in Rome to inquire how they wish me to dispose of your presence in Italy. Oh yes, one other item, I will immediately start proceedings for defrocking you as a clergy member of the Catholic Church."

As the red blotch began to form on the archbishop left cheek, the pope added, "You pompous, ugly man. You don't deserve to wash the feet of Father Budi Susanto. Yes, he may have black skin, but he is no fool, nor is he stupid. He simply worshiped you, more than he loved himself. However, you were so engrossed in your own importance; you never once noticed his dedication. Shame on you. You are not only a disgrace to the Catholic Church; you are also a disgrace to humanity. You will have a great deal to answer for, both to man and God, but your greatest sin, one you will be judged harshly for, is the unjust way you used and manipulated another human being, my dearest friend, Father Budi Susanto."

All the participants at this meeting remained silent as the five Swiss Guards escorted the former archbishop out of the pope's office. The only sound came from the alcove in the pope's office, where Father Susanto remained in a fetal position, sobbing.

Epilogue

There was a lot of press coverage once the scandal became public. Donations began to pour into Build Africa Together. Schoolchildren around the world were sending their spending money to the humanitarian agency in care of the Vatican, accompanied with original pictures they had drawn of African people. Other organizations and agencies wrote to Build Africa Together, inquiring how they could assist. Donations from foundations, multi-national corporations, schools, institutions, and individuals amounted to $88 million over the following year.

The Peter's pence Collection over the years had consistently amounted to approximately eight million dollars each year. After the story of how big agri-businesses had tried to stop Build Africa Together, the Pope's Peter's pence collection rose consistently over the next four years averaging thirteen million-plus dollars a year.

The pope had been lobbying Western European nations with modest success, but after the agricultural scandal became public, the combined donations from Western Europe countries amounted to $3.6 billion.

The Federal Trade Commission sent the Vatican the $14 million dollars used to frame Roscoe Ayala, including the payoffs to Colonel McGruder and Archbishop MacCarthy. Two weeks later, Pope Francis Xavier received the four million-dollar fines from each of the seven agriculture firms involved.

Build Africa Together became the recipient of just under two billion dollars directly related to the archbishop's plan to destroy the project's activities in Africa.

Along with the fines, there was sufficient evidence to arraign, prosecute, and administer a twenty-four-month jail sentence to the former Archbishop MacCarthy. Three agricultural executives who had direct contact with the archbishop received sixteen-month jail sentences in America and the United Kingdom.

The former archbishop received early release for good behavior from his two-year jail sentence in 2014. It was rumored that the defrocked prelate was living an itinerant life in the beach resort areas of Costa Rica. His personality traits remained unchanged, even though he was now dependent on others for his lonely existence.

Roscoe Ayala, Amarie Maalout, Vice Admiral Jack Fisher, Rick Kinsley, and Jon Edwards left the project at the end of their two-year assignment. A former Home Secretary from the United Kingdom and an African independence leader from Kenya replaced the current co-managers. Vice Admiral Fisher convinced two recently retired naval officers to take over the leadership of B.A.T. 1 & 2 for the next two-year tour of duty.

After their retirement, two CIA agents, who had been undercover in Pakistan, accepted a two-year tour of duty, replacing Rick and Jon.

Roscoe and Amarie were generally pleased with the progress made over the past two years in Africa. However, they were very disappointed in the continued slow evolution toward a governmental structure in Somalia. In 2014, the Islamic jihadist group commonly referred to as ISIL or

ISIS, moved into the Somalia areas formally controlled by al-Shabab and the warlord and militia groups.

The clan families in Somalia grudgingly accepted B. A. T.'s presence in their country but remained opposed to collaborative efforts to join or support the democratic initiatives that were beginning to emerge in their country.

Amarie convinced Pope Francis Xavier to enlist the services of two highly regarded and influential Somali writers/historians: Lidwien Kapteijns, author of the book, Clan Cleansing in Somalia, and Nuruddin Farah, author of a document titled "Hiding in Plain Sight," which showed the benefits of a Somalian democratic governmental structure, which included clan family members.

The one tragic victim of Build Africa Together was Father Budi Susanto who was hospitalized in March, 2013, after which he was under the direct care of Dr. Cloise Box, a Canadian psychiatrist who specialized in the treatment of brainwashed victims. Father Susanto was able to return to his position as the pope's secretary in November 2013, fully recovered but minus his jovial personality.

Doctor Adair remained with Build Africa Together for four more years. He resigned his position in 2017, after the last house in the tropical savannas was built and occupied. During this time in Africa, there was considerable worldwide publicity about the young autistic genius and his connection to the earth through his shoeless feet.

Jem Adair returned to Wales, living with his parents and his sister Matilda for three years. During this period, he remained active as a highly paid consultant to many countries in the area of natural resources. His father became his business manager, investing his considerable earnings in a secure retirement account.

Doctor Adair decided to return to Africa in 2021, when a newly created agency, the Federation of African Presidents, offered him the position of Administrator of African Natural Resources. He settled in a residence in Cape Town, South Africa, where the new agency was located. In 2023, there were fifty-four independent countries in Africa, not including Somaliland, which is recognized as an independent country.

Membership in the Federation of African Presidents realized a steadily increase in participation; in 2023 membership was listed at forty-six African presidents. The federation published its first official document regarding the future of a functioning Africa: *Member presidents have the responsibility to work with neighboring countries, sharing ideas and peacefully cooperating on all matters affecting their countries. Member presidents will declare that all Africans have a right to enjoy liberty, and the independence to pursue their own destinies.*

Also, in the year 2023, the seventh of the two-year leadership rotations, continued its emphasis on African security. The two co-managers of that two-year rotation had as one of their main objectives the promotion of voter registration for African citizens, as more and more African political leaders were moving their countries toward a democratic form of government.

FOOTNOTES

1. SOLAR THERMAL POWER PLANT

2. AFRICAN INTRA-CONTINENTAL HIGHWAY

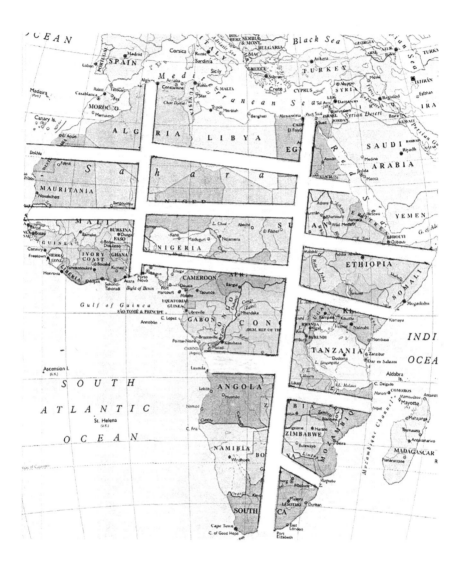

3. AFRICAN UNDERGROUND WATER AQUIFERS

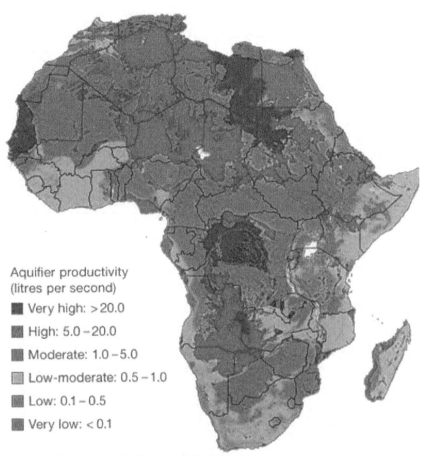

Aquifer productivity
(litres per second)

■ Very high: > 20.0

■ High: 5.0 – 20.0

■ Moderate: 1.0 – 5.0

▨ Low-moderate: 0.5 – 1.0

▨ Low: 0.1 – 0.5

■ Very low: < 0.1

Source: Environmental Research Letters

Researchers estimate that reserves of groundwater across the continent are 100 times the amount found on its surface

By Ted Thornhill

PUBLISHED: 19:20 EST, 21 April 2012 | Updated: 19:22 EST, 21 April 2012

Huge reserves of underground water in some of the driest parts of Africa could provide a buffer against the effects of climate change for years to come, scientists said.

Researchers from the British Geological Survey and University College London have for the first time mapped the aquifers, or groundwater, across the continent and the amount they hold.

'The largest groundwater volumes are found in the large sedimentary aquifers in the North African countries Libya, Algeria, Egypt and Sudan,' the scientists said in their paper.

4. MASH TYPE HOSPITALS FUNDED BY BUILD AFRICA TOGETHER

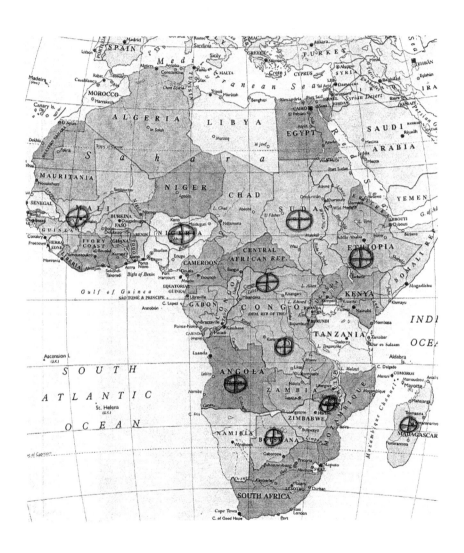

5. LOCATION of MASHTYPE TENT HOSPITALS PAID FOR BY The WORLD BANK

6. MAP OF AFRICA'S TROPICAL SAVANNAS

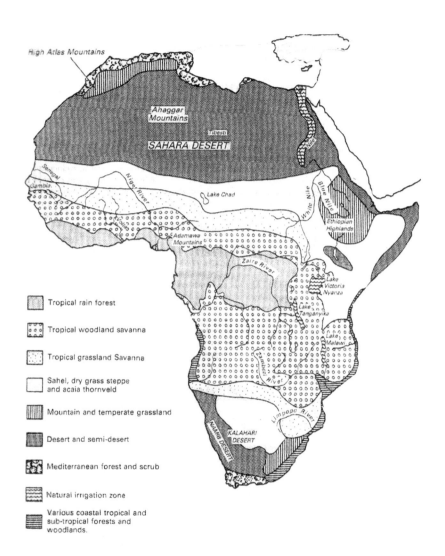

High Atles Mountains

Ahaggar Mountains

Tibesti

SAHARA DESERT

Senegal

Gambia

Niger River

Lake Chad

White Nile

Blue Nile

Ethiopian Highlands

Adamawa Mountains

Zaire River

Lake Victoria Nyanza

Lake Tanganyika

Lake Malawi

Zambezi River

Limpopo River

NAMIB DESERT

KALAHARI DESERT

Tropical rain forest

Tropical woodland savanna

Tropical grassland Savanna

Sahel, dry grass steppe and acaia thornveld

Mountain and temperate grassland

Desert and semi-desert

Mediterranean forest and scrub

Natural irrigation zone

Various coastal tropical and sub-tropical forests and woodlands.

Peter D. Cimini

Peter D. Cimini received bachelor's and master's degrees in education from New York University in 1954. He taught in New York public schools for six years. In 1960, he was offered a teaching position in the Clarkstown, New York public schools. In his third year there he was named by the local Kiwanis organization Teacher of the Year. Then in 1970 he was recruited by the Newington, Connecticut Board of Education to become a curriculum coordinator.

As a curriculum coordinator for twenty-five years in Newington, Connecticut, he found that writing curriculum was his most gratifying task. During this period in Newington, Peter published twelve articles in professional journals as well as writing articles for the Hartford Courant.

He retired from his coordinator position in 1996 and began to write his first novel, "The Secret Sin of Opi," on the topic of missing and exploited children, which was published in 2010 and is still available on Amazon.

In 2017, he began writing his second novel, "The Man Who Transformed Africa," published in 2020.

Made in the USA
Middletown, DE
02 February 2022

59318791R00275